AMERICAN HISTORY AND ITS
GEOGRAPHIC CONDITIONS

"So much is certain: history
lies not near but in nature."
CARL RITTER

AMERICAN HISTORY AND ITS GEOGRAPHIC CONDITIONS

BY

ELLEN CHURCHILL SEMPLE

Late Professor of Anthropogeography, Clark University
Author of "Influences of Geographic Environment"
and "The Geography of the Mediterranean Region"

REVISED IN COLLABORATION WITH THE AUTHOR

BY

CLARENCE FIELDEN JONES

Professor of Economic Geography, Clark University
Associate Editor of "Economic Geography" Author of
"Commerce of South America" and "South America"

NEW YORK / RUSSELL & RUSSELL

PREFACE TO THE REVISED EDITION

American History and Its Geographic Conditions, "a pioneer work and still preëminent in its field," defines the relationship between historical movements in the United States and the natural environment as the stage on which history unfolds; it emphasizes the relation of coasts, islands, rivers, mountains, vegetation, and soils in the exploration, settlement, and early development of the United States and in the expansion of the American people from a small nation on the eastern rim of a continent to a continental power, a power of the western hemisphere, of the Pacific ocean and of the world.

In view of the enormous expansion of the United States during the past several decades, an up-to-date volume on the relationships of geography to historical evolution becomes especially valuable in the twentieth-century world with its many new and complex problems. In the revision of the volume the authors have retained the original organization and method of treatment of the text. The original author, Ellen C. Semple, has made contributions to improve or clarify certain historical aspects of the subject; Clarence F. Jones is responsible for the detailed work of revision and for the addition of all economic material designed to bring the book up-to-date.

Two features have been added to the volume: a supplementary reading list of more than 240 references and a list of literary readings. The supplementary readings do not represent a definitive list on American history and its geographic conditions. They embrace the salient features of the several chapters and are arranged by the major sections of each chapter.   This arrangement makes possible specific assignments on the different portions of the chapters.   References have been selected to give not only historical development but also the geographic relationships to such developments.   The list of literary readings is merely typical and suggestive; it is designed to interest the student in broad selective reading of rich material on geographic relationships in general literature.   These lists assume special significance in view of the enormous amount of literature being produced in American history, both academic and fictional.

The authors are indebted to Dr. Charles Gooze for careful work in connection with the revision of the text, in proof-reading, checking materials and indexing, and to Katheryne C. Thomas for a critical reading of the manuscript and for making valuable suggestions.

ELLEN CHURCHILL SEMPLE
CLARENCE FIELDEN JONES

CONTENTS

MAPS

CHAPTER I

THE ATLANTIC STATES OF EUROPE THE DISCOVERERS AND COLONIZERS OF AMERICA

THE most important geographical fact in the past history of the United States has been their location on the Atlantic opposite Europe; and the most important geographical fact in lending a distinctive character to their future history probably will be their location between the North Atlantic and the North Pacific, between the mainsprings of western and occidental civilizations and culture.

RELATION OF MEDIEVAL EUROPE TO THE FAR EAST

Until the end of the fifteenth century, Europe was dominated by its position as part of the continental triad of the eastern hemisphere. In spite of the long, indented coastline and considerable maritime development of Europe, its navigation was mainly coastwise, not oceanic; and its sea travel was everywhere supplemented on the great routes by land travel, up or down river valleys and across deserts or steppes. A land of the temperate zone, it sought the tropical products of the Orient.[1] Thither the way was easy: the Indian Ocean stretched out two welcoming arms, the Red Sea and the Persian Gulf, towards the Mediterranean; the Tigris and Euphrates rivers rested their light finger touch on the highlands of Armenia near the basin of the Euxine; and into the Mediterranean Europe dropped a fringe of

[1] Principal commodities moving from Asia to Europe included:
(a) Spices: pepper from India and Ceylon; cloves, nutmegs, and allspice from Banda-Benda and other small volcanic islands with basalt soil, high precipitation,

peninsulas, which gave her ample contact with its waters. Thus, for the easy-going trade of the Middle Ages, communication with the Orient was in general satisfactory. The Mediterranean was an open highway; and to the east, if the Suez route was temporarily blocked, more goods came by way of the Euphrates and Antioch, or by Trebizond and the Black Sea; or the silks and teas of China could be deposited at Batum, the eastern port of the Euxine, after a long journey across the highlands of Central Asia, down the valley of the Oxus, across the Caspian Sea, and along that deep furrow between the Great Caucasus and the Anti-Caucasus mountains which forms a natural highway to the Black Sea.

But wherever a water route is interrupted by a land barrier, as in the isthmuses of Panama and Suez; or where a continuous water route is constricted to a narrow passway, as in the Strait of Gibraltar, the English Channel between Calais and Dover, the Bosphorus, the Strait of Bab-el-Mandeb, and the Straits of Malacca, we find points of strategic importance which give to their masters the power to tie up the arteries of travel. The eastern coast region of the Mediterranean from Antioch to Alexandria partakes of the nature of an isthmus, while Constantinople

high even temperature; cinnamon from Ceylon and India; ginger from India and China.

(b) Stones: diamonds from India; rubies from Ceylon, western India and Persia; garnets and topaz from Persia; pearls from the waters southeast of India near Ceylon and the Persian Gulf.

(c) Fabrics: old cotton fabrics from the west coast of Calicut, India; silks from China.

(d) Indigo, Brazil wood, aloe-wood, and sandal-wood from India.

The principal articles moving from Europe to Asia included woolen goods, linen goods, silver, quicksilver, tin, copper, lead, amber, wines and glassware.

(*Encyclopædia Biblica*, IV (1903), 5145–93.

Cheyney, Edward P., *European Background of American History 1300–1600*, New York, 1904, pp. 3–21.)

is in a position to block the Trebizond and Batum routes. With the Saracen conquest of Egypt and Syria in the seventh and eighth centuries, European trade with the Orient on the southern routes was cut off; the trade was forced to rely on the Bosphorus passway alone, until the crusades again opened the roads through Syria and Egypt.[2]

After their expulsion from Constantinople in 1261, the Venetians transferred their eastern commerce to Alexandria, and after the capture of Constantinople by the Turks in 1453, Egypt for a time enjoyed almost a complete monopoly of the eastern trade. Amid the Mongol and Turkish convulsions along the caravan routes the monsoon passage was the one channel that remained open from India.[3] Long before the development of the Ottoman Navy and the final seizure of Egypt in 1516–17, which completely disrupted the trade, frequent political disturbances, the mounting prices of articles, and frequent delays in transit caused trade to decline greatly.[4]

[2] Semple, Ellen Churchill, "The Ancient Piedmont Route of Northern Mesopotamia," *Geographical Review*, VIII (1919), 153–79; reference on pp. 177–78.

[3] Hunter, Sir W. W., *History of British India*, New York, 1899, pp. 17–53; reference on p. 49.

[4] The conditions of trade on the Egyptian–Monsoon route are typical of the adversities to commerce in the centuries before the collapse of the trade. Navigation in the northern Red Sea and especially in the Gulf of Suez was perilous and difficult, owing to (1) marked tidal circulation in the gulfs of Suez and Akabah, (2) transverse currents moving down the two gulfs, driven by strong or violent winds, northwest winds in the Gulf of Suez, and north or northeast winds in the Gulf of Akabah, (3) the southwest monsoon in the Arabian Sea which draws out water from the Gulf of Aden and depresses the level of the water three feet at the head of the Red Sea, further complicating the currents there, (4) the fringe of coral reefs bordering the shores of the Red Sea, and (5) the short sailing season to and from the Arabian Sea during the period of the reversing monsoons.

Hence, under Greek, Roman, and Saracen rule in Egypt, when Venice handled the eastern trade from Alexandria, oriental products sought the Mediterranean by the "Grand Detour." They came up the Red Sea to Berenice (24° N.L.) and thence by caravan for eleven days to Caenopolis or Coptos on the Nile; or to Leucos Limen (Kosseir) at 26° N.L. and thence straight west by caravan over a well-equipped trail to Coptos or Caenopolis, a journey of five to seven days for donkey or camel. At

EUROPE TURNS TOWARD THE ATLANTIC

Owing to these difficulties in obtaining the coveted articles of the East, Europe gazed longingly, despairingly towards the old avenues to the Orient, whither its face had been set so long; then reluctantly, at first almost hopelessly, it looked towards the Atlantic, on which hitherto its back had been turned, and asked the momentous question whether the ocean could afford a new route to the Indies and Cathay.

Thus was initiated the westward movement. It was participated in by all the Atlantic nations of Europe and by only these; in it the maritime powers of the inland basins took no share. Landlocked seas have always been the nurseries of maritime development, but nurseries they have remained. In the fifteenth century Europe could boast two groups of genuine sea powers, the Italian cities in the Mediterranean and the Hanse towns in the North Sea and the Baltic, each the product of its geographical environment, born of the union of great inland routes of trade with the indented coast of a tideless sea.[5] But with the effort to discover ocean routes to the Orient began the Atlantic period in history, in contrast to the Mediterranean period which preceded it. Then there came upon the scene of

Coptos or a near-by Nile port the goods were transferred to Nile boats, and went by river downstream to Alexandria.

Aside from caravan costs, traffic charges were heavy because of frequent breaking of bulk, transit duties on all goods both entering and leaving Egypt, *ad valorem* duties imposed at all provincial frontiers where custom houses were maintained or where a bridge of boats blocked the passage, and frequent bribes. These irksome tolls and duties burdened and delayed traffic all during the Middle Ages when Venice exploited the Egyptian trade out of Alexandria, and furnished a strong argument for exploring the outside sea route to India.

[5] Semple, E. C., "Development of the Hanse Towns in Relation to their Geographical Environment," *Bulletin of the American Geographical Society*, XXXI (1899), No. 3, pp. 236-55.

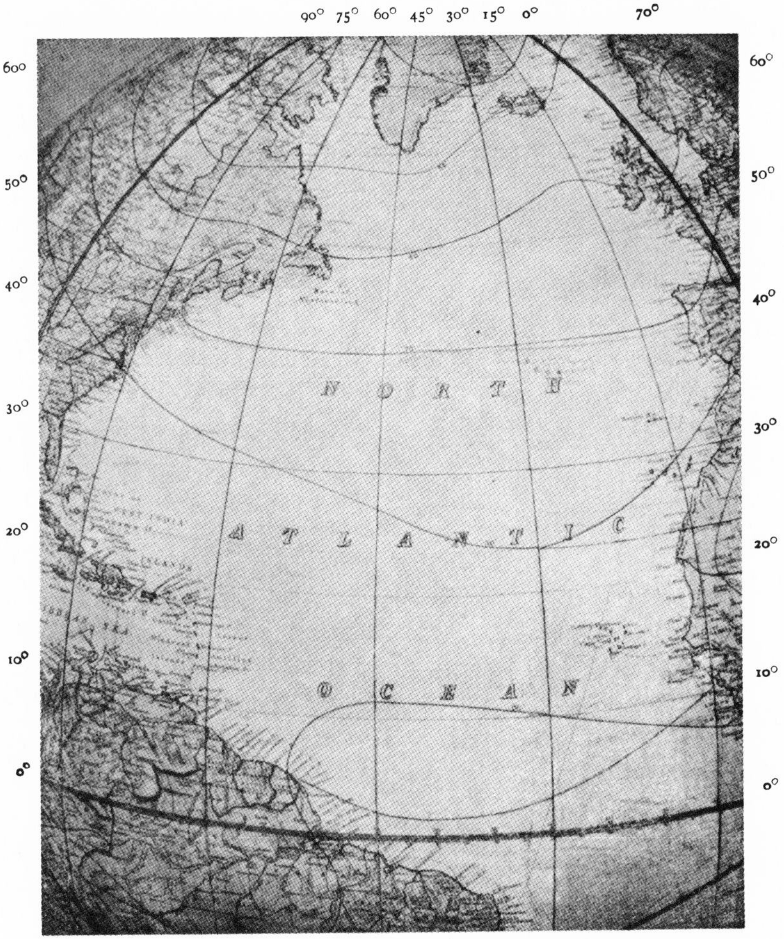

FIG. I. THE NORTH ATLANTIC BASIN

On the North Atlantic Basin nature bestowed conditions that favored voyages. Though 3600 miles wide in the southern part, winds, ocean currents and islands facilitated advance along northwest Africa. In the north the narrow width, limited contact with Arctic waters, and islands as stepping stones aided the Northmen in reaching America early.

history other maritime powers, trained in a severer school of seamanship, accustomed to look out upon the landless horizon of the *Mare Tenebrosum*, yet heirs to all the knowledge of navigation and cosmography their Mediterranean neighbors could give them, stimulated and guided by Florentine and Genoese and Venetian map-makers, pilots, and sea captains. In order there rose the Norse, Portugal, Spain, England, France, and Holland. These nations had the start in the race towards the west; and when they realized that the new Occident was not the old Orient, their geographical position gave them the best opportunities the earth could offer for wealth and dominion. Why this was so an analysis of the geographical features of the Atlantic will make clear.

The Influence of the Atlantic. West of the Dark Continent and the Light Continent lies a long body of water whose area is only one half that of the Pacific, though its drainage basin is more than double that of the larger ocean (Fig. 1). The Atlantic, by the gigantic tendrils of its rivers, lays hold upon the Rockies and the Andes, the plains of Central Russia and the highlands of Abyssinia, and hence draws to itself by mere force of gravity the trade from the heart of the bordering continents. Its shape is approximately that of the letter "S," the stricture in the middle, formed by the approach of Cape St. Roque and the Sierra Leone coast of Africa, dividing the ocean into two well-defined basins. On the northern basin, which Europe faces, nature has bestowed all her favors. Though 3600 miles wide at its broadest part between Morocco and Florida, between Norway and Greenland it contracts to less than half that width and has therefore only limited contact with the chilling waters of the Arctic Ocean. In contrast to the smooth contour of the South

Atlantic, the northern basin has countless indentations great and small, is bordered by vast landlocked seas, like the Mediterranean, the Baltic with the gulfs of Bothnia and Finland, the Gulf of Mexico, Gulf of St. Lawrence, and Hudson Bay, which carry the ocean into the interior of the continents and lay upon the bordering lands the vivifying touch of the sea.

The Atlantic as a whole has a coast-line of fifty-five thousand miles, as long as that of the Pacific and Indian oceans taken together. This is due almost entirely to its numerous inlets, for it is island poor. The countries whose shores it washes have the ample contact with the sea which leads to a seafaring life; but except in its great inlets, like the Mediterranean, it lacks the islands which early tempt to bold maritime enterprise. It is a significant fact that the ocean was first crossed in its narrowest part, in the only place where the islands are grouped like distant stepping-stones from shore to shore.

The Northmen. The Northmen early became acquainted with the Hebrides, Orkneys, Shetlands, and Faroes, from which they passed to Iceland, thence to Greenland, and thence to Newfoundland or Cape Breton Island and the continent of America. Lured to the ocean by the outlying islands, bred to the sea by their deep-running fiords and their steep mountains, which denied them more than a narrow foothold upon the land, on the sea also they were forced to eke out by fisheries the slender subsistence which the country afforded. Only the small deposit plains of gravel and sand at the heads of the fiords yielded level surface for agriculture, while conditions of climate further limited the products of the soil. When we consider that Norway today has only 2.2 per cent of its area in arable land

and .8 per cent in permanent grass,[6] we can realize that in the early centuries, with its primitive systems of husbandry, population must soon have pressed upon the limits of subsistence.

It is the tendency of all people thus placed on a narrow hem of land between mountain and sea to establish maritime colonies, even where a warmer climate makes nature more generous. Phœnicians and Greeks dotted the Mediterranean coasts with their settlements, and Malays today permeate the island world southeast of Asia; while the Northmen planted themselves on every available coast and island, and swept the shores of Europe from the White Sea to the Black. Their daring voyages were possible because their vessels were stronger and swifter than the Spanish and Portuguese caravels of five centuries later. In this sea-born genius for shipbuilding they suggest the Haida Indians of the Queen Charlotte Islands, who make their canoes on what a sailor would call beautiful lines, and in them venture out a thousand miles into the open Pacific.

But the colonizing enterprises of the Northmen in the ninth and tenth centuries were too numerous and scattered, the climatic conditions of Vinland too harsh for a small and remote settlement in the midst of hostile Indians, and the population of the mother country too sparse to produce any lasting results from these early transoceanic voyages.[7] Hence the effective discovery of America had to wait for five centuries, to be made by nations farther south, to whom better conditions of climate and soil had given larger populations, and who also enjoyed ample contact with the

---

[6] Norway, *Statistical Survey in Europa*, I (1930), 515; Statistics for 1928.

[7] Thördarson, M., "The Vinland Voyages," *Research Series No. 18*, American Geographical Society, New York, 1930, pp. 1–68.

sea, but who faced the broadest stretch of the Atlantic and made their voyages into the vast unknown. But they, too, were led across the threshold of the ocean by a few outlying islands.

Portugal. The nearer groups of the Madeira and Canaries had been known for centuries, though we hear of an expedition sent out in 1341 by Alphonso IV of Portugal to rediscover the Fortunate Islands (Canaries). Lying near Africa, in the path of the trade winds and only a little to the south of the Strait of Gibraltar, they naturally came early into the realm of geographical knowledge. The Azores, a thousand miles west of Portugal, seem to have been visited first in 1147 by an Arabian navigator, who set out on his voyage of discovery from the port of Lisbon, at that time the Moorish stronghold of power and commerce. From 1346 they appear upon the maps of Europe, and seem to have had chance visitors from that time until their so-called rediscovery in 1431 by one of the expeditions of Prince Henry of Portugal. The long voyages to all these remote islands educated the timid sailor of the fifteenth century in maritime enterprise. Also, the Cape Verde Islands, ten degrees farther south, served to direct the course of the Portuguese navigator Cabral, when, standing farther out to sea than was customary for vessels following the Cape route to India, and drifting or driven farther westward than he realized, he came to the coast of South America, which here lies directly in the path of the southern equatorial current, and only ten degrees west of the longitude of the Cape Verde Islands.[8]

[8] This protrusion of the South American continent forty degrees east of the Bahamas, and therefore east of the "Line of Demarcation" laid down by the Pope, Alexander VI, threw Brazil to Portugal and gave that power its sole domain in the New World.

That Portugal should have been the pioneer in the search for the "outside" passage to the Indies and should have followed the southern route was intimately connected with its geographical location. Through the Mediterranean, Portugal had felt the influence of the oriental trade for centuries; by its outpost position on the ocean and its long coast-line facing west and south, Portugal was dominated by the Atlantic; its relief and soil restricted the arable land; it was held from expansion to the east by Spain; its navigation was favored by southward-flowing currents and strong summer winds; while its maritime enterprise was attracted by the proximity of Africa and the outlying islands to the southwest, which the Portuguese rediscovered. The resolution of all these geographical forces was the search for the African sea route to the Orient. Minor forces also contributed to this end. Portugal, like Aragon and Old Castile, being remote from the center of Saracen dominion in southeastern Spain, was held by a weaker grasp and was therefore able to free itself sooner. Lisbon was liberated in 1341, a century and a half before Spain had accomplished the reconquest of its territory, and therefore could turn to other tasks. Moreover, Moorish neighbors helped to develop the seamanship of Portugal in naval warfare, for Portuguese vessels in pursuit of Mussulman pirates became accustomed to sail down the western coast of Africa. Afterwards such voyages were continued for commerce, just as the sequel to Prince Henry's military expedition into Morocco, where he learned of the gold-laden caravans from the Guinea coast to Mediterranean ports, was his endeavor to reach the Gold Coast by sea. From that time, in his sea-bound castle of Sagres where the promontory of St. Vincent carries Portugal territory far out into the ocean,

Henry the Navigator, watching his ships outbound from the neighboring harbor of Lagos, gazing out into the Atlantic for the return of his storm-beaten caravels, is symbolic of Europe in the fifteenth century.[9]

Spain. From Lisbon, Lagos, and Sagres the fever of maritime discovery spread along the coast to Palos, Cadiz, and Seville. Many men, like Christopher Columbus, his brother Bartholomew, and Magellan, learned much in the service of Portugal before they made their great discoveries for Spain. Columbus's sojourn in Lisbon, at that time the center of nautical science in Europe, strengthened his convictions of the feasibility of his plan to sail west. Added impulse was given his purpose in 1471 by the expedition of Santarem and Escobar which rounded the elbow of the Guinea Gulf and disclosed the southern trend of the African coast. This information occasioned probably the simultaneous inquiry of Columbus and King Alphonso V of Portugal to Toscanelli in regard to a shorter transoceanic route to the Indies. Though the southern route was sure to be long, Portugal was committed to it, and Columbus turned to Spain, where Portuguese achievement had aroused maritime enthusiasm and the spirit of rivalry which would welcome the strange proposition. And then, on the south-

---

[9] The steps in the discovery of the route around Africa: Gil Eannes rounded Cape Bojador in 1434; Nuno Tristam at Cape Blanca, 1441; Diniz Diaz beyond Cape Verde, 1445; nearly thirty years of trade in slaves and gold on the Guinea Coast; Santarem voyage of 1471 showed southward trend of Guinea Coast; Diego Cam at the Congo, 1484; Bartholomew Dias rounded the Cape of Good Hope, 1486; Vasco da Gama discovered all-water route to India, 1497–99.

Note to Fig. 2:

If this map were used by Columbus on his first voyage, the misconceptions embodied in the map aided him in his eventful voyage; his landing place in the New World, as well as his final starting point, was governed by it; Columbus followed closely the parallel of the Canary Islands; he deviated from it only twice. Columbus really made three great discoveries: the New World, the best route for sailing vessels from Europe to the Americas, and the best route from the West Indies to Europe.

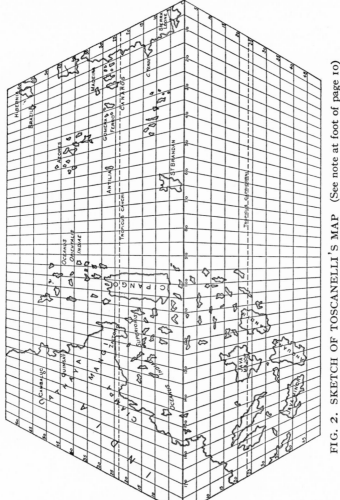

FIG. 2. SKETCH OF TOSCANELLI'S MAP (See note at foot of page 10)

western coast of Spain, in the ports of Cadiz, Palos, and San Lucar de Barrameda, was concentrated the life of the country for the next hundred years.

As with the Northmen and the Portuguese, islands pointed the way for Columbus. Only the group of the Canaries belonged to Spain, but it was fortunately situated within the belt of the northeast trade winds and on the twenty-eighth parallel, which happened to be also the latitude of the northern end of Cipango, according to its supposed location in the western Atlantic as set down in Toscanelli's map (Fig. 2). Since the lack of chronometers in the fifteenth century made the calculation of longitude very inaccurate, it was the custom for navigators to sail due north or south to the parallel of their proposed destination and then shape their course directly east or west.[10] Thus the Canaries were the first objective of Columbus in his outward voyage, and, when he steered thence, served to determine the Bahamas as the first landing-place in the New World. This island outpost and the beneficent trade wind combined to make the voyage into the unknown of as short duration as possible for the timid and mutinous spirits of the Spanish crew. The Cape Verde Islands, ten degrees farther south, formed the turn in the road in the third voyage of Columbus, whence his southwesterly course brought him into all the horrors of the equatorial belt of calms.

The safety and ease of the first route of Columbus, the mistaken idea that the Spice Isles were still to be found in the tropical regions of the western Atlantic, the search for a possible water passage through the continental barrier, the

[10] Fiske, John, *The Discovery of America*, Boston, 1892, I, 315–16; Nunn, G. E., "The Geographical Conceptions of Columbus," *Research Series No. 14*, American Geographical Society, New York, 1924, pp. 30–53, and map opposite page 50.

discovery of the Pacific, and their conquests of the Aztecs and the Incas combined to hold the Spanish in the Gulf of Mexico and the Caribbean Sea, especially when Mexico and Peru were found to yield gold. Their explorations, therefore, extended around these two bodies of water, with some sporadic voyages farther north up the east Atlantic coast, while their conquests spread in a half-century from California [11] to the Maule River in Chile and the Mendoza region in Argentina.[12] The marked southwestward trend of the South American coast below the Tropic of Capricorn made it evident that this part of the country, according to the papal bull, must belong to Spain. Though the year 1516 brought the Rio de la Plata into the realm of geographical knowledge, permanent settlement was made at Buenos Aires in 1580 only after two unsuccessful attempts. Then settlement was made by *gauchos* from Asunción and Santa Fé, Asunción having been founded in 1536 to provide a way station to Peru. In this settlement, established without direct order from the crown, trade directly to Spain by sea was prohibited by the ban of 1599 under penalty of death and forfeiture of property. Only through Lima and Panama could settlers communicate with Spain,[13] which focused activities in the region of Panama.

England. England, the next Atlantic power of Europe to take part in the westward movement, had its maritime development predetermined by its geographical conditions. Its long coast-line and abundant harbor facilities encouraged the nautical proclivities of its population, which was made

---

[11] Bourne, E. G., *Spain in America*, New York, 1904, pp. 149-74.

[12] Dawson, T. C., *The South American Republics*, New York, 1903, I, 135, and II, 15.

[13] *Documents para la Historia Argentina*, Buenos Aires, 1915, tomo V, "Comercio de Indias" (1713-78), pp. 41-48.

up of oversea elements — Anglo-Saxons, Danes, and Norman French. As an island, its earliest means of defensive warfare lay in the navy of King Alfred. Later its merchant vessels found a near market in the ports of Norway, and its fishing-smacks drew in their nets off the coast of Iceland. Looking towards the western waters was Bristol, at the end of the fifteenth century the chief seaport of the island. Hither came the Genoese Cabot, and hence sailed the first trans-Atlantic expedition of the English. Cabot's instructions excluded the southern course, probably to avoid encroaching on the maritime field of Spain and Portugal; so he sailed directly west, and came to the coast of Labrador or Cape Breton. His course lay westward approximately along the fifty-fourth parallel, where the distance from shore to shore, in consequence of the eastward projection of North America and the general convergence of the continents towards the north, is only about two thousand miles. But while his voyage was little over half as long as that of Columbus, the prevailing currents of ocean and air were against him in the outward passage.

Exploration of North America in the higher latitudes lay near to England as a result of its own northern location, just as in the case of the Norse discoveries, but the early English voyages, like those of the Vikings, were not followed up by European explorers because of the harsh climatic conditions of the bleak coasts thus reached. At a later date, however, the search for the Northwest Passage, when it came to be limited to Arctic regions, fell naturally to English navigators, such as Frobisher, Davis, Baffin, and Hudson. Thus was established England's claim to the subpolar regions of the continent; but they remained barren until Charles II in 1667 granted to the Hudson's Bay

Company a charter to Prince Rupert and his associates for the purpose of discovering a short northwest passage across the American continent to the Pacific and the "South Seas," which promised a briefer voyage to China and the Orient, and also for developing trade in furs, minerals, and other commodities.

British Rupert Land comprised all the territory draining into Hudson's Bay. The territory extended on the north from the Melville Peninsula to the eastern end of Great Slave Lake, and thence southwest enclosing the valleys of Nelson and Saskatchewan rivers to their source in the Rocky Mountains of British Columbia. It was confined on the south by the Laurentides, which here approached James Bay and provided only a low and rather narrow barrier between Rupert Land and the St. Lawrence–Great Lakes valley occupied by the French until 1763. Hudson Bay was accessible only at its north end through Hudson Straits. The sub-arctic location of its shores and hinterlands insured heavy fine pelts, but the trading season was limited to the short summer, so that the factories of the Hudson's Bay Company in general were placed at the mouths of rivers which served as harbors.[14] The Hudson's Bay Company, whose traders operated among the Indian tribes of the interior, came into collision with the French voyageurs, who were pushing up from the St. Lawrence and its northern tributaries for the northern furs.

France. The English, however, had met the French before in the New World on the Banks of Newfoundland. From northwestern France two peninsulas of ragged contour project into the Atlantic and the Channel; and from the

[14] Pinkerton, Robert, *The Hudson's Bay Company*, New York, 1931, pp. 88, 90–91.

days of Cæsar and famous *Veneti*, Brittany [15] and Normandy have nourished a hardy maritime race who, like the Norse, have been forced to rely in part upon the sea for their means of subsistence. These were the men, born to the sea, who first sailed from France to the western continent. Opposite Brittany and in the same latitude is southeastern Newfoundland, which marks the point of North America's closest approach to Europe south of Greenland. To the Banks of Newfoundland came these Breton and Norman fishermen as early as 1504; they were followed by the Portuguese, attracted thither by the possibility that this land might lie east of the papal meridian, and at a later date by the English, the original discoverers; for fishing-grounds are always the great cosmopolitan areas of the earth. The attempted settlement on Sable Island by the French in 1518,[16] the exploration of the St. Lawrence soon after, and another short-lived colony of 1542–43 near the present site of Quebec,[17] all show that the French took this field for their own. The English were active in the fisheries also; Gilbert's heroic attempt at settlement of Newfoundland in 1578 shows the importance placed on the industry. In 1578 there were one hundred and fifty French fishing-vessels in Newfoundland waters and two hundred Spanish, Portuguese, and English together.[18] The activities of the French were in effect limited to Nova Scotia, the islands about, and the Gulf and River St. Lawrence, though French names

---

[15] Munro, W. B., *Crusaders of New France*, New Haven, 1918, pp. 15–31, "The Voyageur of Brittany."

[16] Parkman, F., *Pioneers of France in the New World*, Boston, 1903, pp. 192–93. "In 1518 Baron de Léry made an abortive attempt at Settlement on Sable Island, where the cattle left by him remained and multiplied." In 1598 La Roche landed forty convicts on the island; five years later only twelve were taken off; the others had died by hunger, cold, and murder. *Ibid.*, pp. 232–33.

[17] *Ibid.*, pp. 221–27.   [18] *Ibid*, pp. 229–31.

along the coast of Maine still bear evidence to their wider claims of territory, based upon voyages of exploration as far south as Cape Cod.

Range of English Activities. Until near the end of the sixteenth century we find the range of English exploration in the New World south of the Norse, north of the French, and far to the north of the Spanish, reproducing the geographical stratification of these nations in Europe. The Canary Islands and the northeast trade winds, as we have seen, conspired to draw Spanish activities somewhat farther south than the Iberian peninsula, and to keep them limited in America between the equator and 30° north latitude, the parallel of St. Augustine. But from that point north to the mouth of the Penobscot River the coast remained debatable ground. Both French and English came hither, drawn out of their natural path at different times, but by the same motive — the prizes which Spanish treasure ships afforded in time of war. There is nothing like naval warfare to turn the political geography of the earth topsy-turvy. When war broke out between France and Spain in 1521, French cruisers were attracted southwestward to make depredations on Spanish caravels as they set out from the Mexican ports; and one of these cruisers under Verrazano, after having relieved a galleon of its rich cargo not far from its home port, set westward from the Madeira Islands to make discoveries for the benefit of France, and explored the American coast from Cape Fear to the Piscataqua River. But no permanent results followed from this venture.

The first English navigators to appear in the tropical waters of the western Atlantic were the slave traders, drawn thither to find a market among the Spanish colonies for their human merchandise. Sir John Hawkins was bringing slaves from the Guinea coast to meet the steady demand in this region from 1562 to 1567; but his traffic was interrupted soon afterwards by the outbreak of war with Philip II of Spain. Then English privateers began to wait for Spanish vessels in the western Atlantic, and thus became accustomed to the southern route and to these remote coasts. But the English had a motive leading them to combine with their naval and commercial expeditions the more substantial colonial ventures. The loss of Calais in 1557 ended England's hope of continental territory; it was a blow to her "balance of power" idea all the more serious in view of the vast dominions of Spain and the aggressive territorial policy of France. The loss might be made good in the New World. The war was scarcely begun when, in 1578, Sir Humphrey Gilbert sailed with his seven ships from Plymouth to found a colony in that problematical land of "Norumbega," which, however, he never reached. The year 1584 saw the birth of Raleigh's design to "plant an English nation in America," while at home was found in abundance the raw material out of which colonies could be made, a superfluous population induced recently by retrograde economic measures, and persistently by the limited area of the little island kingdom. For a long time and with few exceptions the colonial expeditions from England followed the southern route by way of the Canary Islands on their outbound voyages, although it was long and tedious. The reason is to be sought either in the help given by the northeast trade winds in the southern latitudes, and the difficulty presented by the prevailing westerlies farther north; or in the preference of the early navigators for the route made familiar by their adventures on the Spanish main.

Thus, separated by almost a century from the explorations of the Cabots, was initiated the second phase of England's oversea enterprises; and in a hundred and fifty years her permanent settlements occupied a narrow strip of coast almost continuously from Georgia to Nova Scotia. As both extremities of this line overlapped the claims of their neighbors, the English came into conflict with the Spanish on the south, where St. Augustine and Savannah were alternate objects of attack; and with the French on the north, where the settlements of both nations in Maine and Nova Scotia suffered from the mutual hostilities. Within this area the English had to suppress the colonial ventures of the Dutch, the last of the Atlantic powers of Europe to take part in the westward movement.

Holland. In the events establishing the colonial empire of Holland, geographic conditions were the leading factors. By its location at the northern end of the great trade route up the Rhone and Rhine valleys from the Mediterranean, this country, through the Hanseatic League, became the distributing-point in northern Europe for oriental products. When Portugal got control of the Asiatic trade, the commercial dealings of the Dutch were transferred from Venice and Genoa to Lisbon. But when the union of Spain and Portugal under Holland's hereditary enemy, Philip II, excluded Dutch vessels from the mouth of the Tagus, the merchantmen of the Rhine began to contend for a share in the land of the East Indies. The long coast-line of Holland, its numerous harbors, rich and active seaports, readier access to the Atlantic, and previous experience in the open ocean gained in the long voyages to Portugal, gave to the Dutch cities a broader horizon than the inclosed basin of the Baltic afforded the German members of the Hanseatic

League, and hence fitted them for wider maritime enterprise.

Not until the end of the sixteenth century, therefore, did the Dutch appear upon the high seas. Henry Hudson's discovery of the Hudson River in 1609 and his report on its opportunity for fur trading led them to appropriate Manhattan Island at the mouth of the stream and the great angle of the American coast between Delaware Bay and the Connecticut River. Meanwhile the English colonies were spreading along two natural geographical lines which converged upon the Dutch holdings. From the east, the New England settlements were rapidly throwing out one frontier station after another along the protected waterway of Long Island Sound, so that the year 1639 saw an unbroken line from Newport to Stamford and the modest beginnings of Greenwich, which was within thirty miles of New Amsterdam. From the south, Virginia and Maryland colonists were spreading up towards the head of Chesapeake Bay, where it approaches within twenty miles of the mouth of the Delaware River. From his trading-post on Kent Island, the Manhattan of upper Chesapeake Bay, William Claiborne was pushing up the Susquehanna River as early as 1631 to compete with the Dutch for the peltries of the Northwest. Moreover, the Dutch holdings occupied territory included in the original Virginia grant. The English were aware of the commercial and strategic value of the Hudson, as well as the danger attached to the separation of their two areas of colonization by a foreign power. So the fate of New Netherland was sealed.

The Acquisition of New Netherland. Geographical conditions made the acquisition of New Netherland the most important political event up to this time in the history of the English colonies in America. The natural highway of the St. Lawrence and the Great Lakes brought the French up to the back doors of New York and Pennsylvania, the two colonies carved out of the Dutch territory. From the head waters of the Ohio to those of the Hudson, French and English frontiers met. Lake Champlain with the Richelieu River to the north, and the Mohawk with Lake Ontario to the northwest, made two open, easy thoroughfares for army or trader between Canada and New York. Here no forest wilderness intervened to form a barrier, as it did between the New England settlements and the lower St. Lawrence. Contact was therefore immediate and, in consequence of the northwestern fur trade, of vital importance. Conflict was certain. Against the hostilities of the French, New York became the bulwark of the colonies, whom it helped to unite by demanding their aid against the common enemy. Thus it became the keystone in the arch of the English settlements, which was made all the stronger by the pressure of French aggression from above.

CHAPTER II

THE RIVERS OF NORTH AMERICA IN EARLY EXPLORATION AND SETTLEMENT

THE early European navigators did not find their voyages of discovery limited by the coast of North America; back of the sea-like bays, back of the bay-like estuaries, they met the tide-mingled flood of the great American rivers. Sea navigation passes without break into river navigation. Nature draws no sharp line between stream and ocean. The tide moves up the Potomac almost as far as Washington, and the waters of the Hudson at Newburgh are brackish; while the fresh, muddy current of the Orinoco is carried fifty miles out to sea. Size has differentiated ocean vessels from river steamers, though deep canals in some places extend the landward reach of the sea and diminish this distinction; but the small craft of the early navigators dropped their anchors and their barnacles into the broad, quiet flood of the American rivers, beyond the reach of storm and tide.

Rivers have always been the great intermediaries between land and sea, for in the ocean all find their common destination. Alexander's discovery of the Indus led by almost inevitable sequence to the rediscovery of the eastern sea route. The St. Lawrence brought the French from the Atlantic into the Great Lake Basin of North America, and the hardy explorers had scarcely launched their canoes upon the tributary waters of the upper Mississippi before they were planting the flag of France on the Gulf of Mexico at its mouth.

Relation of Rivers to Accessibility of Continents. The

accessibility of continents is determined by the navigability of their rivers, and this in turn is a matter of continental build. From the huge, monotonous hulk of the African plateau the rivers plunge down the steep escarpment within a few miles of the narrow plain of the coast; only where the Nile leaves its last terrace seven hundred miles inland was the Dark Continent early opened to the light. The vast intaglios of the Euphrates, Indus, and Ganges valleys have served as highways into southern Asia. The structure of the Americas is characterized by long mountain ranges connected by trough-like valleys, continental in size and drained by streams which in flood-time look like inlets of the sea. Into the Atlantic most of these mighty currents are poured, affording waterways from the ocean into the heart of the continents. The chief Atlantic streams of North America are found between 25° and 50° north latitude, in the most desirable part of the temperate zone. Furthermore, North America presents to the Atlantic a long, low, coastal plain, and down its gentle slope pour the easy-going currents of its drainage rivers. Only in southeastern New England does a narrowing of the lowland belt shorten the course and hasten the current of the streams, thus destroying their value for navigation. From the mouth of the St. Lawrence, therefore, to the mouth of the Rio Grande the eastern side of North America invited exploration.

During the sixteenth and the early part of the seventeenth century, there are to be distinguished three great movements in the eastern and northern part of the continent: the development of the banks fisheries which held to the coast, the search for the Northwest Passage, and the pursuit of the fur trade. Two of these penetrated into the interior.[1] All

---

[1] Ratzel, F., Zur Kustenentwiokelung Jahresber. d. Geograph. Gesellschaft in Munich, 1894.

were profoundly influenced by geographic conditions. Accompanying the search for the Passage was the development of the lucrative fur trade. Shortly, in the profits derived from the trade the original motive was all but lost.

The Banks Fisheries. From Cape Cod to Cape Race natural conditions combined to stimulate the fisheries industries. The Labrador current, which sweeps around this angle of the continent, is the natural habitat of the cod, the mackerel, and the herring. The neighboring coast, fringed with fiords and dotted with outlying islands, afforded harbors and fishing-stations in abundance. In the land itself, poor soil and bleak climate refused to the early colonist more than a niggardly subsistence, but the sturdy pine forests, toughened by cold and nourished by rain, put into his hand the material for his fishing-smack.[2]

A line from Quebec to Boston defines the base of the peninsula which forms the back country to most of this coast. It is a limited area, drained from north to south where its dimension is least. The rivers are therefore small, and hence did not adequately open up the back country for the fur trade, that great resource of the American pioneer. Thus the supply of peltries which each stream could command was soon exhausted.

The Search for the Northwest Passage. The search for the Northwest Passage took the explorers into every inlet and up every river. These men came from a continent less than half as large as North America, and their eyes were trained to the smaller dimensions of Europe.[3] In the prevailing estuaries of American rivers, with their salty tide, they saw

---

[2] See Chapter III and the Selected Readings for Chapter III for a full discussion of the banks fisheries and their significance.

[3] Ratzel, F., *Anthropogeographie*, Stuttgart, 1891, Part I, p. 248.

possible channels which, like the Strait of Gibraltar and the Bosphorus, might lead to an ulterior sea. A man accustomed to the small streams of England might well explore the broad, sluggish course of the James River, as Newport did in 1608, to find a passage to a western ocean; yet mariners, in general, were quick to recognize the true character of the estuaries and rivers they entered, as did Henry Hudson in his trip up the Hudson River in 1609.[4]

In Canada the search for the Northwest Passage was pursued longer. The only great waterway in the temperate zone westward into the heart of the continent is afforded by the St. Lawrence and the chain of the Great Lakes. Here the hope of reaching the fabled "Sea of Verrazano" had more to feed upon because of the length of the magnificent waterway already discovered. Therefore, nearly sixty years after the English Hudson and Baffin were limiting their search for the Northwest Passage to Arctic seas, where alone it was to be found, the problem of a water route to Cathay was luring LaSalle to the head streams of the Ohio and the Mississippi. It is significant that all exploration and colonization in North America has been westward from its "Europe-fronting shore." Even the Mississippi, though first reached near its mouth by the Spanish, was effectively approached and appropriated through its westward-flowing tributaries. Moreover, this approach which gave possession was made in its northern course by the Wisconsin River, at a point whence the distance east to the Atlantic shore is greatest. Not the wintry silence of the frozen north, nor river rapids, nor storm-swept lakes, nor swamp-covered portages, nor two thousand miles of travel

[4] Asher, G. M., *Henry Hudson the Navigator, the Original Documents*, Hakluyt Society, London, 1860; Journal of the Third Voyage, pp. 75–93.

sufficed to check the westward-moving tide. The search for
the Northwest Passage, therefore, made the early navigators
familiar with the interior waters; but as the futility of their
quest became apparent, the knowledge acquired in the
process was of great value.

Rivers and the Fur Trade. If an oceanic waterway was
not to be found in the interior, furs were. It is surprising
with what rapidity the desire of the Europeans moved from
the Passage to peltries. The best and most abundant furs
were to be reached only up the channels of the rivers; for
the indiscriminate killing of animals, young as well as old,
female as well as male, and the growing wariness of the
creatures made the fur fields rapidly recede from the coast.
Rivers were the only highways into the interior, and up the
rivers, preferably those flowing from the north, went the
American colonist — the trapper, trader, and voyageur
always in advance. The history of every colony testifies to
this fact. In 1627, William Claiborne, of Jamestown, had
begun to trade up the Potomac and Susquehanna rivers.
The Dutch came to America for the sake of the peltries, and
up the courses of the rivers they were drawn. Landing first
on Manhattan Island at the mouth of the Hudson, they had
a small settlement there in 1613 to control this highway into
the back country. Two years later they had built a post on
a small island just below Albany; by 1623, Fort Aurania was
constructed on the mainland near by; and 1661 saw the
beginning of Schenectady at the rapids of the Mohawk.
The distribution of their other settlements betrays the same
motive and the same characteristics: they were primarily
trading-posts, were limited to the other two great rivers of
the vicinity, the Delaware and the Connecticut, and were
located well upstream. At Fort Nassau, near where

Philadelphia now stands, the Dutch traders gathered in the furs of the Schuylkill and the middle and upper Delaware; Fort Good Hope on the Connecticut, near the present site of Hartford, enabled them to meet halfway the beaver-laden canoes of their savage customers. But the Dutch were shortsighted enough not to secure to themselves the natural commanding positions at the entrance of these streams, as they did in the case of the Hudson; so when John Winthrop, Jr., of Boston, in 1635 built Fort Saybrook at the mouth of the Connecticut, they were shut out of that river and forced to relinquish their upstream post. But when later a small colony of Swedes appropriated the western shore of the Delaware estuary, the Dutch, now grown wiser, overcame them and annexed their territory.

The Plymouth colony in 1634 had established a large trade with the Indians of the Connecticut and Kennebec rivers. But, owing to the smallness of the New England territory and the lack of great rivers, furs soon became scarce along the coast, and the traffic retreated rapidly up the few considerable streams, where the business was ruined by concentration of the traders and over-competition. Broad areas, widely scattered and remote posts, belong to the nature of the fur trade. Springfield, a frontier settle-ment on the Connecticut founded in 1636, was for a short time one of the best points for beaver, but by 1645 the market was spoiled by over-competition;[5] and Sir Richard Saltonstall and others endeavored to secure a monopoly of the right to establish trading-posts farther north than those already existing, while the Springfield colonists were forced to resort to the duller and less lucrative occupation of

[5] Weeden, W. B., *Economic and Social History of New England*, Boston, 1891, I, 14.

agriculture. With the exception of the Connecticut, therefore, which added fertile meadow lands to the attraction of the fur trade, the streams of New England, in consequence of their limited basins and rapid-broken courses, scarcely affected early settlement; while the larger rivers of the country carried far into the interior the vessel of the explorer, the canoe of the trader, and the shallop of the colonist. At Albany on the Hudson the traffic in peltries finally concentrated with far-reaching political results.

In Canada traffic in peltries sprang up along the shores of Acadia side by side with the fisheries and in the central basin of Hudson Bay; but in Canada, as elsewhere in North America, the presence of large rivers determined its progress into the interior. Moreover, the location of these streams to the north, and their connection with the large interior lakes bordering on the vast forest of the bleak Northwest, gave the French in the St. Lawrence–Great Lake country and the English in the Hudson Bay Basin access to fields yielding furs of finer quality and longer staple than any before known; while the remoteness, vastness, and harsh climate of the region promised to insure it against excessive exploitation.

An infant colony, in order to survive, must command some source of large profits, such as tobacco yielded to the Chespeake Bay settlements, the fisheries to New England, sugar and spirits to the West Indies. The reason is to be found in the remoteness of its market, the increased cost of such commodities as it buys in exchange, and the necessity of some indubitable allurement, like the prospect of wealth, in the new country to tempt settlers to make the long voyage from their native land and face the hardships of the wilderness. The glaciated soil of eastern Canada could

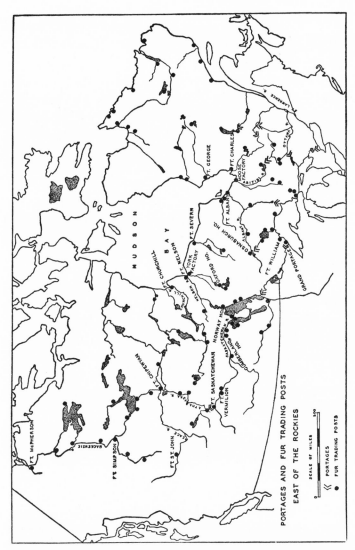

FIG. 3. PORTAGES BETWEEN THE HUDSON BAY BASIN AND THE GREAT LAKES—ST. LAWRENCE AND FUR TRADING POSTS

The many low short portages between the rivers of Hudson Bay and the Great Lakes — St. Lawrence system favored communication. The British located their chief factories at the mouths of the Hudson Bay and James Bay rivers and relied upon the Indians of the interior to bring in the furs.

promise no great fertility, its bleak climate no luxuriant vegetation; but there was money in peltries. Hence the up-stream advance of trading-post and settlement went on with amazing rapidity. Significantly enough, the long stretch of the St. Lawrence gulf and estuary was left almost unmarred by human habitation. Only where the gloomy gorge of the Saguenay River opened up an avenue north-westward to the Hudson Bay country and its rich furs, and where the Ottawa pointed the way and focused the great traffic in pelts from the Northwest did the trading-posts of Tadousac and Montreal break the solitude of the lower St. Lawrence. This westward movement of the French brought them into conflict with the English in the Hudson Bay Basin.

The English commanded the central basin of Hudson Bay for seagoing ships, but the cold northern half of the region supported little tree growth and provided few furs. The southern parts of Hudson Bay and James Bay were sur-rounded by a broad zone of deltas and swamps furnishing no game either for food or pelts; they discouraged the north-western plain and forest Indians, unaccustomed to canoe travel, from making the month-long journey to the British Hudson Bay ports under constant threat of starvation. The English ships could not penetrate up the mud-choked streams like the Churchill and Nelson. Hence the British located their forts at the mouths of the Churchill, Nelson (York Factory), the Severn, and also the mouths of the Albany, Moose, and Rupert rivers flowing into James Bay (Fig. 3). The Blackfeet forest Indians of the Canadian Rockies and the piedmont commanded large supplies of furs and transferred these to the Assiniboines of the Canadian Plains, by whom they were carried by canoe along the great east-west waterway of the Saskatchewan, Lake Winnipeg, and the Nelson River to York Factory on Hudson Bay. But the danger of starvation in the 'muskrat swamp' belt, and the loss of life and pelts in the twenty-three rapids to be traversed greatly increased the cost of the furs at York Factory.[6]

French Canada enjoyed facilities for river navigation unknown to Rupert Land. The St. Lawrence, Ottawa, Saguenay, and the Great Lakes carried big boats which brought the French trading goods from Europe far inland to Montreal. Abundant birch bark and other woods furnished materials for the voyageurs' canoes on smaller streams. French commodities, especially brandy, were assembled at Quebec or Montreal for the traders, and the pelts were exported thence when the ships returned to France in late summer. Large vessels, thirty-six feet long and with big cargo capacity, could be carried over the portages, as between Lake Ontario and Lake Erie, by ten men. Smaller vessels, thirty feet long and two feet deep, could be carried by two or three men, while a canoe was a slight burden for a single man.[7] The typical voyageur, usually a half-breed, had powerful chest and arm muscles, since his paddle was his sole reliance; and if his frail craft was shattered on the rocks of a rapid, he was skillful in constructing a new canoe.

All trade goods for the French fur trade went inland to Montreal, and were distributed thence to outlying fur stations two or three thousand miles in the interior; because the French soon learned they made larger profits by going inland to the Indians, and buying from them the pick of the furs at the lowest prices. Hence the French traders and

[6] Pinkerton, Robert, *The Hudson's Bay Company*, New York, 1931, pp. 88, 90–91.
[7] Pinkerton, *op. cit.*, chap. XXVI, pp. 230–37, 240–47.

later the North-West Fur Company of Montreal competed successfully with the Hudson's Bay Company, which a few decades after its organization lost money heavily.[8]

The distribution of the Canadian rivers in relation to the St. Lawrence–Great Lakes system and the Saskatchewan and upper Mackenzie systems enabled the French and the North-West Company to encircle the Hudson's Bay territory with a series of fur stations, which intercepted the best pelts at low prices and permitted only inferior specimens to reach the Hudson's Bay Company forts on the coast. The St. Lawrence, the Ottawa, and the Great Lakes opened a series of waterways to Grand Portage at the head of Lake Superior, whence an easy track led across the watershed to an arm of Lake Winnipeg in the Hudson Bay territory. The first big fur-trade rendezvous was established by the French traders at Basquia on the Saskatchewan River northwest of Lake Winnipeg. Here the Indians assembled in great numbers with their finest pelts, and sold them in large quantities in order to purchase the French brandy, besides the guns and ammunition on which they had come to rely. Basquia was later known as Cumberland House, when about 1800 the North-West Fur Company of Montreal assumed the work and the policy of the early French traders, while enlarging the scope. From the upper Saskatchewan short portages led to the rich pelt country of the head waters of the Athabasca River, Great Slave Lake, and the Peace River in the present territory of Alberta, and even to the sources of the Fraser and Columbia.

Hence the North-West Company drew their furs all the way from Great Slave Lake to the upper Columbia River, setting up fort after fort, wherever the profits loomed large.

[8] Pinkerton *op. cit.*, chap. XXVI, pp. 115–26, 230–34.

In contrast, the Hudson's Bay Company had few fur stations more than two hundred miles from the coast, and only one or two of these were powerless to compete with the large and strong organization of the North-West Company. Indeed, the older company achieved wealth and success only after consolidation with the vigorous Scotch and French Canadian members of the Montreal Company.[9] Depletion of furs followed wherever the Indians harvested the winter crops, because they killed to excess and were stimulated by the competing companies. Monopoly was normally a basic condition of the fur trade, if it was to survive. Hence the trappers extended their area and began encroaching on the Louisiana country of the young United States, finally penetrating into the Oregon territory until excluded by treaty.

RIVERS AND THE FRENCH SETTLEMENTS

In eastern Canada the first settlements were made at the mouth of the river in 1608, at Quebec, Beaupré, Beauport, and the Island of Orleans. By 1670 there were missions, each the center of a busy trade, at the outlets of Lakes Superior and Michigan, and farther west at the head of Green Bay. As the waterways determined the landward stretch of the French claim, so they fixed the proportions of the *habitant's* land grant and the location of his cabin. His farm was always on the river, which served as the highroad. River frontage was in demand, therefore, so his land grant was very narrow, measuring its width by the foot and its depth by the mile. His dwelling faced the stream, and hence was close to that of his neighbors. Thus the settlements were strung out in long, thin lines on the margins of the rivers. "One could have seen nearly every house in

[9] Pinkerton, *op. cit.*, pp. 115–26, 230–34; 140, 156–57.

Canada by paddling a canoe up the St. Lawrence and Richelieu." [10] The riparian grouping of the colonists, though eminently convenient for the Indian trade, made defense and government difficult. Like all natural forces, this geographical control of the rivers was so strong that it nullified royal decrees designed to concentrate the inhabitants and form villages.

Lakes and Low Divides. Missionary zeal and dreams of far-reaching empire were factors in the westward movement of the French; the fur trade, on the other hand, was a determinant, because it became the sole support of settlement and fort in all the wide region of Canada. But the landward expansion of commerce and Church and State was permitted and controlled by the Canadian lakes and rivers. The recurrent westward search for the problematical "great water" of the Indian anticipated the trader as it had done in the beginning. Then the remotest trading-post became a base for the next outward expedition of the explorer. And the passage from the Lakes to the Mississippi was made almost as easily as that from the Atlantic to the Lakes. This was the result of geographical conditions.

The mighty trough which runs through the center of the North American continent, from the Arctic Ocean to the Gulf of Mexico is met halfway between these points by a lesser valley to the eastward occupied by the Great Lakes.

[10] Parkman, F., *The Old Régime in Canada*, Boston, 1901, p. 297.

Note to Fig. 4:

The distribution and number of portages between the Great Lakes and the rivers of the Mississippi system, and the ease with which they could be traversed accounted in large measure for the early hold of the French upon the interior of the continent and for their ability to encircle the Hudson Bay territory with a series of fur stations, which intercepted the best pelts of the interior and permitted only inferior pelts to reach the posts of the Hudson's Bay Company on the coast. Many of those portages, used by the Indians and the French traders, later became the routes of military roads, canals, railways, and important highways.

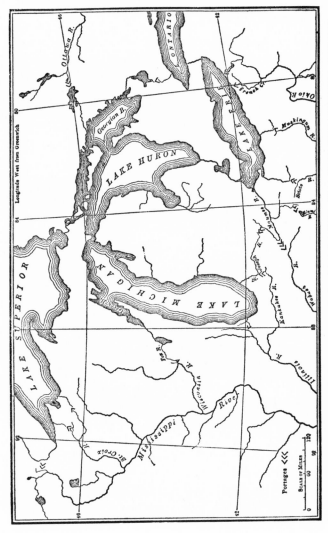

FIG. 4. PORTAGES BETWEEN THE GREAT LAKES AND THE MISSISSIPPI SYSTEM

(See note at foot of page 34)

The rim dividing these two basins is low and narrow, running close to the margin of the Lakes. West of Superior and Michigan the ill-defined watershed is flooded in a wet season; and at all times the ponds and pools and the endless meanderings of the connecting streams tell of a drainage system unfinished because of too slight incline. Hence the transition from the Lakes to the small affluents of the Mississippi tributaries was easy, especially as the French early adopted the canoe of the Indian as eminently suited to the low, narrow divides of the region. In flood-time there was an unbroken waterway; but the rule was to paddle up a short stream flowing into one of the Great Lakes, carry the canoe over a portage one to ten miles in length, and then launch it on a stream beyond, to float down to the all-receiving bosom of the Mississippi. The great number of the portages both offered a choice to the traders, especially advantageous in time of war with one or the other of the Indian tribes inhabiting this region, and enormously increased the voyageur's sphere of activity by opening up to him all the country drained by the Ohio and Mississippi (Fig. 4).

Discovery and Use of Portages. The order in which these portages were discovered [11] and used by the French was determined in part by the political neighborhood of the hostile Iroquois along the southern shores of the nearer lakes, and in part by geographical conditions. Up to 1670 the westward route of the canoe fleets was up Lakes Ontario, Erie, and Huron, to the westernmost outpost at Michillimackinac on the Strait of Mackinaw. This trading-station could be reached also by a more direct northern route from Montreal up the Ottawa River, across to Lake Nipissing and Georgian Bay — a route which was often used when the Iroquois were on the war-path about Ontario and Erie. Further

[11] Winsor, J., *The Mississippi Basin*, Boston, 1895, p. 22.

progress thence naturally led up the waterways afforded by Lake Superior and Lake Michigan to the portages which the Indian described as leading to the western waters. The consequence was that the passages earliest known were those remotest from the Canadian settlements. The first carry route used by the French led from the head of Green Bay up Fox River, across the northern part of Lake Winnebago, and along the upper Fox River for sixty or seventy miles to a narrow portage of two miles, leading to the head of the Wisconsin River.[12] This was the route followed by Marquette and the fur-trader Joliet in 1673, when they explored the Mississippi to the mouth of the Arkansas. The other of these earlier portages was across the narrow, lake-dotted watershed between the St. Louis River, which flows into the western extremity of Lake Superior, and the easternmost bend of the Mississippi.

By the end of the seventeenth century the portages at the head of Lake Michigan were the best known. There were a number of these close together. The Chicago River, the lesser and greater Calumet, and the St. Joseph all led by short carries to the Des Plaines and Kankakee branches of the Illinois. The Lake Erie portages, though affording nearer, more direct routes by the Ohio tributaries to the Mississippi, came into use only in the eighteenth century, and here, too, the progress was from west to east. When the French from their base in the newly founded Detroit (1701) were able to hold the neighboring Iroquois in check, the Maumee River with its portages west to the St. Joseph and the Wabash was open to travel; afterwards the portages from Lake Erie to the Big Miami, Scioto, and Muskingum were rendered safe. When in the middle of the eighteenth century the French began to draw their lines closer around

[12] Winsor, J., *op. cit.*, p. 22.

the back of the English settlements, that from Presque Isle (site of Erie) to French Creek and the Allegheny River marked the entrance to the fortified route of the French to their post at the forks of the Ohio, where Pittsburgh now stands.

Having swept westward up the broad highway of the Great Lakes to the upper reaches of the Ohio and Mississippi, the French went to work more slowly to secure all the portages to these rivers and to occupy every strategic point at the extremities of the Lakes. Forts Frontenac (Kingston), Niagara, Rouillé (Toronto), and Detroit were designed to command the Lakes, as Fort St. Louis on the upper Illinois and the post of Outianon on the upper Wabash controlled the Chicago and Maumee portages; while Vincennes, Cahokia, and Kaskaskia completed the line of connection with the lower Mississippi.

The vast area thus opened up to the French by their possession of the two great waterways of the continent led to the ultimate shipwreck of their colonial venture, because the large extent of the territory lured them to exploit its trade rather than make permanent settlements. They spread themselves thin over an enormous area, yielding to the danger of too great expansion. Their hold upon the country was akin to that of the small, widely scattered Indian tribes, whose manner of life they came to imitate and whose economic methods they adopted. Superficial use of a country's resources always means sparse population and therefore a weak hold upon the land.

RIVERS AND THE ENGLISH SETTLEMENTS

The compact settlements of the English made a surer basis for military operations than did the scattered posts of

the French.   The English had no mighty waterway to tempt
them into the remote lands of the abundant furs.   The
peltries came to them on the upper Hudson and the Mohawk; but everywhere else the fertile river valleys of the
narrow Atlantic plain rooted them in the soil, or numerous
harbors and neighboring fishing-grounds bound them to the
coast.   Their advance towards the interior was therefore a
slow heel-and-toe process, and never lost its connection with
the tide-swept shore.[13]

As the French settlements in North America were dominated by two great rivers, the English were controlled by the
larger and smaller indentations of the coast, together with
the streams draining into them.   Coming from their island
home with the object of making permanent settlements,
they met geographical conditions which combined to
strengthen them in the purpose.   The need of keeping in
touch with the mother country, at first for supplies and later
for commerce, and the equal need of getting beyond the
sandy beaches and rocky shores of the coast to the more
fertile soil as well as to the trade of the interior, were the
two motives determining the distribution of their colonies.
Under the influence of the first, their settlements were
grouped in inclosed sea-basins which carried their vessels by
protected waterways as far as possible into the land.   Massachusetts Bay, Narragansett Bay, Long Island Sound, New
York Bay with Raritan Bay, Delaware Bay with the Delaware estuary, Chesapeake Bay, Albemarle with Pamlico
Sound, marked each the beginning of one, in some cases
two, of the original colonies.   The same principle of selection was shown in the geographical distribution of the
French settlements in Acadia, where the Bay of Fundy and
Penobscot Bay comprised the majority of their fishing-

[13] Tyler, L. G., *England in America*, New York, 1904, pp. 34, 118, 196, and 229.

stations and trading-posts, and their three agricultural villages of Port Royal, Beaubassin, and Les Mines.

All of these inlets answered the requirement of contact with the sea; the rivers flowing into them answered the other requirement of broad contact with the land. Some of these bays, like Massachusetts and Narragansett, which received no affluents, gave to their settlements preëminently the stamp of coast communities. In such the advance of the population towards the interior was very slow, especially as there were almost no fertile alluvial bottoms to vary the monotony of a stubborn glacial soil and to tempt to agricultural expansion. But wherever navigable rivers flowed into these inlets of the sea, we notice the predominance of settlement at or near their mouths and a steady advance of population up their valleys. The mouth, and also in general the lower course of a river, afforded safe harborage for the small craft of the colonial period, while the back country was made accessible by the main stream and the ramifications of its creeks for canoe travel. A settlement thus located on a river commanded the Indian trade of its whole basin, and could easily export the products of its fields and forests.

The instructions of the London Company to the officers of their first expedition, sent to Virginia in 1606, point out another advantage of a river location well up towards the head of sea navigation: "Such a place you may perchance find one hundred miles from the rivers' mouth, and the further up the better, for if you sit down near the entrance, except it be in some island that is strong by nature, an enemy that may approach you on even ground may easily pull you out." [14] This caution was dictated by fear of coast attack from rival

[14] Fiske, J., *Old Virginia and Her Neighbours*, Boston, 1897, I, 72.

colonies of other European nations. The destruction of Ribault's colony at the mouth of the St. John's River in Florida by the Spanish, and later French depredations upon English settlements on the Maine coast, showed the wisdom of this precaution.

The river-made peninsulas of Maryland, Virginia, and North Carolina formed a geographical environment which influenced profoundly the development of these colonies. Here a mild climate, abundant alluvial bottoms, navigable streams, and a network of creeks combined to further agricultural expansion. Twelve years after the founding of Jamestown twenty-five miles from the mouth of the James River, the plantations extended up that water-course for seventy miles, spreading out four or six miles from either bank. In a few years more (1624) population had pushed up the stream to the present site of Richmond and across the peninsula between the James and the York. The intervening waterways and the series of rivers made it easy to expand laterally, so that by 1663 we find the Virginians had spread northward to meet the Maryland colony on the Potomac, and southward to the Chowan Peninsula on Albemarle Sound.[15] The ramifying streams brought almost all the plantations of this tidewater country in contact with the sea. It was customary for every planter to have his own wharf where he shipped tobacco or corn in exchange for the merchandise of Europe or the salted codfish of New England. Plantations on the upper reaches of small affluents were always able to send their produce downstream in canoes to the nearest head of navigation. Canoe and shallop became the coach of state .and the vehicle for neighborly visits, while every plantation was its own seaport.

[15] Bruce, P. A., *Economic History of Virginia in the Seventeenth Century*, New York, 1907, I, 103–05, 326, 341, 418, and 452.

The result of these geographical conditions was a wide and evenly distributed rural population, lack of roads, and absence of large commercial towns. Nevertheless, certain natural features lying beyond the limits of Chesapeake Bay caused the rise of a bustling city at each extremity of this basin. The head of Chesapeake Bay just failed to touch the territory of Pennsylvania, much to William Penn's disappointment, for his colony had no coast and its one seaport town, Philadelphia, was quite on the eastern border. Hence much flour, farm produce, and quantities of valuable furs from the interior of Pennsylvania found their way down the Susquehanna River to Baltimore for export. This town, founded in 1729, grew so rapidly that in 1770 its population numbered twenty thousand. At the other end of the bay Norfolk came to be a fairly active seaport. Two different geographic factors were operating here. The town became an outlet for the produce of the Albemarle Sound country, whose rivers had their navigation spoiled by the prevalent sand-bars, and whose fine lumber from the pine barrens met a steady demand in Virginia, as the tide-water country was stripped of its forests. Furthermore, the location of Norfolk at the mouth of Chesapeake Bay gave it a certain commercial advantage and attracted the West Indies trade in sugar, molasses, and rum, which were exchanged for pork and beef of the Sound country, and subsequently marketed in the river plantations.[16]

Thus the early development of the French and English colonies in America was profoundly influenced by the watercourses. The New England settlements, committed by their geographical conditions to fisheries and a coastwise trade, found great compensation for their lack of rivers in

[16] Fiske, J., *loc. cit.*, p. 211.

the protected waterway of Long Island Sound. Their geographical location at the northern end of the English colonies
and the inevitable encroachment of their fishermen and
traders upon the shores of Acadia brought them into conflict
with the French and made them the natural bulwark against
French aggression in this locality, just as the Hudson and
the Mohawk in the middle section lent this same character
to New York.

CHAPTER III

THE INFLUENCE OF THE APPALACHIAN BARRIER UPON COLONIAL HISTORY

HISTORY shows us by repeated instances that the geographical conditions most favorable for the early development of a people are such as secure to it a certain amount of isolation. For this reason, a highly articulated continent like Europe has proved a forcing-house for nations. Almost every people there has grown up, shut off from its neighbors by barriers of mountain or sea. Confined to a limited area, protected from without by bulwarks of Nature's own making, population increased rapidly and civilization moved with strides under the strongly interactive life. The people soon filled out their natural territory, then began to crowd it, pressing upon the limits of subsistence, and perfecting their political and social organization in the effort to avoid the friction incident to greater density of population. Local life grew in intensity and the sense of statehood was early developed. An increasing industrial and commercial activity endeavored to supply from abroad the deficit of food for the growing number of consumers; while the population, already redundant, began to expand beyond its natural environment and overflow into other lands.[1]

Isolation of English Colonies. Of the three leading colonizing nations which came to North America from Europe, one appropriated the only part of this continent which could afford geographic isolation in any way approximating that

[1] Shaler, N. S., *Nature and Man in America*, New York, 1904, p. 152; Ratzel, F., *Anthropographie*, Stuttgart, 2d ed. 1898, Part I, p. 249.

which it had enjoyed in Europe. That people were the English. At the end of the first century of permanent settlement they found themselves in possession of a narrow strip of coast, shut off from the interior of the country by an almost unbroken mountain wall. Sea and watershed drew their boundary lines and constituted at the same time their frontier defenses. Only one border was really open, that to the south along the Spanish possessions in Florida. The English were therefore in a naturally defined area, isolated enough to lend them the protection and cohesion which colonial life so much needs, affording the long line of coast which could give to this maritime people its most favorable environment, large enough for growth and strength, but small enough to secure concentration and to guard against the evils of excessive expansion.

Beyond this seaboard country lay the great valley of the continent, shut in by the upheaved masses of the Appalachian and Rocky Mountain systems, a vast basin unbroken save by the faint traceries of its winding streams. Here Nature offered no obstruction, afforded no protection. The two natural highways into this country, the St. Lawrence on the east and the Mississippi to the south, came into the hands of the French, and consequently gave them control of this extensive territory. It proved, however, too large for them to hold; the very extent of it scattered their population, tempted to the adventurous, half-nomadic occupation of the fur-trader rather than the sedentary life of the colonist. Here were seen fortified trading-posts instead of the agricultural villages which dotted the seaward slope of the Alleghenies.

The people who came to the New World to "plant an English nation in America" had experienced at home the economic evils of overcrowding. They realized that here was a chance to make a living; and in so far their motive was wholesomely selfish. They went to work accordingly to get an industrial hold on American soil. The narrow strip of land between the Atlantic and the mountains favored and strengthened their purpose. The Appalachian barrier narrowed their horizon and shut out the great beyond; it took away the temptation to wide expansion which was defeating the political aims of the Spanish and the French, and transformed the hunter into the farmer, the gentleman adventurer into the tobacco-grower. Territory that is held industrially in all its extent is held strongly. The less dispersed the population, the fewer are the avenues for invasion and the more solid is the front which the country presents to attack. The mountain wall gave to the Thirteen Colonies a certain solidarity which they would not have otherwise possessed — a solidarity which fought for them in the Revolution.

CHARACTER OF APPALACHIAN SYSTEM

The Appalachian system, which presented such an insuperable barrier to the early colonists, extends from the thickly wooded mountains of northern Maine to the pine-covered hills of Alabama. It consists in general of parallel ranges, altogether some three hundred miles in width, which stretch along with only one considerable break in all their length of fifteen hundred miles. A mantle of primeval forest with a singularly dense undergrowth contributed further to make them impassable. The backwoodsman had fairly to carve a path for himself through this wall of living green. In consequence, the tidewater country had its long-established colonies before anything of the mountains was known. The rivers flowing down the eastern slope were not navigable far back from the coast and therefore did not afford ready access into the interior; but when followed to their head waters they were found to disclose excellent passes. This was especially true of the southern portion of the system, but even here the disposition of the passes involved long, circuitous routes to reach the western slope; for, one range passed, the next one presented a similar barrier and the longitudinal valleys between had to be traversed before another gap could be found. The Pennsylvanians gained access to the Ohio by the West Branch of the Susquehanna, and also by another route farther south from the Juniata to a tributary stream of the Allegheny. The Virginians, though, found a more direct way up the valley of the Potomac and thence by a short portage to the Youghiogeny. Among the broken hills of the southern end of the Alleghenies, an almost level route was frequented by the traders from the Carolinas and Virginia seeking the Cherokee villages; it was known from the earliest times, but had only a limited use, because it was too remote from the northwestern Indians who commanded the all-important fur trade.

Hudson–Mohawk Gateway. The only important break in this mountain wall was to be found in the natural depression of the Hudson and Mohawk valleys,[2] where the pass into the interior is only about four hundred and forty-five feet above sea-level. This route was also able to tap the northwestern fur trade, then in the hands of the French. Furthermore, trails led from the Mohawk and Genesee to the upper Allegheny, and thence to the Ohio and Mississippi. For this

[2] Brigham, A. P., "The Eastern Gateway of the United States," *The Geographical Journal*, XIII (1899), 513–24.

reason it became apparent at an early date that the Mohawk and Hudson valleys formed the key to the Northwest, as the meeting-place of the Allegheny and Monongahela was in reality the "Gateway of the West." By the geography of eastern America, therefore, these rivers were cut out for battle-grounds in all colonial wars between the English and the French, just as the head streams of the Po and Ebro leading down from the passes of the Alps and Pyrenees have been the scenes of conflict in every northern invasion of Italy and Spain since the days of Hannibal and Roland.

FIG. 5. THE MOHAWK VALLEY AND LAKE CHAMPLAIN REGION

The Hudson–Mohawk and Hudson–Champlain depressions afford the only important break in the Appalachian mountain wall; they have played a striking rôle in history: Indian trails, route of the trader and trapper, battle-grounds in the colonial wars and the War of 1812, routes of canals and the great westward migration; sites of power developments and manufactures of a great variety, and lines of railways and modern highways.

Early importance of Hudson–Mohawk Depression. The French, who felt that the heart of the continent was in jeopardy, kept a sharp eye on these avenues to the West. They could attack the English most easily along the Mohawk valley and at the southern end of the mountains; but at both these points the English had a buffer state between themselves and the enemy in the Iroquois tribes in the north and the Cherokees in the south, both of which nations were attached to British interests. The chronic jealousy between the French and English took an acute form when the French discovered that the Mohawk Valley was getting too large a share of the northwestern fur trade (Fig. 5). Consequently, by a long series of wars, they endeavored to drive the English out of this region altogether. The enemy were at a long distance from the middle and southern colonies, which were further guarded by the wall of the Alleghenies; so that, with the exception of one or two sporadic attacks, they were left undisturbed by the struggle going on to the north of them. On the colonies along the Hudson and in New England, though, the attacks were almost incessant. In the French and Indian War nearly every foot of the upper Hudson was fought over as far as Lake Champlain, and the route up the Mohawk to Oswego was almost as bitterly contested. This history repeated itself in the Revolutionary War. Both in the French wars and in the Revolution the Six Nations who inhabited this region rendered valuable aid to the British. In the earlier wars particularly, the fact that they occupied a strategic position gave them a power and importance out of all proportion to their numbers.

Expulsion of Indians. The British early ingratiated themselves with the Iroquois and Cherokees, that they might have these Indians as outposts against the French. But the rest of the tribes on the seaboard were not treated with any undue consideration, for they were not a numerous and therefore not a dangerous enemy; and they were prevented by the mountains from making any combination with the far more populous tribes of the Mississippi Valley. The members of savages with whom the settlers had to contend were small. The Indians of southern New England were exterminated in two short wars. The Delawares were dislodged from their original home and emigrated beyond the mountains. The Tuscaroras were made to evacuate their holdings in North Carolina. Living in the narrow area of the tidewater country, it was unavoidable that the Indians should soon feel the encroachments of the whites; and it was equally certain that they would suffer defeat, when it came to a conflict, in consequence of the weakness of the tribes. Fortunately for the young colonies, the Alleghenies protected them against the depredations of the wild, half-nomadic Indians of the Northwest, and of the fierce Appalachian tribes of the southern Mississippi.

LINES OF DEVELOPMENT IN DIFFERENT COLONIES

Hemmed in thus by the mountains, for the first one hundred and fifty years of their occupancy the English settlers were limited to the tidewater region of the Atlantic coast. This seaboard country presented in its different portions different aspects, which had a corresponding effect upon the colonists.

In New England the lowland belt is only from fifty to eighty miles wide; but it gradually broadens as it continues southward, until in the Carolinas the mountains are two hundred and fifty miles from the sea. The area adapted to settlement was therefore more extensive in the South than in the North. Furthermore, the northern district had suffered glaciation; it was covered with a heavy deposit of boulders, which had to be removed at the cost of infinite labor before the land was ready for cultivation. The hardest work had to be done before a plow could be used; but this once over, the soil could be tilled for a long time without giving signs of exhaustion.[3] This fact, together with the small area at their command, preserved to the settlers the contracted territorial ideas which they had brought with them from the mother country, and served to root them in the soil. In addition, the wealth of the sea, the abundant forests of easily worked timbers, and the numerous protected harbors served to hold them to the border of the sea. Consequently the people of New England developed little of the tendency to expansion which later became a characteristic of the American people.

That tendency developed farther south. Here the larger unobstructed area invited it, and the leading occupation of the settlers — tobacco-culture — made it a necessity. At a time when artificial fertilizing was almost unknown, the production of the better kinds of tobacco demanded a virgin soil. The planters were therefore led to take up as large tracts as possible. The only preparation was "girdling" the trees, the primitive mode of clearing the land which the colonists learned from the Indians. Land so prepared was planted in tobacco for three years, and afterwards in corn. This method of cultivation, expedient in view of the abundance of arable land, was superficial, and the materials taken from the soil were never replaced. By this system of agriculture, the evils of which were further accentuated by slave labor, low lands were exhausted in eight years, fields less favorably situated in three. Ceasing to yield, they were abandoned and allowed to revert again to a state of nature. More forest was cleared for the plow, and the settlements

[3] Shaler, N. S., *op. cit.*, p. 225.

invaded the wilderness.   In 1685, "although the population
of Virginia did not exceed the number of inhabitants in the
single parish of Stepney, London, nevertheless they had
acquired ownership in plantations that spread over the
same area as England itself." [4]   Thus developed that spirit
of expansion which early in the eighteenth century led the
settlers to hammer at the gates of the mountain wall on
their western frontier, and to resent the claims of the
French that the British possessions were limited by the
crest of the Alleghenies.

It was therefore not a matter of chance that the first
protest against the French forts on the Ohio was made by a
governor of Virginia.   Towards the gap in the ridge of the
Alleghenies between the head waters of the Youghiogeny
and the Potomac, French and English were approaching up
the flanking valleys.   Fort Cumberland was Maryland's
frontier defense on the upper Potomac to guard this strategic point; Fort Necessity and the battle of Great Meadows
represented the effort of the Virginians to secure the western
approach to the dividing range, just as Braddock's march
by this same route a year later was aimed at Fort Duquesne,
which commanded all the river approaches from the west to
the mountain rampart of Pennsylvania, Maryland, and
northern Virginia.

The Virginians in the battle of Great Meadows took the
initiative in the French and Indian War before the declaration of hostilities.   Men like Byrd of Westover and
Governor Spotswood appreciated the character of the
mountains as a bulwark against the enemy, and realized the
necessity of making themselves masters of its passes before
the French should do so.   They knew that their expansion

[4] Bruce, P. A., *op. cit.*, I, 424.

over these mountains was inevitable; therefore the sea-to-sea claims of the English were to them of vital importance. This view was shared also by the colonists of Pennsylvania and New York because they, too, lived under similar conditions of expansion; but the people of New England, on the other hand, were indifferent to the disposition of the western country. They seemed quite satisfied with the line of the Alleghenies as a boundary, if the trade with the western Indians could be secured. Their standpoint was therefore provincial, in contrast to the continental conceptions of the middle and southern colonies.

The policy of the latter prevailed and the whole line of settlements from Maine to South Carolina was levied on for its support in the French and Indian War. This was the first time in their history that all the colonies acted together; this was the first time that there was a common American interest at stake. Hitherto none had combined, except the New England colonies, where the geographical conditions made for greater density of population, and a certain degree of isolation emphasized their community of interests. The southern colonies, with their widely scattered plantations, did not at first have much to do with each other or with their northern neighbors. Blocked by the mountains in their growth towards the west, however, they were finally compelled to expand laterally and fill up the stretches of forest which originally separated them. The effect of the Appalachian barrier was therefore to keep the population within clearly defined limits and lend it that density which means strength. In 1700 "it was possible to ride from Portland, Maine, to southern Virginia, sleeping each night at some considerable village." [5]

[5] Shaler, N. S., *op. cit.*, p. 199.

With the rapid increase of population characteristic of colonial life, the limited extent of the country which would repay cultivation, and the prevailing wasteful methods of agriculture, it was to be expected that the supply of arable land would eventually be exhausted, and the activities of the colonist necessarily directed into other channels. This condition was reached first in New England, so that its people were early forced into industrial and maritime enterprise. Manufactories for the most common articles of consumption were established; the forests were levied on for shipbuilding, and American vessels were soon doing all the carrying trade between the colonies.

EFFECT OF BARRIER IN KEEPING COLONIES UNDER CONTROL OF ENGLAND

The Appalachian barrier had the effect, therefore, of keeping the colonies to the hem of the continent. It limited them to a strip of coast, where they were most easily retained under British domination. If they had expanded at an earlier date to the west, England would have found it a much more difficult task to make its power felt over all the area settled. The mere element of distance in a new, unbroken country would have complicated greatly the machinery of government, while diminishing its efficiency. Furthermore, it would have generated in a larger proportion of the population the spirit of the frontier, that is, the spirit of independence. Disaffection towards the mother country would have developed slowly as a chronic disease; and we may think it would have been a long time before the feeling could have gathered strength to break out in rebellion. As it was, held under the thumb of the British government, disaffection took on the form of an acute attack, and rapidly ran its course from protest to rebellion, from rebellion to independence. More than this, when the conflict did come the colonies were all of one mind, no matter from what section they came. The spirit of union which animated them can be attributed in no small degree to their close contiguity, while their occupation of a contracted area with their two and a half million population enabled them to operate in a solid mass against the enemy.

The Colonies as Peripheral Holdings. In revolting against England the American colonies followed a recognized law of political geography. They constituted the remote western frontier of Europe; and a tendency towards defection manifests itself in all peripheral holdings.[6] History is full of examples. The causes are deep-seated. Differences of geographical conditions, of climate, soil, economic methods, and therefore of political and social ideas, rapidly differentiate colonists from the parent nation. Moreover, mere distance increases greatly the difficulty of governmental control, even in this day of rapid communication. More than a hundred years ago Burke stated this politico-geographical law in terms that cannot be improved upon. "The last cause of this disobedient spirit in the colonies... is deep laid in the natural constitution of things. Three thousand miles of ocean lie between you and them. No contrivance can prevent the effect of this distance in weakening government. Seas roll and months pass between the order and the execution; and the want of a speedy explanation of a single point is enough to defeat a whole system.... Nothing more happens to you than does to all nations who have extensive empire; and it happens in all the forms in which empire can

[6] Ratzel, F., *Anthropogeographie*, Stuttgart, 1898, p. 219.

be thrown. In large bodies, the circulation of power must be less vigorous at the extremities. Nature has said it. The Turk cannot govern Egypt and Arabia and Kurdistan as he governs Thrace; nor has he the same dominion in Crimea and Algiers which he has at Brusa and Smyrna." [7]

Remoteness of Colonies. This is the statement of the law from the standpoint of the governing power; those on the far-away periphery also were affected by their remoteness from the center of authority. The colonists found it difficult to get a hearing in England; distance dulled the edge and weakened the force of their protests — this by a psychological law. They found it irksome, often detrimental to their interests, to wait months for the ratification in England of colonial laws. Compelled often by sudden crises to act without authority in consequence of their remoteness, the colonists developed a spirit of initiative and independence. When the outbreak came, England for the first time learned the expense and difficulty of an arm's-length war. Time and space fought on the side of the Americans.

GEOGRAPHICAL CONDITIONS AND CAMPAIGNS

With the opening of hostilities, geographical conditions directed campaigns and influenced the result of battles. The valley of the Hudson made the natural line of communication between Canada and the British fleet on the coast, and at the same time formed the land connection between New England and the other colonies. As the British had full control of the sea, the colonial armies could move only by land routes. Hence the Hudson River was of vital importance to both sides, and from the first both sides

[7] Burke, E., *Speech on Conciliation*, London, 1854, I, 468.

aimed at its control.   The seizure of Crown Point and Ticonderoga at the start enabled the Americans to command the line of communication with Canada.   The British operations to gain the Hudson followed three geographical lines.   By the Champlain route and the Mohawk Valley two armies from Canada advanced towards Albany, where they were to form a conjunction with troops coming up the Hudson.   The naval battle off Valcour Island in Lake Champlain, and later the capture of Ticonderoga and Fort Edward, traced the British advance to the Hudson from the north; Bemis Heights, Stillwater, and Saratoga, the attempted retreat along the same route.   On the Mohawk Valley route, Oswego, Fort Stanwix — which corresponded in its geographico-strategic location to Fort Cumberland on the upper Potomac — and Oriskany marked the conflict between the British and American forces.   The approach from the south began with the operations at the mouth of the Hudson.   Here the siege of Brooklyn Heights, battles of Harlem Heights and White Plains, with the capture of Fort Washington, gave the British the control of Manhattan and the lower Hudson.   But the success of the Americans in cutting the British lines of communication with Canada along the Mohawk and Lake Champlain, and Washington's tactics to prevent Howe's moving up the Hudson, frustrated British effort to control eastern New York.

The colonies by their position on the long, narrow border of the American continent had an extensive sea frontier, which was open to the attack of the British fleet.   Consequently much of the Revolutionary War was fought on or near the coast.   The coast towns of New England were cannonaded and levied on for supplies by the British frigates.   Charleston, South Carolina, and Savannah were

taken by naval attack, and the fleet assisted in the capture
of New York.   With the exception of Canada, the British
had no base on the land frontier, so they had to establish
their base at coast points accessible to their ships.   And if
their armies advanced into the interior, a threat to their line
of communication with the sea would bring them hurrying
to the coast.   Washington's occupation of Morristown
Heights in January, 1776, enabled him to prevent the
enemy from crossing New Jersey to take Philadelphia,
because he was in a position to cut them off from their
supplies.   The campaigns of Cornwallis and Tarleton in the
Piedmont country of North and South Carolina were terminated chiefly by the threat to their lines of communication with the coast.   The final overthrow came when, by
the advent of the French fleet, the Americans were able to
invest the position of Cornwallis at Yorktown by water as
well as by land.

The barrier of the Appalachians kept the American
armies facing eastward.   The colonies braced themselves
against the mountains and fought towards the sea.   The
bulwark at their back protected them from the onslaughts
of the western Indians, who were stirred to hostilities by
British agents.   Only the few settlements beyond the
mountains in Kentucky and Tennessee were exposed to this
danger; but as they were debarred in general from participation in the eastern campaigns, they could give the
Indians their undivided attention.

For a hundred and fifty years the American people were
dammed up against the mountain barrier.   But the energies
aroused by the prosecution of a successful war, and the
snapping of the cords which held the colonies in leash to
England, enabled the mass of American life to rush through

the breaches in the mountains, down to the Mississippi and beyond; until in half the time it had taken the people to reach the crest of the Alleghenies, they were planting their towns on the genial coast of the Pacific.

CHAPTER IV

THE WESTWARD MOVEMENT IN RELATION TO THE PHYSIOGRAPHIC FEATURES OF THE APPALACHIAN SYSTEM

A Mountain System as a Barrier. A mountain system is always a barrier; this character it maintains in a greater or less degree according to its physiographic features. A single high massive range like the Himalayas, or a double snow-crowned rampart like the Great Caucasus and Anti-Caucasus, or a series of parallel earth-folds like the Alps, are enduring obstacles to intercourse, whose resistance is measured largely by their height and width. The number, distribution, and elevation of its passes also affect the barrier nature of a mountain. A comparatively low range like the Pyrenees, which lifts an even sky-line unbroken by any deep gap or notch, is a wall without breach or door, while the many easy and evenly distributed passes of the Alps have reduced the difficulty of communication between the plains to the north and south. Finally, the presence of transverse river valleys leading up like natural roads to these lofty portals in the mountain wall facilitate transmontane travel, and their absence leaves many an excellent pass unutilized.

The general with his army, the pack-laden trader, the migrating settler, and the engineer laying out the course of a railroad, see in a mountain range only a challenge of their energy and endurance; and they straightway search for the lowest dip in the crest by which to cross. The pass points the easiest road across the ridge, and therefore becomes the focus of all established highways on either slope. Along its narrow, rugged channel pours a tide of humanity, drawn thither by some dream of good beyond, while on the flanking summits reigns the solitude of primeval forest or the eternal snows.[1]

Mountains which spread out on a broad base with a succession of parallel ranges must be crossed by a succession of passes determining more or less circuitous routes. This is the case in the Austrian Alps and in the Hindu Kush along the caravan road from Peshawar in the Punjab to Balkh in the plains of northern Afghanistan. But sometimes powerful drainage streams have carved their valleys straight across the axis of the corrugated upland and opened up natural highways to a single pass, which thus dominates a system several hundred miles wide. The valley of the Ticino from Lake Maggiore and of the Reuss from Lake Lucerne form an unbroken ascent to the St. Gotthard, the only point in which the central Alps can be crossed by one pass. But even where streams have not cut reëntrant valleys into the heart of the mountain system, but furrow only the outermost slope, they mark the avenue of easiest approach to the gaps above. Navigable in their lower course, they expedite travel; as the grade grows steeper, however, rapids demand portages, and later canals, but always the rugged gorge above furnishes a foothold for the trail to the summit.

By river valley and pass migrating races and individuals have found their way over mountain barriers. The Gap of Belfort, connecting the long valleys of the Rhone and the

[1] Semple, E. C., "Mountain Passes: A Study in Anthropogeography," *Bulletin of the American Geographical Society*, XXXIII (1901), 124–37, and 191–203; and Ratzel, F., *Politische Geographie*, Liepzig, 1897, p. 685, and *Anthropogeographie*, Stuttgart, 1891, Part I, pp. 420, 424.

Rhine, has been the historic route of migration and travel between the North Sea and the Mediterranean. The Brenner Pass was the Alpine portal by which the Cimbri swept down into the valley of the Po; and the breaches in the eastern Alps determined the line of Rome's expansion to the Danube, just as later they exposed her to the inroads of the Goths and Huns. The Russians pushed southward from the sandy plains of Turkestan up the Heri Rud and Murghab rivers to the low dips in the western Hindu Kush which form the "Gates of Herat"; and eastward by the valleys of the Syr Daria and the Oxus they have stretched their power to the snowy passes of the Tyan Shan and the Pamir, and beyond to Mongolia. In the same way, gaps and rivers enabled the American colonists to cross the Appalachian barrier. The location and distribution of these natural passways determined which colonies should furnish the largest quota of the pioneers, and also what should be the destination of those early winners of the West. To see how this geographic control operated, an analysis of the Appalachian topography is necessary.

The Appalachian System. The Appalachian system is peculiar in that it consists of a long central zone of depression, bordered on the southeast by the Appalachian Mountains proper, and on the northwest by the Allegheny and Cumberland plateaus.[2] This central trough, known as the Great Appalachian Valley, is sunk several hundred feet below the highlands on either side, but its surface is diversified by intermittent series of parallel, even-crested ridges, which rise, one beyond the other, like successive waves of the sea, across the whole seventy-five miles of the valley's width (Fig. 6). The Blue Ridge, which forms the eastern

² Read pp. 46–49.

rim of the Great Valley, is a range of gentle slope and rounded crest, notched at frequent intervals by gaps a thousand feet deep, or cut through by flaring river gorges. The western rim is the Allegheny Front, the bold, forbidding escarpment of the Allegheny and Cumberland plateaus, whose rugged surface, scoured and furrowed by drainage streams, runs off into the low plains of the prairies and the Great Lakes. The height of the Appalachian system increases from the north towards the south; but the average elevation of the ranges, which is only from three to four thousand feet, is nowhere sufficient to constitute a great obstacle. It is the long, unbroken extent of the system and its great width of three hundred miles which make it a barrier.

This character would be far more pronounced were it not for the drainage streams of the upland. The Appalachian rivers cut across the grain of the mountains from west to east or east to west, only intermittently controlled by the ranges and following the trend of the longitudinal valleys. The reason for this physiographic discordance is to be found in the geologic history of the highlands. The transverse river channels are older than the mountains themselves, and as the nascent ranges slowly protruded their crests, or were left in relief by erosion, cut through them in flaring watergaps. The northern rivers, like the Delaware, Susquehanna, Potomac, and James, have their sources on the Allegheny Plateau, cut through the Allegheny Front, the ranges of the Great Valley, and the Blue Ridge or its northern extension, South Mountain, and empty into the Atlantic Ocean, while their head waters interlock with those of the Ohio along inconspicuous divides to the west. The southern rivers take an opposite course. They rise, as the

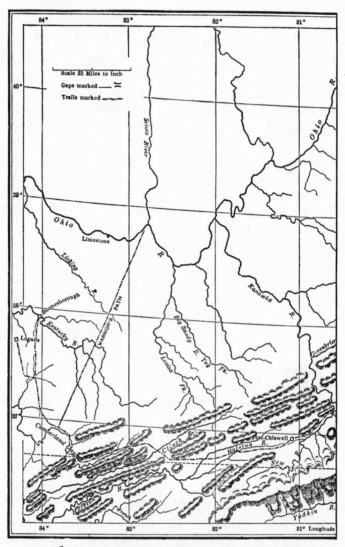

FIG. 6. THE APPALACHIAN SYSTEM AND TRANS-

Though made of parallel belts of Piedmont, Blue Ridge, Great Valley and Allegheny–
Cumberland Plateaus, the transverse rivers, wind gaps, and low interstream divides
facilitated westward migration over two sets of routes. What effect did the location

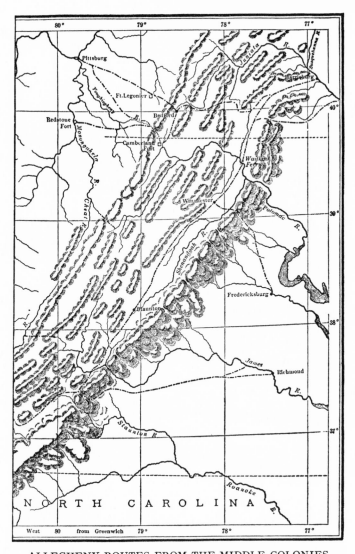

ALLEGHENY ROUTES FROM THE MIDDLE COLONIES

of the gaps in the different ridges have upon the direction of movement? In the early westward movement why was the Cumberland Gap route the chief one used?

Watauga, Nolichucky, Holston, French Broad, and New River, on the eastern rim of the system in North Carolina or, as in the case of the New, even on the seaward side of the Blue Ridge, carve their way westward through every barrier, and flow out as the Tennessee and Kanawha into the Ohio. Their sources interlace with those of the Yadkin and Catawba, which furrow the eastern slopes of the Blue Ridge to the Atlantic; and among the Allegheny ridges of West Virginia, the Greenbrier, a northern tributary of the Kanawha, is separated from the head waters of the James River only by a narrow range tracing the Allegheny Front, crossed by the Chespeake and Ohio Railroad.

The divides within the Great Valley are peculiar in being distinct from the Allegheny ridges; for this reason they are intricate and little elevated above the general level, so that it is easy to pass down the whole length of this trough from the Susquehanna to the Tennessee, merely by following the lateral branches of these and of the intervening streams as they flow along the minor longitudinal vales of the whole system.   Hence the outbound pathfinders to the west were able to enter the Great Valley by the Susquehanna, Juniata, Potomac, James, or Roanoke, turn right or left up a lateral branch, ascend a notched gap or low watershed to the next transverse river within the valley, and following it to its source pass over to some westward flowing stream.   In this way he could cross the Appalachians in almost any direction.

The eastern head waters of the Tennessee, after leaving the high open valleys just to the west of the Blue Ridge, had to cut through the broad, complex belt of the Unaka Mountains in deep gorges, which afforded no easy passway and were further dangerous on account of the hostile Cherokees. Hence North Carolina pioneers from the upper Watauga and Nolichucky valleys found readier connection with the west through the New River and the Virginia routes to the northern tributaries of the Tennessee. And for over a hundred years the Unakas remained an obstacle to deflect the tide of emigration.

SLOW PROGRESS OF COLONIAL FRONTIER

The westward progress of the colonial frontier in early times was slow. Bound to the coast by the need of ready sea communication, in 1700 the settlements embraced all the tidewater country up to the "fall line," the outer limit of the Piedmont Plateau and the first interruption to river navigation; the frontier was somewhat farther inland, about fifty miles to the east of the Blue Ridge. But by 1750 the far-ranging traders were building their lonely cabins in the murmurous solitude of the great Appalachian forests, while their pack-horses were loosening the rocks on the mountain passes beyond, and their bateaux were burdening the waters of the Ohio, Great Miami, Wabash, and Sandusky Bay.[3]

The successful ending of the French and Indian War, which extended England's territory in America to the Mississippi (1763), was the signal for a western advance of the population; but at the outbreak of hostilities (1755) the frontier of settlement described a rough curve, which reached its easternmost points in New York and Georgia, and its westernmost on the Greenbrier and Holston rivers.

In New York. Conditions of physical and political geography determined this frontier line. In New York the advance up the Mohawk Valley moved at a snail's pace as compared with the leap of settlement from Manhattan

[3] Winsor, J., *The Mississippi Basin*, Boston, 1895, pp. 243, 249.

Island to Albany. From Schenectady some late-coming Germans pushed the narrow valley zone of civilization constituting New York first to Palatine Bridge and Stone Arabia (near Canajoharie), then in 1723 to German Flats along the upper Mohawk between Little Falls and Utica. The Catskill and Adirondack mountains on either side, too inaccessible in those roadless days, were left uninhabited. From 1723 till 1784 there was no advance of settlement in central New York, for, though the country was fertile, the location was too exposed to French aggression; and after the removal of this danger, the relatively dense population of the Iroquois tribes was an effective barrier to expansion. Thus political neighbors held back the frontier of settlement.

In Pennsylvania.   In eastern Pennsylvania, where the Appalachian trough is easily accessible in consequence of dips and breaks in the mountain wall, settlers early spread into the Cumberland and Lebanon valleys, and founded Easton, Bethlehem, Reading, Carlisle, and Shippensburg, while the traders had pushed up the Susquehanna to Wyoming and across the "Endless Mountains" by the Juniata, in whose upland valleys they were marking their "tomahawk claims" and preparing for permanent settlement.[4] But this western part of the Great Appalachian Valley is much broken by linear ridges and little adapted for agriculture. Hence the tide of frontier settlers, who were made up chiefly of Scotch-Irish and German late-comers to the New World, spread southward along the line of least resistance into the broad open Valley of Virginia. A few passed thence by the gap of the Roanoke River to the head streams of the Yadkin in the Piedmont of North Carolina.

In the Great Valley.   Both these regions received acces-

[4] Winsor, J., *op. cit.*, p. 258.

sions also from the tidewater portion of the southern colonies. Especially in Virginia, as the large estates predominated more and more, the small proprietors, unable to compete with the plantation system of the tidewater, moved westward and southwestward into the Piedmont and mountain regions, where other economic conditions prevailed, and thus by natural selection added to the democratic element of the frontier. The broad, fertile Shenandoah Valley was easily accessible to these through the low passes of the Blue Ridge between the Potomac and the Roanoke, and hence drew steadily if not extensively from the tidewater sources; but it received the greater part of its population by the nature-made highway leading down from the north. The geographical order of its settlement indicates this. The first clearing was made in 1732 near the present town of Winchester, about thirty-two miles from the Potomac, by one Joist Hite, who came in from Pennsylvania and who was soon followed by sixteen families from the same state. Two years later some cabins and cornfields appeared in the vast encasing forest about twenty-eight miles farther up the valley in the vicinity of the modern Woodstock; and from then till 1740 the tide advanced rapidly up to the sources of the Shenandoah River, and beyond to where the head waters of the James and the Roanoke interlace with those of the westward flowing New River.

In 1755, just before the outbreak of the French and Indian War, Winchester, Staunton or Augusta Court House, as it was then called, and Fincastle were distant frontier posts; but fifty miles beyond, the westward flowing streams, readily accessible from Virginia, showed the remotest habitations of all the colonies. Colonel Wilson's mill on Cheat River was reached by a twenty-mile trace from the South Branch of the Potomac.   Just to the southwest there were a few cabins and clearings on the Greenbrier.⁵   William English or Ingles, with a few other Scotch-Irish and a group of Dunkards, had their outlying dwellings on the upper New far up the Valley of Virginia; and just across the divide to the south the enterprising Stalnaker — his name tells his origin — was building his cabin on a head stream of the Holston near the present Tennessee boundary, when Dr. Walker passed that way in 1750 to explore the lands of Kentucky.   In North Carolina at this time the remotest settlements were along the sources of the Yadkin; but just beyond were the westward flowing streams of the Tennessee, and here the Watauga and Nolichucky valleys in 1758 saw the first stockades across the Blue Ridge south of the Virginia line.⁶

So long as colonies were limited to the tidewater, Piedmont, and the eastern part of the Great Valley in Pennsylvania, the Appalachians were an effective barrier against the western Indians; but when the enterprising settlers began pushing out to the inner ranges of the mountains and contesting the territorial claims of the French beyond, the latter stirred up the savages to depredations upon the outlying settlements.   Then every stream which opened a route into the mountains from the west became an Indian war-path; and between 1754 and 1759 every mountain pass or divide at their sources began to bristle with English fort or stockade to check these onslaughts.   In this period a whole line of such strongholds was erected — Ligonier on the Loyalhanna branch of the Allegheny near the pass from

⁵ Evans's map, made in 1755, reproduced by T. Pownall, in his *Topographical Description of North America* (1776); *Journal of Dr. Thomas Walker*, in Filson Club Publications, No. 13, pp. 38–41.

⁶ Roosevelt, T., *Winning of the West*, New York, 1903, I, 170–72.

the Juniata, Fort Cumberland on the upper Potomac, Fort Chissel in the Valley of Virginia on the divide between the New River and the Holston, Colonel Byrd's fort at Long Island on the upper Holston in East Tennessee, and a hundred miles farther south Fort Loudoun at the junction of the Jellico and Watauga rivers. These remote military outposts and the scattered clearings about them were from a hundred to a hundred and fifty miles west of the frontier of continuous settlement in Virginia and North Carolina.

CHARACTER OF EARLY FRONTIER SETTLEMENTS

In the tidewater and Piedmont regions, the general movement of the population was northwest along the course of the drainage streams, at right angles to the coast; but, within the mountains, population advanced down the longitudinal valleys, along a northeast-southwest line, parallel with the trend of the Appalachian system, and it swept along in its tide all the little tributary streams of outbound settlers who crossed the Blue Ridge. The consequence was that while the tidewater regions of the colonies kept each its distinctive character, born of distinct old-world sources and diverse environments, the backwoods population of the mountains, from the Wyoming Valley to the Yadkin, showed a wide mingling of ethnic elements — Dutch, German, Huguenot French, Scotch-Irish, and English — which obliterated the distinctive types of the coast, while the prevailing similarity of their geographic environment operated to produce the new type of the backwoods. From northern Pennsylvania to Georgia, the whole Piedmont and mountain tract gave its stamp to the life of this forest frontier. Mountain economy, based upon the small farm, did not

permit the development of large estates, with the concomitant industrial system of slavery and aristocratic
organization of society. Difficulty of transportation to the
coast prevented trade on a large scale and the amassing of
wealth. Without social classes and wealth, democracy
reigned supreme. The daily struggle for existence amid the
dangers of the wilderness produced a race of men, sturdy in
their self-reliance, self-respecting in their independence,
quick to think, strong to act, and above all filled with the
spirit of enterprise. Their remoteness from the arm of the
law led them to frame laws for themselves, or to take the
law into their own hands. Therefore with impartiality
they were prone to deal summarily with horse-thieves and
tax-gatherers. But their hardihood and fertility of resource,
practical and political, fitted them to be pioneers and
founders of states in the more distant wilderness beyond.

THE EARLY WESTWARD MOVEMENT

When the westward movement came, the base of its
advance was geographically defined. The isolation of New
England excluded it from it. New York also took no share
in it because of its French and Iroquois neighbors. Moreover, after the war with France, England was bound to
regard the rights of its Indian allies. Therefore, by the
treaty of Fort Stanwix in 1768, though the Iroquois ceded
the western lands lying between the Tennessee and the
Ohio, from Kittanning on the Allegheny the "Property
Line" defining the frontier of white settlement turned eastward along the West Branch of the Susquehanna, crossed by
a small creek to the North Branch, then to the elbow of the
Delaware at the present site of Deposit, from which it

turned directly north along the Unadilla branch of the Susquehanna to a point midway between Fort Stanwix and Lake Oneida. Western New York was thus secured to the Iroquois; but even after the Revolution, which had made the Six Nations the enemy of the colonists, the retention of the Lake posts till 1796 by the British and the strength and number of the Indians themselves deterred the advance of settlements, which in 1800 scarcely extended to the Genesee River.

Around the southern end of the Appalachian Mountains an almost level route led to the Mississippi Valley, but here, as in the north, the Indians barred all western advance. Creeks and Cherokees were stirred by the Spanish, who acquired Louisiana in 1762, to drive the colonists in this region back to the coast. Later, crowded to the south and east by the encroachments of the whites in Tennessee and the infant state of Alabama, these Indians were able to limit Georgia's frontier of settlement to the Altamaha and Ocmulgee rivers as late as 1820.

Expansion of the Middle Colonies. Pennsylvania, Maryland, Virginia, and North Carolina, therefore, were the only participants in the early westward movement. In the three southern colonies, land-hunger resulting from existing agricultural methods supplied the motive, while in Pennsylvania the far-ranging traders had drawn attention to the fertile regions beyond the mountains. Individuals from this colony and from Virginia were prominent in the land companies which from 1750 were trying to secure patents to large areas on the "Western Waters." [7] Furthermore, the provincial governments, with the approval of the British

---

[7] Monette, J. W., *History of the Valley of the Mississippi*, New York, 1848, I, 348.

crown, issued innumerable warrants for land as pay for
military service in the war with the French and with
Pontiac; such claims were to be located along the Ohio,
within the charter limits of Virginia and Pennsylvania.
Later, the young Republic, rich in land but poor in specie,
paid off in the same way a part of the debt incurred in the
Revolution, and thus gave a new impulse to the outmoving
tide.

Geographical conditions favored the expansion of the
middle colonies. Their long line of western frontier was a
chord subtending the rude arc formed by the Tennessee and
Ohio rivers. The head waters of these streams or of their
tributaries opened so many gateways to the transmontane
lands. The broad territory between the two rivers had been
ceded to the English by the Indians at Fort Stanwix (1768).
Reserved by the savages as a hunting-ground, and having,
therefore, no permanent Indian settlements, it opened a line
of least resistance for colonial expansion; while its fertile soil,
agreeable climate, and abundant salt-springs afforded all
essentials for pioneer homes.

The topography of the Appalachians and their two distinct drainage systems determined that the northern routes
should converge where the Allegheny Plateau is spanned by
the forks of the Ohio, and the southern where the Tennessee,
Kanawha, and, just between the two, Cumberland Gap
open portals to the West.

The Routes to Pittsburgh. Three routes met at Pittsburgh:
one from Philadelphia by the West Branch of the Susquehanna, a forty-mile portage over the divide, and Toby
Creek to the Allegheny at Kittanning; a second farther
south, also from Philadelphia, by the Juniata tributary of
the Susquehanna, or by a more direct trace known as

Forbes's Road [8] from Carlisle through Shippensburg, Fort
Lyttleton, and Fort Bedford to the upper Juniata, thence by
an easy mountain pass to the Loyalhanna River by Fort
Ligonier and on down the Allegheny or across the low
dividing ridge to the forks of the Ohio; and a third up the
Potomac to Fort Cumberland and thence by Braddock's
road over the divide to the Youghiogeny or to Redstone Old
Fort on the Monongahela.   This was the natural line of
connection with Alexandria and Baltimore.   On these
northern routes water-carriage predominated.   Navigation
on both the Susquehanna and Potomac was interrupted by
rapids; but for early canoe travel this obstacle was not
serious.   As the transmontane region became settled, however, the Potomac was improved by canalization and a
better road shortened the distance between Fort Cumberland and Redstone.   The traders said that Alexandria was
four hundred miles nearer the fur-fields than any other
Atlantic port.[9]   Therefore Baltimore received a large part
of the bulky exports from the back country, while Philadelphia furnished to the western trade most of the manufactured supplies, which were sent by a more direct wagon-
road three hundred miles across the mountains.

[8] The following table, taken from the records of the tollgate keeper at Fort Loudon,
gives a good picture of the use of the Forbes Road in 1830 and 1834:

Type of Traffic	1830	1834
Broad-wheel wagons	6,641	6,359
Narrow-wheel wagons	495	374
Single-horse wagons	761	1,243
Carriages	128	107
Two-horse wagons	318	779
Riding horses	3,116	2,817
Draft horses	39,824	42,330
Heads of cattle	5,834	6,457
Sheep	2,180	2,852
Hogs	1,180	2,852

(*Chicago Tribune*, July 13, 1924.)

[9] Winsor, J., *The Westward Movement*, Boston, 1897, p. 508.

Once over the mountains, the pioneer continued his journey westward from Pittsburgh by flatboat or keelboat down the Ohio.   But as there was no established carrying business on the river at this time, the supply of even these primitive means of transportation was uncertain, all the more as, once at their downstream destination, they were unfit to stem the swift current on a return voyage.   The emigrant, therefore, was often compelled to wait a month or more before he could get a boat built; for workmen were scarce.   His troubles were not over when his rude craft was launched.   Danger from Indian attack was constant and imminent.   But after the Revolution and Wayne's defeat of the northern savages in 1794, and especially after the opening up of the Northwest, the Ohio route was much used, except for the return trip to the East.   The current that bore the outbound settler down the tide of the western waters was his obstacle when he turned his face towards the coast.   Hence this difficulty and the horror of Indian attack deflected much of the westward movement to the land route from southwestern Virginia by Cumberland Gap.   The intervening trail from the head streams of the James River to the Greenbrier tributary of the Kanawha, and the rugged portal opened to the same river and to the Tug Fork of the Big Sandy by the deep cañon of the New, seem to have been little used by the pioneers.   Buffalo trace and Indian war-path had pointed out the easiest way across the mountain barrier, and these the backwoodsman followed.   The Big Sandy and New River route was the common war-path of the Shawnees when making incursions from Ohio into the territory of their relentless foes, the Catawbas of North Carolina, because it was the most direct line from the villages along the Scioto; but the light equipment of savage warriors permitted rougher traveling than the pack-horses and cattle herds of the outbound settler.

The Cumberland Gap Route — Wilderness Road. The Cumberland Gap route was the natural avenue to the West for emigrants from Virginia and the Carolinas, but it was preferred also by colonists from Philadelphia when they carried little baggage, though the distance from that city to the interior of Kentucky was eight hundred miles. From Philadelphia an established line of travel led across the Potomac by Wadkin's Ferry, and up the Valley of Virginia along the old war-trail of the Iroquois and Cherokee, over the low watershed to the New River. The pioneer crossed that stream and continued up its western affluent, Reed Creek, which on an almost level divide interlocks with the head streams of the Holston. Here the western trail was joined by another path from Richmond, Virginia, and here at the "forks of the road" was Fort Chissel, the blockhouse built in 1758 to hold the Cherokees in check. At this point began the Wilderness Road. The distance to Cumberland Gap was two hundred miles.

From the upper Holston, the Wilderness Road turned west, and by a maze of gaps and their approaching streams which furrowed the mountain sides, it crossed the parallel ranges of Clinch, Powell, and Walden mountains to the Powell River, and turned down this valley to Cumberland Gap, an old "wind-gap" which opened an easy gateway (1600 feet elevation) through Cumberland Mountain to the West. Just beyond the pass the frontiersman struck the "Warriors Path," an Indian trail which ran between the Shawnee villages at the mouth of the Scioto in Ohio and the Cherokee lands in eastern Tennessee. The Wilderness Road, as tracked in 1775 by Daniel Boone for Colonel

Henderson, followed this Indian trail across the ford of the
Cumberland, where this river breaks through Pine Mountain, and down the stream for a few miles to Flat Lick; but
here it turned northwest, and followed a buffalo trace along
the ridges over to Rockcastle River.   In Kentucky the
pioneer, following the example of the buffalo, avoided the
immediate watercourses; for in contrast to the broad basins
of the Allegheny rivers, these streams had carved out the
surface of the Cumberland Plateau into deep V-shaped
valleys, which afforded only precarious foothold for the
traveler and necessitated continuous crossing of their
rushing currents.

By buffalo trace the road continued north from the
Rockcastle River through Boone's Gap in the rugged barrier
of the Big Hill range (present route of the Louisville and
Nashville Railroad) to Otter Creek and the Kentucky River
at Fort Boonesborough, thence to Lexington and the
smiling lands of the Bluegrass.   From Rockcastle River
another branch of the Wilderness Road, blazed by Logan in
1775, turned northwest and, by a natural gateway near
Crab Orchard, reached level land near the present town of
Stanford, where Logan built Station St. Asaphs.   This
track became more important than Boone's trail to the
north because it led more directly to the attractive level
lands of Kentucky, and, passing through Danville, Bardstown, and Bullitt's Lick, terminated at the Falls of the
Ohio, whence was the readiest connection with the old
French trading-posts on the Mississippi and the Wabash.

The route taken by Robertson to the Tennessee country
followed the Wilderness Road beyond Cumberland Gap, and
then turned southwest, guided largely by buffalo traces
seeking pools and salt-licks, to the "bend of the Cumber-

land" where Nashville grew up; but the women, children, and baggage for the new settlement made a long and dangerous journey in flatboats, dugouts, and canoes down the winding course of the Tennessee River to the Ohio, and up the Cumberland to the little stockade on the bluffs. But later (1783) a new road fiom the confluence of the Holston and the Clinch rivers passed by easy ascent over Cumberland Mountain to the valley of the Cumberland and Nashville. This route was joined by a trail also from North Carolina, and at the mouth of the French Broad River by still another from South Carolina. Thus several roads from the east converged upon the upper Tennessee, just as Cumberland Gap was a plexus of other routes aiming at Kentucky and the West.[10]

At first only blazed trails through the great wilderness, then traces trodden out more plainly by the feet of pioneers and pack-horses, impassable to wagons, these transmontane roads offered no easy conditions for travel. The floor of the Great Valley in southern Virginia rises to 1700 feet and the linear ranges to be crossed were in general only 600 or 800 feet higher; but each in turn barred the western horizon like a wall, and only here and there were their even sky-lines notched by a gap. These gaps were never opposite one another in the successive ranges, so the traveler had to take a circuitous way up and down the intervening valleys from pass to pass. He had to ford trough streams and mountain creeks, which one summer rain might raise to rushing torrents. For food he depended upon game or the cattle which he drove along with him, while an outlying habitation occasionally supplied him with bacon and corn-meal. The danger of attack from the Cherokees, stirred to hostility first

[10] Out of 400,000 people, who went West from 1775 to 1800, 300,000 used the Cumberland Gap route.

by the French and later by the Spanish, was always there, but never so imminent as the perils on the Ohio from the Shawnees.   But in spite of dangers and hardships, the trail through the wilderness had its joys — the charm of the wondrous Appalachian forests, the flicker of sunlight through the high-reaching trees, the plunge into a tunnel of

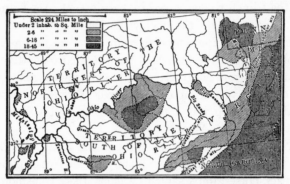

FIG. 7. TRANS–ALLEGHENY SETTLEMENTS IN 1790

The early trans-Allegheny settlements were largely south of the Ohio, opposite the seaboard areas whence the settlers had come, in line with the chief routes of migration, in open woodlands formerly held as Indian hunting ground and in fertile limestone regions and river valleys.

green through the tender spring underbrush, the sense of strong, pulsing life with the upward climb, finally the deep-drawn breath on the summit before the outstretched billows of land, and the hope of opportunity beyond.

TRANS-ALLEGHENY SETTLEMENTS IN RELATION TO HIGHWAYS

The distribution of trans-Allegheny population in 1790 was in close relation with the western highways.   Pennsylvania settlements formed a continuous line from the Juniata to the Allegheny, Monongahela, and Ohio almost to the mouth of the Muskingum River (Fig. 7). In Virginia there was an unbroken area of settlement to the western rim of the Great Appalachian Valley; but beyond the Greenbrier and the New, the frontiersman had passed by the rugged country of the Cumberland Plateau along the upper Kanawha to make a small settlement at its mouth. The frontier farms and villages in the parallel valleys of the Holston and the Clinch merged into "the independent state of Franklin." Downstream moved the tide of settlement. Where the Holston and French Broad unite to form the Tennessee, White and Conner in 1787 located a warrant of land which they had received as pay for military service in the Revolution, and about their fort the town of Knoxville was laid out soon afterwards. In 1785 a settlement was attempted at the Muscle Shoals of the Tennessee River in northern Alabama, and a few years later Sevier and others secured a grant of land for settlement just south of the Shoals. The attraction here was a geographical one. The obstruction to navigation by the rapids necessitated a carry at this point, which therefore became a halting-place for travelers. Furthermore, the Big Bear River, a southern tributary of the Tennessee, connected by a short portage with the head streams of the Tombigbee and Yazoo, thus opening up lines of trade with the lower Mississippi and Mobile Bay.

To the west Nashville, whose eighty or ninety cabins were a center for the five thousand pioneers settled for eighty miles along the river, was a product partly of the waterway formed by the Tennessee and the Cumberland, and partly of the land routes through the gaps in the Cumberland range. In the same manner the Kentucky settlements were born of the Ohio and the Wilderness

Road.   The Cumberland and Kentucky settlements were separated from the frontier of civilization in Virginia by a wide zone of wilderness, the rugged upland of the Cumberland Plateau, a region condemned by its geographical conditions to isolation, poverty, and a retarded civilization.[11]   With the exception of Louisville at the Falls of the Ohio, the Kentucky settlements avoided the main streams, but chose the smaller affluents and rich undulating country between.   Filson's map (1784) shows fifty-two villages and eighteen scattered houses.   One large group, with Lexington as a center, spread over the land between Elkhorn Creek and the Kentucky River and showed a few outlying stations on the South Fork of the Licking; another group, including Danville and Harrod's Town, was located within easy reach of Dick's River, a southern tributary of the Kentucky; and a third to the west stretched along the upper forks of Salt River, where Bardstown was the backwoods metropolis, and merged into the closer settlements along Beargrass Creek and the Falls of the Ohio.   The geographical distribution of the early Kentucky population brings into relief the home-making motive in striking contrast to the purely trading instinct which determined the location of the French settlements across the Ohio to the north.

TRANS-ALLEGHENY SETTLEMENTS IN THE REVOLUTION

With the outbreak of the Revolutionary War these trans-Allegheny settlements took on a peculiar political importance.   They were a wedge driven into the great West, which was claimed by the colonies on the ground of their

---

[11] Semple, E. C., "The Anglo-Saxons of the Kentucky Mountains." *Bulletin of the American Geographical Society*, XLII (1910), 561–94.

sea-to-sea charters, claimed also by the British by the treaty of 1763 and the royal proclamation reserving the transmontane country as crown lands, and the Quebec Bill (1774) bringing the region north of the Ohio under the jurisdiction of Canada. But the Americans were on the ground. Virginia, pushed on by the pressure of land-hunger and facing the open doors along her mountain frontier, on which the best western highways converged, insisted more than any other colony upon the terms of its sea-to-sea charter. It was Virginia who invested Clark with a commission to conquer the Illinois country, but it was this man from the backwoods settlements who proposed the scheme. The capture of Kaskaskia swept the British from the West. They had now no fort or garrison between the Lakes and the Gulf. In the face of enormous difficulty, Clark maintained his hold upon the Illinois country. The sparse population of the West afforded a scanty supply of troops to guard a frontier reaching from the Mississippi to the upper Ohio. The remoteness of the region and the barrier of the mountains interfered with the transportation of reinforcements and supplies from the East. Munitions and food came even to Fort Pitt from the Spanish at New Orleans up the Mississippi. The possession of the Illinois and Kentucky country annulled the proclamation of 1763 and the Quebec Bill, and influenced the final negotiations for peace. Though the extension of the young Republic to the Mississippi was based formally in these negotiations upon the charter bounds, the presence in these western lands of a vigorous people who had made good their title by axe and plow and rifle constituted a more solid claim to the debated territory than the yellow parchments of dead monarchs or living potentates.

CHAPTER V

GEOGRAPHICAL ENVIRONMENT OF THE
EARLY TRANS–ALLEGHENY SETTLEMENTS

THE trans-Allegheny settlements had been planted in the center of a country which comprised five eighths of the territory of the young United States. Barred from the East by the Appalachian Mountains, it sloped gently from the plateaus westward to the Mississippi and southward to the Gulf of Mexico, its surface broken only by low hills or undulating upland. A canoe could travel from Lake Erie to Mobile Bay through the heart of the region, with only two portages, one at the sources of the Wabash, and the other between the Tombigbee and the Tennessee; while on its western margin the Mississippi furnished a waterway from its northern to its southern frontier. The Ohio and its tributaries aggregate twelve thousand miles of streams which in early times afforded transportation routes and facilitated the movement of men and produce.

ENVIRONMENT IN RELATION TO SETTLEMENTS

Fertile Land.   The abundance of land, the lack of barriers, and the easy river connection, all made for expansion of western population. The vacant space between the Cumberland and the Kentucky was soon filled up; settlements were strung along the Ohio, like beads on a cord, from the Big Sandy to western Pennsylvania, while in the Northwest Territory scattered cabins up the course of the Muskingum, Scioto, Great and Little Miami rivers indicated the lines population was following. In the frontier of a country is to be found always the index of its growth or decay. A rapid advance of the boundary, whether of settlement or political control, speaks of vigorous, abundant forces behind demanding an enlarged field of activity: a retrogression or caving-in of the frontier points to declining powers, inadequate strength.[1] Along the western waters all was activity, eager advance, yearning for a farther beyond. Here appeared that uncramped, undiscouraged development which has given the distinctive stamp to American life.

The abundance of land was reflected in the generous soil of the transmontane country. North of the Ohio, the surface is underlaid by a thick mantle of glacial drift formed from rocks of a chemical nature to supply food for plants. The timberless character of the country enabled settlement to go on at a rapid rate, unretarded by the slow work of cutting down forests and clearing out stumps. South of the Ohio and beyond the rim of the Cumberland Plateau with its poor land, the blue limestone outcrops, furnishing to the subsoil a large supply of plant food. This has made the fame of the Bluegrass region of Kentucky. It underlies also southwestern Ohio and Tennessee to the northern border of Alabama; but owing to the covering of glacial drift in the north and the sandier character of this rock in the south, the soil is less fertile than in Kentucky.[2] The southwestern parts of Kentucky and Tennessee are underlaid by Subcarboniferous limestone, which enriches the soil almost as much as does the Silurian. The Gulf slope of this western country is a fertile silt-made plain, built up from the débris

[1] Ratzel, F., *Anthropogeographie*, Stuttgart, 1891, Part I, pp. 260–63.

[2] Shaler, N. S., *United States of America*, New York, 1894, I, 105, 106. Out of nearly 400,000 people west of the Appalachians in 1783, the Blue Grass region had 320,000.

of limy or clayey rocks, and hence far richer than the crystalline detritus which covers the surface of the Atlantic plain.

Climate. An abundant rainfall well distributed through the year, a temperate climate varied by cold, dry winds which sweep down the great trough of the continent from the northwest, and warm, moist winds from the Gulf, a long, warm summer for the growing crops, all united to mitigate the hardships of pioneer life and to keep up the courage of the home-maker in the wilderness.

CHARACTER OF FRONTIER PEOPLE AND SETTLEMENTS

The men who grew up in this westward facing country were the first genuine Americans. The seaboard population were Europeans living on American soil under English control, bred to English luxuries which were supplied by English manufactories. In time of danger English armies had been in part their resource, and the English treasury paid in part the costs of colonial wars. American soil and the barrier of the Atlantic had modified European institutions and character in the hands and persons of the colonists somewhat;[3] but their gaze was seaward, towards the English palace and council hall where their destiny was decided. Volney, a Frenchman traveling in this country in 1796, discerned the difference of standpoint between the people of the tidewater and the over-mountain region. "The inhabitants of the Atlantic coast call the whole of this the Back Country, thus denoting their moral aspect, constantly

---

[3] Turner, F. J., "The Significance of the Frontier in American History," *Annual Report of the American Historical Association* for 1893.

turned towards Europe, the cradle and the focus of their interests. It was a singular, though natural circumstance, that I had scarcely crossed the Alleghanies, before I heard the borderers of the great Kanhaway and the Ohio give in their turn the name of Back Country to the Atlantic coast, which shows that their geographical situation has given their views and interests a new direction, conformable to that of the waters which afford them means of conveyance towards the Gulf of Mexico." [4]

In the cabin clearings of the western wilderness, beyond the barrier of the mountains, English institutions took on a new stamp of republicanism, society became more purely democratic, and the new-born American looked only to his own strong arm for aid, to his own strong intellect for counsel. Separation from old-world traditions, a return to close contact with nature, the stripping off of non-essentials, growth under conditions of uncramped development and untried possibilities — these made the sturdy, youthful American of the western wilds. Old-world methods and ideas must be transformed to survive in new-world conditions,[5] and the conditions modify the man along with his methods. The change may appear at first to be retrogression, but it is only the step backward for the long running-jump.

The successful ending of the Revolutionary War had focused the eyes of the Americans on their own country. Then the possibilities of the young West began to loom up, especially in view of the economic depression of the tide-water region following the long war. Warrants and military

4 Volney, C. F., *View of the Climate and Soil of the United States of America*, London, 1804, p. 21.

5 Roscher, W. H., *Nationalökonomik des Ackerbaues*, Leipzig, 1888, p. 104.

scrip for western lands guided thither the discharged soldier from New England to South Carolina. The outbound population to the Kentucky and Cumberland became more composite in its character than that of the old backwoods on the Piedmont and Blue Ridge frontier. It included the same racial elements and in addition more varied American constituents, which beyond the mountains forgot their colonial allegiance, whether to the aristocratic capital of Charleston or the Puritan township of Connecticut, lost their old sectional feelings, and instead substituted allegiance to the national government and the sectionalism of the over-mountain men as opposed to the seaboard states.

Isolation and Trade. Upon these early western settlements isolation set its stamp. Range after range of mountains, mile after mile of rugged plateau separated them from the seats of civilization and government. Land and water routes were beset by Indians, and even the homeward-leading rivers beat back with their increasing currents the pirogue of the eastbound Westerner. The great streams of the Mississippi Valley made the settlements more accessible to their British neighbors to the north, and their Spanish neighbors to the west and south; but this accessibility was disadvantageous rather than otherwise. Detroit and the navigable waterway of the St. Lawrence and the Great Lakes played the same part in the history of the young West as did New Orleans and the Mississippi. Both cities were the center of plots to incite the Indians — northwest and southwest — against the backwoods frontier, to construct the intervening savage tribes into buffer states against the expansion and aggression of the colonists, to invade American territory for illicit trade, and finally to tempt the frontiersmen to defection by promises of the needed river outlet for their produce to the sea. By the retention of the Lake posts for twelve years after the peace of 1783, the British kept their hold on the fur trade in the Northwest Territory. Moreover, they secured permission from the Spanish to trade on the western bank of the upper Mississippi, and this necessitated their passing to and fro on American soil by way of the Chicago portage or by the Wisconsin River to the post at Prairie du Chien. In consequence of this trespassing the American trade at Vincennes was greatly reduced.[6]

From the south, the Spanish traded up the Alabama and Tombigbee rivers from Mobile across the thirty-first degree, north latitude, which had been agreed upon in the treaty of 1783 as the northern boundary of West Florida, and over the three-mile portage to the basin of the Tennessee; and traders from Pensacola were doing a thriving business with the Creeks and Cherokees to the northeast. From New Orleans and other Spanish posts along the Mississippi, traders were encroaching on American territory, especially up the Illinois River where they shared the field with Canadian rivals, while the officials on the Gulf were obstructing or inhibiting the navigation of the Mississippi to the western pioneers and hounding on the southern savages to attack.

Indians and Method of Settlement. On either side of the western wedge of settlement lay a broad zone of Indians, whom the expansion and encroachments of the whites, as well as the incitement supplied by British and Spanish, made the natural foe of the settler. They were as much a part of his environment as the fertile soil and the far-reaching wilderness. They controlled in part his social organization, taught him new modes of warfare, and modified his character. A frontier is never a line but always a shifting zone of

[6] Winsor, J., *The Westward Movement*, Boston, 1897, p. 416.

assimilation, where an amalgamation of races, manners, institutions, and morals, more or less complete, takes place.[7] The English pioneers in the wilderness retained their sedentary occupation of the land, in contrast to the nomadic habits of the French traders; settled in more or less strongly compacted groups, which were further consolidated locally and politically by the danger of the all-surrounding savage; and thus retained an inner environment which was civilized. The line between them and the savage was therefore strictly drawn: half-breeds were rare. But the outer environment was all of the wilderness and the Indian, and to this the man of the Cumberland and Kentucky yielded himself. He lived in great part by the chase, dressed in buckskin and furs, wore the moccasins of the redman, adopted his scalping-knife and tomahawk, and waged against him a war of extermination, with all its savage features of ambush and scalping, and all its brutalizing effects.[8] In view of the ever-present danger of Indian attack, the basal organization of pioneer communities was military. The settlement was the stockade or station — a fortified village; militia service in the common defense became the first duty of the citizen. Representation in the early Kentucky conventions to consider separation from Virginia was made on the basis of military companies.

Necessaries of Life. The common remoteness and the conditions of wilderness life laid their equalizing touch upon all. Equality of opportunity and resource, identity of tasks and of dangers, and the simplicity imposed upon all precluded classes, and in the mass developed vigor, enterprise,

---

[7] Ratzel, F., *Anthropogeographie*, Stuttgart, 1891, Part I, p. 265.

[8] Monette, J. W., *History of the Valley of the Mississippi*, New York, 1848, II, chap. 1.

and independence. The backwoodsman had what the forests and clearings could furnish, and little more. Wooden vessels of all kinds, whether turned or coopered, were in common use. Owing to the great cost of transportation over the mountains, hardware was rare. Houses were built without nails, and even shingles were put on with oak pins.[9] Linen was made from the lint of nettles, and buffalo wool was the raw material for cloth. Furs became the medium of exchange, though after the Revolution "there was some paper money in the country which had not depreciated more than one half, as it had at the seat of Government." [10] This fact speaks eloquently for the isolation of the region. At first salt was imported at almost prohibitive prices; but soon the pioneer began to boil water from the saline springs which abounded, and later learned to bore for richer brine. At Bullitt's Lick on Salt River in Kentucky, a regular industry was started, and supplied the frontier communities from the Ohio to the Cumberland.

The products of the country which were bartered for eastern merchandise were primarily those of the wilderness — hides, furs, ginseng, snakeroot and bear's-grease; or of a frontier country with abundant pasture land or forest range, such as horses, hogs, salted pork, lard, tallow, and dried beef. Very soon the fertile soil began to yield abundant crops. Tobacco, corn, flour, whiskey, flax, and rope from the hemp-fields were ready for export. Before the treaty of 1783, when Spain was friendly, much of this produce went down the Mississippi and found a ready market in New Orleans. Only the most valuable part would bear the cost of up-stream and over-mountain transportation to the eastern seaboard.

[9] Collins, R. H., *History of Kentucky*, Louisville, 1877, I, 516.
[10] Marshall, H., *History of Kentucky*, Frankfort (U.S.A.), 1824, I, 150.

Early Manufactures. The high price of commodities imported by this route forced the backwoods settlements to
institute manufactures at a surprisingly early date, so that
here in one small area were to be seen all the stages of economic development — savage, pastoral, agricultural, and
industrial. The line of manufactures was determined by
the domestic supply of raw materials and the most pressing
need of the settlers. Retarded by the selfish policy of England, manufactures along the seaboard scarcely antedated
the appearance of industries in this free western country.
Iron was found in great abundance on the westward slope
of the Allegheny Plateau along the Monongahela, Youghiogeny, and Cheat rivers, and the big demand for it along
the frontier caused the erection of furnaces and iron works
as early as 1788.[11] Lexington, Kentucky, had a cut-nail
factory in 1801, and Georgetown a ropewalk and fulling-mill
in 1789.[12]

The first spinning-jenny after the Hargreave type in
America was operated at Philadelphia in 1775; a cotton
factory was established at Beverly, Massachusetts, in 1787,
at Providence in 1788, and in Pawtucket, Rhode Island, in
1790.[13] A society for the encouragement of manufactures
was organized in Danville, Kentucky, in 1789, under the
auspices of Judge Harry Innes and other prominent men,
who in 1790 started the first cotton factory in the West.
The carding, spinning, and weaving machines were purchased in Philadelphia, where they were manufactured,
carried over the mountains at great expense to Pittsburgh,
and down the Ohio to Louisville, whence they were hauled

[11] Monette, J. W., *op. cit.*, II, 199.
[12] Collins, R. H., *loc. cit.*, I, 516.
[13] Weeden, W. B., *Economic and Social History of New England*, Boston, 1891, II,
848.

to Danville. The raw cotton was produced in the Cumberland River settlements, and for several years was a regular article of trade between the two communities; some was also raised in Kentucky. The four skilled workmen and the manager were imported from Philadelphia, and John Brown, congressman from the Kentucky district of Virginia, who negotiated the purchase of the machines and the contract with the workmen, explained to Judge Innes, in a letter of May 25, 1790, that a certain irritating delay would never have occurred "did not a disposition prevail with some in this place to prevent the emigration of Manufacturers and the establishment of Factories in the Western country." [14] Here speaks the new sectionalism. Already some of the wiser heads in the East had predicted that, if the federal government failed to secure by treaty with Spain the free navigation of the Mississippi for the transmontane settlers and an outlet for their agricultural products, these communities would be early forced into industrial ventures, and so rendered economically independent of the northern seaboard states, who hoped to find in them a market, and yet, for selfish reasons, desired the closure of the Mississippi.

THE MISSISSIPPI HIGHWAY

Nature had done everything to open up Kentucky, Tennessee, and the growing Northwest Territory towards the south. Ramifying through this whole country was the Ohio with its tributaries, affording easy access to the Mississippi and the natural market in semi-tropical New Orleans. Old established routes of trade passed their door; and the

[14] Todd, G. W., *The First Cotton Factory in the West.* An unpublished paper read before the Filson Club, March, 1898, based upon unpublished letters and papers by Judge Harry Innes, great-grandfather of Mr. Todd.

reckless, jovial French voyageur, with his gaudy backwoods dress and his fiddle, was still passing down the Wabash or Miami from the Lake country to trade at Louisville, St. Louis, and New Orleans. With the cessation of the British and Indian wars, and with the increasing tide of immigration, the Ohio route from the East grew in importance. Brownville, laid out at Redstone Old Fort on the Monongahela in 1785, and Pittsburgh as the starting-points for the downstream journey, became lively distributing-centers for the western country. In both places an active boat-building industry supplied boats for the hundreds of emigrants who arrived every week from the East, and also for the regular trade on the river. Kentucky offered more to settlers than the country across the Ohio; and now they began to fill the northern part of the state which had been left vacant because of its exposure to the attacks of the Shawnees from the Scioto. Now the old war-trail of the savages along the outer rim of the Cumberland Plateau from the mouth of Limestone Creek to the Kentucky River settlements became a highway of trade. Limestone became the point of debarkation of men and goods for central Kentucky, and four miles back from the Ohio, on the top of the steep ridge facing the river, grew up the town of Washington. Here large wagons for the interior started with loads too heavy to be hauled up the steep slope. The Falls of the Ohio made Louisville a natural port for the upper river, as also the head of navigation for the lower stream. The town was furthermore the western terminus of the Wilderness Road. Hence it afforded unusual facilities for trade.

In those early days commerce moved in wide circles. The western pioneer from Nashville or Brownville passed down the Cumberland or the Monongahela with his own produce in his own boats to the Ohio, thence down the Mississippi to New Orleans, where his cargo was sold or exchanged. From there he went by sea to Cuba for further sales, and then embarked for New York, Philadelphia, or Baltimore, where his money was reinvested in manufactured articles. These he transported over the mountains at a cost of three dollars per hundredweight, to sell them in the scattered markets of the Ohio basin, after having been absent from four to six months. The result of such circular tours was large financial profit and a broad experience of life which made these men of the backwoods in a sense the cosmo- politans of the country. Smaller boats, laden with fine commodities of slight bulk and great value, sometimes made the return trip up the Mississippi from New Orleans to Louisville. This took forty days or more. The barges, which were equipped with sails and oars, were helped on by the prevailing south winds and the eddying up-currents at the bends of the river.

Policy of Open Mississippi. For the first decade of their history, the Kentucky and Cumberland settlements relied chiefly on Pittsburgh and the Ohio for the limited trade they could furnish or command; but as the population increased, and the rich fields began to respond to systematic culture, New Orleans was looked to as the natural market for western products, and as a source of supply for foreign and domestic products not to be secured nearer home. Therefore, when at the close of the Revolution Spain laid claim to both sides of the Mississippi River as far north as Kentucky, to the exclusive control of its navigation, and to the right to impose transit and harbor duties; [15] and when in 1787 Jay, the secre- tary of foreign affairs, was about to make a treaty with

---

[15] Spain closed the river to the western settlement from 1783 to 1795.

Spain conceding this right, bitter protests came from the transmontane settlements. In view of the increasing trade the barrier of the Appalachians made the outlet of the Mississippi a vital question. Collot in 1796, computing the expense of transportation by the Potomac and other over-mountain routes as compared with the Mississippi, found that goods could be conveyed from Philadelphia to Kentucky at a cost of 33 per cent *ad valorem*, and from New Orleans to the Illinois of only 4 to 4½ per cent.[16] Moreover, the difference in climate and consequently of products between Louisiana and the Ohio country made each a market for the other; and the Gulf region, with that lack of diversification of products which characterizes all new countries, was confining itself to cotton, sugar, and molasses. From 1785 to 1795 the exorbitant duties on American commerce descending the Mississippi and the oppressive commercial regulations imposed by the Spanish brought stagnation on the river, while in the frontier settlements from the Tennessee to the Allegheny it was the moving cause in the separatist movement. But other causes were operating also.

SEPARATIST TENDENCIES

Causes. Along this whole western frontier appeared that tendency towards defection which we have found to be characteristic of all peripheral holdings. The causes lay in the remoteness of the settlements, the barrier of the Appalachians, and the closure of the western outlet. Geographical conditions had produced here a people with different point of view, needs, and interests from those of the seaboard. Their situation reproduced in essential features that

[16] Winsor, J., *The Westward Movement*, Boston, 1897, p. 508.

of the colonists before the Revolution. In the constantly recurring Indian wars, troops and munitions from the tide-water capitals always arrived late, delay was dangerous, and the frontiersmen had to act on their own responsibility. The East did not appreciate the attitude of the frontier towards the Indian: the frontier saw the futility of Indian treaties, blamed the national authorities for talking and bribing instead of fighting while American settlements were being ravaged by the savages, and resented the course of the national agents in ignoring state and private agreements with the natives. Peace came to the frontier only when a punitive expedition from the Holston or Cumberland or Kentucky or Ohio, unauthorized by state or national authorities, used the only arguments appreciated by the Indians. The bloody raids of the savages in 1786 called forth reprisals when George Rogers Clark, Benjamin Logan, and Simon Kenton led expeditions against the Shawnees north of the Ohio, and Robertson with a hundred and thirty hardy followers sallied out from the Cumberland settlement to visit retribution on some marauding Creeks and Chero-kees who had intrenched themselves near the bend of the Tennessee. Requisition was made upon the settlers for pack-horses and supplies, ranging from salt to lead, with which to equip these forces.

Such expeditions, being of the nature of private enter-prises, did not have their expenses defrayed by the govern-ment. The costs fell, therefore, as an unequally distributed charge upon the communities, who felt in consequence the injustice of being taxed while their effective and constant military service went unpaid. The excise taxes were a spe-cial grievance and led to the Whiskey Rebellion in western Pennsylvania, and to milder protests elsewhere along the transmontane frontier. The surplus corn in the remote settlements, being of large bulk in relation to its value, could not stand the heavy cost of transportation across the mountains until it had been converted into whiskey. Here a nature-made law was confronting a human one, as it continues to do in the isolated regions of the southern Appalachians today. In Pennsylvania the law was resisted as unjust, and as in the mountains today, the Eighteenth Amendment is evaded by the moonshine still. Similar geographical conditions produce similar results. In other respects the burden of distant tidewater control rested heavily upon the frontiersmen. They had their local courts for minor cases, but all the more important civil and criminal cases and all appealed suits had to be carried to the tidewater capitals for trial. This involved a journey of from three to five hundred miles, much expense, and long delay. On account of courts and taxes, therefore, the pioneers desired separate state governments. But most of all they desired the representation in Congress which would give them a voice in the pending negotiations with Spain regarding the navigation of the Mississippi.

Independent States. All along the frontier from western Pennsylvania to the Tennessee River the spirit of independent statehood was rife.[17] Some of the frontier communities wished to establish their states with boundaries geographically determined, ignoring the charter lines of the old colonies. They were guided by the principle of ready communication. The Watauga settlements in western North Carolina proposed to combine with the Virginia settlements farther up the valley of the Holston and along

[17] Turner, F. J., "Western State-Making in the Revolutionary Era," *American History Review*, I (1895), Nos. 1 and 2.

the New to form the state of Franklin,[18] because together they formed a geographical whole. As Nashville, through the river and the southern branch of the Wilderness Road from Crab Orchard, stood in closer communication with her northern than her eastern neighbors, there was talk of the union of the Cumberland with the Kentucky settlements to form the State of Transylvania.

Blocked by the Eastern states in their efforts to secure independent statehood, disgusted by the short-sighted policy of the federal government which threatened to sacrifice the interest of the over-mountain communities in the free navigation of the Mississippi, and exasperated by its desultory efforts to stand on its rights with Spain, while the commerce of the Mississippi was being ruined by the depredations of Spanish officials on vessels which attempted to descend the river without their permission, these pioneer settlements finally developed a separatist movement of a different nature, which aimed at union with any foreign power, Spanish or British, promising to give them an outlet to the sea. The temptation was very near, and it was geographically determined.

The Mississippi as a Bond of Union. Every river system forms an unbroken whole and therefore serves as a natural bond of union between those living among its remotest sources and those settled at its mouth.[19] The direction of its flow guides the drift of commercial intercourse and the trend of political combination. For twenty years the politics of our western country centered about "the Island of New Orleans." The pioneers were under the geographical

[18] Muzzey, D. S., *The United States of America*, Boston, 1922, I, 291. Map showing "Projects for New Western States in the Revolutionary Era."

[19] Ratzel, F., *Anthropogeographie*, Stuttgart, 1891, Part I, pp. 344, 345.

control of the western waters. Their rivers carried them on downward currents to the Mississippi and the Gulf, where the Spanish offered free navigation and trade. From the Ohio the winding courses of its northern tributaries carried them to easy portages leading to the vast waterway of the Lakes and the St. Lawrence. Between them and their blundering Congress in the East stretched a mountain wall three hundred miles wide. In the colder, undeveloped north they could find a near market, as in the warmer, half-developed south, while the market to the east was cut off by a mountain barrier. There was another alternative, rather ideal in its character but favored by geographical conditions: union with the British and a downstream conquest of New Orleans. This possibility was held over the head of the Spanish Intendant on the Gulf. Spanish influence was felt more in Tennessee and Kentucky, British in Kentucky and the infant settlements of the Northwest Territory, where the Muskingum country had its Colonel Wilkinson in General Parsons.

All such intrigues ceased with the promulgation of Pinckney's treaty in 1795 which secured the free and unlimited navigation of the Mississippi, the right of deposit at New Orleans free from Spanish control, protection to American ships on the river, and the territory north of $31°$.[20] The ultimate result of the Mississippi outlet, the discussion it aroused, and the benefits it bestowed, was the purchase of Louisiana eight years later.

[20] Bemis, S. F., *Pinckney's Treaty*, The Johns Hopkins Press, 1926, pp. 394-400.

CHAPTER VI

THE LOUISIANA PURCHASE IN THE LIGHT
OF GEOGRAPHIC CONDITIONS

Rivers as Boundaries. For twenty years after the treaty of 1783 the Mississippi was accepted as the western boundary of the United States. But a river is not a barrier and therefore never a scientific boundary; it is merely a convenient line of demarcation,[1] uncertain at best on account of its shifting bed. The plantations on the meanders of the lower Mississippi belong now to one, now to the other of the contiguous states, as the mighty stream straightens its course after the almost annual overflow. The Rio Grande is anything but a satisfactory boundary between the United States and Mexico. Dry for many months of the year, it bears no semblance of a barrier; then it is suddenly filled with a resistless current which cuts a new channel for itself, leaving many square miles of Mexican territory on its northern bank, and in turn cutting off Texas ranchers from their native state. The result is a new survey or endless controversies as to whether Texas or Mexico is to claim certain dislodged pieces of land.

The political frontier line which is run along a river is an artificial one, for every drainage system forms an unbroken whole. The common destination of the tributary streams makes it as easy to cross as to follow the structural axis of the basin. The water journey on the Mississippi from Cairo, Illinois, to St. Paul, Minnesota, and return presents about the same difficulty as the round trip from Cincinnati to

[1] Ratzel, F., *Anthropogeographie*, Stuttgart, 1899, 2d ed., I, 349–52.

Kansas City by way of the Ohio and Missouri.   To migration and to conquest a river presents no obstacle.   Within the Tigris–Euphrates Valley three great monarchies — Assyrian, Babylonian, and Persian — arose, and each in turn extended its dominion over the whole basin.   To the Romans, the Danube and Rhine as their northern frontier had the value chiefly of established lines in the unexplored wilderness of the interior.   But even the Romans found it necessary to acquire the highlands forming the watershed between the Rhine and the Neckar, and Dacia to the north of the Danube.   The Danube formed the northern Turkish frontier in 1444, but in twenty years the empire had taken in Wallachia across the river and by 1672 embraced the whole basin of the Danube up beyond Budapest.   When the empire began to decline, the frontier dropped back down the river to Belgrade (1700), but still held both sides of the valley.

Even more surely than conquest does migration tend to hold the two slopes of a river basin.   Before the westward movement of the Germans, both banks of the Rhine were held by the Gauls, whose villages in some instances were bisected by the river, just as Rome arose on both sides of the Tiber.   Then in a like manner the Teutons spread over the whole long, deep trough of the Rhine valley.   Across the Rhine, Meuse, and Seine the early Franks spread into northern Gaul, and they occupied the Valley of the Rhone through the pass of Belfort.   The population of all these river basins show the admixture of that tall, blond race, while the surrounding highlands harbor the darker, shorter race constituting the earlier inhabitants of the land.[2]

A boundary of race or language cuts across the axis of a

[2] Ripley, W. Z., *The Races of Europe*, New York, 1899. Maps, pp. 143, 147.

river basin; rarely is it defined by the stream itself, and then only for a short distance. Where the Elbe flows through the low plains of North Germany, across its whole valley the population is the pure Teutonic type — fair, tall, long-headed; a broad zone of a more brunette type occupies its middle course across the uplands of Saxony; while its upper course, hemmed in by the Erz and Riesen Mountains, shows the broad-headed, short people of the Bohemian plateau.[3] Lines of ethnical demarcation, therefore, cut the Elbe Valley transversely, not longitudinally. The whole valley of the Danube from the Drave northward to the Austrian boundary is Hungarian. From the Drave mouth to the Iron Gate it is Serbo-Croatian on either bank, as is also its western tributary, the Save. The linguistic boundary of German cuts across the Danube between Vienna and Budapest.[4] The German-Romansch line of speech crosses the upper Inn at the entrance to the Engadine, and the upper Rhine near Ilanz, some twenty miles above Chur.[5] So in America, the lower St. Lawrence is French and the upper stream is English. This linguistic boundary is one of the few scars on a political body to be found in this country; such scars, being made in general in the youth of our nation, soon healed over and were obliterated.

THE MISSISSIPPI AS A BOUNDARY

The boundary line of the Mississippi was never more than a scratch at best, as we shall see, for as a race frontier it was only an imaginary line. As soon as the enterprising Westerners reached the Mississippi, they were on it and across it.

[3] Ripley, W. Z., *The Races of Europe*, New York, 1899. Map, p. 222.
[4] *Ibid.*, maps, pp. 403, 429.   [5] *Ibid.*, map, p. 284.

The trans-Allegheny rivers made the requisite conditions for a rapid expansion of population, and the convergence of the Ohio, Tennessee, and Cumberland upon the Mississippi guided the three incoming tides of settlers towards the great central stream.   As early as 1788–89, between 800 and 900 boats went down the Ohio past Fort Harmar (Marietta), carrying 20,000 people, with 7000 horses, 3000 cows, 900 sheep, and 600 wagons.[6]   This does not take into account the trains of pioneers whose feet were treading out a broader trail along the Wilderness Road, or the large accessions to the Cumberland settlements after the cessation of the Indian wars.   The numbers of the western people were ominous to the Spanish power beyond the Mississippi; more ominous still were their spacial ideas.   Already the bigness of the West was being absorbed into their mental constitution. The mighty sweep of the western waters, the interminable stretch of the northwestern prairies, the boundless extent of the Appalachian forests, were giving to these men from the narrow Atlantic plain new standards of measure.   Five to ten thousand acres became the desirable, almost the usual size of a farm, until the land was pretty well taken up.   A river voyage of a thousand miles was a commonplace matter, and even a land journey of five hundred miles on foot or horseback along the Chickasaw Trace from Fort Adams, the southernmost post of the United States on the Mississippi, to Nashville was nothing to brag of.   It was made every year by the returning traders with their money from the river trips to New Orleans.

Early Settlements Along the Mississippi.   In 1800 the western settlements extended down the Ohio almost as far as the mouth of the Cumberland.   There were besides two

[6] Winsor, J., *The Westward Movement*, Boston, 1897, p. 372.

remote outlying strips of settlement along the Mississippi, the form and location of which were significant. The northern one was in the western part of the present state of Illinois and formed a narrow band along the Mississippi from near the mouth of the Illinois River southward beyond the Kaskaskia. Its nuclei were to be found in the old French settlements of Cahokia and Kaskaskia, and the attraction was the opportunity of trade with St. Louis and Ste. Genevieve on the Spanish side of the river, where could be obtained foreign articles of luxury from New Orleans or skins and furs which found their way down from the upper Missouri.

The other group was known as the Natchez District and stretched along the bluffs of the Mississippi for a hundred miles between the Spanish line of demarcation and the Yazoo delta. Its population of about six thousand, including slaves, was distributed in several large settlements along the Bayou Pierre, Cole's Creek, St. Catherine, Second Creek, Honochitto, Buffalo Creek, and Big Black River, most of them within ten or fifteen miles of the Mississippi. The District contained a nucleus of English settlement, dating from the period of 1763–1783, when the British held West Florida and were trying to divert some of the commerce of the Mississippi by way of the Iberville River, which was to be canalled, and Lake Ponchartrain to Mobile or Pensacola.[7] There were new accessions of American population after the treaty of 1783, which secured the region to the United States, though the Spanish did not yield the control which they had assumed by encroachment until 1798. The proximity of Natchez to the Spanish boundary made it the most convenient point for trade with New Orleans, and

[7] Winsor, J., op. cit., p. 32.

it was the starting-point of the old wilderness trail to the Cumberland settlements for the returning river men. The bluffs above the Mississippi afforded a more hygienic and less malarial situation than the low bottom-lands either above or below. The elements of the population were characteristically those of a frontier region in this locality — Anglo-Americans from the old British Florida, a few French who had become dissatisfied with Spanish rule in Louisiana, a remnant of Spaniards, and an increasing proportion of Westerners.

The nature of a frontier as a zone of commingling elements has been described above. The composite character of the Natchez population was duplicated on the west side of the Mississippi with the proportions of the Latin and Saxon constituents reversed. In the barge and flatboat life on the mighty stream itself, the two races were in all probability about equally represented. Not more completely did the Ohio and the Missouri mingle their currents in the central channel than their burdens of craft and men and mer-- chandise. Here was the cosmopolitan life of the country — river men from the Holston and the Allegheny, newly arrived New Englanders from the Muskingum settlements, French, British, and Scotch traders from the Illinois River, and French voyageurs with a few Spaniards, chiefly officials, from the Louisiana side. Busy was the trade on the river. By it New Orleans and Brownville were linked together. The Creole city drew its flour, grain, and salted meat from the Ohio country, its vegetables from the Natchez District, so that when suspension of the American right of deposit at New Orleans put a quietus on the river traffic, it nearly starved.

In Upper Louisiana, French and American elements predominated in the long strip of settlements which bordered the Mississippi from St. Charles and St. Louis to New Madrid. Some of the French had belonged originally to the east side of the river, and had migrated from the Wabash and Illinois when this region was acquired by England in 1763. American settlers were tempted across to New Madrid by Governor Miro of Louisiana in 1787 by large grants of land and promises of free navigation of the Mississippi, and under the same allurements many from the Holston and Cumberland emigrated to West Florida. By the census of 1799, the population of St. Louis was 925, St. Charles 875, Ste. Genevieve 949, New Bourbon 560, Cape Girardeau 521, and New Madrid 782, all of them river towns. The fact that Upper Louisiana had increased its population much more rapidly than the remainder of the province [8] was due largely to the steady influx of American colonists.

Westward Movement of Settlers. A regular extra-territorial expansion was going on: the backwoodsmen were anticipating the movement of the flag: the race, by an anthropogeographical law, was spreading from the downward to the upward slope of the river valley. The trans-Mississippi country had a stronger attraction for the pioneer than the region north of the Ohio; the climate and soil were better adapted to the crops which he was accustomed to raise with slave labor, and there slavery was not forbidden. Somewhere between 1797 and 1799, Daniel Boone, having lost his lands in Kentucky by a defective title, moved to Spanish territory and took up his residence in the Femme Osage settlement, about forty-five miles west of St. Louis. His son, Daniel Boone, Jr., had preceded him thither, and other of his married children soon followed him.[9] Captain Merri-

[8] Monette, J. W., *op. cit.*, I, 545.
[9] Hartley, C. B., *Life of Daniel Boone*, Philadelphia, 1865, pp. 308–24.

wether Lewis, in the spring of 1804, found in this settlement thirty or forty families from the United States, and another smaller group of American emigrants on the Bon Homme Creek a few miles to the east.[10]　All the river towns were getting accessions from the eastern side of the Mississippi.

Lower Louisiana was more remote from the American frontier of continuous settlement, and hence its population showed a smaller admixture of the American element.　This was found chiefly in New Orleans, where the advantage of trade attracted the enterprising merchant from the United States.　There was an occasional American planter between the Mississippi and the Ouachita, and some American immigrants at Natchitoches far up the Red River; while a band of adventurers, under Philip Nolan, in 1800 penetrated to the Brazos River in the present state of Texas.　There they had set up their cabins, and were occupied in catching wild horses, till they themselves were captured in 1801 by Spanish officials.[11]

The zone of assimilation which constituted the American-Spanish frontier was shifting ominously to the western side of the political line of demarcation.　Louisiana was in danger of being inundated by the oncoming flood of western settlers. The Intendant at New Orleans became alarmed, and in 1799 issued regulations to discourage American immigration in every way; and in 1802 the king of Spain prohibited any grant of land to a citizen of the United States.[12]

[10] Coues, E., *History of the Lewis and Clark Expedition*, Washington, 1876, I, 7.
[11] Roosevelt, T., *op. cit.*, IV, 266.
[10] Monette, J. W., *op. cit.*, II, 541, 546.

INTEREST OF DIFFERENT NATIONS IN LOUISIANA

The expansion of the Westerners and the oneness of the great river valley were working together for the acquisition of Louisiana by the United States. Race power and geographical condition were operating to the same end. Jefferson understood this. In January, 1803, he urged upon Congress the desirability of purchasing from the Chickasaw Indians a strip of territory along the Mississippi, north of the Yazoo, in order to possess "a respectable breadth of country on that river [the Mississippi] from our southern limit to the Illinois at least, so that we present as firm a front on that as on our eastern border." [13] And again, he affirms his faith in the policy of putting off the day of contending for the possession of New Orleans "till we are stronger in ourselves and stronger in allies, but especially till we have planted such a population on the Mississippi as will be able to do their own business." [14]

Historians are fond of insisting that the acquisition of the Louisiana country was fortuitous, depending upon half a dozen chances. The great factors of a nation's development are not set in operation by the whim of a First Consul or the uncertain events of a distant war. The purchase of Louisiana was the occasion, not the cause of the acquisition of the trans-Mississippi country. That must have come sooner or later. Even if the French had established themselves in Louisiana, they could not long have resisted the operation of geographic factors and the enterprising spirit of the western people, itself in part a product of environment.

[13] Ford, P. L., *Writings of Thomas Jefferson*, VIII. Confidential Message to Congress on the Expedition to the Pacific, January 18, 1803.

[14] *Ibid.* Letter to John Bacon, April 30, 1803.

The trans-Mississippi region, hopelessly arid beyond the one-hundredth meridian, could never have supported a large enough population to resist the Americans, with whom the common navigation of the Mississippi would soon have brought them to blows. At the moment negotiations for the purchase were pending, the breadth of the Atlantic rendered formidable an uprising of the blacks in San Domingo and lost France that island. Napoleon applied the geographical principle involved to a possible French colony in Louisiana, further jeopardized by a foreign war. Had England conquered Louisiana from France — the chance which Napoleon feared — even her superior colonizing methods could not have made the country support a population large enough to cope with the thickly planted American settlements in the wide, rich, well watered regions to the east. In a conflict between a cis-Mississippi and a trans-Mississippi power, the former had every geographical condition in its favor — coast-line, rivers, climate, soil, and habitable area. The Americans were destined to hold the West. The purchase hastened and facilitated the process.

For the time being, the United States could not have had safer neighbors in the Louisiana country than the Spanish. They were too weak to be aggressive, and too unprogressive to offer serious competition to American trade. Jefferson's only fear was lest they should be too feeble to hold the country "until our population can be sufficiently advanced to gain it from them piece by piece." The arbitrary suspension of the right of deposit at New Orleans in 1788, and again in 1802 sufficed to indicate the annoyance and hardship to which the Americans would be exposed so long as the key to the western commerce was in any hands but their own. The excitement over this violation of the treaty rights

was greatest in the West, and here it was tremendous.
Kentucky and Tennessee in 1799 could with difficulty be re-
strained by the federal authorities from sending out an independent expedition to capture New Orleans. Here spoke
the self-reliant, dauntless spirit of the backwoods. In 1802,
the President was flooded with protests and memorials from
the whole transmontane country. Stirred even more by the
rumors of the cession of Louisiana to France, Kentucky and
Tennessee called for immediate action, and Governor Claiborne of the Mississippi Territory offered to raise in his
district alone a sufficient number of volunteers to seize New
Orleans before it should be transferred to French hands.

The prospect of having these new neighbors in the Louisiana country was not reassuring.[15]   The French were at
this time the mightiest nation in Europe. Their recent
training had not made them pacific, and the restless, energetic, impulsive temperament of the people was sure to produce friction when they and the Americans met on the waters
of the Mississippi. "There is on the globe one single spot,"
said Jefferson, "the possessor of which is our natural and
habitual enemy. It is New Orleans, through which the
produce of three-eighths of our territory must pass to
market, and from its fertility it will, ere long, yield more than
half of our whole produce and contain more than half our
inhabitants. France placing herself in that door assumes
to us the attitude of defiance…. The day that France takes
possession of New Orleans fixes the sentence which is to re-
strain her forever within her low-water mark. It seals the

[15] This is clearly stated in "that the acquisition of Louisiana was a leading motive
for the diplomatic disturbances of the period, 1795–1800, and that the desire to control this territory was conspicuous among the causes in bringing about the Treaty of
1800 between France and America." James, J. A., "Louisiana as a Factor in American Diplomacy, 1795–1800," *Mississippi Valley Historical Review*, I (1914–15), 44.

union of two nations who in conjunction can maintain exclusive possession of the ocean. From that moment we must marry ourselves to the British fleet and nation." [16] These measures were not desired, but would be forced upon the United States "as necessarily as any other cause, by the laws of nature, brings on its necessary effect." If the French insisted upon holding Louisiana, the cession of the Floridas and the Island of New Orleans might reconcile the Americans by guaranteeing their free access to the Gulf of Mexico. The transit duties on all commerce passing in or out of Mobile Bay also had been working a hardship upon the small Tombigbee settlements, but the key to the Mississippi was the crucial thing.

Napoleon's dreams of colonial empire had to be relinquished. The rebellion of the negroes in San Domingo demonstrated the futility of oversea domination for France at this time. British naval power and the British army in Canada made evident the impossibility of holding Louisiana in the event of war with England. French agents represented to Napoleon the great difficulties of an upstream campaign from New Orleans to protect the distant settlements in Upper Louisiana against the aggressions of the Americans, and the ease of a downstream conquest of Lower Louisiana by the determined Westerners. To the insight of the First Consul into geographical situations, it was clearly futile to retain Louisiana and relinquish New Orleans, which was the key to the whole province. But the dominant factors in the alienation of this western empire was the broad Atlantic and the island-born naval power of the English. Thus, in every motive for the sale as for the

[16] Ford. P. L., *Writings of Thomas Jefferson*, VIII. Letter to Robert Livingston, April 18, 1803.

purchase of Louisiana, the geographic factor was the strongest.

RESULTS OF THE ACQUISITION OF LOUISIANA

The retrocession of Louisiana to France had been made by Spain reluctantly, but the presence of a strong buffer state between Mexico and the expanding United States was undoubtedly a compensation.[17]   With the annexation of Louisiana to American territory, however, the situation of Spanish holdings in the northern continent was seriously affected.   Nearly the whole sweep of the Gulf and Caribbean coast from the Guianas around to Porto Rico was in the hands of Spain, except the five-hundred mile stretch of the Louisiana littoral between the mouth of the Sabine and the Mississippi; but this possessed an importance out of all proportion to its length.   The significance of a coast is determined largely by the extent and character of its hinterland.   Back of the Louisiana coast lay the vast Mississippi basin, now wholly American, like a great funnel whose mouth was at New Orleans.   The pressure from the back country was sure to be enormous and eventually to burst the bonds of Spanish restriction on the Gulf coast.   The Spanish holdings in Florida and Mexico were now severed, and that at a strategic point.   If Louis XIV, from his base in Canada, had succeeded in his plan of conquering the Hudson Valley and intercluding the two lines of English coast in America, the politico geographical situation would have been analogous.

Expansion Along the Gulf.   According to the Purchase treaty, as understood in the United States,[18] the Louisiana

[17] Roosevelt, T., *op. cit.*, IV, 207.
[18] Hart, A. B., *Foundation of American Foreign Policy*, New York, 1901, p. 97.

province was to comprise the original French holding from the Rio Grande del Norte to the Perdido River, which defines the western boundary of the present state of Florida. But Spain, with the instinct of self-preservation, tried to ·restrict these limits as much as possible, transferred only that part of the Louisiana coast lying between the Sabine and the Mississippi, together with the Island of New Orleans on the east bank of the river, planted new colonies in eastern Texas and new posts along this frontier, and began to encroach with an armed force along the Sabine and the Red, with the secret purpose of making the Red River the eastern boundary of Mexico [19] and thus excluding the United States from the Gulf except at New Orleans.

As well might they have tried to dam the mouth of the Mississippi. Rivers and nations strive equally to reach the sea. Soon after the occupation of Louisiana by the United States, its Gulf coast was stretched eastward to the Pearl River. What was known as the Baton Rouge District of West Florida had a population made up largely of English, dating from the British supremacy in this region, and Americans who had come in from the Cumberland country and the Natchez settlement near by. A revolt in the Baton Rouge District and an appeal to the United States for annexation to the Territory of New Orleans brought the American flag to the Pearl River. The exigencies of war carried it to the Perdido, when England, countenanced by Spain, undertook to use the Florida coast as a military base during the War of 1812,[20] and Congress, to defeat this project, ordered its occupation and annexation to the Territory of Mississippi. Purchase in 1819 secured East Florida, and

[19] Monette, J. W., *op. cit.*, II, 461.
[20] Monette, J. W., *op. cit.*, I, 83–85.

expansion of American settlers to the southwest finally extended the Gulf coast of the United States to the Rio Grande.

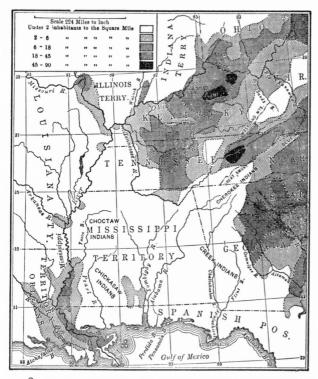

FIG. 8. DISTRIBUTION OF RURAL POPULATION IN THE MISSISSIPPI VALLEY IN 1810

The distribution of population shows the influence of river highways, of the older settlements in Kentucky and Tennessee, and of Indian occupied lands.

Inrush of Settlers. The extension of the federal authority over the province of Louisiana was the signal for an inrush of American settlers, both from the eastern and the western states (Fig. 8). Six months before the transfer hundreds had collected on the Cumberland for the purpose. The distribution of population in 1815 in the New Orleans Ter- ritory, which comprised the present state of Louisiana, is instructive as illustrating the geographic control of water- courses. The greater portion of the 90,000 inhabitants was found along the Mississippi for seventy miles above and thirty miles below New Orleans. Most of these were Creole French, with a slight sprinkling of Americans. There was a dense French population on the Bayou Lefourche for fifty miles below its efflux from the Mississippi, on the Bayou Teche for fifty miles below Opelousas, and on several bayous west of the Atchafalaya in the same neighborhood. The French occupied the Red River continuously up to Alexan- dria, less compactly as far as Natchitoches, while there were some scattered dwellings higher up the stream as also upon its northern tributary, the Ouachita, above the present town of Monroe.[21] The first comers had therefore selected the rich alluvial bottoms, generally within fifty miles of the Mis- sissippi, which formed the chief highway of the country.

In the old Florida parishes on the east bank the Americans predominated. They were to be found elsewhere chiefly in New Orleans and certain coast towns, though their planta- tions were scattered sparsely east of the Ouachita and north of the Red, just opposite the dense American center in the old Natchez District. The French occupation of the present state of Louisiana had progressed from the coast inland, and therefore had fixed upon the lower courses of the rivers. The American immigrants were later comers, and advanced from the interior of the continent; hence they located inland on the upper courses of the streams, excepting those merchants who were attracted to the seaports.

[21] Monette, J. W., op. cit., II, 516.

As the wild lands in the old West were taken up, and steam navigation on the rivers facilitated expansion, population poured across the Mississippi until in 1840 it occupied a broad band up and down that stream, defined on the west by the ninety-fifth meridian and the Sabine River, and reaching from Iowa to the Gulf.

Attitude of the East.   Thus the purchase of Louisiana was abundantly justified, if only on the ground of American capacity for expansion; but the acquisition of so vast a territory was bitterly opposed in the middle states and in New England, the natural habitat of the provincial point of view. The reasons advanced were the preponderance of the South and West in the future councils of the nation, as this large area should be carved up into states; and the possible formation of an independent confederacy, embracing the whole Mississippi basin and thus curtailing the extent and strength of the original Union.[22] It was argued that the course of the river would divert western interests from the East to the South. The same fear had been set forth by the East at the time of the negotiation of the Jay treaty as a reason for accepting the occlusion of the Mississippi as a means of counteracting the separatist tendency of the transmontane settlements.

Influence on Expansion to Continental Power.   Fortunately the narrow policy of the New England statesmen secured no adequate following. The acquisition of Louisiana destined the United States for a continental power. The Republic was born synchronously with the idea of national empire and large territorial dominion. "Young countries know no exclusion from the sea; they are wont rather to

[22] Ford, P. L., *Writings of Thomas Jefferson*, VIII.   Letter to J. C. Breckenridge, April 12, 1803.

grow from the sea landwards and if possible onwards till they reach the sea again." [23]   All the countries of North America, except little San Salvador, have a foothold on either ocean, sometimes the very smallness of this foothold indicating its importance.

In South America physiographical conditions have been adverse to such sea-to-sea expansion, except at the northern and southern extremities of the continent where the mighty rampart of the Andes sinks into the ocean.   Colombia has a broad base on the Pacific and the Caribbean Sea; and where the Straits of Magellan cut through the continent, the bare rim of the mainland is held by aggressive Chile to the detriment of Argentina.   The wall-like barrier of the Andes, rising from no gently sloping plateau as do the Rockies, presented a most formidable obstacle to expansion from the east, while the tropical climate of the greater part of South America served to emphasize the indolent temperaments of the Latin half-breed population.   Though the upland valleys were early occupied from the western coast, the mountain district of the Cordilleras could not soon produce a pressure of population sufficient to mount the snowy ranges and overflow into the great river valleys on the Atlantic side. But the Pacific states reach out towards the east, and the number of boundary disputes on the Atlantic slope of the Andes is significant.

Russia, the youngest country of Europe to develop under geographical conditions of continental expansion, from a small inland area has pushed its frontiers to the Baltic, the Black Sea, and the Pacific.

Lewis and Clark Search for Overland Route for Commerce. Four months before the Louisiana Purchase was consum-

[23] Ratzel, F., *Politische Geographie der Vereinigten Staaten*, 1893, p. 1.

mated, the Lewis and Clark expedition was planned to prepare the way for American expansion to the Pacific by discovering the best overland route for commerce.   Jefferson
wished to exploit the advantages of the great system of river
communication across the continent; he realized the unify-
ing power of the Missouri in creating an interest for the
United States in the far West.   "The river Missouri and the
tribes inhabiting it are not as well known as is rendered desirable by their connexion with the Mississippi, and consequently with us." [24]   He complained that the furs and
peltries of the remote Northwest were carried off by the
British traders through Canada by a far less perfect system
of inland navigation which was interrupted by innumerable
portages and shut up by ice much of the year; whereas these
products of the northwestern forest ought naturally to reach
the Atlantic through American waterways.   Lewis was instructed, therefore, to explore the Missouri carefully, and
follow any of its principal streams which might afford the
readiest communication across the mountains with the
Columbia and the Pacific Ocean.

Prolonged Frontier Conditions.   The Mississippi Valley
was destined to become the core of the nation as it was of
the continent.   Its fertile soil would support a dense population, and its cheap waterways were to prove of inestimable
value for a young, agricultural people.   The acquisition of
the new West prolonged greatly the most distinctive feature
of American anthropo-geographic conditions — the abundance of free land.[25]   A nation is influenced not only by the
topography, but by the size of its territory.   The presence of

[24] Ford, P. L., *Writings of Thomas Jefferson*, VIII.   Confidential Message to
Congress, January 18, 1803.

[25] Turner, F. J., "Significance of the Frontier in American History," *National
Herbart Society Yearbook*, No. 5 (1899), pp. 7–41.

the new West reacted most wholesomely upon the East and the old West: the stimulating effect of inexhaustible opportunity never allowed American energy to abate, and the democratic spirit of the ever youthful frontier fostered the spirit of democracy and youth in the whole nation. The abundance of unoccupied land beyond the Mississippi afforded a solution of the Indian question, and prevented it from ever reaching an acute stage. Some of the Indian purchases were doubtless delayed because of the new outlet for the white population; but when made, were simplified by the transfer of the tribes to new hunting-fields beyond the Mississippi. Thus the western half of the great valley brought more room to the eastern half.

CHAPTER VII

GEOGRAPHY OF THE ATLANTIC COAST IN RELATION TO THE DEVELOPMENT OF AMERICAN SEA POWER

WHILE western settlement was spreading up the lower reaches of the Missouri, Arkansas, and Ouachita in 1810, the center of population for the whole country lay at the eastern foot of the Blue Ridge, forty miles northwest of Washington and the tidal floods of Chesapeake Bay. Even as late as 1830, the star which marks the westward course of population on the census maps had not passed beyond the head waters of the Potomac; it still lingered with the waters draining into the Atlantic, thus showing the ocean's power of attraction, even after the nation by the acquisition of Louisiana had committed itself to continental dominion (see Fig. 22). The influence of the Appalachian barrier, as we have seen, was to limit the British colonies to the coastal plain, and in certain regions to stimulate maritime development because of the limited supply of easily exploited natural resources on the narrow shelf of the continent. When fur-fields and corn-fields gave out, enterprising spirits sought a new field of activity on the sea.

The attraction of the abundant lands in the Louisiana country was not felt immediately. Enterprise and capital do not change their direction so rapidly. The decade of 1830 and 1840 witnessed a decline in the American merchant marine and a widespread movement of population which pushed the western frontier to the ninety-fifth meridian, where it lingered for many years. Then our development became continental as opposed to maritime or extra-continental. "In the present century we see the effects arising from the opening of the Mississippi Valley to our Atlantic coast peoples in the gradual decadence of our shipping interests.... Although there have been many influences at work in the diversion of our people from maritime life, it seems on the whole that the most important cause is to be found in the way opened to enterprising people through the ready access which this century has given to the central fields of the continent. This phase over, we may expect reversion to maritime life on the Atlantic coast." [1] Such a development is taking place as a result of the changes ushered in by the World War, the increased industrialization of the country, and mounting foreign investments.

EARLY DOMINANCE OF THE SEA

Through all the colonial period and for the first four decades of the Republic, the United States was dominated by the ocean. Geographical location and a variety of geographical conditions determined the maritime character of the nation.

A String of Settlements. The original Thirteen Colonies were a long cordon of settlements along the Atlantic, stretching from the St. Croix River in the north to the St. Mary's in the south; they had length but not breadth, and this length was washed by the tides of the ocean. Each colony had ample contact with the sea, and developed along the lines of its sea connection. Travel from colony to colony by land crossed the watercourses at right angles; only in exceptional cases could it make use of these natural highways of a

[1] Shaler, N. S., *Nature and Man in America*, New York, 1904, p. 200.

young community.   Inter-colonial travel and traffic therefore went by sea, and the coastwise trade became a great
artery through which circulated the common life of the
nascent people, contributing to that solidarity which made
their strength.

Harbors.   Of harbors there were plenty, from one end of
the coast to the other.   The Atlantic shore of the United
States is characterized by multiplicity of small indentations
and paucity of large ones.   In this respect it presents a contrast to Europe.   Chesapeake Bay and Long Island Sound
are the only partially inclosed bodies of water considerable
in size, and even they run parallel to the coast and so contribute comparatively little to opening up the back country.
This office was performed by the Atlantic rivers with their
estuaries, which sufficed to carry maritime influences well
into the heart of the narrow zone of settlement.

Peninsulas and Islands.   A paucity of large inlets means
a paucity of peninsulas.   In the domain of the United
States we can count only the Delaware–Maryland arm of
land, southern New Jersey, the southeastern projection of
Massachusetts, and at a later date Florida, which, however,
owing to its poverty of harbors, has contributed little to the
maritime development of the country.   The United States
has also few segregated areas in the form of islands; it lies between the great island regions of the Atlantic, between Newfoundland, Cape Breton, Prince Edward, and Anticosti to
the north, and the vast loop of the Antilles to the south.
Thus the continental location of the United States is emphasized.[2]   Such islands as it has are close inshore, a part of the
general contour of the country.   They are fragments of the
mainland cut off by glacial action and subsidence, as those

[2] Ratzel, F., *Politische Geographie der Vereinigten Staaten*, 1893, p. 29.

along the fiord regions of Maine; or long bars of deposit which inclose the coast with few interruptions from Sandy Hook to the Rio Grande. Only Long Island by its size and Nantucket by its comparative remoteness have achieved an independent or individual existence. The presence of foreign powers in all the islands to the north and south and even those off the coast, as the Bermudas, Bahamas, and Antilles, has been a distinct factor in the naval and military history of the United States, demonstrating the disadvantages of a purely continental location.

Geographical Location and Resources. Length of coastline and abundance of harbors united with a third geographical condition, namely, location, to make the Americans from the start a seafaring people. They held a central position on the rim of the populous and progressive North Atlantic Basin, and in this position New England occupied the choice place. Trade followed the great sweep of the Gulf Stream, the North Atlantic Drift, and the returning Equatorial Current past the shores of Newfoundland, Great Britain, Spain, Africa, the Canary Islands, West Indies, and up the coast of the United States. This path the American schooners followed, helped onward by the currents and their causing winds, visiting in turn all the markets passed and completing with profit the great circuit of trade. Not England itself had a more advantageous position for the commerce of the North Atlantic, if we except its proximity to the isolated maritime field of the Baltic. Located in the temperate zone, the colonies, as later the states, were under the necessity of importing tropical products from the West Indies, among whose islands American vessels threaded their way, carrying in exchange the substantial foodstuffs of the North. As a new country with an abundance of surplus products from forest, field, and shore, it demanded the manufactured wares of Europe, while that continent in turn clamored for the raw materials of America. To both these important markets colonial America held a near and central position. These are the large features of her geographical location. A more detailed analysis of early American exchanges will reveal other advantages which can be attributed in great part to conditions of climate, soil, and physical features obtaining in the states themselves, or in the markets which their merchantmen sought along the current paths of the pathless ocean.

Within the area of the Thirteen Colonies there were differences of natural conditions sufficient to diversify their activities and their products, to make land interests predominate in one section and maritime in the other, and that in spite of the fact that both regions had ample contact with the sea. The geographical environment of a people consists of all the natural conditions to which they are subjected, not merely a part. A coast region shows always the interplay of the forces of land and of sea. According to the fertility and extent of arable soil, or to the abundance and availability of harbors combined with an unproductive or limited back country, now the agricultural phase of development, now the maritime prevails, following the law of the resolution of forces.

Example of Jews and Phœnicians. A one-sided view of environment in the study of geography is disastrous, as shown by the conclusions of a writer, who says: "The evidence of history is, however, strongly against the assumption that geographical facilities alone will make a people maritime. The Phœnicians and the Jews dwelt side by side on the same coast, but they made very different uses of their opportunities. The Phœnicians filled the Meditteranean with their commerce.... The Jews never developed any aptitude for the sea." [3]

These two peoples made a different use of their opportunities because their opportunities were essentially different, both as to the land and as to their respective coasts. The Jews inhabited a broad band of field and pasture stretching westward from the Syrian desert, but reaching the Mediterranean only southward from the promontory of Mount Carmel; here the coast is one smooth, unbroken stretch, even the tiny estuaries of its streams being filled up by the current-borne sand swept northward from the Nile delta. The coast afforded no harbors, while the back country with its varied, abundant crops, rich orchards, but scanty forests, offered every inducement to an agricultural life. The Phœnicians occupied a narrow hem of land between the solid range of the Lebanon Mountains and the sea. The port of Sidon was only fifteen miles distant from the summit of the range (four thousand feet). Expansion to the eastward was practically impossible; only across the hill country of Samaria, where expansion was possible, did the Phœnicians stretch their dominion through the mountain barrier to the inner range of Mount Hermon. The coast which they held north of Mount Carmel, in contrast to that of the Jews, was somewhat broken and irregular from the fact that the roots of the mountains here intruded upon the sea. An occasional harbor, an inshore islet making a protected roadstead, and outlying Cyprus, invited to maritime life. On the slopes of Lebanon, which condensed the moisture brought in by the prevailing southwestern winds, grew the magnificent cedars which furnished the material for the Phœnician

[3] George, H. B., *The Relations of Geography and History*, Oxford, 1901, p. 76.

fleets. But the steep hillsides would grow little else. Hence geographical conditions both of the sea and of the land combined to make a maritime race of the Phœnicians, an inland people of the Jews.[4]

THE MARITIME DEVELOPMENT OF NEW ENGLAND

Such a contrast was presented by the Atlantic shore of America and with much the same result. In New England the deeply embayed coast, the narrowness of the lowland belt, the glaciated soil, the power resources of the plunging streams, the heavy forest growth, and the abundance of fish in the coastal waters were all geographic factors operating to develop maritime life. In New York and Raritan bays similar conditions, combined with favorable routes of communication with the interior, produced a region of natural seaports with the attendant nautical activity. Philadelphia near the mouth of the Delaware River and Baltimore commanding the Susquehanna outlet became the ports for eastern Pennsylvania. But southward from this point, in spite of bays, sounds, inlets, and deep river mouths, the sea loses its ascendency in controlling the activities of the people, and the extensive, fertile soil of the southern states determines their agricultural development. By length of coast-line the southern colonies were kept in contact with oversea influences, but the profits of tobacco and rice crops withheld their investments from the carrying-trade, which they therefore left to others, notably New England. Even today the southern states own less than a tenth of the ships under our flag.[5]

[4] Smith, G. A., *Historical Geography of the Holy Land*, London, 1895, pp. 76–85 and 127–35.

[5] *Merchant Marine Statistics, 1930*, Bureau of Navigation, Department of Commerce, Washington, 1930, p. 4.

The great navigators of the world have always been those nations living in small, half-barren coast countries, or in larger countries with only a limited fertile area, but lying near to larger fruitful regions for whose products they could play the part of middleman, or exchange the harvest of their seas.   Such peoples were the Phœnicians, Carthaginians, Greeks, Latins, English, the burghers of the Hanse towns, and the Norwegians.   The rocky, indented coast of New England produced the great maritime carriers of the New World, with whom even British merchantmen found it difficult to compete.   The ports of Massachusetts Bay are four degrees of longitude nearer to England than is Philadelphia, nine degrees nearer than Charleston, South Carolina; therefore they had distinct advantages in the trade with the island kingdom which, by reason of its limited area and denuded forest lands, made a steady demand for the raw products of America.   Especially it needed masts, spars, and lumber for the royal navy from the northern forests of New England. These materials the colonists also worked up assiduously for their own marine, so that shipbuilding for home uses and exportation became one of the earliest and most important industries of the northeast coast.

Shipbuilding.   The geographical distribution of early shipbuilding ports in New England shows the dispersion of maritime interests along the whole coast, as opposed to the concentration at a few favored points in later times; it tells of abundant forests near all the shipyards, of the splash of waterfall and the whir of sawmill almost mingling with the roar of the surf on the shore.   In the period from 1620 to 1750 we find vessels being launched at numerous towns along the coast from Cape Ann to the Connecticut River — at Gloucester, Salem, Marblehead, Medford, Dorchester,

Boston, Plymouth, Portsmouth and Newport in Rhode Island, Westerly on the estuary of the Pawcatuck, and New London.

But after 1750 the lumber supply near the older ports was exhausted, and the shipbuilding industry began to concentrate along the shores of northeastern Massachusetts, New Hampshire, and the nearer coast of Maine. Wells, Maine, built a schooner of eighty-eight tons in 1767, but the greater center of shipbuilding activity was on the Piscataqua River, where vessels were turned out at the rate of two hundred a year. The abundant forests furnished the lumber; the cordage, anchors, and canvas to equip the vessels came from England, though Portsmouth started up three ropewalks at this time. Naval stores, such as tar, pitch, and turpentine, came from the northern woods or the forests of North Carolina. As the Piscataqua began to need all its lumber resources for the construction of ships, the center of export of masts and spars moved eastward from Portsmouth to Portland, Maine, evidencing the relationship between forests and commerce.[6]

Reading the early commercial history of New England, one seems never to get away from the sound of the shipbuilder's hammer and the rush of the launching vessel as she "schoons" on the waves. Massachusetts employed a fleet of two hundred vessels as early as 1709, and sold on an average one hundred a year to merchants of London and elsewhere.[7] Shipbuilding was inspected by the government, such was the pride in the industry, and builders were granted special privileges in several ports. Other lines of manu-

[6] Weeden, W. B., *Economic and Social History of New England*, Boston, 1891, II. 765, 766.

[7] *Ibid.*, I, 366.

factures which started up before 1650 remained undeveloped because this one great industry absorbed the energies and capital of the population. American ships were the cheapest and best afloat. Philadelphia, which was advantageously situated near the Appalachian forests and also near the sea, turned out the best-finished vessels, but New England's were the fleetest and staunchest.

Such an important field of activity was offered by the American merchant service that it attracted a superior class of men both for officers and crews. A vessel which started out with the highly composite cargo of an American ship, to visit the markets on the great circle of trade from Newfoundland around to Barbados, required a master who understood the possibility of every market both for selling and buying, and was alert to pick up a bit of freight business between the foreign ports which he might happen to pass. For this reason the personnel of American seamen was far superior to that of the British in the eighteenth and early part of the nineteenth century. The consequence was that American vessels were the favorite carriers on the ocean. They were the fastest, safest, took better care of their goods, loaded and unloaded most quickly. This reduced for them the rate of insurance, and enabled them to select the most valuable freight at the highest profit.[8]

Influence of Banks Fisheries. The shipbuilding industry of New England was stimulated especially by the proximity of the extensive fishing-grounds off the northeast coast of North America, where the submarine plateau of the Grand Banks pastured the finny herds of the ocean. Fisheries have always been the original inducement for men to go to sea, and they continue today to be the training-school of

[8] Shaler, N. S., *op. cit.*, I, 551, 552.

seamen. Boston alone in 1664 had three hundred boats fishing in the waters about Cape Sable; and there were fifteen hundred fishermen casting in their nets off the Isles of Shoals.[9] Cod became the staple of New England exports. Salted and packed, it found a ready and extensive market. The choicest fish were sent to the Catholic countries of southern Europe where the regular fast-days occasioned a steady demand, just as they had done in the fifteenth century for the salt herring of the great Hanse fisheries.[10] The medium quality was kept for home consumption, and the refuse fish was carried in great quantities to feed the slaves on the sugar plantations of the West Indies. This trade was carried on regularly with the British holdings in the Antilles, and illicitly but extensively with the French and Spanish colonies. The limited area of these islands and the more profitable use of their soil for a few semi-tropical products necessitated the importation from the American colonies of foodstuffs, which presupposed larger areas for agriculture and pasturage, as well as proximity to the northern fish. At the outbreak of the Revolution, the interruption of commercial dealings with the West Indies almost annihilated the fisheries and likewise the slaves, for thousands of these unfortunates died of starvation in a few years.

Whaling. Cod and mackerel, however, were not the only prizes that lured the American fisherman upon the water. In the early colonial days the right or baleen whale frequented these coasts, and a spout offshore was the signal for the launching of boats for the attack. In case a dead whale drifted to land, riparian rights, defined by law, decided the

[9] Weeden, W. B., *op. cit.*, I, 245.
[10] Schaefer, D., *Die Hansestädte und König Waldemar von Dänemark*, Fischer. Jena, 1879, p. 256.

ownership of the prize. But soon the drift whales decreased, and in consequence sloops and other small craft began to seek their prey, especially the sperm whale, in the open ocean, and a regular industry developed. This seems to have been concentrated chiefly on the southeastern coast of New England. The leaders were Nantucket, Long Island, and New Bedford; Providence, Warren, and Newport in Rhode Island, Dartmouth and the Cape Cod district participated. Boston took no very active part, though it was the chief port for the commerce in the products of the whale.

Deep-sea whaling demanded larger vessels, both for safety and to hold the big cargo of bone and oil. These ranged first from the Bahama Islands northward to Baffin Bay and Davis Strait, then across to the Azores and the Guinea coast. New England soon led the world in this industry; and when the whale was exterminated in the North and South Atlantic, its vessels followed it to the Pacific and Arctic. Whalebone and oil became important items in domestic and foreign exchanges. Of five thousand tons of whale-oil imported into London in 1763, nearly three fifths belonged to American owners, while forty tons of bone were deposited in the same market in 1761 and 1762.[11] Thus ships, lumber, fish, whale-oil and bone, New England's contributions to the world's exchanges, were intimately connected with its geographical location and natural features of coast-line, climate, and soil.

THE CURRENTS OF TRADE

Intercolonial Trade. Geographical conditions, as we have shown above, determined that inter-colonial communication should be largely by sea. This prepared the way for a pe-

[11] Weeden, W. B., *op. cit.*, II, 746.

culiarly active coasting-trade, especially as every district of the Atlantic slope was highly differentiated as to its products in consequence of varied natural conditions. The geographical control in the activities of New England and the southern states has been considered. New York and Philadelphia, by reason of their extensive interior connections through the Hudson, the Delaware, and the Susquehanna, were the natural ports for the fur trade. New York, Pennsylvania, and northern Maryland were the chief wheat-producing countries. New England, with the early exhaustion of its limited farm-land, soon (1745) found it necessary to import wheat,[12] and the southern states found it more profitable economy to get cereals from the North. South Carolina utilized its swamps for rice, and North Carolina, which long held the place of a frontier country to the older Virginia, contributed to commerce the products of a frontier region — lumber, naval stores, cattle, and leather.

The most active agents in the early coasting-trade were the Dutch of New Amsterdam, whose central position in the angle of the continent gave them peculiar advantages; but they soon found active competitors in the New Englanders, as soon as these later comers began to adapt themselves to their environment. The absence of great inlets along the western shore of the Atlantic had the effect that the American coastwise commerce was not thalassic but oceanic. It made wide sweeps, and in truth was intimately associated with the foreign trade. Just before the outbreak of the Revolution Rhode Island alone had three hundred and fifty-two vessels coasting from Newfoundland to Georgia.[13] The small coasting-craft did a continuous drop-in business from port to port. The southern states wanted fish from the

---

[12] Weeden, W. B., *op. cit.*, II, 507.　　[13] *Ibid.*, 761.

Grand Banks, European wares and wines from Boston, West Indian molasses, sugar, and rum from the New Haven docks, and wheat from New York and Pennsylvania; while tar from Albemarle Sound and tobacco from the Chesapeake in turn went up to fortify the hulls of the ships and the souls of the skippers off the Grand Banks. Often a homebound vessel from a tour in the Caribbean Sea would stop at Norfolk and exchange a part of its semi-tropical cargo for tobacco. Thus the coastwise trade shaded off into the foreign trade with the near-by Antilles.

West Indian Trade. But the commerce which was most remunerative and most regular was that with the West Indies. The islands demanded things which the colonies could give them or bring them, and they gave in exchange products which commanded a ready market. Besides fish, salted meats, and flour, they wanted horses in large numbers for the cane-crushing mills of Barbados and other sugar districts, barrel and pipe staves for their sugar and molasses, boards and houses ready framed to be set up, and lastly they wanted slaves. The slave trade, particularly, was profitable and delightfully simple in its reciprocity aspects. Moreover, it stimulated the industrial development of New England by introducing the manufacture of rum in enormous quantities. Made of inferior molasses which the Indies themselves furnished in vast quantities, rum was distilled chiefly at Boston and in the twenty-two still-houses of Newport, and then went to buy the kidnapped negroes on the Guinea coast and introduce the residual inhabitants to the advantages of civilization. The slaves, who were rescued from the debauching effects of the rum, closely and carefully packed as it behooves valuable merchandise, made a short voyage to the Antilles, were distributed among the British,

French, and Spanish plantations, or were brought farther north to supply the slave-markets of the southern states, without contaminating the soil of New England, or by their presence disturbing the placid conscience of even such a liberty-loving trader as Peter Faneuil.

The chief places interested in the West Indian trade were Ipswich, Salem, Boston, Newport, New London, New Haven, Windsor, and New York. We notice that Long Island Sound points, which were slow in participating in colonial maritime activity, became important in the West Indian trade. The wealth of New Haven was based largely on its commerce with Barbados. New England vessels visited with little discrimination British, Spanish, French, and Dutch holdings in the Caribbean region; for the Navigation Laws were too carelessly enforced to limit the commercial field of the enterprising Yankee trader. Outbound vessels from the American coast generally carried an extra supply of staves and a number of coopers, who were busied setting up barrels and hogsheads to hold the return cargo of sugar and molasses. The same vessels brought in also indigo, cotton, mahogany, dyewoods, silver, and Spanish iron, the last two being items of Spain's trade with her own possessions. New England, always in need of salt for the fish industry, at one time tried importing this article from the Tortugas of the Gulf, but it proved an unsatisfactory variety for preserving fish, and New England continued thereafter to rely upon the Mediterranean supply, which was shipped chiefly at Malaga.

European Trade. As England's commercial policy permitted the colonies to trade with all European countries south of Cape Finisterre in such commodities as the country did not produce, American merchantmen did a thriving business with Spain, Portugal, and, on the return voyage, with the Madeira and Canary Islands. These countries being Catholic wanted fish, and being great wine-producers wanted staves, both of which the colonies gladly furnished for salt, wine, oil, and fruits. Once in these regions, it was a simple matter to run down the African coast for gold-dust, ivory, and slaves.

Late Development of New York's Trade. Geographical conditions determined New England as the great maritime region of America. New York's limited though valuable coast, and the retardation of its back country by the proximity of the hostile French, and later by the retention of British posts on the Lakes, prevented early maritime development. In the middle of the eighteenth century, the entrances and clearances in the ports of Philadelphia and New York combined were just equal to those of Boston alone. In 1731, when Pennsylvania owned 6000 tons of shipping, Massachusetts had nearly 38,000 tons, one half of which was employed in European trade. In early history, the port of New York had to share honors with Perth Amboy, which attracted trade on account of its nearness to the sea and its superior advantages for avoiding the import and excise taxes;[14] but with the expansion of population along the shores of Ontario and Erie, the activity along this frontier in the War of 1812, and the consequent construction of the Erie Canal, the port of New York attained that preeminence marked out for it by its position before the "eastern gateway of the United States."

Privateering. A merchant marine becomes in time of war an important factor in national defense and aggression. It

[14] Brodhead, J. R., *History of the State of New York*, New York, 1853, II, 392 and 460.

furnishes seamen, transports, its vessels are converted into armed cruisers, or are fitted out with letters of marque to prey upon the enemy's commerce. Colonial privateers did effective service in the Spanish and French wars, for it was easy to intercept French supply ships or merchantmen in the Gulf of St. Lawrence, or Spanish vessels on their way to the Antilles. In the Revolution, the supremacy of English sea power left any regular naval warfare out of the question for the young Republic. However, the great number of its merchant ships and seamen, whose occupation was for the time destroyed; their familiarity with the secluded ports and island hiding-places of the coast; moreover, England's necessity of exporting its supplies in this oversea war, while it held a naval base on the mainland only at two points, New York and Newport, all combined to make a situation in which privateering could be most effective, while affording to the merchant marine means of partially recouping their losses. Therefore we find that Boston had three hundred and sixty-five vessels commissioned for this semi-piratical service, Salem about a hundred and eighty, Rhode Island some two hundred, though right under the nose of the British guns at Newport — while other New England ports frequently sent out vessels. That they went to some purpose is evidenced by the fact that in 1776 the rate of marine insurance between England and the West Indies rose to twenty-three per cent. The vessels which the national government put into the service were most effective as cruisers on the high seas, while the colonial cruisers, with the privateers, were employed in the same way inshore. The prize cargoes of military and naval supplies which were thus brought in did much to relieve the needs of the colonies, which, in consequence of their previous dependence upon

England, were almost destitute of the simplest means for carrying on the struggle. From Cape Breton to Martinique these gadflies of the ocean stung, preyed upon, and almost stampeded English commerce.

Pacific Ocean Trade.   Just as the achievement of independence was the signal for territorial expansion on the part of the Americans, so it marked the beginning of a pronounced maritime expansion. England was to be no longer the middleman in the trade with the Orient. American merchantmen, discouraged by the British attempts to curtail their trade with the West Indies, but encouraged by discriminating duties in their favor, found their way to Canton and the East Indies, stopping *en route* in the Indian Ocean to trade at Bourbon and Mauritius, which had been opened by France to American commerce. This trade owes its beginning to a New York ship in 1784, the Empress of China, which completed the round trip in two years, and made a handsome profit. A Boston ship, in 1788, following in the track of the whalers in the Pacific, began trading cutlery, iron ware, nails, clothing, beads, molasses, rum, and muskets to the Indians of the northwest coast of America for furs, which it carried across to Canton and exchanged for Chinese products especially silk and tea. In 1790 the China trade accounted for one-seventh of the country's imports; in it the British offered no competition. It brought the greatest profits of any branch of our trade, founded the fortunes of a long line of merchants from Salem to Philadelphia, and attracted the best ships and the finest seamen of the seaboard.[15]   From 1804 to 1809 a total of one hundred and fifty-

---

[15] Dulles, F. R., *The Old China Trade*, Boston, 1930, pp. 49, 76.   In five years, 1797 to 1802, one ship returned to Boston with a fortune swollen from $7000 to $70,000; many ships on the first voyage paid for the total cost of the vessel and left a profit of from $20,000 to $80,000.

four American vessels sailed to Canton. Between 1784 and 1844 New York and Boston led in the China trade, with more than all other ports together.

The search for articles to barter led to the discovery of many islands of the Pacific which became regular ports of call; the islands furnished sandal-wood, coral beads, mother of pearl, *bêche de mer*, edible birds' nests, and other products. In the trade the Hawaiian Islands became an important wintering place for ships engaged in the fur trade of the Pacific coast; they also encouraged profitable barter. The islands furnished abundant fresh vegetables, fruits, fowls, and hogs for scurvy-stricken sailors and sweet-smelling sandal-wood which found a profitable market among Chinese merchants at Canton. Hawaiians bartered it for iron and anything made of iron as this mineral was lacking in the volcanic islands and its nearest source was the American continent two thousand miles away.[16] In the years of the China trade, New England vessels were to be seen constantly in the Spanish ports of California, where they outnumbered all other foreign merchantmen; they first drew the attention of the national government to the need of a foothold on the Pacific.

The exclusion of English competition by the Navigation Laws and superior facilities for shipbuilding enabled the states to exploit all the advantages of their location and natural equipment for maritime ascendency. While in the period from 1789 to 1793 their proportion of the carrying trade of the country rose from twenty-five per cent to seventy-nine per cent, by 1810 they had absorbed eighty-nine per cent. Interests so important and operating in such

[16] *Ibid.*, pp. 66–71. Reckless destruction of the sandal-wood forests, reducing the power of the islands to barter, so reduced the trade that by 1822 the islands had ceased to be an important port of call.

a wide field required the protection which only a navy could give.   Depredations on American commerce by French vessels in the West Indies in 1793 was the occasion for the construction of the first warships by the new Union and for the reprisals which taught the French manners.   Similar outrages by the corsairs of the Barbary States, just outside the Strait of Gibraltar, gave the youthful navy, in 1803, that experience in conducting a campaign which prepared it for the more serious contest of 1812.

CHAPTER VIII

GEOGRAPHY OF SEA AND LAND OPERATIONS
IN THE WAR OF 1812

IN THE War of 1812, even more than in the Revolution, the United States felt the advantages of its remote geographical location and large area. The three million people who had fought the War of Independence had increased in 1810 to over seven millions, a consequence of the abundant land and resources of a new country, its encouragement of natural increase, and attraction to immigrants. The line of inhabited coast was only little longer than in 1780, but the land frontier of continuous settlement slanted southwest from Lake Champlain to the mouth of the Ohio, and from that point southeast to the St. Mary's River, which marked the northern border of Spanish Florida. Outside of this 2900 mile frontier were isolated areas of settlement, every one of which, except the Mississippi group between the Ohio and the Missouri, figured in the War of 1812 — Detroit, Mackinaw, Prairie du Chien, Fort Dearborn (Chicago), New Orleans, and Forts Mims and Bowyer, which guarded the approaches to the Tombigbee settlements.

A Frontier War. From the geographical standpoint, the distinguishing characteristic of this war lay in the fact that it was limited strictly to the frontiers, both land and marine. Only in the attacks on Washington, Baltimore, and New Orleans, which, by reason of their tidewater location, can be set down as coast towns, did invasion penetrate more than a few miles from the sea; while on the land frontier, where there was no waterway to aid, the British hesitated to advance even this far from their base upon the border. It was therefore a peripheral war, and left the mass of the country undisturbed. This could have been the case only in a country of large area and isolated location, or in a land like England, with only marine frontiers defended by a strong navy. Thus even the taking of Washington, the capital, lost its military significance, because it only scratched the skin of the country and left the great body unimpaired.

Opposition to the War. In view of the maritime development of the United States at this time, the impressment of American seamen into British service had to be checked. Six thousand Americans on English naval vessels tells how the English had improved their opportunities. The war was undertaken, therefore, to vindicate the rights chiefly of the maritime states, and yet it was just these states which opposed the war. Hostilities meant the interruption of navigation and the destruction of their commerce; but they preferred to lose their mariners rather than their money. Hence the sectionalism of parties in their attitude towards this war was clearly drawn. In the opposition was found all of New England, with the exception of the coastless state of Vermont, a large part of New York, and the majority of New Jersey and Delaware. The South and West supported the war, though Maryland, showing the conflict of land and sea interests, cast three votes against it.[1] The leader in the opposition, as was to be expected, was Massachusetts, moved by its dominant maritime interests.

The war was probably distasteful to New York because it would suffer not only in its port, but also in its northern

---

[1] Ingersoll, C. J., *Second War of the United States with England*, Philadelphia, 1845, I, 48-65.

frontier, which, together with that of Vermont and the northeastern corner of Ohio, constituted the only settled area of the United States contiguous with the Canadian border. This was the old danger-line from Champlain to Presque Isle (Erie) which had been made conspicuous in the French wars and in the Revolution; and now with the advance of population it extended westward to Detroit. Moreover, in contrast to the natural indifference of French Canada in this conflict, the Americans felt the animosity of their neighbors in the adjoining province of Ontario. These were loyalists who had withdrawn from the United States after the Revolution. Opposed to mingling with the French element in the older eastern part of Canada, like all late comers in America, they were located in the west, and were granted tracts of land by the British government in the remote district north of Lake Ontario, where they formed the nucleus of the later political division of Upper Canada.[2]

GEOGRAPHICAL CONDITIONS IN THE WAR ALONG THE CANADIAN FRONTIER

It was along this line that hostilities began, though war had been declared because of maritime outrages. But the youth and weakness of the American navy, and the strength of the British in our waters, with their naval stations at Halifax, the Bermudas, Saint Lucia, Barbados, and Jamaica, whence they could blockade our coasts, necessitated the opening of the campaign with an attack on Canada. But here, again, geographical conditions determined that the war should be in large part naval; fleet and infantry were to combine. Lakes Ontario, Erie, St. Clair, and Champlain

[2] Morris, H. C., *History of Colonization*, New York, 1904, II, 98.

were the scene of these water operations; and the two short, detached lines of the Niagara and Detroit rivers, where the land frontiers converged, became strategic areas of continued military activity in hand to hand encounters.

Along this inland frontier the British had the advantage. The St. Lawrence afforded them a protected line of communication with the naval and military stores of Canada and England, and hence brought the frontier nearer to the treasury and troops of England than were the Americans to the Hudson. The Mohawk route with its imperfect and interrupted navigation, though it had served well for the birch canoes and furry cargoes of the colonial wilderness, was ill adapted to the transportation of heavy guns. Moreover, the outlet of this route was the mouth of the Oswego River, and supplies for the naval base at Sacket Harbor at the easternmost end of Lake Ontario had to run the gauntlet of British ships which issued from their station at Kingston near by; while Kingston, by its position at the effluence of the St. Lawrence, secured the British line of communication on that river. For both sides the control of these inland waters was of the utmost importance, because upon it depended the supplies of all the Niagara and Detroit River posts.

Fort Malden and Detroit. The land position of the British, too, had some geographical advantages. Lake Ontario laps over the end of Lake Erie in such a way as to make a small rectangular peninsula of the British territory along the Niagara River; and this formation is duplicated at the western extremity of Ontario Province along the Detroit River by the same relative position of Lake Erie and Lake St. Clair. The position of the British, flanked by the Lakes, was peculiarly protected along these two rivers, which, by their shortness, isolation, controlling positions, and their

exceptional character as the only settled land frontiers west
of the St. Lawrence, were immediately endowed with strategic importance.   The British post of Fort Malden particularly, by its location on an angle of land at the mouth of the
Detroit River, was able to cut off reinforcements moving to
Detroit by land and supplies coming by water from the
American settlements at the eastern end of Lake Erie.

The long arrow-shaped wedge of Upper Canada brought
the British at Malden far into American possessions, enabled
them to cut off the upper lakes from Erie, and gave them an
administrative center on the northwestern frontier for stirring up the Indians all the way from the Wisconsin River to
Sandusky Bay.   Detroit was the post whence the efforts of
the British might be frustrated: hence its strategic importance and the early movement of American forces towards
this point.   The capture of the sole American boat on Lake
Erie as it was going up the Detroit River with the supplies
of the troops from the Maumee, the defeat at Huron River
of the reinforcements for Detroit, the capture of the post,
the two battles on the Raisin River, and the advance of the
British to Sandusky River, show the disadvantage of Detroit's position, remote from the frontier of continuous settlement, while British ships held the control of Lake Erie.
To maintain an effective line of communication by a long detour around the western end of Lake Erie through pathless
forests was almost impossible.   And the British, masters of
Lake Erie, were able to seize the remote post of Mackinaw,
whose position was made hopeless by the interruption of its
line of communication through Detroit.   Indian allies
seized Fort Dearborn and Prairie du Chien, though a relief
party coming up the Mississippi from St. Louis endeavored
to save this post at the mouth of the Wisconsin.

Perry on Lake Erie. While these successes were falling to the enemy, Perry was doing the impossible at Presque Isle — converting a forest into a navy. The falls of the Niagara

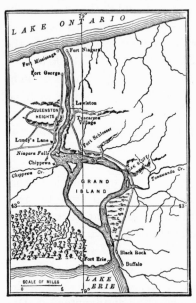

FIG. 9. THE NIAGARA RIVER
FRONTIER, 1812–1814

necessitated the construction and maintenance of separate flotillas on Lakes Ontario and Erie, thus increasing the expense and difficulty of war on the inland waters. The one American ship on Erie had been captured. The British at Fort Erie prevented supplies and a few purchased ships from coming out of the upper Niagara River to Presque Isle. Out of the green woods of Erie, therefore, from hull to mast grew Perry's fleet in 1813; there it was equipped and manned, though supplies had to be hauled over blazed tracks through the forest, and remoteness made it difficult to get seamen. But before the summer was over, this Rhode Island man with his high-seas experience wrested the control of the lake from the provincial seamen of Canada, cut off the British supplies, and cleared the way for the American advance on Malden, with the consequent retreat of the enemy from this post and Detroit, and their defeat at the Battle of the Thames.

The Niagara Frontier. The remoteness of Detroit and the isolation of Lake Erie, due to the interruption of navigation at Niagara Falls, made this region drop out of the conflict as soon as it was retaken from the British. The really strategic frontier was the Niagara River, and here focused the land operations of the war (Fig. 9). Here was the battle of Queenstown Heights, the attack on Fort George, the capture of Fort Erie, the battle of Chippewa Creek and of Lundy's Lane on the Canada side; and on the American the capture of Fort Niagara and the burning of Youngstown, Lewiston, Manchester, Black Rock, and Buffalo. As the fate of the Niagara posts on both sides depended upon the maintenance of navigation on Lake Ontario, and as the fleets were pretty evenly matched, neither dared risk an engagement without decided advantages of wind and position. Too much was at stake. Hence warfare on Lake Ontario was colorless because it lacked a decisive battle. The body of water was so small and distances so short that it was always possible for either Americans or English to avoid an engagement by running into a home port and taking refuge under the land batteries. For this reason seizure of stores in course of transportation up the Lake, and predatory descents like those upon Oswego, Sacket Harbor, Toronto, or Burlington Bay made up the story of Ontario warfare.

Champlain–Hudson Lowland and Provost's Invasion. The possible prize the British hoped to gain by successes on the Great Lakes was the future exclusive right of navigation, by which the British could have retarded the whole development of the Northwest: hence the concentration of military activities on Lake Ontario. The old Champlain route, which had figured prominently heretofore in every war across the Canadian boundary, by reason of its detached lo-

cation played a smaller part in the hostilities of 1812. But
when the temporary cessation of the Napoleonic War in
1814 released the English troops from service on the Continent, and large reinforcements were sent to Canada for an
invasion of New York, this shortest line of communication
between the St. Lawrence and the Hudson became the line
of march.

The route of the invading army from Canada was flanked
for a long distance by the Richelieu River and Lake Champlain, so a flotilla of ships accompanied the land forces to
carry supplies and at the same time lend protection. Hence
both the land and water route had to be contested by the
Americans. In anticipation of such an invasion, a flotilla
had been stationed on Lake Champlain, but the body of
water was so long and narrow that cruising was out of the
question; so the vessels took up their position inshore near
the land forces, which were stationed along the Saranac
River to check the enemy's advance. Modern warfare is
largely a science of communications and transportation.
Hence the defeat of the British ships on Champlain was the
signal for the retreat of the British army. Here, as on Lake
Erie, a naval victory was of supreme importance to the
Americans, because of the difficulty of constructing a new
fleet on this isolated body of water, were the first one destroyed. Defeat would have put them in the position of the
British after Perry's victory.

GEOGRAPHICAL CONDITIONS IN THE WAR ON THE MARITIME FRONTIER

It was not possible for the United States to sustain any
considerable damages along a land frontier which through

Maine and New Hampshire was a primeval wilderness and from Vermont westward was only sparsely settled, and which, moreover, by its very shortness left only a limited area exposed to attack; but the long and densely populated sea frontier presented a vulnerable surface to the onslaughts of the British navy. From one extremity of the coast to the other, and from the beginning to the end of the war the enemy's ships made their depredations. England's great sea power enabled it to blockade all the principal harbors from Maine to Chesapeake Bay, with the result that several new American vessels which were being built never got to sea. This had been the case before in the Revolution. The fisheries of New England were almost broken up and the foreign commerce of the eastern states was totally destroyed. Stonington, Connecticut, and Lewiston on Delaware Bay were bombarded. The salt-works on Cape Cod saved their buildings by a ransom.

In Chesapeake Bay depredations extended from Norfolk to Havre de Grace at the mouth of the Susquehanna. The estuaries of the Patapsco and Patuxent afforded easy lines of approach to Baltimore and Washington, and the Potomac carried the British fleet to Alexandria. Thus the waterways of Chesapeake Bay and its estuaries, together with the weak-kneed resistance of the militia which met the invading force at Bladensburg before the city of Washington, enabled the enemy to penetrate farther into the interior than at any other point along the whole coast.

Farther south, the coast of North Carolina was protected from naval attack by the "skaergard" of the offshore sand-reefs, for the only place to suffer was the village of Portsmouth, which occupies an exposed position on the Ocracoke Inlet into Pamlico Sound. The South Carolina coast was

plundered by the British ships after the defeat at New
Orleans, where the enemy made their greatest demonstration during the war.   From the island of Jamaica came the
expedition — a fleet of fifty vessels carrying twelve thousand
troops.   Lakes Borgne and Ponchartrain and the numerous
bayous offered many avenues of approach to the city, whose
position was therefore even more exposed than had been
that of Washington.   But it was defended by troops of the
backwoods and Jackson, the man of the frontier, the man of
initiative and resource, the man who waited not for prece-
dent.   Still breathless from his unauthorized punitive attack upon the Spanish in Pensacola, who had aided the British in an attack upon the Americans at Fort Bowyer, he
hurried back to New Orleans.   He seized the cotton bales of
protesting merchants to build his barricade, and afterwards
paid the fine imposed for this high-handed, high-minded act.
The bayous he obstructed.   He set up batteries at the mouth
of the Bayou Sauvage and far down the Mississippi to block
approach from Lake Borgne and the Gulf.   Then his men
behind their cotton bales, flanked by river and marsh, showed
what kind of marksmanship the military school of the backwoods produced.

It is fair to say that the only valiant work of this war was
done by the infantry, regulars and volunteers, trained on the
frontier, and the mariners who had learned their lesson on
the high seas.   Geographical environment, making the necessity and opportunity, had in both cases brought forth a
sturdy product.   From Newfoundland fishermen, Nantucket
whalers, New England sailors, merchantmen, captains, and
American shipbuilders was combined a navy that could deal
some heavy blows even to the sea power of England.   The
British fleet was big enough to blockade every American

port, but it did not know well enough the secrets of the shore to prevent the escape of sea-rovers, some belonging to the navy, but far more fitted out by private enterprise to prey upon British commerce. American privateers swarmed on every sea, while the navy, both men and ships, was recruited from the merchant marine.

GEOGRAPHICAL DISTRIBUTION OF NAVAL ENGAGEMENTS

The sea-fights of this war, if studied merely in their chronological sequence as presented in the ordinary school histories, leave only a confused impression, of which the student, young or old, retains little at all and less that is valuable. But an analysis of the geographical distribution of these engagements reveals a wide underlying system which explains their purpose and brings order out of apparent chaos.

Off the American Coast. Two important ports of the British on the American continent were Quebec and Halifax, one their supply station for the war along the Canadian frontier, and the other their chief naval base in American waters. Hence American vessels cruising to the southeast of Cape Breton Island were likely to intercept supply ships for these two points; furthermore, they were in the path of home-bound English merchant ships returning heavy laden from Caribbean ports. But before the American cruisers could reach this strategic position on the high seas, they had to run the gantlet of the enemy's ships coming out from Halifax.

In the light of these geographical conditions, observe some of the important naval engagements of this war. Captain Broke, with the British vessels Shannon and Tenedos, was instructed to watch the American coast east of Cape Cod and prevent the escape of the four chief American frigates from the harbor of Boston.[3] Two of these slipped by him, but a challenge lured Lawrence in the Chesapeake to single combat, with the result of the encounter near Boston, the defeat of the Chesapeake, and the taking of the prize to Halifax. The Constitution, which had been hanging about the entrance to the Gulf of St. Lawrence off Sable Island in August, 1813, was victorious in a terrific fight with the British ship-of-war Guerrière southeast of this point (41° N.L., 55° W.L.). About halfway between Bermuda and Halifax (37° N.L., 65° W.L.) the American sloop-of-war Wasp two months later fell in with the Frolic, which was convoying a homeward bound fleet of six British merchant-men of the Honduras trade. In the conflict the Wasp was successful, but the victor and its prize were immediately captured by the Poictiers and taken to Bermuda.

The proximity of the British bases to the American coast enabled [4] both regular ships and privateers to make depre-dations on American commerce. Hence some of our vessels were kept on the eastern coast to guard against this threat-ening danger. The ship Enterprise, of the United States, in the summer of 1813, captured the Boxer from the Bay of Fundy off Penguin Point in Maine, then cruised south and took the British privateer Mars off the coast of Florida. In the same vicinity the Peacock from New York captured the Epervier, and carried it into Savannah, the nearest Amer-ican port. Vessels from these southern ports also used to lie in wait offshore for Jamaica convoys.

[3] McMaster, J. B., *History of the People of the United States*, New York, 1902, IV, 91.

[4] For distribution of British naval bases, see Mahan, A. T., *Influence of Sea Power in History*, Boston, 1894, map, p. 532.

At the Ocean Crossroads.   Farther south, in the great tropical highway of the trade-winds, from one side of the Atlantic to the other, there were rich prizes to be secured in the British ships bound for the Caribbean holdings, and also those turning southward from Cape St. Roque to round the Horn for the East Indies.   Therefore some of the fiercest engagements of the war took place along this path of the Indiamen.   The vessel United States took the Macedonian a few miles west of the Canary Islands.   The Hornet captured the British ship Peacock off the coast of British Guiana, and the Southampton captured the American Vixen among the West Indies.   Thirty miles off the northeast coast of Brazil, where the searoad forked to the West and the East Indies, the Java, bound for the Orient, made a valiant resistance to the Constitution, but was captured and then burned, because there was no American port sufficiently near where it might be taken for repairs.   The United States suffered in this war because of its strictly continental position and its consequent lack of naval bases away from its own shores.   Captain Porter in the Essex made a prize of the British packet Nocton, just northeast of Cape St. Roque.   As English influence was dominant on the whole South American coast, and the United States had no depot in that region, Captain Porter turned south and rounded the Horn to levy for supplies on the English whalers in the South Pacific, who always went well provided, and at the same time to protect American whalers who were at the mercy of English cruisers.   Off the coast of Chile, among the Galapagos Islands and as far west as the Marquesas group he cruised, capturing whalers and privateers, but finally off Valparaiso he had an engagement with the British ships Phœbe and Cherub and was taken.

Depredations on British vessels in English waters constituted natural reprisals. There we find the Argus making a daring cruise off the coast of England and Ireland, capturing twenty merchantmen, until she herself is captured by the British Pelican. Then her place is taken by Wasp II, which captures the Reindeer and puts into the friendly port of L'Orient on the coast of Brittany. This was the only remote region where the Americans had a friendly harbor into which they could go for supplies or repairs, or to sell their prizes. Elsewhere prizes had to be manned by the conquering ship or destroyed at sea.

Even after peace had been declared, war lingered upon the sea along the trade-wind track of the Indiamen. The Constitution captured two British vessels off the southwestern coast of Portugal, and the Hornet took the British Penguin off the coast of Brazil.

THE RESULTS OF THE WAR

The results of the war were far-reaching in their effects on the United States. As the war was one largely of independence we first gained our rights on the sea — free seas and the non-impressment of American seamen. During the three years of the war, fourteen hundred British vessels were taken, together with several thousand seamen and rich cargoes. Though the Americans, too, lost heavily, the spirit of maritime enterprise was kept alive and the quality of American seamanship was proved. The coastwise and foreign trade was greatly reduced in the period of hostilities, but by 1819 the reaction set in, and American vessels were doing seventy-eight per cent of the country's carrying-trade; and from 1820 to 1830 they reached their high-water mark of ninety per cent.

The war emancipated the country from the belief that it had to depend upon European countries. It strengthened the bond of union and increased the spirit of nationality. It was the cause of the immediate establishment of the Second National Bank; it encouraged manufacturing greatly and initiated the protective tariff.

The war was a signal for a marked increase and movement of population and internal improvements. The concentration of activities along the Canadian frontier opened up the Mohawk country and the Great Lakes. After 1830, the center of population moved across the Allegheny Mountains; the development of the country became more continental, and attracted landward the activity of the people. In six years, 1816 to 1821, the territorial population increased so rapidly that a new state was added each year. The Erie Canal, a necessity that had been made apparent by the War of 1812, became a channel through which flowed a westward-streaming tide of population, pushing the national center of gravity farther from the coast and through which returned a huge movement of the produce of the West. In the South the slave power, searching for unexhausted lands which would repay cultivation under an extensive system of agriculture, was spreading over a large interior area. Hence the ascendancy of the maritime coast declined until the time when, the industrial conquest of a vast country having been accomplished, there should come an extra-continental development, seeking new markets and foreign bases of commercial activity.

CHAPTER IX

SPREAD OF POPULATION IN THE MISSISSIPPI VALLEY AS AFFECTED BY GEOGRAPHIC CONDITIONS

THE westward expansion of the American people has been marked by a slow advance from tidewater to "fall line," and from "fall line" across the Alleghenies; a rapid progress downstream to the Mississippi and upstream along its western tributaries to the margin of the arid belt; a leap across the Great Plains and the Rockies to the Pacific, long accepted as the outer edge of American dominion, until a faltering step was planted on the Hawaiian Islands, and a bold stride took the flag across the Pacific to the Philippines.

CAUSES OF EXPANSION INTO THE MISSISSIPPI VALLEY

For twenty-five years after the conclusion of the War of 1812 there was a pronounced movement of population into the Mississippi Valley. In 1790 only five per cent of the population of the United States was west of the mountains; in 1820 twenty-five per cent. There were 2,225,000 people in 1820 in the West; the numbers increased to 4,625,000 in 1830 and to 6,330,000 in 1840. This great movement was due to the release of new forces after the cessation of hostilities; the final defeat of Tecumseh's warriors in the Northwest as allies of the British and Jackson's successful quietus upon the Creeks and Cherokees, who had long checked the expansion of Georgia and Alabama; the acquisition of the

Floridas by which the Gulf states came into their own, geographically speaking; finally the forced opening-up of western New York incident to the military operations of the War of 1812 on its frontier and the consequent construction of the Erie Canal. The strategic necessity of an exclusively American waterway to Lake Erie in the event of another war with Canada, because of the serious difficulties and delays recently experienced in forwarding supplies to the front, and the immediate demand for better means of transportation through the Mohawk thoroughfare for men going west and products coming east, called for the union of the Hudson and Lake Erie. Steam navigation on lake and river, well established at this time, was developing the full usefulness of the interior waterways, both as avenues of immigration and means of exportation; men came in one season, and the products of their fields went out the next. Moreover, a strong tide of immigration from Europe, set in motion by the subsidence of the Napoleonic wars just at this time, found its way to the unoccupied lands of the Mississippi valley.

Influence of Rivers on Movement. All of these causes combined started a movement towards the great central basin so strong that it went far before its energy exhausted itself (Fig. 10). This is the explanation of the fact that the period from 1810 to 1820 blocked out the work of expansion which the next two decades were occupied in completing.[1] As has been shown before, the degree of life or movement in a people is indicated by the advance of its frontier, the truest index to which is found in the bulges of its outer line of settlement. In American history the noticeable fact is that these bulges have almost always been along the course of rivers.

[1] *Eleventh Census of the United States Population,* I, xxii.

In the early eighteenth century these protrusions followed the Mohawk and Potomac, and later extended over the adjacent watershed, halting along the ultramontane river sources when these occupied fertile valleys, as in the case of the Youghiogeny, Monongahela, and Holston, or passing over a more rugged plateau area to the smiling plains of the middle courses, as in the case of the Kentucky and Cumberland settlements.

In 1820 the frontier protrusions took the form of long fingers, which seemed to point the line of advance along the waterways of the country. These fingers were longer, more slender, more eager, so to speak, south of the Ohio and west of the Mississippi, attesting their origin in the population of the South Atlantic states, in whom had long been bred the spirit of expansion. One finger crooked around the western rim of Lake Erie to Lake St. Clair, and ten years later touched the outlet of Lake Huron. Up the Wabash and the Kaskaskia, up the Mississippi, almost to the mouth of the Des Moines, up the Missouri two-thirds across the present state of that name, up the Arkansas, the Ouachita, and the Red, pointed these sign posts of western migration, while corresponding lines of settlement down the Pearl, Pascagoula, Tombigbee, Alabama, and Chattahoochee led the way to the Gulf. Rivers present the lines of least resistance to the incoming colonist, and afterwards lend themselves to his economic needs.[2]

[2] A potent influence in directing the course of migration was the introduction of steam navigation on the western rivers. Steam navigation was first introduced on the Ohio in 1811. The second boat was built in 1813, and the fourth in 1816. The one built in 1816 was the first to descend the river to New Orleans and return. By 1820 seventy-two churned the turbid waters of the Mississippi, by 1830 two hundred and thirty and by 1848 there were twelve hundred. By 1835 more than sixty tributaries of the Mississippi were used for steam navigation. Myer, B. H., *History of Transportation in the United States Before 1860*, Washington, 1917, pp. 94–116, 129 280 ff.; *Eleventh Census, Transportation*, II, 395 ff.

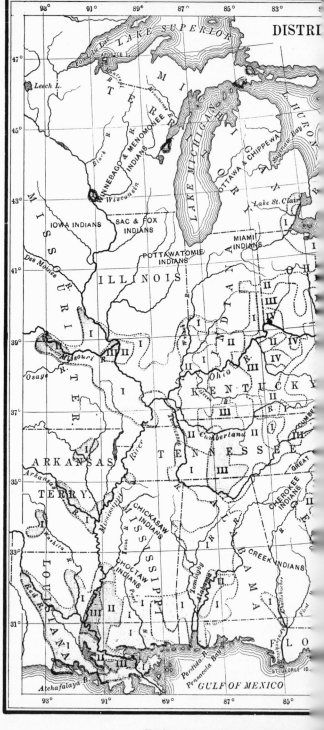

FIG. 10. DISTRIBUTION

A study of the map brings out the influence on the westward
lands and fertile soil areas. In the Appalachian regio

OF POPULATION
820

Miles to inch

LEGEND

Under 2 inhab. to the Sq. Mile

2	6	,,	,,	,,	,,	,,	I
6	18	,,	,,	,,	,,	,,	II
18	45	,,	,,	,,	,,	,,	III
45	90	,,	,,	,,	,,	,,	IV
·90 and over	,,	,,	,,	,,	V

★ Center of
Population

*Cities over 8000 inhabitants in solid color
in circles proportionate to population.*

ULATION IN 1820

rivers, lakes, national roads, swamps, location of Indian
graphy accounts for the areas of few people.

FACTORS ACCOUNTING FOR VACANT SPOTS

Within this ragged frontier are numerous vacant spots. These are often rough mountain regions, as in the Adirondacks in New York, the Allegheny Plateau in northwestern Pennsylvania, and the Cumberland Plateau in West Virginia and East Tennessee. Two decades later similar islands of unpeopled areas are found in the Ozark Mountains of northern Arkansas and southern Missouri, where a rugged hill country with poor soil repelled settlement. Vacant spots of this class began to contract and eventually were filled up, but their scars are still left in the sparsity and retarded development of their populations even today. Other vacant spots also were due to geographical causes, such as the swamps in northwestern Ohio, western Indiana, southern Georgia, and along the Gulf coast of the southern states; the flood-plains in the lower course of several Mississippi tributaries, like the St. Francis, White, and Yazoo, which periodic overflows and continual malaria made unfit for settlement until an accumulation of capital and men justified the construction of levees. Here, too, the scars have lingered in the form of a sparser population. Elsewhere areas of severe climate, small streams unfit for steam navigation, and dense forests rendering the preparation of the ground for agriculture more difficult were long left uninhabited. These causes checked the landward advance of population in Maine, especially after the decline of wooden ships; and for the same reasons, farther west, the incoming tide of settlement set towards Michigan and Wisconsin only to forty-three degrees north latitude, and then was deflected towards the trans-Mississippi country with its fertile prairies and navigable streams. Much of this northern forest region is empty today except for an occasional winter logging-camp, mining camp, or the cottage of the summer sportsman.

The other vacant spots on the maps showing density of population from 1820 to 1840 were due to the presence of Indian tribes who held large tracts of fertile land in the natural path of expansion of some of the oldest settlements. Choctaws and Chickasaws prevented Tennessee settlement from extending to the Mississippi River, and kept the population of Mississippi crowded down in the southwest corner of the territory. Farther east, the Cherokees and Creeks blocked Georgia's advance and crowded upon the flank of Alabama; though the latter state, placed between these two great Indian areas, had developed more rapidly during its short existence than its two neighbors, Georgia and Mississippi, which enjoyed far greater geographical advantages. Georgia's population, dammed up against this Indian barrier, overflowed into the valley of the Chattahoochee and moved down its channel into Florida. In northern Illinois, the Sac, Fox, and Pottawatomie tribes delayed settlement in large areas of fertile land which they held.

The decade from 1830 to 1840 saw the title to all these Indian lands gradually extinguished by the federal government and the tribes themselves removed to the Indian Territory. Within two or three years thereafter, the area thus relinquished was covered with a comparatively dense population, and in the next decade was as thickly settled as any parts of these states. Here there were no scars because no adverse natural conditions.[3]

---

[3] For general subject of vacant areas, see *Eleventh Census of the United States, Population*, I, xxviii. Also, *Treaties of the United States with the Several Indian Tribes*, 1778–1837, Washington, 1837, pp. 391, 497, 633.

MOVEMENT INTO THE NORTHWEST TERRITORY

The elements of population moving into the Northwest Territory, as likewise their distribution, were determined largely by its two great geographical lines of approach. New England, New York, New Jersey, and Pennsylvania furnished most of the early and later settlers; these entered the country by the Cumberland Road and the Ohio River route, and the route of the Mohawk depression into the northern part of Ohio, stretching a band of settlement along the whole southern shore of Lake Erie as early as 1820. But beyond, the northern parts of Ohio, Indiana, and Illinois were cut off from the influx of population coming from Lake Erie because of the swamps covering the uncertain watershed of the Maumee, Wabash, and St. Joseph rivers. The southern parts of these states received considerable accessions of population from neighboring Kentucky and Tennessee. Some of the southern immigrants with anti-slavery sympathies were attracted thither by the free-state clause in the Ordinance of 1787; others by the chronic land-hunger of the day.

Position of Illinois. The geographical position of Illinois was interesting in 1818. With the exception of a group of fur-traders at the lonely station on the Chicago River, all its population was concentrated in the extreme southern part, where focused the Missouri, Mississippi, the Ohio, Cumberland, and Tennessee rivers, and with them the influence of the South and West. Here was a strategic area for military and political purposes. In 1818 Illinois applied for entrance as a state. The Ordinance of 1787 provided that the northern boundary of the north Ohio states was to follow a line drawn through the southern bend of Lake Michigan,

thus excluding from Illinois the post at Chicago which was
to be the outlet of the already projected Illinois and Michigan Canal.   The withdrawal of the western and southern
states from the Union was even then a possibility ever
present to men's minds.   Therefore it was decided to give
Illinois a goodly shore-line on Lake Michigan in order to
strengthen its northern line of connection, which the Erie
Canal was relied on to perfect, and thereby weaken its dependence upon the South and West.   Hence a politico-
geographical necessity traced the northern boundary of
Illinois.[4]

Effect of Erie Canal.   The opening of the Erie Canal in
1825 exerted a strong influence throughout the Lake region,
and soon afterwards other canals across the low watersheds
southward to the Ohio opened up a hitherto inaccessible
country.   Into this region, especially after the removal of
the Indians to the west, poured a stream of immigrants from
the eastern states and from Europe, especially Germany.
Between 1820 and 1840 the states north of the Ohio and east
of the Mississippi increased as a whole over three hundred
and sixty per cent.[5]   The frontier of continuous settlement
outlined an almost wholly compact area along the forty-
third degree of latitude; while isolated cabins and farms
beaded the shore of Lake Michigan and indicated the future
line of expansion (Fig. 11).

The New York, New England, and German elements
brought with them the staid, contracted ideals of the old
Atlantic seaboard and of Europe; they tended to settle on
moderate and equal-sized farms on the uplands between the
streams, put solid improvements on their land, reflecting

[4] Ford, T., *History of Illinois*, Chicago, 1854, pp. 22–24.
[5] Sparks, E. E., *Expansion of the American People*, Chicago, 1900, p. 268.

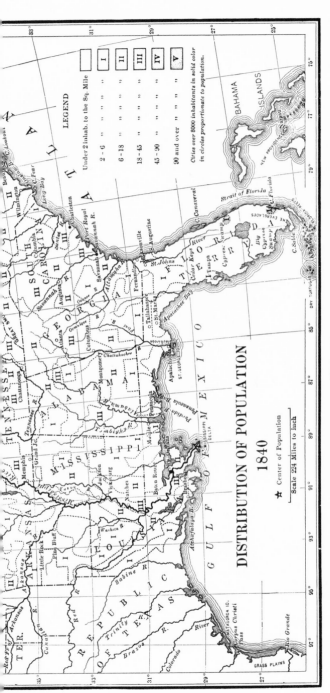

DISTRIBUTION OF POPULATION
1840

★ Center of Population

Scale 224 Miles to Inch

LEGEND

Under 2 inhab. to the Sq. Mile
I   2 - 6   " " " " "
II   6 - 18   " " " " "
III   18 - 45   " " " " "
IV   45 - 90   " " " " "
V   90 and over   " " " " "

Cities over 8000 inhabitants in solid color
in circles proportionate to population.

FIG. II.

their sedentary purpose, while only a slow, compact protrusion of their frontier registered their advance at the cost of the wilderness. The trans-Mississippi Westerners, on the other hand, with the half nomadic instinct bred from many migrations, and inherited from their Virginia and Carolina forbears, strung out their settlements along watercourses whence a fresh movement was easy, put up temporary buildings which could be abandoned without a pang,[6] left the upland region between unoccupied, and strode forward into the up-river country with the glory of the sunset in their faces and the yearning for the bigness of the prairies in their hearts.

EXPANSION BETWEEN OHIO AND THE GULF

Expansion between the Ohio and the Gulf went on at the same time as that in the Northwest Territory. The small group of settlements between the Natchez District and the Yazoo delta formed the nucleus of the state of Mississippi, as those on the Tombigbee did of Alabama. The purchase of Louisiana attracted immigrants to this region, but they were forced to take the long roundabout river journey by the Ohio or Tennessee and Mississippi. And such as came this way were generally from North Carolina, Virginia, Kentucky, and Tennessee. Accessions from the nearer source of Georgia and South Carolina were excluded by the barrier of the hostile Creeks, until Jackson's victory in 1814 rendered travel across their country less dangerous, and the natural highway around the southern end of the Appalachians could come into use. Hence by 1820 the Tombigbee settlements had grown and spread until they coalesced with those on the

[6] Flint, T., *The Last Ten Years in the Valley of the Mississippi*, Boston, 1826, p. 48.

bend of the Tennessee and the expanding area of civilization in southern Mississippi.

Kentucky and Tennessee at this time were cut off from the Mississippi by a wedge of the Chickasaw tribe which extended as far as the Ohio between the Mississippi and the Tennessee. But in 1820 the claim of the Indians was extinguished and immigrants poured into the Chickasaw Purchase, and soon by the Obion, Forked Deer, Hatchie, and Wolf rivers reached the long desired lands on the Mississippi. The southern boundary of Tennessee (35° N.L.) marked the limit of the Chickasaw Purchase, so expansion was checked at this line until 1838, when all the southern tribes were removed to the Indian Territory. Then from the already densely populated Chickasaw Purchase, immigrants rushed into northern Mississippi. The new lands thus opened were peopled chiefly by their neighbors, Georgia, the Carolinas, and more particularly Tennessee, which has been called the "mother of states," because it contributed more to the new settlements in the Mississippi valley than any other state in the Union. From Tennessee came an important part of the population of northern Alabama, Mississippi, and Florida, as also a large portion of the early settlers of Missouri, Arkansas, and Texas.[7] To all of these states it holds a central position, and from its borders radiate the rivers making them accessible.

MOVEMENT INTO THE TRANS-MISSISSIPPI COUNTRY

It was in the trans-Mississippi country, however, and especially in Missouri, that expansion was most active from

[7] Monette, J. W., *History of the Valley of the Mississippi*, Boston, 1846, p. 48.

1810 to 1840. To the unbounded West came all those restless spirits in whom opportunities for migration had aroused all the *Wanderlust* long dormant from the opiate of a sedentary civilization, and to whom movement had become a habit of life. On they came, the more vigorous and daring pushing on to the western rim of the Mississippi valley to set their beaver-traps on the head streams of the Pacific rivers; the less daring taking up prairie land beyond the outskirts of settlement on which to graze their cattle, and erecting a temporary shelter to be occupied until a more industrious and permanent race of agricultural settlers began to press upon their rear. Then they moved on, hunting, trapping, rounding up their cattle, planting an occasional field, but always more assimilated to the wilderness beyond them than to the civilization behind. The greater part of the population belonged to this class. The West was peopled by a sort of staccato movement. Immigrants built cabins and laid fences; but before the wood was seasoned or the fresh rails darkened by exposure, the place was sold, and the wheel-tracks of the canvas-covered wagon going to meet the advancing afternoon shadows told the wide destination of the migrant family. Thus the frontier zone broadened until it reached the margin of the arid belt; then a partial recoil set in.

Into Missouri. Along the Mississippi boundary of Missouri was the gathering of the waters; higher turned the Ohio with its vast tributaries, the Illinois, and the Missouri. The Mississippi furnished communication with the Gulf below, and with the Green Bay and Chicago portages above. Missouri was accessible to American settlers from the Lakes to the Gulf, and straight across its broad territory ran the natural highway of its own mighty stream. Every section of the United States, therefore, contributed to the population of this nascent state, though some sections more than others.

The old trading intercourse between the early trans-Allegheny commonwealths and the French settlements on the west bank of the Mississippi made the Missouri country the natural destination of restless backwoodsmen like Daniel Boone and his sons. The right of property in slaves, guaranteed by the Purchase treaty to the original French inhabitants of Louisiana, fixed Missouri's future as a slave state, and enabled it to receive accessions of population from all the other slave states which the Ohio could deposit at its doors. Its chief sources of population were therefore Kentucky, Tennessee, Virginia, and North Carolina; the states just north of the Ohio, also, yielded emigrants who were lured westward by the current of "La belle Rivière." [8] Other settlers came from New England by way of the Erie Canal, the Great Lakes, and the Illinois River; and in 1833 came some thirty thousand frugal and industrious Germans.[9] As early as 1820 Flint had found in the Girardeau district a substantial settlement of Germans, some of whom had come directly from the Fatherland, but the greater portion from Pennsylvania and North Carolina.[10] After the introduction of steam navigation, foreign emigrants began to land at New Orleans and ascend the Mississippi by steamboat to this western country,[11] while they poured in by the thousands from the northern waterway of the Lakes.

In the distribution of population in Missouri, the geographic control of the rivers was the dominant factor up to

[8] Monette, J. W., *op. cit.*, p. 553.   [9] *Ibid.*, p. 554.
[10] Flint, T., *op. cit.*, p. 233.
[11] Bromwell, W. J., *History of Immigration*, New York, 1856; see New Orleans in list of ports between 1820 and 1840.
Monette, J. W., *op. cit.*, p. 567.

1830. Settlements spread in a narrow belt up the Mississippi and the Des Moines to the northern boundary of the state; in a broader zone up the Missouri, chiefly on its northern or prairie side, to the western frontier defined by the elbow of this great river; and in a still broader band along the small western affluents of the Mississippi, especially the Meramec, and the head streams of the Whitewater and St. Francis, just above the swamps in which these rivers lose themselves in the southeastern part of the state. The hilly country of the upper Whitewater and St. Francis extends eastward as the Cape Girardeau country, early selected by the French for settlement; it is fertile, thickly timbered, well watered, furnishing pure streams and mill-sites, and for these reasons early attracted colonists while the still richer alluvial bottoms remained untouched.[12] Mill-sites were a rarity in this level country. For a long time maize was pounded in a mortar by hand. In 1825 steam-mills were introduced in St. Louis, but elsewhere treadmills worked by oxen or horses did the work,[13] and lumber was costly because of the lack of water-power sawmills.

At a time when only the rivers with their rich bottoms, flanking prairies, and natural highways, could boast a population of from two to six to the square mile, the ranger and the rancher, nevertheless, were setting up cabins and fences in remoter parts of Missouri. Flint says that as early as 1818 there were white settlers in the wilderness near the western state line between the Arkansas River and Missouri, a hundred miles from any settlement. Thither they had gone to secure a fresh range for their cattle, or merely the "elbow-room" which was the first demand of the backwoodsman.

[12] Flint, T., *op. cit.*, p. 232.   [13] *Ibid.*, p. 211.

By 1840 population was distributed evenly but sparsely over the whole state except in the rough hill country of the south-central portion.   A uniformly fertile soil resting on an underlying limestone rock, abundant rainfall, temperate climate, a country too level to present any obstacle to expansion, either on its surface or in the current of its streams, diversified by forest and prairie, the natural focus of the Illinois, Wabash, Ohio, Tennessee, and Mississippi river routes — no wonder that Missouri increased in population.   Here grew the whole range of our northern agricultural crops, and the labor, so difficult to secure in a new country, was here supplied in part by slaves.   The staple crops were wheat and hemp; the former was sent down the Mississippi in large quantities as flour to New Orleans, and the latter, either as raw material or manufactured into bagging and rope, was exported to Kentucky.[14]   St. Louis became the great emporium for the commerce and manufacture of the upper Mississippi, the depot of the western fur trade which the Missouri River system brought to its doors, and the eastern terminus of the Santa Fé trade which was carried on via the Missouri River to Independence, and thence by means of caravan across the American desert.   St. Louis, by its command of the great inland water routes, early developed the manufacture of steamboat supplies, steam machinery, and finally by 1844 rivaled Pittsburgh, Cincinnati, and Louisville in the construction of superior steamboats.[15]

Into Iowa.   As Missouri filled up, and as settlements between 1830 and 1840 were spreading from northern Illinois and from the southwestern nucleus of that state, the natural expansion of these three areas of population was creating the beginning of Iowa.   No artificial state line or the demarking

[14] Monette, J. W., *op. cit.*, pp. 553–54.   [15] *Ibid.*, p. 558.

course of the Mississippi ever really separated the settlements distinguished for administrative purposes as Illinois, Missouri, and Iowa Territory. In 1832 the government purchased from the Indians nearly all the land within fifty miles of the west bank of the Mississippi, from the Des Moines to the mouth of the Wisconsin River on the north. The beautiful, fertile prairie country was immediately taken up by pioneers. Even in 1830 Illinois and Missouri had overflowed into the little angle between the Des Moines and Mississippi rivers; but now settlement spread rapidly north to Burlington and Salem, and by 1840 this southeast corner of Iowa was the most densely populated portion of the territory. It merged into a belt of similar density, which extended up the Illinois River and over to the end of Lake Michigan, thereby suggesting the avenue of approach.

At about the same time as the planting of Burlington (1833), Dubuque was founded nearly two hundred miles farther up the Mississippi, and became a center of distribution for the northern part of the newly purchased area. Its location coincided with the western end of a band of denser settlement which defined a broad belt of rich lead-mines extending along the northern border of Illinois and over into southwestern Wisconsin. These mines had been worked by Indians and French traders from early times, but the rush thither began in 1823, when they were described as the richest mines in the world. The chief diggings were at Galena and the vicinity in Illinois, and were pretty well distributed over the present counties of Grant, Lafayette, and Iowa in Wisconsin, while rich mines were found across the Mississippi, about Dubuque.[16] Hence the birth of this city followed closely on that of Galena in 1826.

[16] Peck, J. M., *A Guide for Emigrants in Illinois and Missouri*, Boston, 1831, pp. 132–34.

Population advanced rapidly up the drainage streams of Iowa, covered the whole area of the Black Hawk Purchase by 1836, and was encroaching on the Indians' lands to the west, so that the government in 1837 extended the western boundary by a new purchase from the Sacs and Foxes. A new and strong tide of immigration, begun in 1839, carried population far up the Red Cedar and Des Moines rivers, and on the western frontier up the Missouri beyond the present site of Council Bluffs, while a vacant spot between the eastern and western groups showed the geographic control of the Iowa rivers in determining the location of settlements.

As Iowa lay north of the Missouri Compromise line, the movement thither was from free states. The route of the Erie Canal and the Great Lakes brought immigrants from New York and New England, and foreign elements from Germany, France, and Great Britain, who, with their small capital, could find no place in the industrial system of the South. The Ohio also delivered its contribution of settlers from the free states on its northern bank.

The movement of population, at least after 1820, was in general from free state to free, and from slave state to slave. This was true in the Northwest Territory and in Iowa, as we have seen. Missouri, occupying an intermediate position between the two sections and convenient to the Ohio and the northern routes, drew from both sections, but chiefly from the region south of the Ohio. Arkansas and Louisiana by their geographical location belonged to the slave power. They recruited their population from the older and more densely settled commonwealths of Kentucky and Tennessee, and from the wealthy planters of Mississippi, Alabama, South Carolina, and Georgia, who were seeking new, unexhausted lands for the employment of their slaves. These, therefore, generally crowded into the rich bottoms where cotton, sugar, and maize would flourish.

Into Arkansas. Emigration to Arkansas went on very slowly until after the Indian Territory was erected as a separate district (1824), but from 1830 until 1835 the population doubled. This was the period when Mississippi, Alabama, and Georgia were feeling their expansion blocked by the presence of the Indians in the extensive areas within their boundaries, and when the final purchase and removal of 1838 had not yet brought them relief. Louisiana, being an older state, had less unclaimed land to offer the newcomer than its neighbor to the north.

The population of Arkansas in 1820 was 10,000. These were distributed in one narrow, detached line of settlement along the Mississippi near the mouth of the St. Francis, and in another fifty miles below the mouth of the Arkansas; in a broader line following the Arkansas upward from a point fifty-five miles above its confluence with the Mississippi, the area of cypress swamp, bayou network, and ox-bow lakes which told the story of widespread and long-continued overflow.[17] This first point of safe habitation — leaving out of consideration ague and fever — was occupied by the Post of Arkansas, in early days the administrative center of the territory. A line of continuous settlement extended from here to about forty miles above the present site of Little Rock; but beyond that, far up the Arkansas, the "Mulberry Settlement" in the hill country of the western frontier told of the energy of the pioneer and his desire to get out of the malarial bottoms. Two other detached settlements indicated the same need, one in the north among the highlands of the White River, and another in the southwest, known as Mount

[17] Flint, T., *op. cit.*, pp. 252–54.

Prairie, on the tableland between the main Ouachita and its tributary, the little Missouri.[18]

With the new accessions of population, these centers expanded until at certain points they coalesced, but elsewhere were separated by vacant areas of mountain, swamp, and flood land, while the line of the Arkansas valley rapidly carried settlement to the pleasant hill country in the northwest, bordering on the Indian Territory. In 1835 rich planters were attracted to the southwest corner of the territory where the deep meanders of the Red River furnished rich bottoms suited to cotton and maize.[19]

The soil along all the great streams of Arkansas was the richest alluvium and practically inexhaustible. The extensive prairies and hill country also, by the decay of their bedrocks, had an excellent soil, which eventually was found to yield good crops of cotton, but in the pioneer days of the state was taken up by the grazing element. A warm climate, abundant rainfall, and accessibility to the Mississippi secured to Arkansas both crops and a market.

Into Louisiana. Similar geographical conditions and similar results obtained in Louisiana. Here too were swamp, alluvium, prairie, and pine woods. "The people in the pine woods raise cattle by the hundreds and thousands — are poor, satisfied, and healthy. In the bottoms are the sugar and cotton plantations with wealth and sickness." The prairie country west of Opelousas and the upper Bayou Teche was devoted chiefly to cattle, partly to cotton and sugar plantations. The lowlands were mainly swamps, so that we find the valley population distributed in belts from two to three miles wide along the elevated margins or broad nature-made dikes of the watercourses. Here, as in the

[18] Flint, T., *op. cit.*, pp. 265–66.   [19] Monette, J. W., *op. cit.*, p. 555.

river peninsulas of old Virginia, the planters were able to load their produce of sugar, molasses, and cotton immediately on steamers at their own wharves. This is Louisiana as Flint saw it in 1823.[20] In 1836 a fresh tide of settlers, avoiding the swamp regions of the coast, spread into the arable lands southwest of the Bayou Teche and along the head waters of the small Gulf streams as far as the Sabine. This represented chiefly a natural expansion southward of the Red River zone of settlement, and it was supplemented by an advance of planters at this time into the fine cotton region of the upper Red, Ouachita, Black, and Tensas rivers, all in the northern part of the state. The settled areas along the Mississippi and the Red now merged into those of Arkansas, as shown in the census map of 1840. The abrupt line defining the northwestern frontier of Louisiana settlement represents the political separateness of the country beyond, but it conceals the important fact that the expansion of the American people, though not of the American government, had gone far beyond the limits of the Sabine.

EXPANSION INTO THE DOMAIN OF MEXICO—TEXAS

The subject of early trans-Mississippi expansion must include that irregular advance of American citizens into the domain of Mexico. We have seen that expansion into Spanish Louisiana foreboded the political fate of that vast territory, which, however, by the rapid shiftings of diplomacy and the clamorous demand of the youthful West, reached its destiny without waiting for the slow operation of the natural law of territorial extension. Thirty years later in Mexico this law, reinforced by other politico-geographical principles,

[20] Flint, T., *op. cit.*, pp. 329–49.

worked itself out to its inevitable conclusion, just as it has
done with slight local variations in the Hawaiian Islands.

Reasons for Expansion. The advance into the Texas province of Mexico was a part of the general westward movement. It was stimulated by the restlessness, enterprise, and
aggressive spirit of the frontier; and it was participated in
largely by the slaveholders of the southwestern states whose
legitimate political expansion was blocked by the Indian
Territory and the Missouri Compromise line, but it also
drew into its sweeping tide representatives from every state
in the Union and emigrants from across the sea. To the
landless, the wide grassy plains and fertile bottoms of
Texas were attraction enough. To the merchant or trader,
Mexico with its belated industries and rudimentary commerce would yield a fortune in a few expeditions. The uncertain claim of the United States government to the trans-
Sabine country before the final understanding of 1819, the
well-known weakness of the far-away power in Madrid, the
attraction of an ill-controlled border region of a foreign country to the rough, lawless elements of our own frontier, probably all united to swell the American population in Texas.

As we have shown before, a frontier is always a zone of assimilation between the contiguous territories. It will lean
more to the one or the other side of the political boundary
line, according to the energy and growth of the national life
behind it. We have seen how, just after the Louisiana
Purchase, Spain, by the energy it displayed in strengthening its hold on the Texas country by settlement, fort, and
garrison, secured the Sabine instead of the Rio Grande as the
eastern frontier of Mexico. The United States had not at
that time accumulated a large enough population in the
southwest to constitute a natural pressure upon the Mexican

frontier. From that time, Spain, seeing the unwisdom of its previous policy of hospitality to American settlers, strove to keep the Texas district uninhabited on the primitive principle of a waste boundary as a barrier against the influx of its restless neighbors. But the principle did not work. It is easier to occupy a vacant land than an inhabited district. On came the Americans, and the zone of assimilation grew wider and wider, extending farther and farther on the Mexican side of the Sabine.

The aggression of the Americans was shown by their share in almost every revolution in Mexico between 1812 and 1817. Officers of the United States Army helped to lead them, and the expeditions supporting them were fitted out at Natchez on the Mississippi, Natchitoches on the upper Red River, and Gaines Ferry on the Sabine. When the treaty of 1819 renounced the claim of the United States to the territory between the Sabine and the Rio Grande, American interests in Texas were already so strong that Henry Clay protested against the agreement. Natchez, from whose doors the Red River led to the Texas frontier, entered its protest against the treaty by sending out an expedition under Dr. James Long to invade Texas. His small force of seventy-five men swelled to three hundred by the time he reached Nacogdoches, fifty miles west of the Sabine. There he issued a Declaration of Independence for Texas, but his enterprise failed of its purpose.[21] In 1820 all Mexico revolted against Spain, and in four years the United States of Mexico was established. At this time it included in its population about three thousand Americans, settled mostly at Nacogdoches, the first town on the highway leading from Natchitoches, and along the road southwest to San Antonio.

[21] McMaster, J. B., *op. cit.*, V, 4-7.

Mexico, anxious to increase her population, now met the spirit of expansion in the American people by issuing large grants of land in Texas. Stephen Austin, originally from Connecticut but more recently from Missouri, secured an enormous tract extending from the highroad between Nacogdoches and San Antonio to the coast between Galveston and Matagorda bays, on which, as *empresario*, he was to settle three hundred families.[22] Other contractors from the trans-Allegheny states, Missouri, Tennessee, Kentucky, and Ohio, or from New York, Ireland, and Scotland, agreed to bring some two thousand families, and received similar grants until almost the entire state was parceled out. This was in 1825; by 1830 there were twenty thousand Americans in Texas. They came by all the ports of the coast and moved up the rivers; or they followed the Ohio and the Mississippi to the Red, which carried them up to the head of steamboat navigation at Natchitoches, or farther still by smaller craft to Shreveport, somewhat nearer the Texas frontier. The eastern border of Texas about the Iyish Bayou was chiefly settled by Americans,[23] and beyond lay the rich boundless prairie on which could be raised fine crops of sugar, cotton, and corn. The genial, salubrious climate, too, had a peculiar attraction for the ague-shaken dwellers of the Mississippi lowlands.

Roads into Texas. Four roads, indicating the amount of intercourse between Texas and the United States, crossed the frontier in 1826: one from Liberty on the Trinidad to Opelousas, Louisiana; another from Liberty, joined at the Sabine by a branch road from Nacogdoches, leading across

[22] McMaster, J. B., *op. cit.*, V, 13.
[23] Flint, T., *History and Geography of the Mississippi Valley*, Cincinnati, 1828, I, 464.

to Alexandria on the Red River; the old highway direct from Nacogdoches to Natchitoches; and a fourth from the former town across the Red River at Fulton to Little Rock, Arkansas.[24]

Factors in the Texas Uprising. Mexico became alarmed and withdrew her favors, canceled all except three land grants, forbade further colonization and the importation of slaves; and to check the active trade between the two countries, closed all but one port on the American side and laid heavy import duties on all the manufactured articles needed by the agricultural population of Texas. In the meantime the spirit of expansion was making itself manifest in another way. The United States government was becoming desirous of acquiring this last territory occupied by the American people, as it had followed them into Louisiana and into West Florida. From 1827 to 1829 repeated offers were made by the government at Washington to buy Texas. The reasons advanced were politico-geographical ones. Mexico was too near to New Orleans, the entrepôt of the great American waterway. Much of the Red River and many tributaries of the Arkansas lay in Mexican territory. When the country should become thickly settled, community of interest in the navigation of these streams would give rise to disputes. Clay suggested the Brazos, or the Colorado, or the Rio Grande with the western watershed of the Red and Arkansas rivers as boundary; and when these offers were rejected, he warned Mexico of the possibility of its losing Texas because of the large American contingent there, and the consequent collisions between the two elements of the population which might draw the two republics into war.

[24] McMaster, J. B., *op. cit.*, V, 12. Map of the period, 1900.

Finally the Texas uprising came and a new star dawned for the American flag. The revolt of Mexico against Spain, like the American Revolution, was the repudiation of the central authority by a peripheral state according to the politico-geographical law already stated. Somewhat similar, though somewhat different, too, was the declaration of independence by Texas. In the American colonies there had been little infusion of foreign blood to modify the race: a pure-blood offspring rebelled against parental authority. In Mexico, the ethnic element of the Spanish conquerors had been greatly weakened in its absorption into the large native population. Hence racial differences had combined with new and unfamiliar geographical conditions to differentiate the Mexican from the Spanish, and strengthen the tendency towards disintegration. Texas, too, was a peripheral state, with all its natural tendencies towards defection enhanced by the fact that the dominant race here — dominant by reason of energy, intelligence, wealth, and affiliations, though not by number — was of an imported, alien stock, having no inherited sympathy with the governing power.

The geographical location of Texas on the outskirts of the Mexican territory, remote from the center of the federal authority, with a savage frontier on the north, and an alert, enticing neighbor on the east, put this province much in the situation of the early trans-Allegheny settlements in relation to their mother states of Virginia and North Carolina, and generated the same separatist tendencies with the same threat of defection to a neighboring foreign power. It was difficult to get a hearing before the general government. "Texas is situated twelve hundred miles from the capital of Mexico; and owing to the distance, and state of war in the country ever since we have known it as a Republic, com-

munication could be no other than tedious and uncertain....
All these... have been sufficient to cause so much delay as to
injure Texas materially without the possibility of remedy."
This is an extract from a circular issued in Texas in 1834,
advocating patience and loyalty to the Mexican government. Two years before this Texas had sent in a petition
for independent statehood and separation from the more
densely populated province of Coahuila extending south of
the Rio Grande, on the ground that Indian problems along
her northern frontier threatened a calamity "which nothing
short of a well-regulated government of a free, unshackled,
and independent state can provide against." "The wide
extent of wilderness, forming a natural boundary between
Texas and Coahuila, places an indispensable barrier in the
way of Coahuila's extending the efficient means of defense
she might wish." [25] Furthermore, differences of climate,
soil, and productions, partly also of population, made such
a separation desirable. This line of reasoning might have
emanated from any of the pioneer leaders of the Watauga,
Cumberland, or Kentucky settlements.

Remoteness in turn enabled the Texans to ignore certain
Mexican laws. A long reach weakened the arm of the execu-
tive here as we shall find was also the case in Mexican California. The inhibition of the slave-trade was disregarded
by the Americans in Texas, as was later (1829) the decree
of emancipation of all slaves; and the danger of revolt attending the enforcement of this law was so apparent that a
special decree made it inapplicative in this province. Even
in the days of Spanish supremacy in Mexico, the connection
between Texas and the center had been weak. Control of

[25] Edward, D. B., *History of Texas; the Emigrant's, Farmer's, and Politician's
Guide*, Cincinnati, 1836, pp. 231 and 207.

the province had been administered after a fashion from the remote Chihuahua, five hundred miles even from San Antonio in whose vicinity was the only compact area of Spanish settlement west of the Sabine and Red rivers.   Subsequently the vacant region between these border streams and the Rio Grande was filled by a foreign population, prone to fall apart from the Mexican center by the weight of their own antagonisms, and furthermore drawn in the opposite direction towards the United States by every tie of race and interest. Here attraction on the one side and repulsion on the other operated to the same end.

When the revolt of Texas began, its affiliations with the United States counted for something.   Two companies of New Orleans volunteers, others from Mobile and Kentucky, some eight hundred in all, took a hand in establishing the young republic, while two hundred deserters from the United States army were found serving under the Texas standards; and Sam Houston and Davy Crockett, men who embodied the enterprise and recklessness of the backwoods frontier, made picturesque figures in the Texas war of independence.

Annexation of Texas.   How truly this was in the last analysis a war of unauthorized or individual American expansion, is indicated by the fact that, of the fifty-eight delegates who declared the independence of Texas at New Washington in March, 1836, only three were Mexicans, though Americans constituted only about one fourth of the total population.   Their immediate application for annexation to the United States showed that in their own consciousness they had never really expatriated themselves, but merely had stretched the farming, cattle-tending, trading America out over Texas prairies, with the expectation that the flag would do its smaller part and follow. Therefore, when the admission of the Lone Star State was agitated ten years later, the American mind reverted to the old claim of the United States to the Rio Grande boundary of Louisiana, and argument ran high for the "reannexation of Texas." [26]

[26] Sparks, E. E., *Expansion of the American People*, Chicago, 1900, p. 318.

CHAPTER X

GEOGRAPHIC CONTROL OF EXPANSION INTO THE FAR WEST: THE SOUTHERN ROUTES

THE westward moving frontier of the American people is beyond all doubt the most interesting subject that American history presents. Here is written the fullness of American energy, its daring resourcefulness and ambition; here the rate of national growth registers itself in more telling figures than mere statistics of population; here, with rifle, axe, and plough; with canoe, bullskin boat, pack-horse, and covered-wagon, the man of backwoods and plain shapes the national dream of empire into the sturdy stuff of trading-post, ranch and farm.

The Advance of the Frontier. A frontier is a zone, and the width and character of that zone tells the whole story. A narrow, evenly drawn frontier, like that of the American colonies in 1750 along the eastern foot of the Appalachian barrier, pointed to the balance maintained between the half-developed strength of the nascent people and the power of British dominion reinforced by the geographical control of the mountain wall. By 1800 the frontier had lost its neat outline but had gained in interest. It sent out great bulges and streamers running out from the Appalachian ridges to Lake Ontario and to Erie, and to the Wabash. Its width bespoke a rapid rate of expansion, while farther still, outlying groups of settlement in the Natchez District or opposite the Missouri's mouth, and lonely cabins beyond the Mississippi in Spanish territory led the advance and signaled to the rear to follow over the easy roads which river and prairie afforded.

In 1820 and 1830 the western frontier was more ragged still and formed a fringe with wide intervals up the trans-Mississippi rivers. The map of 1840 shows what seems to be again the neat, narrow frontier zone of arrested growth, a line approaching the ninety-fifth meridian and the northward bend of the Missouri River. Though continuous settlement did pause long at this limit, because it was the outer margin of the arid belt and the eastern boundary of the Indian Territory, nevertheless even before this time, that unofficial America on Texas soil was supreme as far as the Nueces River. American trading-posts at the gates of the Rockies, missions on the Columbia, and ranches on the Willamette had stretched the United States frontier to the Pacific, while individual enterprise was Americanizing the commerce of New Mexico and influencing the politics of Alta California. Never were the accumulated energies of the American people so great, never was its frontier so broad a zone. Over arid plain, snow-capped mountain, and alkaline desert, it stretched from the Missouri to the Pacific, wherever the smoke from the trapper's camp-fire in the Rockies curled upward in the evening air, wherever the trader hobbled his footsore beasts at night in the scant meadows of the western trails, wherever the immigrant staked out his land claim on the banks of the Columbia or the Sacramento. The breadth of this frontier explains the fact that, while continuous settlement paused at the western boundary of Missouri and Iowa in 1850, the United States had made good its claim as far as Puget Sound, and the American flag waved over the presidios of California.

CONDITIONS FAVORING ADVANCE TO THE ROCKIES

Rivers and Plains. To the first stage of this far western expansion nature presented no serious obstacles, though she also afforded no great assistance, such as that rendered by the Ohio River and the Great Lakes in the trans-Allegheny advance. The even, gradual rise of the Great Plains to the foot of the Rocky Mountains made the ascent to an altitude of even five thousand feet almost imperceptible. No forests obstructed progress, and the character of the soil was such that the passage of a few wagons marked out a well-beaten road (Fig. 12). The rivers draining this even slope flowed in parallel courses to the Missouri and Mississippi. They pointed the direct way to the West, and were closely followed by the moving caravans for the sake of their water supply. The cottonwoods growing on their islands or scantily fringing their banks furnished fuel for camp-fires, which otherwise had to be supplied by *bois de vache*, the "buffalo chips" of the plains. The arid and treeless regions of the world everywhere resort to similar fuel — the excrement of camels in the deserts of Arabia and on the rainless plateau of Tibet, *taquia*, the llama dung of the *Altiplano* of Bolivia, cattle dung, with which Kipling's hero, the boy Kim, also cooks his evening meal in the valley of the Indus.

With the exception of the Missouri, the western rivers af-

Note to Fig. 12:

Beyond the Allegheny Mountains, the pioneers carved homesteads out of the mixed hardwood open forests as far west as Missouri; though the forests blocked movement and had to be girdled or cleared for crop land, they provided many materials for the pioneer homestead and sheltered the abundant supply of game. In the Great Plains no forests obstructed passage but strips of trees along the rivers provided fuel, repair timbers and light logs to buoy up the covered wagons at river crossings. The great trans-Rocky Mountain trails spanned the sage brush and creosote bush area of the Great Basin. Compare Figs. 13 and 14. (Courtesy of the United States Department of Agriculture.)

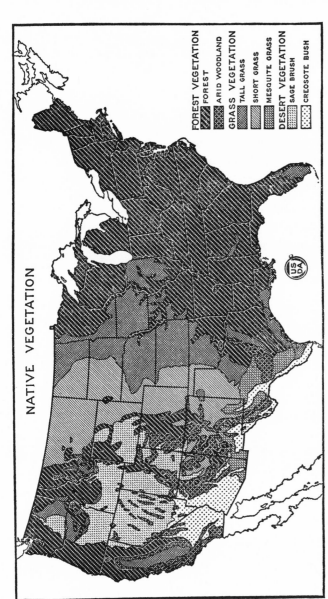

NATIVE VEGETATION

FOREST VEGETATION
FOREST
ARID WOODLAND

GRASS VEGETATION
TALL GRASS
SHORT GRASS
MESQUITE GRASS

DESERT VEGETATION
SAGE BRUSH
CREOSOTE BUSH

FIG. 12. NATIVE VEGETATION OF THE UNITED STATES. (See note at foot of page 184.)

forded no waterways to the emigrant, for they are navigable only in rare, short periods, and only for canoes or very shallow flatboats. Rising in the Rockies they flow directly east through an arid land, receiving no tributaries to increase their volume, while their water is evaporated in the dry air or sucked up by the porous soil. In crossing the broad belts between these rivers the early caravans would often travel a hundred miles without meeting a single permanent watercourse. Hence the trails preferably passed from one river to another somewhere between the ninety-fifth and ninety-eighth meridian on the eastern margin of the arid region, and again by the lateral streams at the base of the Rockies where the beds were still full.

These rivers, owing to their usually scanty volume and consequently weakened currents, possess only slight erosive power; hence they have deposited much detritus in the valleys previously cut in the friable soil of the prairie. Over these sandy plains in time of flood they spread a shallow sheet of water, often two miles wide; but when the flood passes, the river becomes a series of shallow interbraided streams, obstructed by sand-bars and islands. The topography of the country gives a different character to the Missouri. From 48° to 39° north latitude this stream is a lesser Mississippi, occupying a central basin running north and south, and intercepting all the western streams which set out from the mountains on their way to join the Father of Waters. Hence the Missouri is reinforced constantly by new affluents. Moreover, it rises in the extreme north of the Cordilleran plateau, where the mountain system is narrower and in general lower than it is farther south, thus admitting the moisture drifted in by the Pacific westerlies; hence this river has better supplied sources than the Platte and the

Arkansas. Nor is this all. The upper Missouri by its tributaries spans the base of the Rockies from the sources of the Milk River (49° N.L.) to the springs of the Big Horn (43° N.L.), while its own main stream penetrates to the western ranges of the system, thus levying a tribute of water on a wide stretch of the highlands. Hence the Missouri is navigable as far as Fort Benton at the mouth of the Teton River, just below the Great Falls which present an obstacle to further advance.

The sources of the Platte, the Arkansas, and the Red stretch out along the eastern slopes of the Rockies with a narrower span, but their lateral head streams interlace with one another, as the North Fork of the Platte does with the southern affluents of the Yellowstone in the Big Horn and Powder River. Thus it is possible to pass from one of these rivers to another by lateral head streams over easy watersheds along the whole eastern base of the Rocky Mountains. These geographical lines determined the trails of the trappers going north and south in the first half of the past century, and later the route of the railroads which traverse the base of the mountains (Fig. 13).

The superior navigability of the Missouri and its course straight from the great fur-fields of the North, naturally drew the canoe of the trader and trapper up its course first. The Lewis and Clark expedition in 1804 had no difficulty in finding Canadian guides and voyageurs who knew the Missouri as far as the Mandan villages at the great northern elbow of the river. On the upstream voyage, the expedition met a trapper, Vallé, who had spent the winter nine hundred miles up the Cheyenne River at the foot of the Black Mountains.[1] It found also French traders among the Mandan

---

[1] Coues, E., *History of Lewis and Clark Expedition*, Washington, 1893, I, 150.

villages, and several agents of the Northwest Fur Company who had come from their station on the Assiniboine River only a hundred and fifty miles to the north.[2] The course of the Canadian rivers, the Saskatchewan and Assiniboine, here parallels that of the upper Missouri, from which they are separated by only a narrow, lake-dotted watershed; and both systems lead to the springs of the Columbia. These geographical conditions determined the clash of two rival commercial interests on the Pacific coast. No sooner did Lewis find the English trading on the Missouri than he began to speculate whether the Milk, Maria, or some other of its northern affluents might not give the Americans access to Canadian territory on the upper Saskatchewan for trade with the Assiniboine Indians, with whom the English were already doing a lively business.[3]

The Advance of Traders. The advance of the traders up the western streams was rapid. In 1805 the Little Missouri was the remotest point on the Missouri visited by white men; but on his return voyage in 1806, Lewis met two American traders in camp on the White Earth River,[4] and on the lower Missouri he constantly passed strings of canoes on their way to the Platte.[5] Two years later, when Astor's party set out for the mouth of the Columbia to establish their trading-post on the Pacific, Missouri trappers had appropriated all these western streams. The trappers spent the winter among the mountains setting their traps, hunting, and trading with the Indians for buffalo robes; and in the spring took advantage of the annual rise in the shallow rivers to float their cargoes of furs in canoes or barges down

[2] Coues, E., *History of Lewis and Clark Expedition*, Washington, 1893, I, 178, 203.
[3] *Ibid.*, I, 273.   [4] *Ibid.*, II, 1116.
[5] *Ibid.*, II. 1206.

FIG. 13. T

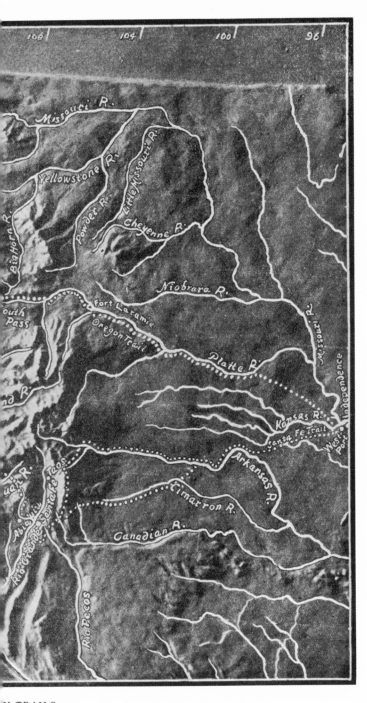

Y TRAILS

to St. Louis. The flood was generally sufficient to carry them to their destination, but not always. Frémont in 1842 met some traders of the American Fur Company who had started out from Fort Laramie on such a voyage down the North Platte. Their boats drew only nine inches of water, and floated rapidly down the full tide for some sixty miles; but then followed wide, shallow reaches, blind channels, and sand-bars, while the river was falling rapidly. There was nothing to be done but to leave their goods on land with a guard, while the rest, with such packs as they could carry, started out on foot for St. Louis.[6]

When the frontier military posts of the United States were still confined to the western boundary of Missouri and Arkansas, trading-stations, those vedettes of civilization, had been planted far up the head waters of all the western rivers, or beyond the Rockies on the sources of the Pacific streams. As early as 1808 the Missouri Fur Company had a station in the mountains at the three forks of the Missouri, but in 1809 its trappers were dislodged by the hostilities of the Blackfeet Indians, so they crossed the Rockies and established a post on the head waters of the Columbia.[7] The Laramie Fork of the North Platte was marked by two such stations, Fort Platte at its mouth and Fort Laramie a little farther upstream. Vrain's Fort and Fort Lancaster, two private posts on the South Fork of the Platte, at an elevation of fifty-four hundred feet,[8] gathered in the furs of the Colorado Rockies, but had rivals just to the south in Bent's Fort on the upper Arkansas, just above the mouth of Purga-

---

[6] Frémont, J. G., *Narrative*, Washington, 1845, p. 17; Parkman, F., *The Oregon Trail*, New York, 1910, pp. 87 and 88.

[7] Irving, W., *Astoria*, New York, 1854, pp. 134 and 178.

[8] Frémont, J. G., *op. cit.*, pp. 35–95; Chittenden, H. M., *The American Fur Trade of the Far West*, New York, 1902, III, 947–70, and map.

tory River, and Barclay's Fort in the Mora valley of the Canadian. All of these posts became later great way stations
in the westward movement. In the wake of the trapper
came the pack-horse or wagon-train of the trader and the
white-roofed caravan of the settler.

Westward Movement of Outfitting Points. In the early
days (1810) St. Louis was the last outfitting point for the
Indian trade of the West; but as steam navigation was introduced and then improved, and as the commerce of the
prairies increased, the outfitting point traveled westward up
the Missouri, first to Franklin, opposite the present town of
Boonville, a hundred miles from the frontier; then, in 1831,
to the new town of Independence, only twelve miles from the
Indian border and two or three miles south of the Missouri;
and, finally, when the steamboat landing at Independence
caved in, just beyond to Westport and Kansas City. These
three places then shared the control of the overland trade.[9]
The northward bend of the Missouri here made this elbow
the natural terminus of the river route to the West. Here
began the prairie trail. The unfitness of the streams for
navigation forced the westward movement to resort to other
means of transportation. Pack-horses and wagon-trains
took the place of canoe and barge and steamboat, dusty
trail over wide grasslands and sandy waste the place of glid-
ing current twixt wooded banks. Independence became a
market for horses, mules, and oxen. Here the Rocky
Mountain trapper could get his simple equipment; but it
was the overland trade with the Mexican town of Santa Fé
which gave to Independence its bustling activity and made
St. Louis the great commercial city of the early West.

[9] Gregg, J., *The Commerce of the Prairies*, Cleveland, 1845, I. 32–33.

THE SANTA FÉ TRAIL AND TRADE

Bases of Trade. Just beyond the eastern rim of the Rockies in the valley of the upper Rio Grande, and opposite a natural gateway in the mountain barrier, lay the old city of Santa Fé, a territorial capital even in the early Spanish days, and under Mexican rule a squalid adobe town of some three thousand inhabitants. The business of the place was considerable, for it supplied almost the whole population of New Mexico, which was distributed in villages and ranches along the valley of the Rio Grande for a hundred miles to the north of Santa Fé and a hundred and forty to the south.[10] Its markets were stocked under the Spanish régime with goods which came up from Vera Cruz and other Gulf ports of Mexico at enormous cost; but after Mexican independence was established, a less exclusive commercial policy was adopted and the overland trade from the United States began. Then every wagon-track and mule-trail across the plains marked the passing of the shuttle weaving northern Mexico and the American Republic into one fabric. The aridity of the prairies called a temporary halt to agricultural expansion, but wider ranging commerce made Las Vegas and Santa Fé American towns in their business quarters.

A few pioneers in the overland trade between 1805 and 1820 had found their way to Santa Fé by various routes — up the Platte and the Arkansas to their sources, over the Colorado ranges, and into the valley of the upper Rio Grande above Taos; but the established Santa Fé trade began in 1822, and after a few experiments as to routes, settled down to what was known as the Santa Fé Trail.

The Santa Fé Trail. Geographical conditions determined

[10] Gregg, J., *op. cit.*, I, 111 and 145.

Independence, Westport, or Kansas City as the start-ing-point of the overland commerce. The east and west course of the Missouri between the frontier and the Missis-sippi made this river the natural western extension of the Ohio route, which brought goods from the manufacturing centers of the country, and for which St. Louis was the natural western depot and distributing-point. North of New Orleans, St. Louis was the only emporium that offered river and land connections with Santa Fé, shorter and better than those of the Gulf city. Arkansas, with its exclusively agricultural interests, developed no commercial center which might have profited by the waterway of the lower Arkansas River, tortuous though it was, and the direct west-ern line along the Canadian River to San Miguel and the gates of Santa Fé. This route from the Arkansas frontier was several days shorter than the northern trail, was open earlier in the spring, with a supply of pasturage for horses which lasted, too, later in the fall; it was better provided with timber along the tributary brooks and less intersected by large streams.[11] For these reasons it was sometimes taken by a belated caravan in the winter-time in preference to the colder northern route. But the preponderance of ad-vantages was along the line of the Ohio, the city of St. Louis, the Missouri, and the upper Arkansas, which therefore de-termined the route of the Santa Fé Trail. This road, eight hundred miles in length from the last outfitting-point at the southern elbow of the Missouri, rising by such imperceptible degrees for three fourths of this distance as to seem quite

[11] Duffus, R. L., *The Santa Fé Trail*, New York, 1930, map opposite page 8z, "Report of Committee appointed to prepare a correct map of the old Santa Fé Trail across Kansas," *Kansas State Historical Society Report* (*1913*), pp. 107–25; Perrine, F. S., "Military Escorts on the Santa Fé Trail," *New Mexico Historical Quarterly*, II (1927), 175–93, 269–304.

level, guided straight across the thirsty stretches of the Great Plains by the eastward-flowing streams, bending then slightly southward to the gate in the mountain wall which opened upon the old Spanish city, made the simplest and most direct connection between the emporium of the middle Mississippi and the distributing-center of the upper Rio Grande valley.

The sudden northward bend of the Arkansas between the ninety-seventh and ninety-eighth meridians brings the upper course of this river parallel with the Kansas and almost directly west of Independence, making its valley the natural supplement by land of the Ohio and Missouri route to New Mexico. The Santa Fé Trail, after crossing a well-watered country to the Arkansas, followed the river westward as far as Bent's Fort in the early days, turned southwest up Timpas Creek and the Purgatory River into the Raton Hills, and over this ridge to the interlocking head streams of the Canadian and Pecos, which led to Las Vegas and San Miguel. Fifty miles northwest across the mountains lay Santa Fé in its hill-locked valley. To the west of San Miguel the outer range of the Rockies is broken up into detached plateaus and ridges, between which the Apache Cañon, a pass three miles long and wide enough for only one wagon, carried the road over the watershed. Thence with a slight dip it dropped to the elevated valley of Santa Fé (7000 feet). It was at the western end of this gap that the Mexican army, in 1846, took its stand to oppose the advance of General Kearney, who had brought his forces from Fort Leavenworth by this route.

Character and Significance of the Trade. For the first year or two of the Santa Fé trade, transportation was confined to pack-horses, which could make their way over the rough hill country at the foot of the Rockies; but when the commerce was developed and wagons were resorted to, the travel left the Arkansas at Cimarron Crossing, just beyond the present Dodge City, and struck southwest across the desert to the Cimarron River, which by a decided northern bend here approaches within fifty miles of the Arkansas. The road led then southwestward up the half-dry Cimarron, and struck the older trail at Las Vegas on the Mora, the most northern affluent of the Canadian River. This became the established line of the Santa Fé Trail. In addition to the easier gradients of the plains, it had the advantage of avoiding the long detour of the upper Arkansas; but the effort of the pioneer caravan to cross the desert to the Cimarron proved almost disastrous, and this stretch was always the scene of suffering for man and beast.

Since the Trail ran along the banks of the western rivers for a great part of the distance, and these, owing to prevailing aridity, received only a few small tributaries, the drainage system of the country placed no serious obstacles in this path of overland commerce. It crossed the unbridged streams by fords in the dry season, when teams had to be doubled to the wagons and lashed across the quicksands to prevent their sinking; in spring freshets by buffalo boats and wagons encased in skins to make them impervious to the water. Out from Independence moved the scattered parties of traders to rendezvous at Council Grove some hundred and fifty miles away on the Neosho, and there to organize their caravan under a captain. Apaches beset the trail to murder and plunder, wolves to prey, and droves of wild horses to stampede the live stock of the train. The wagons were formed into a hollow square at night as defense against the Indian or corral for the animals. Every man had to take his turn at guard duty, according to "the common law of the prairies."

The outgoing caravans were to trade with the non-industrial population of New Mexico; hence their cargoes included every manufactured commodity from salt to silk. The exchanges included specie, gold and silver bullion, gold-dust from the placer mine near Santa Fé, buffalo rugs, furs from western trappers, some wool of poor quality, a few coarse Mexican blankets which could find a market in the American frontier settlements, and immense droves of mules and horses.[12] Most of these were products of a people lingering in the hunting and pastoral stages of civilization. The value of the merchandise exported from the United States after 1826, when wagons were regularly used for transportation, averaged about $140,000 per annum, but it rose to $250,000 in 1831 and 1839, and to $450,000 in 1843. The goods were sold at a great advance, and the profits were doubtless large, but the business was most hazardous. Moreover, it was in the hands of a large number of small dealers, who invested their all in the cargoes of their wagons. The number of men in these yearly caravans was always large in proportion to the transactions, indicating that the human intercourse between the United States and New Mexico was as significant as the commercial.

Soon Americans settled in Santa Fé, monopolized its trade, and then extended their commercial operations over a still greater field. Stretching away for three hundred and twenty miles directly southward, the valley of the Rio Grande, like a deep groove between the flanking ranges, opened a way to Mexico through the water-gap of El Paso

[12] Gregg, J., *op. cit.*, p. 307; Stephens, F. F., "Missouri and the Santa Fé Trade," *Missouri Historical Review*, X (1916), 234–62, and XI (1917), 289–312.

in the mountains. This had been the line of early Spanish expansion northward into New Mexico and the San Luis Valley of Colorado, and became now the route along which American commerce spread to the southward. The Rio Grande is not navigable in this upper course, but the great national highway along its banks carried American traders with their pack-horse trains to El Paso, whence they continued two hundred miles south to Chihuahua, an important administrative and commercial center of northern Mexico. The trade with this place became particularly active and profitable, so that between 1830 and 1840 it absorbed nearly one half the imports of the Missouri caravans.

THE ADVANCE TO THE PACIFIC

Trapper and Trader. Thus American commercial expansion found a natural opening to a market in the south. To the west there was no such point of attraction for the merchant, but for the trapper, the wild, rugged uplands of the Rocky Mountains, their snow-fed streams, and untouched game preserves formed an alluring field of operations. The geographical location of Sante Fé made it a center from which in a wide sweep he could follow his favorite occupation. Therefore in the next advance to the west the trapper was again the pioneer. The trader keeps to a beaten road between two points, but it is the nature of the trapper to penetrate a whole river system, following its main course and the twig-like branches of its head streams, in order to set his traps for beaver or hunt deer in the isolated meadows of the upland valleys.

Influence of Location of Santa Fé. Santa Fé lies at an elevation of seven thousand feet, on the north and south course of the Rio Grande about halfway between two points where this river is closely approached by two westward-flowing streams, the Gila and the Colorado, which themselves unite at the southeastern corner of California. In other words, the Colorado system, by means of the Gila to the south, the Grand River and Gunnison to the north, spans the valley of the Rio Grande from southern New Mexico to southern Colorado. In Santa Fé American energy had a foothold within the rim of the Rockies for further expansion. The well-beaten roads along the banks of the Rio Grande led in either direction to the narrow watersheds beyond which lay the rushing sources of the west-bound rivers. Hence we shall see that Santa Fé, in consequence of its geographical location, became the center of the first sustained expansion to the Pacific; that the two main routes followed were determined by the Gila and the upper Colorado; and that consequently southern California was the first portion of the Pacific coast to experience any regular overland intercourse with the United States.

The Gila Valley. From the Rio Grande in southwestern New Mexico to the sources of the Gila River is only about fifty miles. The watershed is formed by the Mimbres Mountains, which rise only three or four thousand feet above the Rio Grande, here flowing in a valley four thousand feet above the level of the sea. At a very early date there was an established trail over these mountains as far as the Copper Mines, worked by Spanish or New Mexican proprietors, or leased to Americans. They lay twenty miles northwest of the upper Mimbres River, about twenty miles east of the present town of Silver City at an elevation of over six thousand feet, and about thirty-five miles, or a two days' journey, from an eastward bend of the Gila. Pack-mules bringing out the metal and carrying fuel into the mountains for the primitive smelting works had worn a distinct trace. This branched off from the main thoroughfare of the Rio Grande valley at 33° 20′ north latitude near the present village of Palomas and led southwest a four days' journey to the mines. It ran through a beautiful grazing country, over streams flowing down from the Mimbres Mountains, ascended one of these narrow valleys, and crossed the range by a pass so easy that the summit was left behind several miles before the fact was discovered; then down the dry bed of an arroyo to the Rio Mimbres and the mines.[13] Just beyond, the countless branches of the Gila sources harbored beavers in considerable numbers.

The Gila Trail and California. All this region became a natural field of activity for the trappers from Santa Fé; and the direct western course of the Gila in no very long time guided them to the border of California. This was the shortest route across the continent from St. Louis. The marked southeastward bend of the California coast from Cape Mendocino brings San Diego five degrees of longitude farther east than San Francisco, and within twelve degrees of old Fort Union in the Mora valley of the Canadian River. After the cession of all this southwestern country by Mexico in 1848, the first government surveys for a transcontinental railroad were made along the valley of the Gila.

The first overland party to enter California was that of Jedediah Smith in 1826, who took a more northern route from an advance trading-post on Great Salt Lake, southwest to San Diego. But his purpose was merely to explore

[13] Emory, W. H., *Notes of a Military Reconnoissance from Fort Leavenworth in Missouri to San Diego in California.* Made in 1846–47. Ex. Doc. No. 41, Washington, 1848, map and pp. 55–59. *Personal Narrative of James O. Pattie of Kentucky,* Cincinnati, 1831, p. 52.

and therefore his venture may be regarded as a sporadic effort, especially since it did not establish regular communication, as did the early advance from Santa Fé along the Gila route. The pioneers in this movement were the Patties, father and son, in 1827. The career of these men is typical. Natives of Kentucky, they became lumbermen in Missouri, in 1824 joined a trapping and trading expedition to New Mexico, and by the next three years they brought in skins from the Gila more than once. Then the elder Pattie organized a party of thirty trappers at Santa Fé to operate on the Colorado. Only eight of these reached the mouth of the Gila. Thence they floated down the Colorado in canoe-rafts and reached Santa Catalina mission in Lower California in January, 1828.[14] Ewing Young, a Tennessean, came with a party of beaver-hunters from New Mexico in 1830 to exploit the streams of southern California, and again the next year, trapping on the Gila as he went. Jackson in 1831 left Santa Fé by the southern route with nine hired men to buy mules for the Louisiana country.[15] Their route was traversed by several parties in the next few years, for it was always an open one; and in spite of the desert and Apache attacks it was comparatively safe for even small bands of travelers. Some members of all these early parties, after one or two trips, settled in California and planted the first milestones, as it were, of American expansion to the Pacific.

Use of the Gila Trail. The Gila Trail formed the route of Kit Carson's famous ride in 1846 from California, when he came bearing dispatches from Commodore Stockton for the authorities in Washington concerning the part of the Ameri-

[14] Emery, W. H., *op. cit.*, pp. 51–57, 133–37; Bancroft, H. H., *History of California*, San Francisco, 1884, III, 162 and 163.

[15] Bancroft, H. H., *op. cit.*, pp. 174 and 387.

cans in the Mexican War in California; and it was the line of
General Kearny's march the same year to take charge of
the military operations on the Pacific coast. The Trail was
practicable for horses and was well supplied with water, but
farther south the Mimbres Mountains sink into the Sierra
Madre Plateau, which afforded a more arid though almost
level route to the West. Skirting this southern rim of the
Gila basin, it was possible to pass westward at an elevation
of three or four thousand feet, and then drop down to the
regular Gila Trail just above the great bend. Therefore
Kearny sent his wagon-train under Lieutenant Cooke to
follow by this more level path which, once being opened, was
utilized by Californian emigrants in subsequent years.
Moreover, its value as an easy passage for a national railroad
to the Pacific became apparent to W. H. Emory of the Mexican Boundary Commission, and was later a strong motive in
the purchase by the United States of the territory south of
the Gila.[16]

The Spanish Trail. In the meantime, the restless activity of the trapper had pushed northward from Santa Fé to
Albiquiu and along the valley of the little Chama River over
the divide and westward across the sources of the San Juan
to the Dolores and the Colorado; or these same untiring
explorers had moved up the high valley of the Rio Grande
and into the elevated basin (seventy-five hundred to eight
thousand feet elevation) known as the San Luis Valley, from
the northern end of which, by pass and stream-worn gorges,
they traversed all the wild upheaved area of the central
Rockies, and penetrated to all the upper tributaries of the

[16] Emory, W. H., *Report of the United States and Mexico Boundary Commission,*
Washington, 1857, p. 93.
Bancroft, H. H., *Arizona and New Mexico,* San Francisco, 1889, pp. 477 and 478.
Cooke, P. St. G. and Emory W. H., *Report of March from Santa Fé, Mexico, to
San Diego, California,* Washington, 1848, Ex. Doc. No. 41, pp. 553-57.

Colorado — the Gunnison, Grand, and Green rivers. The ranges and the passes were high, but so was the base of the trappers' operations. Taos, the center of trade and population on the upper Rio Grande, was about sixty-five hundred feet above the sea. The head streams of the Colorado system afforded fine hunting-fields, especially near their sources; for the cañon formation of the chief branches and the trunk streams impeded the ubiquitous searching of the trappers. Hence in their progress to more western hunting-grounds, these men of the woods passed along by the minor watersheds and small transverse valleys of the Colorado affluents, avoiding the main streams. When they had reached the inner rim of the Great Basin, the next obvious step was to the Pacific.

William Wolfskill of Kentucky, after trapping and trading extensively for eight years about Santa Fé, fitted out a party in 1830 to trap in California. He set out from Taos by a northerly route, swung around westward across the Grand and Green rivers and over the Wasatch Mountains to the Sevier River. This is a stream of the Great Basin, flowing northward from the divide which the Virgin River, an affluent of the Colorado, drains to the south. Hence his path turned southward up the Sevier, over the mountain rim of the Basin, and southwest down the Virgin. The vast cañons of all these western rivers in their highland course preclude navigation even when the volume of water would permit it. Therefore Wolfskill turned away from the Virgin before reaching the Colorado, and struck out southwest across the wide Mohave Desert and reached the Cajon Pass (4560 feet) in the San Bernardino Range, through which he moved down to Los Angeles.[17]

[17] Bancroft, H. H., *History of California*, San Francisco, 1884, III, 386.

This route came to be known as the Spanish Trail. It settled down to the more direct line up the Chama River and down the Dolores valley to the Grand. This it crossed near the present town of Moab, Utah, where a post-road now leads over the river, and took advantage of a break in the cañon formation of the Green to pass that stream just where the railroad crosses it today.[18] In time it was well defined, for along it moved yearly caravans from Santa Fé to California led by Americans or New Mexicans, bringing woolen fabrics and *sarapes* to exchange for the mules and horses of California or the silks and other choice imports of China.[19] It was the route followed by Frémont on his return from California in 1844. The Mohave section, like all desert trails, zigzagged across the arid waste from one watering-place to another. These were springs, water-holes, or little wells, dug narrow and deep in the dry bed of the Mohave River by wolves, whose keen scent told them of the underground water supply. Sometimes there were stretches of forty or sixty miles without water. It was impossible to miss the Trail here, because it was traced with bones. After a twelve or fifteen hours march without relief, the animals, exhausted by the scorching heat and parched with thirst, would stagger along with drooping head and tail, when suddenly the wild mules which generally accompanied the caravans as return products or reserve pack-animals, would toss their heads with an alert movement, sniff the air, and then start off at a full gallop down the dusty pathway. This brought joy to the men of the Trail, because

[18] Beckwith, E. G., *Senate Report of Explorations and Surveys for a Railroad Route from the Mississippi River to the Pacific*, Washington, 1861, XI, Part 2, map 4; Albert, J. W., *Examination of New Mexico, 1846–47*, Washington, 1848, Ex. Doc. No. 41.

[19] Bancroft, H. H., *History of California*, San Francisco, 1884, III, 395.

they knew there was a surface supply of water a mile or two ahead.

Early American Settlements in California. Such were the two routes, geographically determined, from New Mexico to California. Both had their natural termini in San Diego and Los Angeles. The men who came to this country to trap continued their operations along the river feeders of Tulare Lake and the mountain tributaries of the San Joaquin, and lived the nomadic lives of hunters. Though a steady intercourse was kept up by the annual visits of the Santa Fé traders, these southern routes never became avenues of heavy immigration. The trapper and the trader are not domestic animals; they bring no families with them except mongrel offspring of Indian wives. Mountain and desert acted as a barrier, and the overland infiltration of American elements into California in early days went on very slowly. Only thirty hunters were added to its population between 1831 and 1835, the residuum of the Santa Fé parties and of two other expeditions which came directly across the Sierra Nevada to the Pacific.[20] More Americans came by sea. The New England trading-vessels, which yearly visited this coast in goodly numbers, added more to the American colony, for they were constantly leaving here invalided sailors, deserters, and occasionally a commercial agent. So an American population in California was slowly being recruited, exclusively men who in general married California women. The steady influx which later planted a bit of the United States on California soil was intimately connected with the peopling of the contiguous territory of Oregon, where the United States frontier met that of California.

[20] Bancroft, H. H., *History of California*, San Francisco, 1844, III, 373.

CHAPTER XI

EXPANSION INTO THE FAR WEST BY THE NORTHERN TRAILS

AT THE time the American trappers and traders found their way to the Pacific, California was a foreign possession. This fact, reinforced by the length and difficulty of the journey thither, sufficed to discourage the immigration of families, especially after the rebellion of Texas under American leadership had rendered citizens of the United States undesirable tenants of Mexican soil. Texas, to be sure, had been Mexican domain, but it was close to Louisiana and the Mississippi River. Oregon was as remote as California, and like it was barred by two thousand miles of plains, mountains, and desert; but it was claimed on solid grounds by the United States. Hence in this direction Americans turned when the uneasy spirit of migration began to stir along the Missouri and Mississippi frontier.

BASES OF AMERICAN CLAIMS TO THE OREGON COUNTRY

Discovery and Exploration. The mouth of the Columbia had been discovered by a New England vessel in 1792; it had been reached by the overland exploring expedition of Lewis and Clark in 1805, and occupied temporarily as a trading-point by the fort of the Astor party in 1811. The frequent visits of the New England merchants engaged in the China trade brought the Oregon country more and more into the

American sphere of influence. The line of the Missouri and Columbia first opened the way to the Oregon country; immigration set vigorously into this trans-Rocky America, and from the southward-pointing valley of the Willamette spread over into the vast trough of northern California. Thus California was entered freely at its northern and southern extremities by natural avenues, while on the east the double barrier of the snow-capped Sierras and the vast expanse of the Nevada Desert long excluded immigration.

The Columbia River as a Key to the Northwest. From the point where the Colorado, after a long cañon-bound course, pours its thin, desert-worn current into the Gulf of California, northward to Vancouver Island there is only one river which traverses the whole width of the trans-Rocky region and breaks through the double mountain wall to the sea. This is the Columbia, claimed by the United States and counterclaimed by the British; for both it was the key to western expansion on the Pacific. Its three long arms penetrate to the heart and even to the eastern rim of the Cordilleras; they stretch a mighty span from the head waters of the Athabasca in the north to the sources of the Platte and the Colorado in the south, touching fingers along the Great Divide with the divergent affluents of the Missouri. These Columbia streams, with their slender supply of water and turbulent current, would rarely hear the dip of paddle or ripple of canoe-prow upon their cañon-shadowed surface; but they guided the trail down those rocky slopes from where the mountains doffed their caps of snow and flung wide their giant portals to the march of an invading people.

Missouri River Route and the Lewis and Clark Expedition. The Columbia was first approached from the east through the Missouri, where it takes its rise in the western ranges of the Rockies. The Lewis and Clark expedition therefore followed this river to its forks in the heart of the mountains, continued up the Jefferson, its most westward branch, to the outermost range, whence the Lemhi Pass and an Indian trail led down to the Lemhi branch of the Salmon River.[1] Hopeless of traversing the wide desert by the mad, rock-bound waters of the Salmon, the party turned northward over the range and up the Clark River, which flows between the parallel ranges of the Rockies. Its lateral affluents, corrading transverse valleys, served as intermediary paths over the mountains between the upper Missouri and the central tributaries of the Columbia, just as farther south the Green River branch of the Colorado by its side valleys opened a way over two watersheds for the Oregon Trail from the Sweetwater branch of the North Platte to the Port Neuf and the Snake River at Fort Hall. Such was the part played by the New and the Holston in the early trails across the Alleghenies; and earlier still, such was the anthropogeographical importance in the Alps of the torrent-scoured gorges branching off from the valleys of the Upper Rhine, Rhone, and Inn in the lines of communication between Italy and the northern plains of Switzerland.[2]

The return route of Captain Clark led directly east from the great elbow of the Columbia up the Snake and Clearwater River, over the Bitter Root range by the Lolo Pass, and by the Lou Lou Fork and Blackfoot valley of the Clark River to the Lewis and Clark Pass, down to the little Dearborn River of the Missouri. A well-beaten road marked the whole trail, for it was the path of the western Indians

[1] Coues, E., *Lewis and Clark Expedition*, Washington, 1893, II, 484–93.

[2] Semple, E. C., *Influences of Geographic Environment*, New York, 1911, pp. 537, 539, 549.

coming to hunt buffalo on the plains.[3]   This was the shortest route across the mountains, because the Rockies contract as they near Canada; this route had the longest river approach on a navigable stream, the best mountain pass, the narrowest stretch of desert on the west, and the most direct approach to the great bend of the Columbia, where regular canoe navigation began; but it involved too great a detour to the north.   It was too far from St. Louis and that bustling center of emigrant preparation at the elbow of the Missouri.   Hence we find that the Astor expedition, which set out in 1810 to establish an American trading-station at the mouth of the Columbia, went up the Missouri only to the Grand near the Aricara villages, and then made a short cut by striking out southwest across the plains to the Big Horn branch of the Yellowstone; thence it continued up the Wind River to the great central dome (nine thousand feet) of the Rockies, defined by the Teton, Gros Ventre, and Shoshone ranges.   This it crossed by a single pass to a head stream of the Snake River.

A returning party of Astoria traders a year or two later struck southeast from the upper Snake, and reaching the Green River basin, took advantage of the general dip in this section of the Rockies to reach the Sweetwater, the North Platte, and finally St. Louis.[4]   This was in its main features the route followed later by the Oregon Trail when expansion to the Pacific began in earnest.   The Astoria venture was short-lived because it had to contend with an overland line of communication hopelessly long and difficult, without any base between the Mississippi and the Pacific; with inter-ruptions to its sea communications caused by the War of

[3] Coues, E., *op. cit.*, II, 1060–70.
[4] Irving, W., *Astoria*, New York, 1854, chap. 43–50.

1812; and with territorial encroachments of the British in the aggressive expansion of the Hudson's Bay Company into the valley of the Columbia.

BASES OF BRITISH CLAIMS

Discovery. The claim of the British to the Columbia was geographically based. The east and west line of the Saskatchewan River had at a very early date carried English explorers in Canada to the northern arm of the Columbia among the Selkirk Rockies. Discovery of the mouth of the river, by an international principle which the English themselves had established, gave this great stream to the United States; but its northern source was in the hands of the British. We have seen how easy and natural is downstream expansion. The great trading company had a near base in their fur stations on the upper waters of the Canadian rivers. Wealth, organization, a long-established service, and strong political backing gave them an effectiveness which Astor's American Fur Company lacked. Aided by the happy accident of war, they were able to extinguish by the seizure of Astoria the last spark of life in the American Fur Company on the Columbia. Then they proceeded to take systematic possession of the whole Columbia basin after the manner of the fur-trader which the French in Canada had found effective for a time.

The Fur Trade and the Activities of the Hudson's Bay Company. By 1834 every strategic point at bend or fork of stream, and every center of the great fur-hunting fields in the Rockies was marked by a fortified post. Fort George, on the site of the old Astoria, maintained communications with the sea. Fort Vancouver, the chief administrative post, six miles above the mouth of the Willamette River, exploited the rich farm-lands of that valley to supply the upstream line of forts with bread. Where the wide diverging arms of the Columbia met at the great bend, Fort Walla Walla held a position as vital for the control of this sole western waterway as old Fort Duquesne for the command of the Ohio. It felt the pulse of the wild trapping life from Fort Hall on the upper Snake, drawing in its beaver from the slopes of the Wasatch Mountains, to Fort Colville, far up the Columbia at the foot of the Selkirk Rockies.[5]

As we have seen before, a primeval wilderness, widely separated trading-posts, a sparse population of nomadic trappers half assimilated to the savage life about them, and above all a monopoly, belong to the nature of the fur trade. The influence of the Hudson's Bay Company was sufficient to keep out the English traders and settlers from this great game preserve, and they could undersell the American traders;[6] but they could not exclude American settlers under the agreement of joint occupation made with the United States in 1818. The experience of the French had proved how weak a land tenure was that of the trading-post when contesting claims with a sedentary agricultural population. At first it was only a few American trappers who sifted through the mountain breaches into the Oregon country; but soon a line of dust hovering in the air marked from afar the Oregon Trail. Into the wide gaps between the stations and forts poured an inundating tide of American immigrants, sweeping away the beaver and the game, setting up the claim of plow and sawmill against the weaker title of the trap.

[5] Bancroft, H. H., *History of Oregon*, San Francisco, 1886, I, 6–14.
[6] *Ibid.*, I, 48 and 70.

Rivalry between Hudson's Bay and American Fur Companies. The Hudson's Bay Company, through the natural avenues of the Salmon and Snake rivers, made its power felt as far as Great Salt Lake, the Bear River, and the Green River Basin; but here it came into conflict with American trappers who entered this famous fur-field from every direction, from the upper Rio Grande, Arkansas, North Platte and Sweetwater, and the Wind River branch of the Big Horn. Rivalry was fierce. The American and the Rocky Mountain Fur Company had their traders' rendezvous sometimes on the Wind River, more often on the Green, and sometimes even at Pierre's Hole,[7] a valley just west of the Teton Range and draining into the Henry branch of the Snake; but occasionally American traders pushed into the British rendezvous at Ogden's Hole on Bear River within the Great Basin. All this area of interlocking streams was the battle-ground of rival commercial interests; but though the American got a slight foothold on the westward-flowing streams, encroachment was limited in general to the sources. The Americans had an advantage to the southwest. Ashley of the Rocky Mountain Fur Company made his first rendezvous on the Green River in 1824, entering its valley by the famous South Pass; and the next year founded Fort Ashley on Utah Lake, where he left a hundred men to exploit the peltries of this rich country.[8]

Between 1826 and 1829 there were about six hundred American trappers in the region of the Teton Mountains and Green River, also a great number of the Hudson's Bay Company men.[9] The wild sons of the trail explored every

---

[7] Bancroft, H. H., *History of the Northwest Coast*, San Francisco, 1884, II, 455 and 562.

[8] *Ibid.*, II, 448.   [9] *Ibid.*, II, 459.

upland valley and pass, and opened the mountain paths for others, but there is little evidence that they contributed to the settled population of Oregon until after the dissolution of the American Fur Company in 1840. Furthermore, it was comparatively late before a regular westward movement of population set towards Oregon.

THE INFLUX OF SETTLERS

The first immigration into that country was the result of individual enterprise originating on the Atlantic seaboard, and having nothing in common with a national expansion of the frontier. It was recruited from a population which had left its pioneer days far behind and therefore had un-learned the useful lessons of the wilderness; or it drew upon Canada's ready-made stock of traders and trappers. It came in no small part by sea and relied upon maritime con-nection with the East for supplies, support, and growth. Such was the Astoria party, recruited almost entirely both as to partners, factors, and *engagés* from the Scotchmen and French Canadians of Montreal and Mackinac. Such was the Massachusetts expedition under Wyeth, which came overland in 1832 to establish a trading-post at the mouth of the Columbia. The journey of over a thousand miles from St. Louis to the Snake River in the company of the veteran Sublette and his Rocky Mountain trappers edu-cated the inexperienced but purposeful Wyeth to the most important pioneer requirements. Some of his fantastic equipments, elaborately devised in the scholarly environ-ment of Cambridge, were laughed out of service by the practical men of the plains at the Missouri rendezvous; the rest were exhausted or lost, or discarded when the strength of himself or his pack-animals began to fail, so that his diminished party reached the Columbia almost empty-handed. The vessel which was to bring merchandise around the Horn for his post never arrived; and though a return to the East and reinforcements of his supplies justified him in building his stations on Wapato Island in the lower Colum-bia and at Fort Hall on the Snake, the Hudson's Bay Com-pany was too strongly entrenched in all the Oregon country to suffer this invasion of its trading-grounds.[10]

While the men who knew the ground, the American trappers and traders, were still hanging on the mountain outskirts of the Oregon country, religious enthusiasts in the eastern states were fitting out missionary parties for the uplifting of the western Indian, their zeal being as usual in direct proportion to their ignorance. Such was the be-ginning in 1834 of the Methodist mission in the valley of the Willamette and the Presbyterian stations on the Walla Walla and the Clearwater branch of the Snake River in 1836. The pioneers came overland by the North Platte and the Snake River. The inland location of the Presbyterian missions, the poverty of the country about, and the danger-ous character of the Indians, though at the river terminus of the desert trail, prevented their attracting reinforcements and growing to a settlement. The Willamette mission, accessible to the mouth of the Columbia, drew from Boston and the East by sea the supplies and people which the wide expanse of plain and mountain and desert at that period debarred.[11]

Jason Lee, finding the Indians of the Willamette im-

---

[10] Bancroft, H. H., *History of the Northwest Coast*, San Francisco, 1884, II, 557–64.

[11] Bancroft, H. H., *History of Oregon*, San Francisco, 1884, I, 78–182.

possible and the country highly possible, was converted from missionary to colonizer. His lectures in the United States advocating the settlement and formal appropriation of this western possession before the clutch of the British should be tightened upon it, writings in similar strain of other pioneers who had tried to get a foothold in the Columbia trade, and the discussion of the "Oregon Question" in Congress, served to advertise the trans-Rocky country. Lee, on a return trip to the United States, met his first audience and the first response to his eloquence in the frontier states. In the spring of 1839 two small parties moved out from Illinois on the route to the Columbia,[12] the forerunners of a new westward movement. Here was a genuine expansion from our western frontier, inaugurating the second phase of Oregon immigration.

The Oregon Trail and Migration. Up to this time the settlements in Oregon were an anachronism — our farthest West with the stamp of our farthest East; social, political, and economic ideals of New England storekeeper, mill-owner, preacher, and school-teacher in the vast Cascade forests and the wilderness valleys of the Willamette and Columbia. But the eastern settlers were too few and the Atlantic seaboard too remote for this to last. As the irregular explorations of the West reduced the Oregon Trail to its easiest and final route, the Missouri frontier was brought nearer. The panic of 1837 to 1839 worked hardships on many in the East and caused them to take to the trail to make a new start in a land of promise. By 1840 the rapid occupation of the early western states, the lack of other outlets than the Mississippi and New Orleans, and the consequent gorging of that market without relief for the

[12] Bancroft, H. H., *History of Oregon*, San Francisco, 1884, I, 227-37.

plethora, caused a disastrous drop in the prices of western agricultural products. One Missouri farmer sold a boatload of bacon and lard for a hundred dollars. The Mississippi steamboats at times found in bacon a hot and cheap fuel. So much for living in a country without a seacoast. And the western farmer, with the migratory instinct in his blood, set out without regret and with the desire for adventure to the fertile plains of the Oregon country, whence the wide Pacific highway led to Asiatic markets.

From that time the dust of travel thickened on the Oregon Trail. From Arkansas, Missouri, and Iowa, from Kentucky, Tennessee, and Illinois [13] the pioneers gathered at the rendezvous at Independence, Liberty, St. Joseph, and Council Bluffs, with their heavy moving-wagons and their lowing herds. The party of 1844 consisted of fourteen hundred people; that of 1845 of three thousand souls.[14] The campaign cry "Fifty-four Forty or Fight" attracted many to the promised land. The Trail, twenty-four hundred miles long, led up the Platte and its North Fork to Fort Laramie, around the Black Mountains by the Sweetwater to South Pass [15] (7490 feet elevation), over this dip to the Green River, up the transverse valley of the Black River, by Muddy Creek to a pass over the divide rimming the Bear River Valley on the east.[16] This was the highest point of the whole long trail, 8230 feet elevation.[17] The road dropped down the Bear River to the most northern point of

[13] Bancroft, H. H., *History of Oregon*, San Francisco, 1884, I, 393.

[14] Dale, H. C., "The Organization of the Oregon Emigrating Companies," *Quarterly of the Oregon Historical Society*, XVI (1915), 205–27.

[15] Gilbert, E. W., "South Pass: A Study in Historical Geography of the United States," *The Scottish Geographical Magazine*, XLV (1929), 144–54.

[16] Young, F. G., "The Oregon Trail," *Quarterly of the Oregon Historical Society*, I (1900), 339–70.

[17] Frémont, J. G., *Narrative*, Washington, 1845, pp. 112–16.

its course and then crossed over an insignificant watershed to Port Neuf River and Fort Hall on the Snake. Thus far the way was easy. To South Pass the ascent was so gradual that it was difficult to determine when the summit was reached, and the grassy road to the higher pass over the Bear River divide was only "at times steeper than the national road in the Alleghanies." [18] The pass itself was a good one, and the fertile meadows of the Bear River valley were a natural recruiting ground for the travel-worn caravans.

Fort Hall was twelve hundred miles from Independence and only a little over halfway to the mouth of the Columbia. But the last part of the road was the hardest. For three hundred miles across the desert without a fertile spot or any pasturage, the trail followed the Snake River, whose cañon walls for days together barred the thirsting herds from its rushing waters. From Salmon Falls the road, avoiding a wide bend of the river, cut across the plains to Fort Boise, an intermediate station of the Hudson's Bay Company, whence it continued northward down the Snake again to Burnt River. Now only the thickly wooded range of the Blue Mountains lay between the emigrant and the Columbia. The road turned off up the Burnt River Cañon, over a dividing ridge to the upper Powder River, whose transverse valley pointed the line of easiest ascent up the steep slope. The range once surmounted by double teams, the Umatilla opened an easy path down to the Walla Walla and the great bend of the Columbia. [19]

Four months of continuous traveling, over two thousand

[18] Frémont, J. G., *Narrative*, Washington, 1845, p. 60.

[19] Bancroft, H. H., *History of Oregon*, San Francisco, 1884, I, 400–02; Frémont, J. G., *op. cit.*, pp. 147–66.

miles of weary plodding over plain, mountain, desert, and
mountain again, with two hundred and fifty miles of dangerous navigation on the rapid-swept Columbia; days and
weeks of scanty food and scantier drink, of midday heat and
midnight cold in the plateau desert — these were the tests
which geographical conditions set to the survival of the fittest on the Oregon Trail.   Faint-hearted members of the
caravans turned back at Fort Laramie, Green River, or even
Fort Hall.   In the earlier days wagons were exchanged for
pack-horses at Fort Laramie; but as the road became better
known, the lumbering vehicles were carried farther, to Fort
Hall and finally to the Columbia.   Property was abandoned
all along the route as pack or draught animals dropped from
exhaustion or were used for food.[20]   Even the Columbia did
not bring relief.   The lean and sore-footed herds, the hope
of future ranches and the leather trade with China over the
wide highway of the Pacific, might reach its banks, but they
could not be transported in the frail canoes and bateaux
which shot its rapids.   The only alternative was to sell them
at a sacrifice to the British at Fort Walla Walla, or to start
out on another weary journey over the wall of the Cascade
Mountains along a dangerous trail beset by thieving Indians
who carried off prizes from every herd.

Settlements in Oregon and Washington.   But in spite of all
these obstacles, on they came by the hundred and the thousand, a sturdy western stock, large in the patience and
hospitality born of their experience, broad in their democracy, insistent upon their rights, aggressive and even bluster-
ing in their Americanism.   They settled in the valleys of
the Willamette and its tributaries, on the Nehalem River
flowing into the Pacific, the plains about Astoria, and in

[20] Parkman, F., *The Oregon Trail*, New York, 1901, pp. 101–03.

spite of British protests staked their claims about the head of Puget Sound.[21]   Along the Willamette they found a mixed population.   In the ascendency were the original mission settlers from New York and New England, who in 1843 had been reinforced by small parties from Massachusetts and Maine, coming by sea and well provided with worldly goods.   These had come to set up stores, build mills, and speculate in land.   Living among the men from the East but holding themselves aloof were a considerable number of French Canadians, old employees of Fort Vancouver, who now raised wheat for the post.   These, too, had received accessions from an unexpected source. In 1841 the Hudson's Bay Company, in order to strengthen its hold on the Oregon country, brought out a colony of sixty people from the Red River settlement of Canada by the way of the Saskatchewan to take up land on Puget Sound about the Nisqually River.   But the colonists, finding the soil poor, removed to the Willamette valley, thus defeating the political design of the British and strengthening the American center.

But now the Willamette settlement was inundated by the inpouring tide from the Missouri frontier. The new immigrants by their number were able to remove from Oregon the local stamp of the East and of the Hudson's Bay Company, and to put upon its political and social institutions the stamp of a larger Americanism. "They carried the world of politics on their shoulders." The petty provisional government set up under missionary domination in 1843 they fundamentally altered in 1844 to conform to their own more democratic ideals.

The presence of eight thousand Americans in the Colum-

[21] Bancroft, H. H., *History of Oregon*, San Francisco, 1884, I, 413–15, and 458–64.

bia country in 1845 [22] hastened the settlement of the
"Oregon Question" in 1846. In 1847 more than 4000
migrated to Oregon. The appeals of the Pacific colony for
incorporation in the Union were energetically supported by
the western states, who from 1843 to 1846 assailed the
Senate and Congress with resolutions from general as-
semblies, memorials, and petitions for the political occupation of Oregon. The bond of union between the Columbia
and the Missouri frontier was close, for the geographical
environment of the Mississippi valley had bred the expanding tendencies which peopled the valley of the Willamette. In 1850 the passage of the Oregon Donation Land
Law, giving 640 acres to a married man and 320 acres to a
single man, who settled by December of that year increased
the western tide. Nine-tenths of the early settlers were in
the Willamette valley. In 1820, Oregon, Washington, and
Idaho had 130,000 people; 64,000 were in the Willamette
valley.

THE TIDE TURNS TO THE SACRAMENTO

As the most accessible and choicest land in Oregon was
taken up, an open, direct road made by Nature up the
valley of the Willamette and down the long trough of the
Sacramento invited dissatisfied colonists to seek more
desirable fields in northern California. This was already
a well-beaten trail. Before the coming of the missionary,
the American trapper with well-laden pack-mule had taken
this way up from California to the ready fur market at the
Hudson's Bay Company post of Vancouver.[23] The Cali-

[22] Monette, J. W., *History of the Valley of the Mississippi*, Boston, 1826, I, 569,
footnote.

[23] Bancroft, H. H., *History of the Northwest Coast*, San Francisco, 1884, II, 455.

fornia cattle which stocked the Willamette ranches in the early days helped to beat out this trail,[24] and at all times there was more or less communication. Oregon received a few stray immigrants from California, and California got some of its earliest pioneers, like Sutter, from Oregon; but from 1843 to 1846 every year saw a large party from the Willamette cross the watershed to the Sacramento.

Conflicting Interests in the California Region. Nor was this the only expansion into northern California. Russians and English had already made a commercial invasion of the country from the relatively near bases on the Columbia River and Baranof Island. The Hudson's Bay Company had a post on San Francisco Bay, whence its trappers ranged the upland valleys of the Sierra Nevada. Communication with Fort Vancouver was maintained both by land and sea. The Russian expansion was maritime; it was therefore easy and appeared early. In 1812 it built its trading-post at Ross near Bodega Bay a few miles north of the Golden Gate, and established a sub-station on the Farralone Islands, where from twelve to fifteen hundred fur seals were taken annually for the first few years by the Aleutian hunters in their skin boats or *bidarkas*. The Russians wanted not only furs, whether of sea or land, but also grain and other food supplies which they purchased from the Spanish Californians for their far northern trading-stations on the Alaskan coast.[25]

Lake Superior, Lake Winnipeg, the Saskatchewan, Columbia, Willamette, Sacramento had been the British line of approach to San Francisco Bay; the more open highway of the Pacific along "Russian America" and its islands, that

[24] Bancroft, H. H., *History of Oregon*, San Francisco, 1884, I, chap. 6.
[25] Bancroft, H. H., *History of California*, San Francisco, 1884, I, 298, and 628–35.

of the Slav advance; the Gila River, Spanish Trail, and Oregon Trail, that of the American. The presence of all these foreign elements in this northern province of Mexico points to the broad zone of indefinite frontier characteristic of every new land. Western boundaries were not yet evolved and western territories had not yet been differentiated out of their "indefinite, incoherent homogeneity." The Americans, English, and Russians were all regarded with some apprehension by the Californians, though the advantages of foreign trade overcame their misgivings. It was the United States which on the basis of an as yet unformulated Monroe Doctrine called a halt to Russian expansion on this coast in 1823, when the line of 54° 40′ north latitude was agreed upon as the southern limit of Muscovite dominion in America.

Meanwhile the American element in this extra-United States territory was increasing. The efficacy of informal expansion in Texas was an argument to the practical mind of the American for the application of the same method to California. The public sentiment as to "manifest destiny" was pretty well formulated as early as 1841. Scouting parties of early immigrants, as we have seen, had found the northern and southern breaches in California's mountain wall; but now the advancing army began to cross the vast sandy moat of the Nevada Desert and assail the mighty rampart of the Sierras.

Development of the California Trail. From the time that Ashley and Bonneville had discovered Great Salt Lake and trading-posts had been established there, and on Utah Lake to the south, small bodies of trappers and explorers had been guided by the Humboldt River westward across the desert, and with their slender equipment had managed to scramble over the mountains into the great Valley of California.[26] They discovered many high-laid passes at the heads of the deep-cutting torrents which tore down the steep slope to be sucked up by the bibulous sand below, but none were practicable for a heavy-laden caravan of immigrants. As the accounts of California aroused greater interest in the states, an adventurous body of immigrants under Bidwell and Bartleson in 1841 struck off from the Oregon Trail at the northern bend of the Bear River, followed the course of that stream southward almost to Great Salt Lake, and then turned west, searching for the Mary or Humboldt River, which they found after nearly a month and followed westward to Humboldt Sink. Thence they continued south to the Walker River, by means of its valley struggled up the mountains, crossed the ridge near Sonora Pass (10,115 feet elevation) with untold suffering from cold and starvation, and reached the San Joaquin valley by the Stanislaus River.[27]

The best lands in Oregon were now taken up, and the overflow into California was increasing; hence there were renewed efforts to find a more direct route to the valley of the Sacramento without making the long detour by way of Oregon or Los Angeles. Finally the Truckee Pass in the Sierras was discovered in 1844 and the California Trail settled down to the line of least resistance. It branched off from the Oregon Trail and the Snake River about a hundred miles below Fort Hall, turned southwest up Goose Creek, a southern affluent of the Snake, and over to the head waters

[26] Bancroft, H. H., *History of the Northwest Coast*, San Francisco, 1884, II, 449; and *History of California*, San Francisco, 1884, III, 389–91.

[27] Bidwell, J., "The First Emigrant Train to California," *Century Magazine*, XIX (1890–91), 106–30; Bancroft, H. H., *History of California*, San Francisco, 1884, IV, 269–71.

of the Humboldt River.   Later it left the Oregon Trail at
Bear River.   From Humboldt Sink the road led directly
west to the Truckee River, up this stream to Truckee Pass
(7017 feet) and down the western slope by the American or
Bear River of California to the Sacramento valley.   Sutter's
Fort near the mouth of the Bear River was a distributing-
point for immigrants entering both by the Sacramento
route from Oregon and by the California Trail.   Therefore
this adobe settlement with its various industries formed a
caravanserai, ever filling and emptying its contents into the
Sacramento, Napa, and Sonoma valleys.   With the opening
of the California Trail, the immigrant parties increased in
size and in 1845 began to include families.   Northern California was being Americanized and Sutter's Fort was the
rallying-place.   This trading-post on the frontier, remote
from Mexican control emanating from Monterey or Los
Angeles, accessible to the steady stream of Americans from
the east and north, was in a position to "contribute materially to hasten the success of American occupation." [28]

Relation of California to the United States and Mexico.
But California was much farther from the United States'
frontier than Mexican Texas had been.   Both the length and
natural difficulties of the overland journey precluded immigration on the large scale that had made an Anglo-Saxon
state out of a Latin province on the Sabine and Brazos.   At
the end of 1845 the total foreign male population of California was only 680; but the majority of these were Americans and were collected around and about the Sacramento
valley and San Francisco Bay.

But if California was far from the United States, it was
almost as remote from Mexico, and the Mexicans on the

[28] Bancroft, H. H., *History of California*, San Francisco, 1884, IV, 227.

ground not numerically strong; 6900 for the whole department, 3550 for northern California.[29]   In relation to the
administrative center in the City of Mexico, California was
distinctly a peripheral state with the usual tendencies
towards defection.   Conditions in the northern department
were not understood in the far-away capital.   Mex'can
governors and officials were unsatisfactory.   Hence in 1836
and again in 1844 a successful revolution established the
principle of home rule under national allegiance as against
centralism, while there were advocates of entire independence.   Officials in California ignored instructions for the
control of that department emanating from the capital; and
the federal authorities at the City of Mexico found the
efficiency of their control sadly diminished by poverty,
which complicated the difficulty of maintaining troops in
the remote province.   On many subjects the Californian
and the Mexican point of view differed fundamentally.
When in 1843 American immigration into California began
to increase noticeably, Mexican orders were received excluding such newcomers, prohibiting retail trade by foreigners throughout the republic, and reserving the coasting-
trade to Mexican subjects; but no attempt was made to
enforce these decrees in California.   On the contrary,
American immigrants were well received, obtained land
grants readily; and for the protection of Boston trading-
vessels on the coast, the governor of California levied a duty
on all foreign goods coming in from Mexican ports.[30]   The
long stretch weakened the arm of authority.

The federal sentiment was strongest in the south.   San
Diego fought for centralism in the revolution of 1836, and

[29] Bancroft, H. H., *History of California*, San Francisco, 1844, IV, 649.
[30] *Ibid.*, IV, 380–85, 429, and 555.

Los Angeles was the bulwark of Mexican allegiance against the revolutionary agitations of Monterey and the north.[31] It was southern California which made the only obstinate resistance to American conquest in 1846. This portion of the state had a closer sea connection with the national port of San Blas through the Gulf of California and the Pacific than that enjoyed by Monterey and San Francisco; and it was the natural terminus both of the Gila River Trail uniting it with Santa Fé and Chihuahua, and also of a more southern route leading through the province of Sonora in northern Mexico.

The California of the Sacramento valley and San Francisco Bay, on the other hand, was more isolated from the central authority and more open to American influences coming in by the two northern trails. Unlike the Russian and British traders, the Americans were settled on farms and ranches, had largely monopolized the commerce of the country, and had taken to themselves Californian wives; for until the Truckee Pass alleviated the worst hardships of the California Trail, there were few women among the immigrants. Bonds of property, commerce, and marriage united the American settlers to the Californians, who fully appreciated the advantage to the community of such enterprising elements. A certain assimilation of sentiments undoubtedly followed. When in 1846 the war between the United States and Mexico became imminent, many Californians foresaw the economic benefits which would fall to their country with an American régime. General Vallejo, guardian of the northern frontier and the sturdiest character among Mexican subjects in this region, favored the annexation of Cali-

---

[31] Bancroft, H. H., *History of California*, San Francisco, 1844, III, 613–15, and 629.

fornia to the United States. Everywhere in the north the spirit of resistance to the threatened invasion was lukewarm at best.

Attempts to get California. The United States had been turning covetous eyes towards California since 1835. It needed ports along this mountain-bound coast. Floyd of Virginia in 1822 advocated the occupation of Oregon chiefly to secure the mouth of the Columbia as a harbor for American whaling-vessels. In Jackson's administration an offer was made to purchase that part of California between 37° and 42° north latitude in order to secure San Francisco Bay. A few years later so radical a measure was no longer contemplated. West Florida and Texas had taught the Americans that the expansion of the trader's pack-horse and the rancher's herds was the surest pledge of territorial aggrandizement. They were possessed therefore with a large patience, in spite of eloquent appeals for acquisition from lecture platform and press, while immigration into California went steadily on and did its work. Thus the question of annexation was taking care of itself. Time was the only thing necessary, and the Americans felt they had all the time required.

But the United States government was not napping. The Russians had withdrawn from the field. The thinly scattered trappers and isolated posts of the Hudson's Bay Company in California could not vie with the spreading farms and growing families of the American settlers, but Englishmen who had large claims against the Mexican government for money loans had been for some time negotiating for a cession of territory in California or elsewhere as payment or security for the same.[32] The English govern-

<hr />

[32] Bancroft, H. H., *History of California*, San Francisco, 1884, IV, 298.

ment took no part in this so far as known. Any effort on the part of any foreign power to seize any part of California was to be checked on the basis of the Monroe Doctrine. This was always held in reserve. Towards California the greatest diplomacy was shown. If that province should declare its independence of Mexico, it should be encouraged and supported as a "sister republic," and later invited to join the Union.[33] American settlers and American influence were to be relied upon to dictate the answer.

The American element in California, however, was less patient than the government. When rumors of a war between the United States and Mexico became louder, these men, remote from succor, threatened as some believed with expulsion from their hard-won homes, outnumbered but not outmatched by the Californians, acted upon the instincts of self-help bred on the plains and the frontier. They raised the flag of revolt in the Sacramento, Napa, and Sonoma valleys; and the American colors were flying over Sutter's Fort and the captured Sonoma when Sloat under American orders hauled down the Mexican flag at Monterey on July 11, 1846. Filibuster venture though it was, and complicate though it did the American occupation of the country by antagonizing the Californians, it strengthened Sloat's position on the coast and supported Kearny's troops when they appeared in southern California after their forced march westward along the Gila Trail.

The Treaty of 1848. In the treaty of 1848 the United States forced Mexico to yield up not only New Mexico and California, which American troops had conquered, but all the intervening country from the Rio Grande to the Pacific and from the Gila north to the boundary of Oregon. The

---

[33] Bancroft, H. H., *History of California*, San Francisco, 1844, V, 74 and 196.

lines of communication with the new territory had to be secured. The United States now realized "the manifest destiny" of the American people to occupy the continent from ocean to ocean.

CHAPTER XII

GROWTH OF THE UNITED STATES TO A CONTINENTAL AND WORLD POWER

FROM a narrow strip on the Atlantic littoral, the United States had pushed steadily westward until it had possession of the most desirable stretch of coast on the Pacific. In this advance from ocean to ocean geographic conditions, in the cumulative effects of direct and indirect operation, became factors so strong that just for the sturdy energy of the Anglo-Saxon race they became determinants. A less vigorous people would hardly have responded to the educative influences of this peculiar environment.

GEOGRAPHICAL CONDITIONS AND EXPANSION

The remoteness of the North American continent from the centers of civilization and teeming populations of Europe and Asia had maintained it as a great territorial reserve. Except for the once great centers of Central America, Mexico, and the southwestern United States, it was occupied only by a sparse population whom the want of propitious geographical environment had helped to keep in savagery or the lowest stages of barbarism.[1] Here, for the greater part of the territory north of the Rio Grande, were lacking those small segregated geographical areas which early curb the wandering instincts of a primitive people, bring them to a sedentary life, and then by protecting mountains and seas guard their germinating civilization,

[1] Shaler, N. S., *Nature and Man in America*, New York, 1904, pp. 168–72.

and force its development by the warm interactive life of a contracted territory. Savagery and barbarism mean a scant population, weak tenure of the land, and a fragile bulwark against aggression. Therefore the westward advance of the young republic met only slight hindrance from the indigenous tribes of the country.

The result of this savage occupancy was a country with all the pristine richness of untouched resources. The barrier of the Atlantic was a basis of natural selection among the early colonists, so that in general only the fittest, the robust and enterprising, reached American shores. The abundance of opportunity in this virgin land constantly attracted foreign immigration to reinforce the American population. Easy conditions of earning a livelihood induced early marriages and the consequent large families which became a factor in the expansion of the nation. When with growth of population competition grew stronger and land scarcer, with a fine impatience of these altered economic conditions the dweller of the frontier moved westward to take up unexhausted lands, an unused "range," and also to seek that unconstrained life of the backwoods which has a powerful charm to the natural man. Thus fullness of opportunity bred the migratory instinct, and geographical conditions favored it.

Just as the continental build of most of North America was unpropitious to the development of small detached nations, so it afforded the natural environment for a few great ones. Its topography is marked by large simple features — two parallel mountain systems, their two ocean slopes, and between a vast trough-like area reaching from the Arctic Ocean to the Gulf of Mexico. Small physical features like detached mountain ranges, islands, peninsulas, and deep embayments are scarce, except along part of the Atlantic coast. Nowhere is there a highly diversified surface or a highly articulated coast except in the half-submerged lowlands of the sub-polar regions: shore-line and interior are equally characterized by simplicity and unity. This simplicity is reflected in the few political divisions of the continent.

All the political divisions of North America reach from ocean to ocean, with the exception of little San Salvador. In Mexico and Central America the diminishing width of the continent made such expansion easy, especially since it was guided by military conquest, despite the isolation of fending mountain barrier. The great breadth of the northern section was traversed in Canada before it was in the United States. Here physiographic conditions were all conducive to early expansion, especially when the method was that of the far-ranging voyageur. No mountain barrier like the Appalachian system discouraged early progress. The St. Lawrence owed its great significance in early days to the fact that it alone opened a way from the east into the central valley of the continent. Beyond, the Great Lakes and the low plains of the Saskatchewan carried the early explorer three fourths of the distance across the continent to the foot of the Rockies, which bend rapidly towards the west after entering Canadian territory. Lower passes in the mountains and the absence of deserts, due to the lower level and narrower width of the highlands, further expedited Canadian overland advance. Hence from the Gulf of St. Lawrence to Puget Sound was the easiest and earliest line of expansion from the Atlantic to the Pacific. Furthermore, the severity of the Canadian climate, the consequent smaller incentive to slow agricultural conquest of the country, and the greater temptation to the nomadic exploitation of the fur trade, stimulated the advance towards the west. These conditions of topography and climate explain the fact that the Lewis and Clark expedition made their explorations in the light of data furnished chiefly by Hudson's Bay Company factors.

In the United States geographical features were not quite so favorable, and yet were not adverse to westward expansion. On the threshold of the continent stood the Appalachian barrier, but there were five great routes across or around this; by the St. Lawrence and the Great Lakes, by the Hudson and the Mohawk Valley, by the line of the Potomac and the Ohio, by the Appalachian Valley and Cumberland Gap, and by the open way through northern Georgia. Beyond, the mighty Mississippi system, built for intercourse, gave ready access to the threshold of the Rocky Mountain portals. The great width of the Cordilleras, flanked on the east by arid plains which long kept at arm's length the frontier of continuous settlement, and on the west by wide stretches of desert, drained by cañon-cutting rivers unfit for navigation, and scantily supplied with grass for fodder or wood for camp-fires, greatly increased the difficulty of American expansion.

But difficulty is always a relative term and must be measured by the means of overcoming it. The Alleghenies to a race in its infancy were quite as serious an obstacle as the Rockies to the same race in its prime. Frontier conditions along the Mississippi and Missouri trained a people able to cope with the conditions of the transmontane journey of two thousand miles. Life in the plains and backwoods had become second nature to men from whom the need of luxury had been eliminated. Mere space, unconstrained existence, a buffalo hunt, or an Indian fray was pleasure enough. In the large, fresh environment of the American continent the English race had been born again and now was animated with the irrepressible vigor of a youthful people. A constant change of environment had given them the adaptability of youth; vast opportunity had bred the spirit of venture and enterprise. Nothing seemed impossible and therefore little was impossible.

The advance from the Alleghenies to the Mississippi and from the Mississippi to the Pacific was natural. And in this advance the large and simple structure of the continent kept the Americans one people. Each mountain barrier in turn was regarded as a possible line of political division until the intercourse made possible by gaps and approaching streams was developed by the mechanical power of the people. The spirit of separation in the young trans-Allegheny commonwealths was short-lived. Later on the Pacific coast, the most truly isolated portion of United States territory, the idea was current that California and Oregon were destined by geographic conditions to form an independent state. This sentiment was voiced in Congress more than once.[2] And the prompt survey for a transcontinental railroad after the acquisition of California pointed to the government's fear of losing this peripheral possession. The work of construction was long postponed, however, until in 1862 rumors that the people of the Pacific slope, tired of waiting for overland communication, proposed erecting an independent republic, and the report of a Confederate invasion of New Mexico induced Congress to lend government aid to the Union Pacific Railroad.[3]

[2] McMaster, J. B., *History of the People of the United States*, New York, 1902, V, 26. Bancroft, H. H., *History of Oregon*, San Francisco, 1884, I, 350–80.

[3] Sparks, E. E., *Expansion of the American People*, Chicago, 1900, p. 368.

EXPANSION AND SCIENTIFIC BOUNDARIES

Every forward step in American expansion meant a more scientific boundary. Behind every process of rounding out the contour of our political territory lay the geographical motive. The Mississippi was only a line of demarcation. Long before the Louisiana Purchase or the discovery of the Columbia, Jefferson saw the value of a Pacific front. The line of the Rocky Mountain watershed, especially as reinforced by the desert beyond, was the highly scientific boundary secured with the Louisiana country; but the ocean is the only absolute boundary, and beyond lay the Pacific. A seacoast is valuable chiefly on account of its ports, and of these the slightly indented shore of the Pacific in all its vast length south of Puget Sound afforded few. Entrenched at first on the short strip of coast between 42° north latitude and the Columbia, the United States had only the mouth of the river for a harbor; but the vast inlet of Puget Sound was secured by the compromise of the "Oregon Question," San Francisco Bay by the conquest of California, while by the treaty made with Mexico in 1848 the international boundary line was made to bend slightly south of west between the mouth of the Gila River and the coast in order to include in United States territory the excellent harbor of San Diego. The United States was also guaranteed the free navigation of the Gulf of California and the Colorado River to the confluence of the Gila.

The Gila River boundary, as fixed by the Mexican cession, was corrected by the Gadsden Purchase in 1853 of land to the southern watershed. This again represented an advance from an unscientific to a scientific frontier. The Gila River occupies a depression which divides the northern from the Mexican Cordilleras, and which is "one of the most important topographical features in North America."[4] It possesses a strategic value as a natural passway through the mountains and deserts to the west, and therefore its control could not be shared with another power. The easiest trail, as we have seen, approached it by the southern affluents of the Gila. It was the natural route to the Pacific from the coast of Texas, where the highway of the Gulf landed a west-bound traveler a hundred miles farther on his way than a Missouri steamboat which put him ashore at Kansas City. In the Gila depression the first survey for a transcontinental railroad was made as the most obvious route, and here finally was constructed the Southern Pacific line, on the southern side of the valley. The Gadsden Purchase was decried as a wasteful expenditure of ten million dollars for forty-five thousand square miles of poor land almost unfit for occupation. But never was money better spent. The value of the tract is not to be estimated by its fitness for agriculture, but by its strategic importance as a passway to the Pacific which is always open on account of its lower levels and more southern location, when the northern routes are blocked by snow.

The southern boundary is continued by land along the Rio Grande, which serves as a convenient though rather unreliable line of demarcation. From the mouth of this river the United States territory reaches the sea again. The great westward-bending inlet of the Gulf of Mexico creates a southern coast for the United States, which therefore from Key West to the Rio Grande faces South America and not Europe, though washed by Atlantic waters. Confined at first to the strip between the Sabine River and Lake

[4] Ratzel, F., *Politische Geographie der Vereinigten Staaten*, Leipzig, 1897, p. 33.

Pontchartrain, the republic with persistent effort worked to broaden her base on the Gulf in order to control the natural outlets of her southern and western country, and give it the absolute boundary of the sea.

The eastern and western boundaries of the United States are alike in being entirely oceanic except for part of Maine. The southern boundary is land in its western half, water in its eastern; so too the northern boundary. The international frontier of Canada and the United States extends from Lake Superior overland westward along the forty-ninth parallel to Georgia Strait, whence it continues south and west through Haro and San Juan de Fuca Strait to the Pacific; eastward from northern Minnesota to northern New York the boundary is defined by the Great Lakes, three short connecting rivers, and the broad channel of the St. Lawrence.[5] Though these "Mediterranean Seas" are fresh water, they have played as great a part as a marine highway in opening up the interior of the country as has the Gulf of Mexico, and that in spite of the fact that they receive no great affluent like the Mississippi to enhance their importance.

Everywhere the contour of the United States territory is simple and as far as possible natural. Any line separating it from Canada in the west must be artificial because the valleys, plains, and mountains of the one country continue into the other without topographical division; but the forty-ninth parallel has the advantage of brevity. Moreover, it was easy to draw such an artificial line of political division in the remote, almost uninhabited regions of the Northwest. The international boundary of New England, however, is long, irregular, and follows natural features only for a short

[5] Ratzel, F., *op. cit.*, p. 35.

distance along the St. Lawrence watershed, the St. John and the St. Croix rivers. Contrasted with the northwest frontier and the Mexican boundary, "it marks the contrast in effect of contact with an old and organized state and a politically new and unorganized one." [6]

Such were the limits which the republic wrought out for itself by 1853. The territory which it acquired was confined almost wholly to the mainland. This is its distinguishing characteristic. Its islands are few, small, and close inshore. Island acquisitions were renounced in the struggle for continental aggrandizement, though some lively diplomatic battles were fought for the possession of the outlying fragments in Passamaquoddy Bay in the negotiations fixing the eastern boundary of Maine.

THE UNITED STATES AS AN AMERICAN POWER

Another geographic factor in the growth of the United States to a continental power was to be found in its isolation from Europe. The wide barrier of the Atlantic which furthered political independence stimulated economic independence and a rapid development of natural resources more extensive than intensive. This involved expansion. The young republic of 1776 which turned its back upon the Old World set its face systematically towards its own vast hinterland; it was animated by a continental policy in 1783 in claiming territory beyond the Alleghenies to the Mississippi. This policy was shadowed forth yet more distinctly in the Louisiana Purchase and the Lewis and Clark expedition, and twenty years later reached a novel and lasting expression in the Monroe Doctrine.

[6] Ratzel, *op. cit.*, p. 36.

This national principle was enunciated because geographic conditions made it possible. Geographic isolation suggested and dictated its oldest and fundamental proposition, that of our non-interference in the internal concerns of European powers. "Our detached and distant situation," said Washington, "invites and enables us to pursue a different course" from that of Europe with its international entanglements. "Why forego the advantages of so peculiar a position?"[7] The obvious corollary of this proposition was the non-interference of Europe in American affairs,[8] which could best be secured by calling a halt to European colonization on the American continents and the reassertion of European dominion over successfully rebellious colonies. This principle, foreshadowed again by Jefferson, was formally stated first to meet Russian aggressions on the northwest coast, which the United States hoped to make its own through the Oregon claim, before it was embodied in Monroe's message to Congress in December, 1823; so that it was designed to protect the territorial plans of the nation. It was formally adopted as a national policy to protect the Central and South American republics which had been enabled by a remote peripheral position and the dividing expanse of the Atlantic to secure their independence. The third proposition of the Monroe Doctrine, the purpose of the United States to interpose in defense of the independence of any American nation against any attempted conquest by a European state, was undoubtedly reinforced by the knowledge that geographic isolation would enable the champion to interfere successfully. A broad military base near at hand on the Atlantic, Gulf, and Pacific, as opposed to the remoteness of the European

[7] Washington's Farewell Address, September, 1795.
[8] Foster, J. W., *A Century of American Diplomacy*, Boston, 1900, p. 441.

powers, even with their narrow footholds in the Caribbean Sea, would give to the United States the advantage in any inter-continental war.

The leadership in the American continents assumed by the United States in the enunciation of the Monroe Doctrine has its final basis in geographical conditions. Identical as to the dominant race, Canada and the United States differ only in the seats of their respective dominions; hence climate, soil, location, and natural features have been the differentiating factors in their history. In the contest of expansion which resulted in this leadership, Great Britain was the most dangerous competitor of the United States; it was an American power with large interests in this continent which could be seriously marred by new appropriations of territory by its republican rival. But the center of British power was extra-continental in relation to America: the broad interoceanic belt of Canada was not enough to dominate the western continent. "The United States had all its forces on the ground and no distracting interests in other parts of the world. Hence in all the debatable territory England gave way. Texas was annexed without opposition; Oregon was divided; California was conquered."[9]

The isolation of North America gradually eliminated the lesser European rivals of the United States in the western hemisphere, and enabled her by securing some of their previous holdings on the mainland to carry out her continental policy of compact growth, which made for strength in the struggle with England for continental control. The compact political territory, having little exposed surface as frontier, is less vulnerable than the widely scattered political area, and can expend all its powers at will in any one direc-

[9] Hart, A. B., *The Foundation of American Foreign Policy*, New York, 1901, p. 36.

tion, just as Russia throws its great weight today against the wall of the Hindu Kush, tomorrow against the buffer of Manchuria. The United States has in general directed its efforts at only one thing at a time and that with success, because its energies have not been dissipated as have England's.

Geographical location has been the most powerful factor in this leadership; it has given the United States advantages over both Brazil and Canada, the only other two large territorial powers of the western hemisphere. Canada has, like the American republic, an interoceanic position, but it is too far from the center of things to make its influence felt widely, and has too severe a climate to permit the development of the dense population necessary for strength. Brazil has the fertility and area, but its tropical location will always limit the energy of its people, even if we leave out of consideration the limitations for leadership native to the Latin races; and Brazil's want of a Pacific and Caribbean seacoast must confine its sphere of influence largely to the Atlantic.

The location of the United States makes it the master of the situation. It alone has a location wholly in the temperate zone, stretching from ocean to ocean. Thus it has a population energetic by reason of an invigorating climate and multitudinous because of the large and fertile area of the country. Its extension to the Pacific and the Panama Canal brings it into relation with the western states of South America, while its long coast-line on the Gulf of Mexico makes it the leading Caribbean power. Its position in the North Atlantic opposite Europe makes it the great maritime doorkeeper of the western world. Thus this central belt of the North American continent was geographically determined as the seat of control of the new hemisphere. This destiny was fixed by its colonization by the sturdy Anglo-Saxon race.

THE UNITED STATES A WORLD POWER

The evolution of the place of the United States in world politics is interesting. In its colonial days, America, as merely the western periphery of Europe and an appanage of the Old World, was subjected to all the international forces which swayed her sovereigns. European wars had episodic campaigns on American soil, and provisions as to American territory figured in all their treaties from Ryswick to Paris (1763).[10] For a short time after the Revolution the young republic was embarrassed by some responsibilities to France, heritages from the time it formed a part of the European body politic, which led France to think it might be used as an ally against England. But in the isolation of its new environment, the United States quickly threw off its European connections, worked out its destiny as the foremost American state, became an interoceanic continental power, then a hemisphere power, dominating the international affairs of North and South America.

For a long time this domain absorbed the activities of the United States. Geographic isolation was so strong in its suggestion that there was no temptation to extra-continental political activity; but even in this period of apparent quietude the seeds of further expansion were germinating — expansion which was to lead the United States beyond the confines of its hemisphere, now grown too narrow, to take its place as a world power. Isolation gave to the infant

[10] Hart, A. B., *op. cit.*, p. 3.

giant that protected position which fostered political development on a large scale, just as the segregating environment of the Greek city-states achieved for those a similar development on a small scale, until in these latter days, issuing from the seclusion of its hemisphere, the United States has participated as a world power in an increasing degree in the affairs of the entire globe.

In the multifarious world relationships of the present, the geographic factors of relative isolation continue to assert themselves, despite the growth in complexity of their influence. Until the World War, the country's community of interests with Europe could be epitomized in the act of the early trapper in shipping his furs across the Atlantic. With regard to Asia and Latin America, as well as Canada, if reversed the connection was essentially the same. In the years since the Armistice, the diversity of ties has grown with vertiginous speed. The United States, no longer dominantly a producer of raw materials, but highly developed industrially, quickens the activities of older nations; at the same time, the country gradually and naturally takes to itself many of their affairs. The world-wide reproof to the Hawley-Smoot tariff opened many eyes; even more enlightening is a revelation of the nationality of the foreign protests. In the World Court or League of Nations, whether marked by official participation by the United States or not, American interest will frequently oppose American interest.

Having gained an all-round economic life, the United States, while aiding old countries, has lent a helping hand to the developments in new areas. The amazing growth of American investments in Latin America shows how much the United States has done for this area as well as for others. The riches resulting from vast resources to an undeveloped country meant prolongation of healthy existence. To the United States, also, that good health has had great significance; for it has assured supplies of raw materials of types which this country either cannot produce because of conditions of physical geography or will not produce because of advancing economic age. The wool trade is an outstanding illustration of economic age; coffee aptly exemplifies the interchange resulting from limitations of physical geography.

Towards the ancients of Asia, the attitude of the United States has closely paralleled that of Europe. China and India have been considered primarily as markets for manufactured commodities. Some of their produce the United States used, but the main interest lay in what this country could sell to them. The active concern of the United States in Japanese aggression in Manchuria and China attests the vast importance of the needs of a populous though poverty-stricken country.

Inextricably engaged in commercial and financial activity the world over, the country concomitantly bears the political consequences. Though students and statesmen at Washington and in foreign lands urge the United States to withdraw from European entanglements, Latin-American politics and investments, or other world affairs as quickly as possible, a complete withdrawal is well-nigh impossible with our huge commercial ties and investments.

SIZE AND UTILITY

The size of the United States has been determined largely by the continental build of North America. We have seen how its simple structure facilitated western expansion and preserved the unity of the people. We have seen how the ranks of the future nation were drawn up in compact form along the narrow Atlantic littoral between the mountains and the sea, how the line of march was flanked by the Great Lakes on the north and the Gulf on the south, how the Mississippi carried the outbound conquerors southward to the Gulf and the Ohio tributaries carried them north to the Lakes; how the length of the Mississippi became the base for the next advance. The imperfect geographical knowledge of 1783, supposing the sources of this river to be northwest of the Lake of the Woods, by a happy mistake fixed the incipient point of the northwest boundary beyond the headwaters of the Mississippi, and thereby increased the dimension of the United States along the ninety-fifth meridian.

Confined between the Lakes and the Gulf, the natural outlet of growing powers was towards the west. Had the continent been wider, its width would have been mastered, though perhaps more slowly; had the Mississippi been longer, its greater length could have been as easily controlled, providing its geographical nature remained the same. The effect of the continental build, combined with the constricting influence of the Great Lakes and the Gulf, has been to give the United States a predominant east-and-west direction, with a dimension twice as great as that from north to south; to keep it within relatively narrow zonal limits, away from tropical heat or polar cold, and yet to lend it the enormous area of three million square miles.

Geographic conditions further conspire to make by far the larger part of this area available (Figs. 14 and 15).[11]

[11] In 1924, crop land occupied about 21 per cent of the land area of the United States. Pasture and grazing land, not including woodland pasture, accounted for 44 per cent, and forest or cut-over land about 26 per cent. Of the remaining 9 per cent, 7 per cent lies in waste land — ungrazed deserts and marshes, bare rocks, and sandy beaches — 2 per cent in roads, railroads, cities, parks, etc. (Baker, O. E., "A Graphic Summary of American Agriculture Based Largely on the Census," *Miscellaneous Publication*, No. 105, Department of Agriculture, Washington, 1931, p. 28.)

Through the great central trough of the continent sweep the cold winds of the north and the warm moisture-laden breezes of the Gulf, modifying in turn the climate of Minnesota and of Texas. The narrow width and lower level of the northern Rockies admit the Pacific winds, which bring warmth and moisture to Montana and the Dakotas. There is no other continuous political area of like size which contains so large a proportion of territory adapted to the habitation of man. This huge expanse, through encouraging effort to save time by overcoming mere space, rapidly brought the United States to the front in means for national transport. The development of far-flung systems of transportation and their effectiveness today in vessel, railroad, highway, or air route showed early realization of the principle that the size of a land is to be measured finally in terms of the population it can support and bring to a high degree of civilization; amount and effectiveness of population is the measure of power.

Effect of Size on People. The effect of the size of their country can be traced in the ideas of the American people, which are marked by a certain largeness and daring. The small territorial standards of the early European settlers here became profoundly modified by American continental conditions. The mere area of the individual states increases from the east towards the west. The commonwealths of New England seem pigmies in size compared with the trans-Mississippi states. There are twenty-six states in the smaller half of the country east of the Mississippi, and only

Note to Fig. 14:

Three quarters of the land in farms in the country is in the Mississippi Valley. The distribution of land in farms shows the utility of the plains with an annual rainfall of more than 20 inches. Compare with Figs. 12 and 15. (Courtesy of the United States Department of Agriculture.)

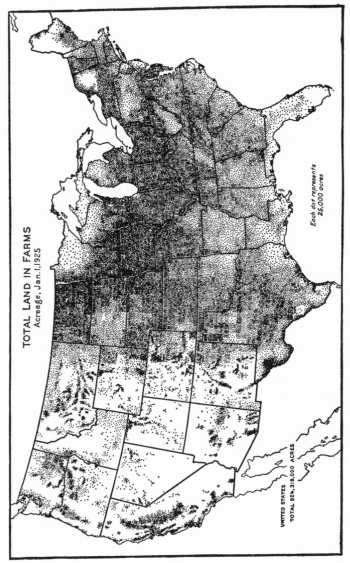

FIG. 14. TOTAL LAND IN FARMS (See note at foot of page 244)

twenty-two west of it. The greater aridity of the western states, their consequent sparsity of population, and also the rapidity with which immigrants spread over them account in part for this larger area. The Senate will always be the legislative stronghold of the eastern states, where representation is based upon units, not on population. The West can therefore look for growing power only in the House, where increasing population will increase their representation.

Everywhere one notices a certain largeness of view in the ordinary Westerner. Even when uncultured and crude from lack of opportunity, he never takes a contracted view of things. He measures things with a big yardstick. The nomadic instinct is still in him, handed down by his emigrant forebears. Wherever he is found, he has always come there from somewhere else. Hence he is never provincial, and he is intensely, broadly American. Distance never appalls him. If he is a Californian, he "steps over the mountains into Nevada," literally on foot if the fancy take him, with as little ado as if he were walking around the corner; or he crosses half the continent by rail or airplane for a two days' visit at Chicago. His point of view is therefore bred of his geographically wide experiences and his intercourse with the other highly mingled populations of the western states.

"The struggle for existence is a struggle for space," says Ratzel. Abundant space in the United States has meant abundant opportunity and a chance for all to rise; it has developed in the Americans a powerful initiative and encouraged the democratic spirit. Thus, as the isolation of

Note to Fig. 15:

From Massachusetts to western Missouri the native forest vegetation has given way to the plow and the reaper; compare with Figs. 12 and 14. (Courtesy of the United States Department of Agriculture.)

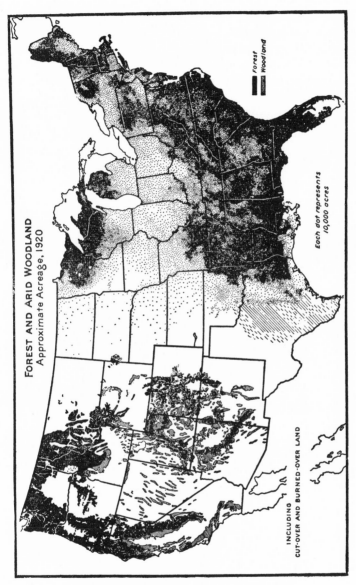

FIG. 15. FOREST AND ARID WOODLAND
(See note at foot of page 246)

North America helped the early colonists to divest themselves of European monarchical principles of government,
so the size of our country has kept classes and masses on a
nearly equal footing by equality of opportunity. Everywhere the "four hundred" tends to recruit itself from the
"four million" near by. The transcontinental expansion of
the American people has made them masters in "the struggle for space."

CHAPTER XIII

THE GEOGRAPHY OF THE INLAND
WATERWAYS

THE simplicity of build which gives to the North American continent its few large features of valley, plain, and mountain range has been the chief determinant in producing its few large groups of navigable rivers; for these are always the product of big, well-watered areas of simple form and gentle slopes. The complex, fragmentary topography of western Europe is too much broken up to develop a great river system. The continental structure of Australia favors a large central system like the Mississippi; but the location of its mountain ranges on the eastern rim, where they intercept the moisture of the trade-winds, robs the wide, interior region of its water. Africa has thousands of miles of navigable waterways high up on the surface of its plateau, but the steep escarpment of this mesa continent bars every river approach from the sea with falls and rapids a few miles back from the coast.

CONTINENTAL BUILD OF NORTH AMERICA
AND INLAND WATERWAYS

Everywhere in North America, except in the western Cordilleras, an easy gradient marks the descent from highland to sea. The natural obstacles to navigation are few and slight. The Ohio from the edge of the Allegheny Mountains to its mouth has only one partial interruption to navigation in the so-called "Falls" at Louisville, over which however, steamers formerly passed for a part of the year.[1] The Missouri pours along its smooth, yellow tide for 2285 miles from the head of navigation at Fort Benton without another break to its mouth, seventeen miles above St. Louis.[2] The gradient of the Mississippi's bed becomes pronounced only above St. Paul, while insignificant watersheds barely suffice to bar the sources of its tributaries from the Laurentine Lakes, or from the Red River of the North which, through Lake Winnipeg, finds its way to Hudson Bay.

Everywhere east of the Rockies the chief drainage systems of the continent approach very near on some low divide at one or several points. Here were located the portages which extended the network of inland commerce in the days of bark canoe and beaver-skin cargo. Here later were built the canals which answered to the demand of spreading settlement and increasing trade, and linked the Atlantic rivers with the St. Lawrence, the Great Lakes, and the eastern branches of the Mississippi. Thus the topography of the country enabled even these abundant water connections to be vastly extended by artificial means. The waterway of the Hudson River, Erie Canal, and Great Lakes has a length of 1360 miles from New York to Duluth. The chief lateral branches of the Mississippi, the Missouri and Ohio, afford river connection from Fort Benton in western Montana to

[1] The falls at Louisville were difficult at all times, and at certain seasons impossible to navigate, not only for early craft, but also for the steamboat; in 1817 it was estimated that five thousand flatboats passed over the falls each year and that three thousand of them required pilots (*Liberty Hall and Cincinnati Gazette*, March 12, 1817). A canal sixty-four feet wide, and with three locks of equal lift at the western end, was completed in 1830 and enlarged in 1921. (*Transportation in the Mississippi and Ohio Valleys*, Transportation Series No. II, War Department, Washington. 1929, pp. 15–19.)

[2] Though a great waterway in steamboat days on the rivers, it is little used today. Above Kansas City it has not a dependable depth in excess of three feet to Sioux City and two and one half feet to Pierre.

Pittsburgh, a distance of 3470 miles, and the old canal links between the Ohio and Lake Erie formerly extended this water route to the Atlantic. The east-and-west direction of the Ohio and Lake route was a strong factor in the union of the early East and West, counterbalancing the centrifugal influence of the Mississippi. And earlier still, the close approach of the Potomac and Ohio, and the ease of intercourse along the highroad between their respective heads of navigation, was one of the chief reasons for locating the national capital at Washington.

The Atlantic rivers, where they are navigable, whether naturally or rendered so by canals, facilitate chiefly an east-and-west connection. The Mississippi system is most important as a highway between the northern and southern borders of the country. Northward from the line of the Ohio and the Missouri, as far as the great bend at Kansas City, this north-and-south connection is manifold. That of the main stream is reinforced by the upper Missouri to the west and by the Illinois and Ohio to the east. Southward from the Ohio only the main stream of the Mississippi forms the conjunction with the Gulf. The value of the Mississippi as a waterway is enhanced greatly by the fact that it traverses the United States across the constricted area between the Lakes and the Gulf, while these two water bodies, fresh and salt, find their value enhanced in turn by the connecting waterway of the mighty stream.[3]

If we leave out of consideration the abrupt eastward projection of the state of Maine, the ninety-seventh meridian is found to mark the medial line of the United States and also the western limit of abundant inland navigation (Fig.16). Corpus Christi, the western terminus of coastwise navigation

[3] Ratzel, F., *Politische Geographie der Vereinigten Staaten*, Leipzig, 1897, p. 19.

on the Gulf, and the heads of navigation on the Red River and the Arkansas are located almost exactly on this ninety-seventh meridian. Beyond this line only the Missouri affords a navigable course to the foot of the Rockies. Scanty rainfall and shallow, shifting beds render the other streams unfit for transportation.

The western part of the United States embraced in the broad band of the Cordilleran upheaval, in consequence of a very complex topography combined with extreme aridity, has developed no long river systems navigable from the sea. Aridity has produced the prevailing cañon formation and the fluctuating volume of water which in the long dry season will float only the shallowest boats. The lower Colorado, after it issues from the Grand Cañon, will carry vessels of eighteen-inch draft from Eldorado in southern Nevada four hundred miles to its mouth. But this sole river outlet to the south has little value because of the desert country and scanty population which it serves. The imprisoned streams and lakes of the Great Basin have been of service merely in furnishing a line of oases which directed the route of the California Trail. Only aridity, due to the encircling mountains, has prevented these streams from developing the volume necessary to cut away the slight opposing barrier, and uniting to a system to find an outlet along the general slope of the Basin to the north.

The gentle curve of the Sierra Nevada and Cascade Mountains marks the eastern limit of the inland waterways of trans-Rocky America. What is found behind the barrier

Note to Fig. 16:

Of vital significance to the explorer, trapper and trader the rivers pointed the way for the advance of the settler, and carried his produce to market. River and canal transportation reached its peak about 1860 before the industrialization of the country and before strangling competition with railways. Compare with Figs. 17 and 30.

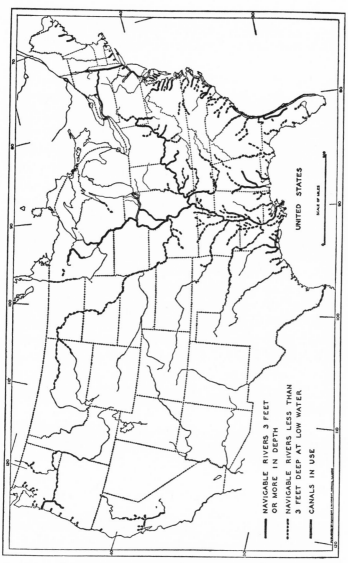

FIG. 16. CANALS AND NAVIGABLE RIVERS OF THE
UNITED STATES   (See note at foot of page 252)

of these ranges counts for little or nothing, and the aggregate of that beyond is only small. Puget Sound, with its nineteen thousand miles of shore-line, owing to its predominant north and south direction, finds its most eastern point only about one hundred and twenty miles from the sea. The Columbia, accessible to ocean vessels a hundred miles from the Pacific, has continuous navigation only a hundred miles farther to the Dalles, where the river rushes down through the narrow gateway of the Cascade Range. The long valley formed by the Sierra Nevada and Cascade Mountains on the east and the Coast Range on the west is occupied in the north by the Willamette, navigable for small steamers and river craft for one hundred and twenty-five miles. Farther south this is continued by the submerged river mouth forming San Francisco Bay with its tributary streams of the Sacramento and San Joaquin, which together afford a north and south waterway of shallow depth for less than three hundred miles. But like Puget Sound, all these rivers except the Columbia, owing to their location in a great longitudinal valley following the axis of the mountains, reach points less than one hundred and twenty-five miles back from the Pacific.

NAVIGABLE WATERWAYS AND ECONOMIC DEVELOPMENT

The abundance of inland waterways in the East and the paucity in the West has greatly differentiated the economic history of these two sections of the United States. Every country of large extent finds its navigable rivers, next to the fertility of its soil, the most important factors of its early development. The one is fundamental to the production of wealth and the other to its distribution and exchange. Small countries with deeply indented coast-lines, like Greece, Norway, England, and areas like New England, can renounce the advantage of big river systems; but in Russia, Argentina, Venezuela, Colombia, the United States, Canada, Egypt, India, and China, the history of the country, political and economic, is indissolubly connected with that of its great rivers. Large areas mean great distances, hence long lines of transportation, which are most easily and cheaply furnished by natural waterways;[4] and the complete exploitation of such natural advantages has been in all times a condition and measure of commercial preëminence. The strength of Venice and the Lombard League found its geographic basis in the Adriatic, the roads across the Alpine passes to the north, east, and west, and the navigation of the Po and Adige. The League of the Rhine towns flourished by reason of the Rhone-Rhine highway across western Europe. The Hanseatic cities from Bruges all the way east to the Russian Novgorod owed their commercial supremacy largely to the great rivers behind them from the Scheldt to the Volga.[5] In France the signal for a marked industrial and commercial development was the construction by Colbert in the seventeenth century of a series of canals across the central plateau of the country, designed to unite the sources of all its radiating streams and perfect a wonderful system of inland waterways. The interior trade of China today moves largely by river and canal; and this country remains the classical example of waterway supremacy. The foreign "spheres of influence" there are

[4] Ratzel, F., *Anthropogeographie*, Stuttgart, 1899, p. 341.

[5] Semple, Ellen C., "Development of the Hanse Towns," *Journal of the American Geographical Society*, XXXI, No. 3 (1899), pp. 236-255.

indicated generally in terms of the great Chinese rivers, because these "spheres" are commercial areas tributary to the river highways.

Early settlement and expansion of population in the United States, falling as it did in a period prior to the rapid development of transportation by means of railroads, and being confined to the well-watered Atlantic slope of the continent, developed, as we have seen in the previous chapters, largely by reason of waterway facilities. Line of river and lake invited and directed the westward movement, distributed the outbound settlers along remote tributaries, and the next year conveyed the produce from the newly opened lands back to the seaboard markets. For every outgoing stream of people to the West, there was a return current of trade, steadily increasing in amount, variety, and value, which moved along these same channels. Later, when railroads were introduced, the inland waterways remained as a cheap competitor of the steel roads, regulating their freight charges particularly in the area from the Lakes to the Gulf and from the Atlantic to the ninety-seventh meridian.

West of the Mississippi. In the trans-Missouri country with its scanty equipment of waterways, geographic conditions have diffentiated greatly the history of transportation. On the margin of the arid belt, canoe, flatboat, and steamer were discarded; pack-horse, ox-cart, and mule team trekked across the endless stretch of prairie and desert. For the West there was nothing between the creeping pace of the canvas-covered wagon and the railway express — that too in a country where time was money and life, if an early snow threatened to block the mountain passes, if the scanty pasturage in the desert oases was all consumed, if the food supply had to be reduced to lighten the burden of the exhausted animals, whose dragging, trembling pace made the desert wider, the hope of water more remote.

Here was the land where the railroad found no competitor, a land moreover of "long hauls" and "through freight," except for the sacks of wool from the scattered highland ranches, and the cases of canned vegetables dropped off at the lonely shacks of the desert road-keepers. Wherever the cheap highways of rivers and lakes are lacking, railroads must develop so much the more rapidly. [6] The sparsity of population along their route diminishes the local business and hence the profits; but the absence of waterway competition facilitates formulation of policy and tariff. Railroads have assumed an incalculable importance in Australia because of the paucity there of permanently navigable streams. Similarly, the Union of South Africa, an extensive area without water communication, has constructed nearly fourteen thousand miles of railroad in spite of the youth of the country and the sparsity of its white population.

In a like manner, our West has developed railroads at an enormous rate, in spite of sparsity of population, owing to the economic necessity of connecting two opposite coasts which serve two areas of trans-oceanic commerce and which supply complementary products. Freed from the regulating control of competing waterways, the western lines early were in the position of a monopoly. Hence the greater danger in their "community of interests" system and the bitter fight against it in the western states. The nearest rival of the overland roads is the Panama Canal, which makes itself felt as far north as the northernmost transcontinental railway.

[6] Ratzel, F., *Anthropogeographie*, Stuttgart, 1899, p. 342.

Twenty-five years after our trans-Rocky expansion had begun in earnest, an overland railroad united the Pacific with the Atlantic seaboard. Transportation development in the far West sprang from the trail to the steel track, omitting the intervening stage of constructed highroad on the one hand and unretarded by the presence of waterways on the other. In the eastern half of the United States, land routes felt everywhere in the early days the severe competition of inland navigation. The abundance of excellent waterways tended to discourage the construction of highroads except such as led across mountain barriers, like the old coach-road from Philadelphia to Pittsburgh, the Cumberland National Road from the head of canal navigation on the Potomac to Wheeling, and the Wilderness Road across the southern Appalachians; or across the axis of the prevailing streams, like the early post-road from New York and Philadelphia southward along the coast to Charleston, South Carolina, or the extension of the Cumberland National Road from Wheeling westward across the northern tributaries of the Ohio through Columbus, Indianapolis, Terre Haute, and Vandalia. New England, owing to its lack of inland navigation, was the part of the country which earliest developed a complete system of turnpikes and later of railroads.

Rivers of the Eastern Seaboard. Abundant waterways therefore mean prevailing water transportation in the early stage of a country's economic development; the larger the size of a country and the greater its distances, so much the stronger its need of inland navigation, the greater the development and the longer the survival of the same. Owing to the narrowness of the Atlantic plain, its southeastward slope, and the "fall line" at no place very far from the coast,

the career of the Atlantic rivers as avenues of transportation
was short in period and limited in extent. Unlike the Hudson and the rivers of New England, they have served only
east and west communication. Intercourse between North
and South was delegated to coastwise navigation, which
here performed the function of the Mississippi boats in the
interior of the land.

The importance of these Atlantic streams was greatest
in colonial days, because, on account of the small sea craft
then in use, there was less distinction technically between
inland and marine navigation. Furthermore, these rivers,
being small, have suffered relatively more from that necessary contraction of navigable waterways which has resulted
everywhere from the substitution of large steamers for the
shallow boats of the early period. Finally, since in all
water transportation the cost falls largely to the expense of
loading and unloading, the small Atlantic rivers are under
the economic disadvantage of the "short haul." Hence
only those have maintained their importance which, like
the Hudson, St. Lawrence, and lower Delaware are navigable
to sea-going vessels.[7]

WATER TRANSPORTATION IN THE
MISSISSIPPI VALLEY

It was in the great valley of the Mississippi that inland
waterways proved to be a most powerful economic and
political factor. This basin, embracing 1,240,000 square
miles, containing 13,910 miles of streams navigable for
present large river craft and having therefore a much
greater mileage in the day of canoe and pirogue, early ex-

[7] Ratzel, F., *Politische Geographie der Vereinigten Staaten*, Leipzig, 1897, p. 539.

ploited its advantages of water communication, all the more because of the rapid expansion of settlement throughout the valley, the increasing distances to be covered, and the sparsity of its population, which could not bear the expense or even furnish the labor for road-making. In the pioneer days it was downstream travel for the emigrant settler to his new home along the Ohio, the Tennessee, and the middle Mississippi, as later for his produce to the market at New Orleans; but increasing economic development with its more extensive exchanges made an insistent demand for more effective upstream navigation, as for more rapid water communication in general. Hence the introduction of steam as a propelling power solved this problem of the swift western waters.

Steamboat Navigation and Commerce. In 1811 the banks of the Ohio first echoed to the stroke of a steamboat's paddle-wheel;[8] and between 1812 and 1836 eight trans-Allegheny states were admitted to the Union. Shipbuilding became an important industry, centered chiefly in Pittsburgh, Cincinnati, Louisville, and St. Louis, though carried on also at Wheeling and Marietta. All of these cities were situated on the east and west waterway of navigation and traffic; they commanded abundant lumber supplies and especially the iron necessary for machinery and construction which then came from the mines on the upper Ohio system; and finally they commanded skilled labor from the influx of northern settlers with industrial habits such as were not to be found in the slaveholding region farther south. Industrially the line of the Ohio was a boundary zone, embracing in its lower course the economic systems of the North

[8] Meyer, B. H., *History of Transportation in the United States before 1860*, Carnegie Institution of Washington, 1917, pp. 102 ff.

and South. New Orleans essayed steamboat building, but never developed it as did the points along the Ohio. Its geographical location, commanding a sea-route to the manufacturing centers of Europe and the North Atlantic states, and a great river highway for the downstream transportation of its food supplies, made the city independent of all craft but sailboat and barge. The upstream men needed the steamers.

In the year 1818 five steamboats were built at Pittsburgh, one at Wheeling, four at Cincinnati, and four at Louisville, or fourteen in all; the next year Louisville built twelve, Cincinnati six, Pittsburgh two, Wheeling one, and New Orleans two, in all twenty-three for the year 1819. The stimulating effect of the long swift currents of the western rivers upon the building of steamboats may be seen by a comparison of the statistics of this industry in the Mississippi valley and along the Atlantic coast and the Great Lakes, where sailing vessels were adequate to the demand of that time. Up to 1820 there had been built upon the Great Lakes four steamers which measured altogether 831.84 tons, and on the Atlantic coast (exclusive of New England) fifty-two steamers measuring 10,564 tons, as against seventy-one steamers measuring 14,207 tons on the rivers of the Mississippi valley. Even in the next decade, when a continuous band of relatively dense population reached to the southern point of Lake Huron, and the Erie Canal had begun to stimulate traffic on these inland seas, only eight steamers were built on the Lakes.[9]

In 1834 there were on the western rivers two hundred and thirty steamboats, with an aggregate tonnage of thirty-

[9] *Eleventh Census of the United States*, Part II, *Transportation by Water, 1890*, pp. 247, 396 and 397.

nine thousand, and in 1842 there were four hundred and fifty boats measuring ninety thousand tons. The number had reached six hundred in 1843, and twelve hundred in 1848. Such a remarkable development reflects the im-portance of great waterways in a new, vast, and highly productive territory. The vessels were built for the least draught of water, and to stem the strong currents of the rivers. They carried heavy freight, which included both agricultural and manufactured products. On the large, elegantly equipped passenger boats, which made regular winter trips between Cincinnati or St. Louis and New Orleans, gay social life with nightly balls gave to river travel on the Mississippi a local color such as it acquired nowhere else. Less than fifty years separated the ripple of the fur-weighted pirogue, paddled along by the voyageur with his buckskin clothes and half-savage habits, from the mo-notonous splash of the big paddle-wheel and the floating palace with its lights, music, and the polished society of the generous Southland.

Ohio River Ports. The business of forwarding the river commerce absorbed much of the capital and the best energy and talent of the larger Ohio river cities. This was especially the case with Louisville, which exploited the advantages of its location at the natural obstruction made by the falls to continuous navigation. Low water on the falls stopped the passage of vessels over these rapids. Louisville therefore was the natural port for the upper Ohio, and the head of navigation for the lower stream. Finally the increasing importance and value of the river traffic rendered it advisable to open a canal around the falls in 1830; but the tolls charged were so exorbitant that boats plying between Louisville and the South loaded and unloaded at Portland just below the rapids, and the peculiarities of Louisville's geographical location remained unaltered.   Meantime, its steamboat captains, who came from the best elements of the community, were amassing fortunes.

St. Louis.   Similarly St. Louis, by its dominating geographical position at the plexus of the western waterways, became an important agent in the commerce of the Mississippi.[10]   Below St. Louis the depth of the Mississippi was six feet or more, above, only between three and five feet. This fact differentiated transportation on the upper and lower river and made St. Louis a point of reshipment.   It became the outfitting-point for the few early steamers which, between 1813 and 1844, carried supplies far up the Mississippi to the Indian traders operating in its upper courses and the troops stationed at Fort Snelling, near the Falls of St. Anthony; for the boats running on the Missouri River to Independence and Council Bluffs with supplies for the overland trails; and for the steamers of the American Fur Company, which up till 1850 were the only ones to penetrate the wilderness of the upper Missouri above Council Bluffs.   Once a year they set out to gather in the harvest of the winter's hunting and trapping, advancing farther and farther upstream as the fur-fields receded — in 1831 to St. Pierre in South Dakota (1175 miles), and in 1832 to Fort Union just above the mouth of the Yellowstone (1740 miles), which long remained the head of navigation.   As population began to spread up the line of the Missouri in western Iowa between 1859 and 1860, a weekly boat ran from St. Louis to Sioux City, the head of navigation for larger vessels; and when this place became the terminus of the Sioux City and Pacific Railroad in 1868, a steamboat

[10] Hall, James, *The West, its Commerce and Navigation*, 1848. pp. 166–04.

company operated in conjunction with it, carrying private, military, and Indian freight to Fort Benton, the final head of navigation.[11]   A treacherous stream, the Missouri took heavy toll among the early steamboats.   The fluctuation in volume and level between the high-water stages of early spring and early summer made snags and sand-bars a constant menace.   Almost two-thirds of the vessels operating on the river in the early days ingloriously terminated service on a hidden obstruction.

Meanwhile the lines of St. Louis commerce were increasing in number and extent, and the amount of its traffic growing from day to day.   In 1845, when river transportation was at its height and had not yet begun to feel the competition of railroads, a report on the river trade of St. Louis during that year records 2050 steamboat arrivals, aggregating 358,045 tons, besides 346 keel and flat boats.   Of the steamers, 250 came from New Orleans, bringing fine merchandise of foreign or New England manufacture to exchange for the flour and bacon of the more northerly states; 406 came from ports along the Ohio and its tributaries, laden with cargoes of agricultural products for the St. Louis market, or with manufactured goods which had come in from the Atlantic seaboard by the eastern canal routes; 298 came from ports along the Illinois River, 643 from the upper Mississippi, 249 from the Missouri River, and 204 from other ports, chiefly Cairo and intermediate points.[12] These figures reflect the commercial development attained by a young country because of its abundant waterways. The same story comes from another source.   Cairo, at the

[11] *Eleventh Census of the United States*, Part II, *Transportation by Water*, 1890, p. 399.
[12] *Ibid.*, p. 397.

confluence of the Ohio and Mississippi, had an excellent location for keeping tally on the river traffic. A record of all vessels passing that point during the year 1840 stated the number as 4566.

Following the progress of steam navigation and the rapid settling of the country, the growth of commerce on the Mississippi system was enormous, and early initiated a demand for national improvements on the watercourse. These were inaugurated by surveys as early as 1819, but the actual improvements began in 1827 and followed rapidly for the next decade. The beneficiaries at this period were the Missouri, Ohio, Wabash, Cumberland, Tennessee, Arkansas, Red, Bayou Teche, and the main Mississippi with the passes at its mouth. In the early days the depth of water in the outlets sufficed for existing vessels, but in 1875 operations were begun to make New Orleans accessible to ocean steamers. A seaport at a great river's mouth is always the converging point for many lines of inland and of marine navigation. The interests of commerce demand that the contact here of river and ocean should be as extensive and perfect as possible. Hence the outlet of a great river system presents a natural field for the expenditure of large sums to this end, especially in a delta region where the branching of channels multiplies the avenues to the sea, but, owing to their tendency to silt up or shift, require artificial aid to keep them open. Therefore in the delta regions of the Rhine, Scheldt, Po, and Adige, as earlier of the Nile, Ganges, and Chinese rivers, water communication with the sea has been extended and secured by means of canals.[13] Similarly in the United States, the government has expended large sums for the improvement of the passes and bayous of the lower

[13] Ratzel, F., *Anthropogeographie*, Stuttgart, 1899, p. 343.

Mississippi. The Eads jetties, constructed in 1875-79 and subsequently improved many times, are a notable instance of huge expenditure. Appropriations have secured the navigability of the many bayous, while canals give New Orleans additional outlets to the Gulf through Lakes Salvador, Ponchartrain, and Borgne. In its network of waterways the Crescent City resembles in some degree Bruges, Amsterdam, Arles, Cairo, and other delta emporiums.

CANALS AND PROGRESS

As the dividing channels of the lower stream suggest this extension of navigable outlets to increase the lines of communication with the great ocean highway, so the spreading branches of a river source which approach or meet other such head waters over a low divide suggest the extension of inland navigation by the union of two drainage systems through canals.

The gentle slopes which so generally characterize the eastern half of the United States, and the long, low line of the watershed separating the drainage basin of the Great Lakes from that of the Hudson and of the Mississippi, made feasible a system of canals completing the "Great Belt" of navigation from St. Lawrence and New York bays to the Gulf. Every early canoe route of river and portage over lake-dotted or swamp-covered watershed to other river or inland lake beyond pointed the line of a possible waterway, whose first surveyor was the redman coming to sell his winter's hunt of fur, or the voyageur outbound with gaudy merchandise to trade in the Indian camps of the interior. Every such trade-route from the Hudson and the Susquehanna to the Northern Lakes, and from the long chain of lakes to the springs of the Ohio and Mississippi, has been the line of a projected or accomplished canal. And just as in the days of the fur trade, the passway of the Mohawk, Wood Creek, Lakes Oneida and Ontario enabled the Dutch and English to draw the peltries of the great Northwest away from the St. Lawrence down to the Hudson, so the Erie Canal has enriched New York with the wheat, lumber, and animal products of the Lake region to the detriment of Montreal and Quebec. Likewise Canada has considered a short-cut ship canal from Georgian Bay through Lake Nipissing to the railroad down the Ottawa River, along the line of the voyageur's interior route in the old days, in order to secure its hold upon the growing wheat export of Manitoba and the Northwest Territories. As yet, the enormous cost of such a route has prevented realization of the early trader's dream. [See map of Great Lakes portages.]

Men like Washington and Jefferson, who were alive to the political as well as the commercial benefits of communication across the country, saw the possibilities of canals in completing the circuit of vast interior waterways.[14] "Extend the inland navigation of the eastern waters — communicate them as near as possible with those which run westward; — open these to the Ohio; — open also such as extend from the Ohio towards Lake Erie; — and we shall not only draw the produce of the western settlers, but the peltry and fur trade of the Lakes also to our ports... binding the people to us by a chain which can never be broken."[15] In 1786 Congress declared all the portages between the

---

[14] Winsor, J., *The Westward Movement*, pp. 248–56.

[15] Washington, letter to Governor Harrison of Virginia. Old South Leaflets, I, No. 16, Boston.

Ohio basin and the Great Lakes common highways. Albert
Gallatin in his famous report of 1808 [16] pointed out the topographical features of the three low watersheds east of the
Mississippi rendering canal communication between the
East and West possible, and also the four necks of land at
the base of the Atlantic peninsulas which could be pierced
to give a shortened and protected passage for coastwise
navigation from Boston to South Carolina. Many of the
canals proposed in his system had already been attempted
or partially constructed by private corporations. The
Dismal Swamp Canal (1785 to 1794) was even then bringing
shingles from the forests of North Carolina in barges of two
feet draft to Chesapeake Bay, and the Carondelet Canal
(1808) had just given New Orleans an outlet to Lake Ponchartrain. When in July, 1825, the Delaware and Hudson
Canal from Port Jervis to Kingston was begun, the Delaware and Chesapeake was well under way. Raritan Bay
was linked to the Delaware River at Bordentown by an
artificial channel across the neck of the New Jersey peninsula in 1838.

The burning question for the consolidation of the country
was communication between the East and the West. The
consideration of Gallatin's plan for a waterway around the
southern end of the Appalachian barrier by a canal five
hundred and fifty miles long, from tidewater in Georgia
across the upper courses of the Chattahoochee and Mobile
rivers to the Mississippi, was postponed by the Indian
occupation of this country until the introduction of railways
had ushered in a more feasible stage of transportation development. The direct course of the Potomac from the
heart of the Allegheny Mountains suggested a canal over

[16] *American State Papers*, Miscellaneous, I, No. 250, Washington, 1834.

the watershed to the sources of the Ohio. The channel was constructed from Washington to Cumberland, but there abandoned as impracticable. The zigzag course of the Pennsylvania rivers across the Appalachian system, the general parallelism of their flow from northwest to southeast, and the interlocking of their tributaries in the high mountain valleys between suggested the utilization of even this mountain topography for canal communication with the Ohio. The Schuylkill, Lehigh, and Lackawanna were canalled along their lower course, but no means were found to extend any one of these links westward across the intervening range to the Susquehanna; so for this stretch a railroad between Philadelphia and Columbia was substituted. The transmontane canal began therefore at Harrisburg, a little farther up the Susquehanna, and followed this stream and its western tributary, the Juniata, to the base of the Allegheny range. There another short railroad over the summit (2491 feet elevation) made the connection with the western canal down the Conemaugh and Allegheny rivers to Pittsburgh. This Portage Railroad, as it was called, took the place of a proposed tunnel canal forty-two miles long.

This circuitous and complex route, made up of river, canal, and railway, though valuable as an outlet for the mineral products of Pennsylvania, could not serve the purpose of a trans-Appalachian canal. That destiny was left for the Mohawk depression, where the mountains drop to an elevation of only four hundred and forty-five feet above ocean level and where the inland objective was not a single river system like the Ohio with a navigable depth of five feet, but a chain of interior seas with coast-line of nearly four thousand miles, navigable to large vessels propelled by steam or sail, and affording in their turn canal communication to all the vast territory contained in the mighty angle of the Ohio and upper Mississippi.

The Erie Canal.   The first suggestion of the Erie Canal came as a proposition in the New York legislature in 1785 for the improvement of inland navigation at various points between Albany and Oswego.   As the idea of a continuous canal developed, Lake Ontario was still regarded as its western terminus.   This was the canal embodied in Gallatin's report, though even in 1808 the superiority of a longer route direct to Lake Erie was discussed and a proposition for its survey made in the New York assembly.   The exploration of this route disclosed the fact that the series of elevated lakes in central New York would exclude the necessity of constructing expensive reservoirs on the summit level, since the canal would occupy the depression which received the outlet streams of these natural basins.   Here was everything needful for a cross-country waterway of three hundred and sixty-three miles; [17] a deep river leading northward from one of the finest ports in the land, a tributary stream from the west flowing down from a broad low mountain gap, lake feeders on the summit, and a terminus on a line of inland seas.

The competition of Lake Ontario and the St. Lawrence was already deflecting the greater part of New York's internal commerce to Canadian ports, and the Susquehanna was carrying off much of its produce to Chesapeake Bay.   Then came the War of 1812, demonstrating the strategic necessity of a protected, wholly American line of water communication with our western frontier, one which should avoid the

---

[17] Today, the canal, under the name New York State Barge Canal, is the main avenue for a system of four hundred and forty miles of canal and three hundred and fifty miles of canalized river and lake, with a minimum depth for the canal proper of twelve feet.

exposed stretch of Lake Ontario and the obstacle of Niagara Falls.   Military as well as commercial considerations dictated the wisdom of extending an arm of this canal up to Lake Champlain, which in the recent hostilities had occupied as dangerous and isolated a position as had Lake Erie at the time of Perry's operations, and which possessed a further strategic importance as a natural avenue from the Canadian boundary.   Another branch from the main canal at Salina to Oswego on Lake Ontario completed the hold of New York on its frontier lakes.   Thus the Hudson River became the channel through which three distinct streams of commerce moved down to the port in New York Bay, when 1825 saw the formal opening of this great interior waterway. The next year, nineteen thousand boats and rafts from the Erie and Champlain canals filed past West Troy on their way down the river.   Shipbuilding grew up as a regular industry on Lake Champlain, to furnish transportation for the staves, shingles, boards, and potashes seeking the big market to the south.   Warehouses sprang up along the canal bank at Buffalo to receive the grain, lumber, rails, whiskey, fur, and peltry to be forwarded to the seaboard, while boats coming through the canal from the east brought cargoes of salt, furniture, and general merchandise to the bustling Lake Erie port.

The Erie Canal fixed the destiny of New York City, forced it rapidly to preëminence as the national port of entry, and as the center of our export trade.   It shifted the great trans-Allegheny route away from the Potomac, out of the belt of the slaveholding, agricultural South to the free, industrial North, and placed it at the back door of New England, whence poured westward a tide of Puritan emigrants, infusing elements of vigorous conscience and energy into all the northern zone of states from the Genesee River to the Missouri and Minnesota. The prairie lands which these new Westerners cultivated were, by means of the Lakes and the Erie Canal, made tributary to the growing metropolis at the mouth of the Hudson. New York became now commercially, as formerly it had been in a military sense, the keystone of the Atlantic shore arch. Baltimore, Philadelphia, and Boston lost much of their importance, and did not regain it even in part until railroads enabled them to reëstablish interior connections.

The local effects in central New York State were equally marked. The farmer found wheat quadrupled in price and the timber from his newly cleared land in reach of the market, for transportation from Buffalo to Albany declined in the twenty-six years after the opening of the canal from $88 to $5.98 a ton. But the farmer about Cleveland or Detroit also profited by these advantages. The consequence was that the price of land along the Erie Canal did not rise as rapidly as was anticipated, because the cheap and abundant prairie lands along the upper lakes were drawn like their products into the market, on the economic principle that every extension of transportation facilities tends to enlarge the area of competition.

However, there was compensation in the industrial impulse given by the abundant water-power developed by the canal and its feeders from the upland lakes. Mills and manufactories of great importance sprang up along the entire length of the New York state canals, as later on the Ohio canals. Especially pails, tubs, and woodenware were fashioned out of the adjacent forest by turning lathes run by water. The manufactured products found a market east and west by the Erie Canal. Water-power though cheap was local and immobile; hence unless it commanded transportation facilities, it had comparatively little value. Along the Erie Canal the water-power was one with the waterway, and for this reason reproduced in part the economico-geographical advantages of New England's early manufacturing towns which were situated along the line where river falls and ocean tide met.

Ohio Canals. Upon the West the Erie Canal had a marked effect, not only by carrying thither new accessions of population and bringing out its produce, but also by stimulating the western states to open up their interiors by canals in order to profit by the through waterway to the East. This influence was first felt in Ohio, where a long lake frontier on the north, narrow width between Lake Erie and the navigable course of the Ohio on the south and east, full-flowing interior rivers, and general location near the western terminus of the canal, suggested the feasibility and advantages of an extensive system of artificial waterways, while its relatively dense population, due to its proximity and accessibility to old centers of settlement in the East, enabled the state to sustain the cost of such improvements. Soon after the work on the Erie Canal had been commenced in 1819, the subject came up before the Ohio legislature. Out of four possible routes — the Great Miami and Maumee valleys, the Sandusky and Scioto rivers, the Cuyahoga and Muskingum, and the Grand and Mahoning — two were chosen. Between 1825 and 1835 the Miami Canal (265 miles) was constructed, uniting Cincinnati with the Maumee, and the Ohio Canal (306 miles), connecting Portsmouth on the Ohio with Cleveland, by way of the Scioto, middle Muskingum, and Cuyahoga valleys. The effect upon the growth and prosperity of the state was enormous, especially of that large central area of prairie farms which had hitherto formed an isolated district, cut off from the highways both of the Ohio and the Lakes, but which now felt the stimulating effect of increased intercourse to the north and to the south. Cleveland and Toledo developed into active lake ports, holding a geographic position similar to that of New York, while Akron, Massillon, and other manufacturing points near the summit level of the canal flourished by reason of the accessible water-power, as did Rome, Syracuse, and Rochester in central New York.

Illinois–Michigan Canal. The stimulating effects of the Erie Canal were felt still farther west. Indiana was eager to take advantage of the low watershed in the northeastern part of its territory to unite the Wabash with the Maumee, and Lake Michigan with Lake Erie; but its plans of internal improvement were so extensive that the sparse population of a new state could not sustain the expense, and works half completed had to be abandoned. The route of the fur-traders from Lake Michigan down the Illinois, which seemed peculiarly adapted to canalization, early (1816) attracted national attention as a military and commercial waterway between the Mississippi and Lake Michigan. The massacre at the mouth of the Chicago River in the War of 1812 emphasized the isolation of the northwest lakes. In 1817, Major Long in his report to Congress regarded such a canal as "first in importance of any in this quarter of the country;" but though projected in 1825, owing to difficulties both technical and financial, it was not opened until 1848, and then proved disappointing as an investment, chiefly because the upper Illinois River needed artificial aid to make it navigable to any but small craft.

The same difficulty was present in the waterway of Green

Bay, Fox River, and the Wisconsin. The canal connecting the great bend of the Wisconsin with the Upper Fox was only two and one third miles long, but the sand-bars of the Wisconsin, the shallow, tortuous course of the Upper Fox, and the numerous rapids necessitating canals on the lower river, robbed this waterway of much of its value, and made it succumb rapidly to railroad competition. These western channels over the Great Lakes watershed, being constructed later (1848–53) than the Erie and Ohio canals, because on the frontier of settlement, felt the deadening grip of the railroad before their traffic had become established, and suffered moreover the disadvantage of reaching less navigable outlets into the Mississippi River.

The "Soo" Canal. The next extension of the Great Lakes waterway to the west was the canal at the Sault Sainte Marie, which made Lake Superior accessible. The Erie Canal, by tapping Lake Erie above Niagara Falls, left to Canada the work of constructing the Welland Canal; but the eighteen feet ascent by lock from Lake Michigan to the level of Lake Superior was a natural task for the United States because of her longer coast-line and hence stronger interests in these more northern lakes. Commercial and military considerations led Canada to construct a similar channel on her side of the line, since Lake Superior is a link in the vast land and water route formed by the Atlantic, St. Lawrence River, Great Lakes, Canadian Pacific Railroad, and Pacific Ocean, which unites England with her colonies in Australia and the Orient.

The "Soo" Canal, opened in 1856, deepened to a ship canal in 1877, deepened again to twenty feet in 1896, and now has a depth of twenty-four and one half feet, developed its full importance only when it reduced the cost of transportation by admitting large vessels. Its consequences then were far-reaching. It aided in bringing about the transfer of the iron industry from the eastern to the western side of the Alleghenies. The iron ore from northern Michigan and Wisconsin is now carried at low freight rates to the manufacturing points in Illinois, Ohio, and western Pennsylvania, but a return westbound traffic in coal from the Erie ports fills the otherwise empty vessels, is carried therefore at a low rate (recently forty cents per net ton) to Duluth, and renders possible the manufacture of iron near the mines.[18] Since 1881 iron ore has furnished far more canal tonnage than all other commodities combined.

While the "Soo" Canal has given great impulse to the manufacturing interests along the southern borders of Lakes Michigan and Erie, it has brought large accession of population to the Lake Superior counties of Michigan, Wisconsin, and Minnesota, stimulated the growth of Lake Superior ports like Duluth, Superior, Two Harbors, and Ashland, and occasioned the development of railroads westward into the Red River valley, whence comes the flour, wheat, and other grains which help swell the freight of the "Soo" traffic, and make it larger in tonnage than the joint total of traffic carried by the Panama and Suez Canals.

Rapidly increasing commerce demanded larger vessels constructed on the most approved pattern and made of steel. The mines near the Lakes provided the material for these and in turn furnished the cargo for the craft when ready for service. The result has been an enormous increase of our

[18] Fairlie, J. A., "The Economic Effects of the Ship Canals," *Annals of the American Academy*, XI, (January, 1898), pp. 54–78.

merchant marine on the Lakes since the deepening of the "Soo" passage. Since 1877, the fleet of lake vessels registered in the United States has grown from 600,000 tons to almost 3,000,000 tons. This fivefold expansion compares favorably with the remarkable growth of the country's ocean fleet, which at its height in 1921 was some four times larger than that of 1877.

Canada and the United States are natural competitors for the commerce of the Great Lakes. The northern country, by a system of deep canals, has fourteen foot navigation from Lake Superior to Montreal. In accordance with the ambitious plans to bring large ocean vessels to the doors of its wheat lands, Canada has expended $125,000,000 on the new Welland Ship Canal. This prodigious enterprise, with a minimum depth of twenty-five feet, in some respects surpasses all other great canals. Montreal suffers, however, from the dangerous navigation of the Lower St. Lawrence, which imposes a very high rate of insurance on vessels bound for Canadian ports. Hence, for example, more Canadian wheat destined overseas seeks the facilities of the Buffalo to New York route than continues on the waterway to Montreal. However, the fact that a large part of the traffic on these inland seas is limited to exchange between Superior and the southern Lakes, and the fact that the raw material worked up in the big manufactures of Illinois, Indiana, Ohio, Michigan, and western Pennsylvania comes out as finished commodities capable of bearing the heavy charges of rail transportation to the seaboard, decrease the amount of freight moving by canal to Atlantic ports and act to the detriment both of New York and Montreal.

Enlargement of the Erie Canal. New York found itself

face to face with the problem of vastly improving the Erie Canal. The railroads, it is true, lessened the significance of the water route to New York City. Nevertheless, they favored also the other Atlantic ports. In consequence, the matter was considered urgent. The port of New York seemed on the way to losing its old preëminence as the great outlet for the interior. Philadelphia, Baltimore, Norfolk, and even New Orleans showed ominous gains. An idea of what so frightened New York may be had in the fact that as early as 1862, agitation began for enlargement of the Canal. Sporadic efforts marked the battle, which was waged chiefly by New York and Buffalo to protect their interests. Reasoning in the vein of the early nineteenth century, protagonists forecast phenomenal benefits for the entire country to result upon consummation of their plans. Determined efforts were made to cause the national government to undertake the project.

Eight states, embracing 416,360 square miles and at the turn of the century a population of 27,150,437, border upon the Great Lakes. An interior sea, the chain of the Great Lakes affords the largest system of deep water inland navigation on the globe. This system, with a general direction east and west, extends from tidewater on the St. Lawrence and, by the Erie Canal, from tidewater at New York 1400 miles into the heart of the continent; from its western extremity at the head of Lake Superior the distance to the Pacific Ocean is only 1700 miles. Towards the close of the nineteenth century, when the agitation became most vehement, the magnificent waterway bore a yearly traffic of 40,000,000 tons, and it served the iron and grain industries, two of the most important economic interests of the United States. Finally, military expediency suggested a deepened canal to offset the inherent dangers of a long unprotected coast-line and the superiority of the Canadian ship canals. To many minds of 1900, therefore, national aid appeared imperative.

Washington, however, failed to consider the matter as one of sufficient national concern to justify a federal undertaking. As a result, the state legislature in 1903 authorized an appropriation of $101,000,000 to convert the Erie into the Barge Canal. To date the program has consumed more than $200,000,000. In the light of prophecies by those favoring it, the Barge Canal, officially opened in 1918, has proved a colossal failure.

No Jeremiah of 1900 could have foreseen the lamentable outcome of the state's huge expenditure. We could not have understood the modern mania for speed in transport. The products of the interior multiplied enormously in variety and bulk, the Mohawk–Hudson route continued to enjoy its unique geographic advantages; but these advantages favored modes of transport other than water. Today, the Barge Canal carries less than the old Erie Canal bore in 1860.

Inadequacy of Waterways and the Rise of the Railroads. The factors leading to the disastrous Barge Canal experiment were evident by 1860. Production simply outstripped the means of distribution. The very greatness of the natural resources of the United States meant an acceleration of the rate at which these resources were exploited. The inland waterways were economically inadequate and the rapid development of the railroads emphasized how far canals had failed to keep pace with the national needs. A traffic interrupted by ice in winter and drought in summer, retarded by slow passage through canal or tortuous river

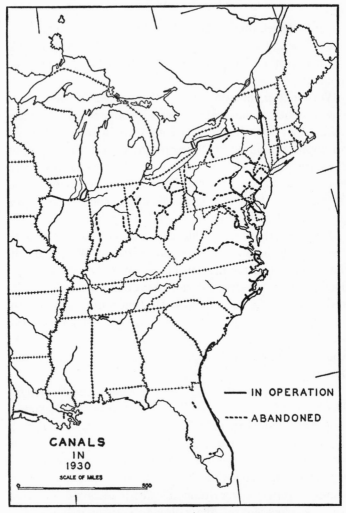

IN OPERATION
---- ABANDONED

CANALS
IN
1930
SCALE OF MILES
0   500

FIG. 17. ABANDONED CANALS — 1930

Canal transportation reached its peak before 1860, before the railways had begun seriously to invade the province of the waterways, and before manufactured wares began to demand better means of transport. The old Erie Canal carried more freight per season than the New York State Barge Canal handles.

course, trammeled by the geographic control of this or that port of outlet regardless of the final destination of the cargo, would not answer the wants of a country which had reached advanced economic development. The palmy days of water transportation in the United States were in the period from 1820 to 1860, when steamboating had improved its facilities, canals had extended the system of inland navigation, and railroads had not yet begun seriously to invade the province of waterways, because the general economic development of the country had not yet passed beyond the agricultural stage (Fig. 17). The bulky but cheap products of forest and farm found their economically appropriate transportation in the low-priced water carriage of that period. But with industrial development came costly manufactured articles of relatively small bulk and large value, which were able to bear the heavier expense of railroad transportation. Hence we find that railroads developed earliest in the industrial areas of this country and waterways retained their value longest in the agricultural and forest regions. Even today rivers maintain their original significance only in economically retarded agricultural regions, as in Arkansas and northern Louisiana, and in the Cumberland plateau, where the government improvements on the Kanawha, Big Sandy, Licking, and Kentucky tributaries of the Ohio, the Caney and Obey branches of the Cumberland, and the head streams of the Tennessee proved a boon to the country. Here a commerce of lumber, railroad ties, barrel staves and shingles has been followed quickly by cargoes of agricultural and mining products, and the appearance of the latter has been the signal for the invading railroad, which seeks always areas of intenser economic activity and the concomitant denser population.

CHAPTER XIV

THE GEOGRAPHY OF THE CIVIL WAR

"CIVILIZATION is at bottom an economic fact," at top an ethical fact. Beneath the economic lie the geographical conditions, and these in the last analysis are factors in the formation of ethical standards. The question of slavery in the United States was primarily a question of climate and soil, a question of rich alluvial valley and fertile coastal plain, with a warm, moist, enervating climate, versus rough mountain upland and glaciated prairie or coast, with a colder, harsher, but more bracing climate. The morale of the institution, like the right of secession, was long a mooted question, until New England, having discovered the economic unfitness of slavery for its boulder-strewn soil, took the lead in the crusade against it. The South, having geographical conditions favorable to the plantation system which alone made slave labor profitable, upheld the institution both on economic and moral grounds.

Various circumstances combined to postpone the South's discovery of the economic unfitness of slavery in its industrial system. The presence of slavery was a deterrent to white immigration into the southern states and encouraged emigration of the unmoneyed whites into the free states, or withdrawal into the mountain region of the southern Appalachians, whither the competition of the plantation method of production could not pursue them. Furthermore, the rapid territorial expansion of the slave power, owing to rapid exhaustion of the soil by the extensive agriculture characteristic of slavery and the consequent need of taking up new lands, stimulated also by the increased demand for cotton which followed the invention of the spinning-jenny, maintained a sparsity of white population, which, being unrelieved by new accessions from without, reduced the competition of the whites among themselves, kept down the beneficent struggle for existence tending to produce a white laboring class, and thus barred the experiment of free labor on the cotton and sugar plantations.

The South thus maintained beyond its time the lavish economic conditions of a new land, namely, extensive area and sparse population.   The relation of the planters to their territory recalls the still more expansive and therefore less economic hold of the fur-trading French Canadians upon their wide country.   In both cases climate and soil, in the South too generous, in the Canadian North too niggardly, combined, moreover, with geographic conditions favoring expansion across the broad Mississippi valley, as along the Great Lakes highway into the vast forest interior, brought about similar economic results.   Hence the South found its basis of political ascendency in its mere extent of territory, and its life and death struggle was made in the United States Senate, while the denser population of the northern states gave them control in the House.

GEOGRAPHICAL CONDITIONS AND ADMISSION OF SLAVE AND FREE STATES

The balanced admission of slave and free states into the Union became a regular feature of political maneuvers; but the North had more raw material in the form of government territory out of which to form states than the South had.   And here, too, geographical conditions played a conspicuous part. The boundary between Pennsylvania and Maryland, running just below the fortieth parallel, was the original Mason and Dixon Line dividing the free and slave states; but by the Ordinance of 1787, forbidding slavery in all territory north of the Ohio, this river became the extension of the line of demarcation, which, therefore, following the southwest course of the stream to its mouth at approximately the thirty-seventh parallel, encroached three degrees southward beyond the original Mason and Dixon Line. The early settlements in southeastern Missouri along the Mississippi at Cape Girardeau and New Madrid, in the days of French and Spanish supremacy here, were located in reference to the Ohio as the great river route from the East. These settlements had to be included in the young state of Missouri as admitted in 1820, and also in the privileges, one of them the right of holding slaves, guaranteed to them by the treaty of the Louisiana Purchase. Hence the Missouri Compromise Line at 36° 30' north latitude can be traced back in its origin to the Ohio.

This line was of vast importance to the North. In 1820 the possible slave area east of the Mississippi, increased by the slave state of Louisiana, was nearly 23 per cent greater than the area devoted to free labor (512,695 square miles as opposed to 417,680 square miles), although the southward trend of the dividing line from 40° to 36° 30' north latitude deprived the slave power of a broad belt of territory. In the triangular area of the Louisiana Purchase, however, with its apex at the Gulf, there was now space for only two other states south of this line, and the westernmost of these was soon devoted to Indian reservations. The recession of the Rocky Mountain watershed farther and farther to the northwest increased so much the domain of the free states.

But the enormous acquisitions of territory following the annexation of Texas and the Mexican War in 1850 meant a possible extension of the slave power to the Pacific, according to the terms of the Missouri Compromise. However, geographic factors came in to wipe out the purely artificial line of 36° 30′ north latitude. California, in consequence of its remote trans-Rocky location, had received no negro element and had been populated largely by emigrants from the northern states or by small farmers from the southern states. Hence it declared as a free state in applying for entrance in 1850, though its southern portion fell within slave territory according to the Missouri Compromise.[1]

The sectional feeling originating in differences of climate and soil was further accentuated by the lack of intercourse between the North and South. The great natural routes of communication, the Potomac–Ohio and the Erie Canal–Great Lakes, as also the chief railroad lines of 1860, ran east and west. Moreover, intercourse along these routes was particularly active because their real termini were to be found, not in Savannah, Charleston, Norfolk, Baltimore, New York, or Boston, but still farther east across the Atlantic in the ports of western Europe. The coast trade between the two rival sections touched only the outer rim of the southern country. Even the north and south course of the Mississippi, strong natural bond as it was in the whole trans-Appalachian region, did not suffice to offset the East's hold upon the states of the old Northwest secured by the double line of the Ohio and the Great Lakes.

[1] McMaster, J. B., *History of the People of the United States*, New York, 1913, VIII, map, p. 190.

BORDER STATES

Nor were the uniting influences of these great routes confined within the boundaries of the free-soil states. Geography knows no rigid lines of demarcation, no sharp transitions. The geographical unity of a river valley tends to be reflected in the homogeneity of its population, a homogeneity not only of constituent race elements but also of institutions and ideals. Hence along the line of the Potomac, Ohio, and Missouri there arose the phenomenon of the "border states," commonwealths not merely located along the northern boundary of the slave territory, but forming in themselves a great zone of assimilation of the conflicting elements to the north and south of them, and showing the inner and outer friction which belongs to every frontier.

Kentucky and Missouri, by reason of soil, climate, their industrial system, and their geographical lines of intercourse with the Gulf country, were in sympathy with the South. Though a large part of their population had come from Virginia, North Carolina, and Maryland, it had been drawn to a great extent from the non-slaveholding yeomen of the Blue Ridge frontier who had moved west by the Wilderness Road. At the same time the Ohio drew from its sources in Pennsylvania and New York northern farmers and artisans, or outbound immigrants and settlers moving along the National Road to Wheeling; many of these it deposited along its southern shores or carried farther west into Missouri, which was receiving similar accession also by way of the Great Lakes. These men of northern or yeoman descent were at best merely tolerant of slavery. When it came to a question of slavery or the Union, their answer was prompt and decisive.[2]

[2] McMaster, J. B., *op. cit.*, VIII, 514.

After a brief civil conflict, Missouri was secured to the Federal side. In Kentucky the strong planter element in the Bluegrass, the aristocracy of the state, was balanced by this yeoman element, by the industrial and foreign residents within its northern border, and especially by the non-slaveholding population in the rough uplands of the Cumberland Plateau. Mountain economy found no place for the negro or plantation cultivation in those sterile hillside farms, pathless forests, and roadless valleys. "The dwellers in the limestone formation, where the soil was rich, gave heavy pro-slavery majorities, while those living on the poorer sandstone soils were generally anti-slavery. This geological distribution of politics was common throughout the South." [3] The whole region of the southern Appalachians had therefore no sympathy with the industrial system of the South; it shared, moreover, in contrast to the aristocratic social organization of the planter community, the democratic spirit characteristic of all mountain people, and likewise their conservatism, which holds to the established order.

Hence when the rupture came between the North and South, the mountains declared for the nation, and thus formed a barrier of disaffection through the center of the southern states, all the more serious because coincident with the physical obstruction of the uplifted ranges. But this area of Union sympathy, because of its poverty, isolation, and remoteness from the Federal base, remained ineffective as regards positive assistance to the operations of the Union armies until after the fall of Chattanooga, though its moral support was always strong. One of the Kentucky mountain counties enjoys the distinction of having furnished to the

[3] Shaler, N. S., *History of Kentucky*, Boston, p. 232.

Federal army the largest quota of troops in proportion to its population of any county in the Union. The uplands of East Tennessee put in a vigorous protest against disunion when that state seceded, and soon after the outbreak of hostilities endeavored to withdraw from the commonwealth. The same thing was true in the mountains of western North Carolina, northern Georgia, Alabama, and even in the hill country of South Carolina.

A wholly mountainous region, dominated through northward-flowing streams by the upper Ohio, West Virginia split off from its parent state. The geographical line of cleavage tells of the natural antagonism between upland and lowland. Long-standing conflict of interests between the tidewater and highland counties of old Virginia prompted schemes of separation prior to 1850, and in that year a new constitution was drawn up to right the grievances of the western section. When the permanent break came in 1861, the first ordinance for the new state adopted at Wheeling included only the counties west of the Allegheny range proper, and drew the boundary line along the mountain crest. The Old Dominion maintained its hold to the south upon the wide, fertile Valley of Virginia and thereby upon the New River, a West Virginia stream; but to the north the younger commonwealth encroached over the proposed dividing ridge east to the Shenandoah or Great North Mountain and its northern extension, the Sleepy Creek range. When erected into a separate state by the bill of Congress, July 10, 1862, West Virginia thus extended only to the western rim of the Shenandoah Valley. This district was geographically a part of the Valley of Virginia, and like it was adapted to plantation culture; but the two counties Berkeley and Jefferson in the lower end of the

Valley, by their outpost location on the bank of the Potomac, were the natural recipients of northern settlers coming down the great trough of the Appalachians. Therefore in the summer of 1863, when most of the Confederate sympathizers were off fighting in the South, these two counties by a vote of the resident population were admitted to West Virginia: hence the erratic eastern boundary of the new state.[4]

The topography of West Virginia made it the sole aggressively loyal state of the border. Kentucky's attitude of declared neutrality was logical in view of the even balance of northern and southern sympathizers within its boundaries, but futile in the light of geographical conditions. A state situated on the outskirts of the scene of the war, like Kansas or Michigan, might have maintained such a neutrality. Wedged in between the Confederacy and the Union, Kentucky stretched its great length east and west from the Appalachians to the Mississippi across the very threshold of the South. Traversing its territory, the Mississippi, Tennessee, and Cumberland rivers opened up parallel avenues for an invading army into the heart of the Confederacy, while Cumberland Gap and the great intermontane valley of east Tennessee afforded a protected high·way from the borders of the Bluegrass country to northern Georgia. Kentucky therefore throughout its length presented a strategic area, which was of paramount importance to the South, moreover, because the Ohio River along its northern border, bridgeless and almost fordless, presented the one strong defensible line in the Mississippi valley. Hence both sides made a dash for the possession of the state, invaded its boundaries in spite of legislative proclamation,

[4] Lewis, V.A., *History of West Virginia*, 1889, pp. 320–25, 355, 373–75, 386, 396.

and forced it from its neutrality. The territory of Kentucky was added to the area of the Union; but the flower of its manhood marched across the border into Tennessee to join the standard of the South.

In Maryland also geographical location was the all-powerful factor in determining the destiny of the state. Here the predominant tidewater area and corresponding planter population made the secessionist feeling very strong; but Maryland's location behind the Potomac made it a highway for the northern troops hurried forward to the defense of the national capital, and therefore insured its prompt occupation by the Federal forces. The security of Washington was not the only object to be gained. The possession of Maryland meant the possession of Chesapeake Bay, a protected sea route to the gaping estuaries of the Virginia rivers.

CAMPAIGNS AND GEOGRAPHICAL CONDITIONS IN THE EAST

The Position of Virginia. The adherence of West Virginia and Maryland to the Union left the Old Dominion state a political peninsula projecting into a sea of hostile territory on the west and north, while the waters of Chesapeake Bay on the east were controlled by the enemy's fleet. This exposed position in itself insured Virginia a large share of the conflicts. To this was added the fact that the apex of its peninsula commanded the Federal capital, while the base sheltered the head of the Confederacy. The country between the Potomac and the James, therefore, became one continuous battle-field in the defensive and aggressive operations of both armies throughout the war.[5]

[5] Muzzey, D. S., *The United States of America*, Ginn & Co., Boston, 1922, I, map, p. 585; Rhodes, J. F., *History of the Civil War, 1861–1865*, New York, 1917, for series of maps on the various campaigns.

Important Geographical Features. The campaigns in Virginia were controlled largely by three geographical features — the north and south reach of Chesapeake Bay, which enabled Federal troops to be transported by sea to any point on the Virginia coast, and later, when command of the James and York rivers was secured, supplies to be carried up to the forces occupied in the operations against Richmond or Petersburg; the southeast course of the Virginia rivers across the lines of advance or retreat; and finally the all important Shenandoah Valley, which, as a protected highway for a northward-marching army, enabled a Confederate force to threaten Washington just as surely as Chesapeake Bay rendered Richmond's position unsafe (Fig. 18). In almost every movement and counter-movement of Federal and Confederate army these three elements of bay, river, and mountain valley played their parts.

A line running through Greenville, Petersburg, Richmond, Hanover, Fredericksburg, Manassas, Fairfax, and Washington indicates with a fair degree of accuracy the "fall line" which divides tidewater from Piedmont in Virginia. East of this line, which marks also the shortest route between the two capitals, the country is low, swampy, and cut by numerous parallel rivers which made the movements of an invading army difficult. Hence, with the exception of those engagements resulting from the advance up the James and York rivers on Richmond from Chesapeake Bay, all the great conflicts on Virginia soil were west of this line of one hundred feet elevation. Moreover, they had a definite situation in reference to the transverse streams, every one of which, from the Rappahannock and Rapidan south to the little Chickahominy and the Appomattox, was a natural line of defense for Richmond.

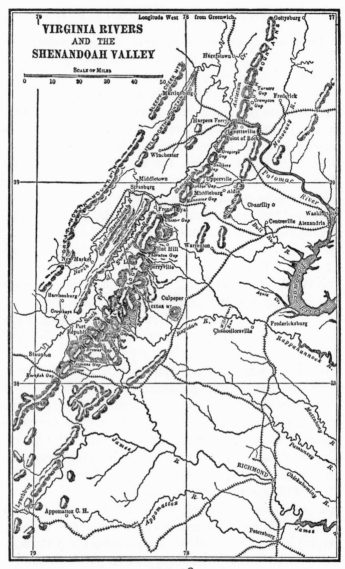

FIG. 18.

These battles of Piedmont Virginia marked the line of invasion which geographical conditions finally forced upon the Federal commanders. McClellan, in the spring of 1862, trying to avoid the difficulties of an advance across the tide-water country, took his army by Chesapeake Bay up the York and the James against Richmond; but the failure of his campaign was due not so much to Lee's valiant defense of the Confederate capital as to the fact that Washington had been left exposed by the withdrawal of the forces to the southeast, whence they could not watch the danger lurking in the Shenandoah Valley. Therefore, when in the fall of 1862 a second advance on Richmond was proposed, McClellan's plan to go by sea again was rejected, and Burnside, who succeeded him in command, selected a route through central Virginia. The southward course of the Potomac was utilized for transportation to the great east-ward bend at Acquia Creek just north of Fredericksburg on the Rappahannock, whose upper course from this point forms a natural extension westward of the line of the lower Potomac. The upper Rappahannock became therefore the Confederate line of defense. The concentration of Lee's forces at Fredericksburg, his entrenched position on the heights which mark the beginning of the Piedmont country, the difficulty and delay of the Federal advance across the Rappahannock by pontoons and ferry-boats while Confederate sharpshooters did their deadly work, all combined to bring about the disastrous repulse of the invading force.

The Rappahannock, about halfway between the two capitals, long remained the line of defense of both Federals and Confederates. Rifle-pits drew furrows along its banks, and pickets bristled at every ford and bridge. The south-ward course of the Potomac from Washington to Acquia and

the possession of Maryland early gave northeast Virginia
into the hands of the Federals; but the Rappahannock
marked the limit where the Confederates could thus be
taken in the east flank. Hence it saw the battle of Fredericksburg in '62, the bloody repulse again at Chancellors-
ville in '63, and the hard-won breach for the advancing
Federals at the battles of the Wilderness in '64.[6]

The line of the Rappahannock was especially advantageous to the Confederates because its head waters led up
to the northern passes in the Blue Ridge which gave access
to the Shenandoah Valley, the third important geographic
factor in the operations in Virginia.   It is the nature of
mountains to lend themselves to strategy.   Their rocky
ramparts conceal the movements of the armies within their
ranges and protect them from unexpected attack.   Their
passes open the way for sudden swoops down upon the
enemy in the plain, and for rapid retreat again, which may
be covered by a small force holding the narrow mountain
gateway against the pursuing enemy.   Mountains are
always primarily barriers; passes, as the breaches in this
barrier, are strategic points having a military and political
history of their own; the longitudinal valleys are the natural
highways, in general easy, along the axis of the upland
region within its guarding walls.

All of these phases came into play in the military history
of the Shenandoah Valley.   As a part of the Great Appalachian Valley, we have seen how, in the period of colonial
expansion, it received population from the Great Valley in
Pennsylvania, and passed on some of its own elements to
the valley of east Tennessee; so now its military history had
definite relations with Hagerstown, Chambersburg, and

[6] Muzzey, D. S., *op cit.*, p. 585.

Carlisle to the north, Wytheville, Knoxville, and Chattanooga to the south. Moreover, the Shenandoah Valley as a factor in the campaigns of the Atlantic plain had a counterpart, with only local variants, in the relation of the valley of east Tennessee to the operations in the Mississippi basin. In each case a mountain barrier and an isolated valley highway flanked the movements in the adjacent lowlands. Cumberland Gap and the pass formed by the Tennessee River at Chattanooga were the two openings in the escarpment wall of the Cumberland Plateau giving access to the valley of east Tennessee, and hence were the two strategic mountain points in the western operations. But the numerous wind gaps which notch the crest of the Blue Ridge every few miles made the Shenandoah Valley much more accessible, enabled the two armies in Virginia to play a game of hide-and-seek in and out behind the barrier, and gave the Confederates opportunity for unexpected dashes through these gateways either for attack or support, as in the case of Joseph Johnston's timely descent through Manassas Gap to reinforce the Southern troops at the first battle of Bull Run.

Napoleon said that Antwerp, as an outlet of the Rhine, was a pistol pointed at the heart of England. Now the deep groove of the Shenandoah was a pistol in the hands of the Confederacy, pointed at the heart of the Union, and from its barrel poured the deadly fire of Jackson's, Lee's, and Early's armies. The northeast and southwest trend of the valley brought its aim against Washington, Hagerstown, and Chambersburg, which therefore more than once felt its devastating fire. The only part of the Union territory east of the Alleghenies to suffer invasion was just this region in front of the Shenandoah opening. Hence it

was always possible for the Confederate leaders to threaten
Washington, and thus create a divertisement to draw off
Federal forces from activities against Richmond, or retard
the concentration of forces against a certain objective point
until the season for them had passed.[7]   This was the purpose of Stonewall Jackson's raid from the Shenandoah in the
spring of 1862.

The Federals, realizing the importance of the Shenandoah
to the Confederacy, endeavored more than once to occupy
it; but every advance up the Valley, by reason of its southwest trend, took them farther and farther from Richmond,
and hence could have no other purpose than merely to clear
this highway of the enemy.   As soon as the Federal troops
were withdrawn, the Confederates poured into it again by
every gap.   In the spring of 1862, while McClellan was advancing on Richmond, General Banks with a Union army
had moved up the Shenandoah as far south as Harrisonburg,
about twenty-four miles north of Staunton.   Stonewall
Jackson with two thousand men, to cut off Banks's retreat,
struck through the Blue Ridge farther north and routed the
Union force which had been placed at Front Royal to guard
Manassas Gap.   Banks succeeded in getting his forces
north to Strasburg, and thence retreated down the Valley,
with Jackson at his heels, across the Potomac.   Union
forces were now summoned to the Valley to drive out the
intruders — Fremont with his army from West Virginia
and McDowell from Fredericksburg, on whose support
McClellan had been counting for his operations against
Richmond.   Then came Jackson's retreat up the Valley,
the battles of Cross Keys and Port Republic, his final

[7] Emerson, F. V., "The Shenandoah Valley and the Civil War," *Journal of School
Geography*, V (June, 1901), 208–14.

escape through the Blue Ridge, and his return to the Confederate army at Richmond.

McClellan's campaign against Richmond, deprived of the necessary reinforcements which Jackson had been engaging in the Shenandoah, was thus a failure, and Lee saw his way clear for an advance on Maryland and the national capital. At the battle of Cedar Mountain, August 9, 1862, just north of the Rapidan, Stonewall Jackson dealt a heavy blow to General Banks, who with Sigel had brought his forces up the Valley from Winchester and Middletown, crossed the Blue Ridge by Luray Gap, and taken position at Sperryville on the upper course of Thornton River, a tributary of the Rappahannock. This position, just in front of the Luray and Thornton gaps, aimed by these passages to maintain a hold on the Shenandoah Valley and block any Confederate movement down this thoroughfare towards the north.[8] At the same time it constituted the western end of the Federal line stretching along the Rappahannock to Fredericksburg and Acquia on the Potomac, and covering the approaches to Washington. The fierce battles on the old Bull Run ground, Centreville, and Chantilly at the close of August traced the route of the Confederate advance to the upper Potomac at Point of Rocks, where Lee's army crossed into Maryland. Here the Potomac is narrow and in general fordable; hence we find the Federal army later invading Virginia in this vicinity at Balls Bluff and Lovettsville. In a few days (September 10) Lee had occupied Hagerstown within the Great Valley of Maryland; but September 14 saw the Federal forces coming to the relief of Hagerstown, fighting their way through Crampton and Turner's gaps in South Mountain, the Maryland extension

[8] *War of the Rebellion, Official Records*, Series I, XII, Part II, 21, 22.

of the Blue Ridge; it saw Lee falling back to where Antietam
Creek flows into the Potomac, to prevent McClellan's
cutting off his retreat, while the next day Stonewall Jackson
seized Harpers Ferry at the confluence of the Shenandoah
and the Potomac, to secure the avenue of escape. The
battle of Antietam, September 17, necessitated the withdrawal of the Confederates, but they found a safe route up
the Shenandoah.

Lee's second invasion of the North in the summer of
1863, following the repulse of the Federals at Fredericksburg,
was made also by the Shenandoah Valley. He led his forces
across the Blue Ridge by the passes at the head of Rappahannock and Rapidan, while Ewell entered the Valley farther
north by way of Chester Gap and drove the enemy before
him out of Winchester, Martinsburg, and across the Potomac. In the meantime Ashby and Snickers gaps in the
Blue Ridge, which were nearest the Federal forces massed
about Washington, were held by General Longstreet, and
General Stuart's cavalry was thrown out in front to guard
the approaches to the same. The engagements at Aldie,
Uppersville, and Middleburg were all battles in the hill
country to render secure the mountain passes behind and
protect Lee's advance down the Shenandoah Valley. Defensive warfare along a mountain barrier, when vigorous
enough, anticipates attack far in front of the passes, and
there deals its blow to the invading enemy, like these Confederate successes before the gaps of the Blue Ridge, or
with a handful of men it defends the pass itself, as the
Confederates at Crampton and Turner's gaps in South
Mountain.[9]

Thus every effort of the Federals to penetrate the moun-

[9] Semple, E. C., "Mountain Passes," *Bulletin of the American Geographical
Society*, XXXIII, Nos. 2 and 3 (1901), pp. 124–37, 191–203.

tains being repulsed by Stuart's cavalry, the Confederate army advanced in security up the Great Appalachian Valley to Hagerstown, Chambersburg, Carlisle, and to within a few miles of Harrisburg.[10]   But now the numerous breaches in the eastern wall of the Great Valley in Pennsylvania enabled the Federals to intercept Lee's lines of communication, just as before Jackson had been able to strike in and threaten Banks's line of retreat.   Therefore Lee turned and marched through South Mountain to meet the advancing Federals at Gettysburg.[11]   After his defeat there the Shenandoah again afforded him a safe avenue of retreat, while Meade with the Federal forces crossed the Potomac near Lovettsville above the Point of Rocks and moved southward to Warrenton, just north of the upper Rappahannock, whence he could watch the passes of the Blue Ridge with the purpose of dealing Lee a final blow as soon as he should show his head through the mountain wall.   It had been Lee's purpose to withdraw to Loudoun County, Virginia by way of Snickers and Ashby gaps, but he was delayed by a sudden rise in the Potomac which made it unfordable, and while his pontoon bridge was being prepared, Meade occupied these passes.   The close succession of openings saved him, however.   He made a feint of crowding his forces through Manassas Gap, drew thither the bulk of the Federal army, and then marching south rapidly to Front Royal, moved out of the mountains by Chester Gap to Culpeper, while Ewell's corps took the Thornton Gap route a few miles farther south and thus avoided the delay of crowding the whole army through one passway.[12]

[10] Morison, S. E., *The Oxford History of the United States*, Oxford University Press, London, 1927, II, map opp. p. 290.

[11] Caldwell, R. G., *A Short History of the American People, 1860–1921*, Putnam, New York, 1927, map opp. p. 112.

[12] *Ibid.*, map opp. p. 68.

Thus the Shenandoah Valley had enabled the Confederate leader to accomplish his purpose of drawing off the Army of the Potomac to the north, diverting and diminishing the forces invading the coast of North Carolina and Virginia, and breaking up the plan of the enemy's campaign by the time the summer was ended.[13]   Finally, when the last advance against Richmond was begun in the spring of 1864 and Grant settled down to the siege of Petersburg, history repeated itself in the Shenandoah Valley.   Federal troops, as before under Banks, were sent up the Valley to prevent a possible demonstration against Washington, were defeated by the Confederates at New Market and driven out, rallied again under a new leader and advanced up the Valley as far as Staunton, and were threatening Lynchburg at the western end of the Confederate line; but being exposed to peril here in the heart of the enemy's country, they retreated over the mountains to West Virginia.   Then, in the hope of making Grant loosen his hold on Petersburg, Lee tried the old expedient of 1862 and 1863.   He ordered General Early with a strong Confederate force to sweep down the Shenandoah Valley, invade Maryland, and threaten Washington. Early came within gunshot of the capital, withdrew into the Valley with trains of plunder, moved northward into Pennsylvania, and once more made unfortunate Chambersburg feel the weight of the Confederate hand.

Then came the final chapter in the military history of the Shenandoah.   Grant was not to be diverted from Petersburg.   He sent General Phil Sheridan to clear the Valley.   This meant not only driving out the Confederate force, but destroying everything which could furnish supplies to the enemy.   Rich in its resources and strong in its loyalty

[13] *War of the Rebellion, Official Records*, Series I, XXVII, Part II, 302–05.

to the Southern cause, the Shenandoah Valley had year after year given of its abundance to the armies of Virginia; but after Sheridan had done his work, this granary of the Confederacy was consumed, the marching and counter-marching ceased, and the peace of desolation settled down upon the Valley.

THE WESTERN RIVERS AND CAMPAIGNS

Just as the Virginia rivers leading up to the passes of the Blue Ridge drew the lines of Federal and Confederate defense in the eastern operations of the Civil War, so in the trans-Allegheny country rivers and mountain passes determined the military lines. The campaigns in the Mississippi valley, though in general quite unconnected with those in the Atlantic plain, were of the nature of a vast flank movement upon the Confederates,[14] by which the southern end of the mountains was turned. Thus the Federals advancing from Georgia and South Carolina were enabled to take the Confederates in the rear, while another force, coming up the side path of the Great Valley from Tennessee, cut off Lee's retreat from Richmond by the southern passes of the Blue Ridge.

In no other war of history, perhaps, have rivers played so prominent a part as in the Rebellion. This importance is reflected in the names of the Federal armies — the "Army of the Potomac," "Army of the James," "Army of the Cumberland," and "Army of the Tennessee." But while the Virginia streams, by their east and west course, simply drew the lines of defense adopted by either side, and with the exception of the lower James figured only by their fords,

[14] Fiske, J., *Mississippi Valley in the Civil War*, Boston, 1900, p. 1.

bridges, sudden rises cutting off advance or retreat, and headstream paths to the mountain gaps, the western rivers, by reason of their large size, navigable character, and predominant north-and-south course, played the far more important rôle of highways for safe and easy water transportation right into the heart of the enemy's country.[15] The great size of the territory constituting the western theater of war, with the consequent long lines of communication to be maintained by the invading Federals, made the western rivers more effective routes of communication than railroads, which could be easily torn up by one of the brilliant raids of the Confederate cavalry. The river routes required no watching, and the immense superiority of the North in steamboat building gave it all the equipment it could need.[16]

From the southern boundary of Illinois the Mississippi led through the Confederacy to the Gulf, while just to the east the Tennessee opened a highway to northern Alabama and the Cumberland into Tennessee. The parallel course of these three rivers therefore made the obvious line of advance for the Federals; and the Ohio, commanding the entrance to these three routes, was the natural objective of the Confederates. Hence the importance to the Southern cause of gaining the adherence of Kentucky, and the inevitable invasion of its neutral soil by both armies. A Confederate army under Polk entered Kentucky and secured the Mississippi by a strong position on the bluffs at Columbus near the Tennessee line, but Grant anticipated any further moves by seizing Paducah, which commanded the mouths of the Tennessee and the Cumberland. Thus the Ohio line of defense was lost by the Confederates; the latter

[15] Muzzey, D. S., *op, cit.*, map, p. 559.   [16] Fiske, J., *op. cit.*, pp. 107 and 194.

therefore drew their line from the Mississippi, where they strengthened the fortifications at Columbus, New Madrid, and Island No. 10, eastward near the Kentucky boundary across the Tennessee and Cumberland rivers at Forts Henry and Donelson to Cumberland Gap, which opened a route of communication with Virginia and, through the Valley of East Tennessee, with Georgia and Alabama.

The fall of Forts Henry and Donelson before Grant's combined land and naval force, and the defeat at Mill Spring, on the upper Cumberland, of the Confederates placed there to hold the connection with Cumberland Gap, compelled the Southern army to evacuate Nashville, abandon the line of the Cumberland, and fall back to their second line much farther south along the bend of the Tennessee. The vital points in this line were Corinth, the junction of two great railroads connecting the Mississippi and the Gulf with Virginia and the Carolinas, and Chattanooga,[17] the southern gateway in the Appalachian wall. The highway of the Tennessee, immediately after the fall of Forts Henry and Donelson, brought the Federal transports and gunboats up the river to Pittsburgh Landing, but the battle of Shiloh fought there retarded the proposed advance upon Corinth. This point was occupied in a few weeks, however, and then the battles of Iuka and Corinth along this line in the fall of 1862 and the battle of Stone River or Murfreesboro, Tennessee, represented the efforts of the Federals to advance east to the mountain gap at Chattanooga.

This point was of the utmost importance to the Confederates. It commanded the approaches to Atlanta and the South Atlantic states, and controlled the intermontane bypath up the Great Appalachian Valley to Virginia and

[17] Caldwell, R. G., *op. cit.*, map opp. p. 124.

central Kentucky.[18]   Through this Shenandoah Valley of the West, the Confederates could throw their invading armies over the Cumberland Mountains into central Kentucky by minor passes, eluding the Federal forces at Cumberland Gap, threaten Frankfort and even Cincinnati, then retreat, driving their captured horses and long wagon-trains of plunder from the rich Bluegrass country, and vanish along the old Wilderness Road into the mountains again, into whose fastnesses few dared to pursue.   Even if the invasion was made by the plains across the middle Cumberland River, as in the case of Bragg's raid in 1862, the Valley of East Tennessee was the safe line of retreat.   Thus it enabled the Confederates, so long as they held Chattanooga, to make a safe flank movement against the Federals in the Mississippi valley, just as the Shenandoah highway gave them this same advantage in Virginia and Maryland.   But in compensation, the Tennessee River in the West, like Chesapeake Bay in the East, gave the Federals easy lines of advance upon the Confederate flanks.

The Federal invasion southward up the Tennessee River was accompanied by a corresponding advance down the Mississippi, because the wedge thus driven into the enemy's territory along the smaller stream rendered insecure or untenable their outlying positions on the Mississippi. Moreover, certain physiographical peculiarities of this river determined that the Confederate withdrawal downstream should be measured by long stretches, because only at rare intervals did its banks present points which could be strongly fortified.   The river winds in gigantic meanders across its vast flood plain, only now and then washing the base of its

[18] Kirke, E., "Chattanooga, the Southern Gateway of the Alleghenies," *Harper's Magazine*, 74 (April, 1887), 659–76.

eastern bluffs, from the top of which its course could be commanded by elevated shore batteries, but whither the fire from passing gunboats could not penetrate. Such points of natural defense were found only at Columbus, Fort Pillow, Memphis, Vicksburg, Grand Gulf, and Port Hudson; and here the Confederates concentrated their efforts at fortification as the price of their hold upon the river. One of these positions relinquished, they had no choice but to fall back, no matter how far, to the next similar point.[19] Only Island No. 10, by its midstream position and geographical location near the fortified point of New Madrid gave them a secure base of another kind whence to contest the passage of the Federal flotillas.

When the loss of Fort Donelson and Fort Henry left the Confederate position at Columbus like a remote island in an enemy's sea, it had to be relinquished, and New Madrid and Island No. 10 became the river outposts. When these fortifications also succumbed to a combined attack of Federal infantry and fleet, the Confederates dropped back to Fort Pillow, which in turn was rendered untenable, owing to the Federal occupation of Corinth far to the south, and had to be abandoned for Memphis. When Memphis yielded to the Federal fleet, the Mississippi was opened four hundred miles down to Vicksburg; but this almost impregnable position on the bluffs two hundred feet above the Mississippi long resisted attack.[20]

Meanwhile the Mississippi was being conquered upstream also from its mouth. After the control of the navigable course of the Tennessee was secured, the next problem of

[19] Fiske, J., *op. cit.*, pp. 181, 182.

[20] Hosmer, J. K., *The Appeal to Arms*, Harpers, New York, 1907, map opp. p. 270; Channing, Edward, *A History of the United States*, Macmillan, New York, 1925, VI, map, p. 548.

the war in the West was the command of the Mississippi, whereby this part of the Confederacy might be cut in twain, much as British control of the Hudson in the Revolution had divided the forces of the colonies. The coast blockade which was maintained along the whole seaboard of the southern states might thus be extended up the river highway on their western flank.[21] The fall of New Orleans before Farragut's fleet gave the key of the river into Federal hands; but the two Union fleets from Memphis and New Orleans failed to take Vicksburg, and the long stretch of river running through the enemy's country was difficult to control with this stronghold in the center unreduced. So the fleets fell back, the one northward to Helena and the other south to New Orleans. The Confederates seized their opportunity and fortified Port Hudson, a few miles above Baton Rouge but below the mouth of the Red River. The five hundred miles of the river now under their control between this point and Helena was to them the most important section. The Red River and the Arkansas brought them men and supplies from the trans-Mississippi states, which constituted the granary of the South, and gave them a secure line of communication through Texas and Mexico with Gulf ports.[22]

But lines were drawn tighter upon the Mississippi. Arkansas Post near the mouth of the Arkansas River was in a position to threaten the communications of Federal army and fleet operating from the north against Vicksburg; hence it had to be reduced. A land force of thirty thousand troops and a flotilla proved just equal to the task, the control of the Arkansas River passed to the Federals, and this artery of the Confederacy was tied up. The Red River, however, the more important avenue to Confederate resources in the

[21] Fiske, J., *op. cit.*, p. 112.　　[22] *Ibid*, p. 183.

West, was safe so long as Vicksburg and Port Hudson, north and south of the river's mouth, were held by southern forces. The problem of the war in the West was the capture of Vicksburg. Its position was almost impregnable in consequence of the bluffs to north, west, and south; the only chance was to attack from the rear by difficult avenues of approach. But when Grant's generalship accomplished this maneuver and the gunboats were maintaining a blockade on the river, the fate of Vicksburg was sealed. Five days after the fall of this stronghold, Port Hudson also yielded, and the Mississippi was a Federal stream bisecting the western Confederacy.

The next move of the war aimed to divide the remainder of the Confederacy along the line of the Appalachians by securing Chattanooga, and thus controlling the lines of communication northward along the valley of East Tennessee with Virginia, and eastward around the southern foot of the mountains with the South Atlantic states.[23] The battle of Murfreesboro was a conflict for the approaches to the Chattanooga gap, just as the battle of Mill Spring in southeastern Kentucky had for its prize the strategic point of Cumberland Gap. The battles of Chickamauga, Lookout Mountain, and Missionary Ridge in the corrugated uplands of northern Georgia gave this passway of the southern Appalachians to the northern armies. The Gulf states were cut off from the Atlantic states of the South, the theater of the war was now reduced to the Atlantic plain, and the national forces closed in around Richmond from the south as well as from the north. Stoneman's raid with a Federal army up the valley of East Tennessee from Knoxville, over the Great Smoky Mountains by the Watauga River, down

[23] Caldwell, R. G., *op. cit.*, map opp. p. 124.

to the Yadkin in North Carolina, and thence along the old pioneer line of communication to the New River and the Valley of Virginia, accomplished the destruction of bridges and railroads along the natural line of Lee's retreat from Richmond and hastened the surrender of the last Confederate army.[24]

Combined Land and Naval Engagements. The Civil War is characterized by an astonishing number of battles fought by combined land and naval forces. Gunboat and infantry charge united in all the great operations along the Cumberland, Tennessee, Mississippi, Arkansas, and Red rivers. The western streams were valuable not only as waterways for transports but as avenues of naval attack. The same phenomenon of combined military forces of land and water is to be noted in almost all the coast attacks. The seaboard cities of the southern states were protected by their prevailing location at the inner end of deep estuaries or bays, which were guarded by island fortifications at the entrances, while often a wide zone of swamp on the land side made difficult any approach from the rear. Hence the attack was usually made by the Federal fleet upon the outer island forts, which were reduced and straightway occupied by land forces from the northern transports. These then aided in maintaining the blockade of the city port in question, which, however, was rarely taken unless like Beaufort, North Carolina, it occupied an exposed position on the outer coast. Only Newbern at the head of the Neuse River estuary, Plymouth near the mouth of the Roanoke River, both in the Sound region of North Carolina, and New Orleans yielded to coast attacks in spite of their retired positions. In all these amphibious military operations we seem to see

[24] *War of the Rebellion, Official Records,* XLIX, Part I, pp. 330–32.

reflected the combination of land and water location in the places attacked.

To the political geographer, the success of the Federal side in the Civil War means the preservation of the large political territory. The evolution of political areas is marked by advance from the small to the large, from the city-state or local principality to the national kingdom or world-empire; it is characterized by increasing aggregation of territory, which minimizes the total amount of political boundaries, extends the area of fraternal feeling, and lessens the artificial barriers to commercial and social intercourse. From the standpoint of political geography, therefore, the disruption of the Union would have been a retrograde step, just as the defeat of the Transvaal meant an advance even for the Transvaal itself, because of its absorption into a larger territorial body.

CHAPTER XV

GEOGRAPHICAL DISTRIBUTION OF IMMIGRATION

IN THE expansion of the United States from a narrow seaboard strip in 1783 to a broad continental territory, three factors were operative — an abundant supply of free land due to continued acquisition of territory, a large foreign immigration, and the building of railroads. These factors were mutually interactive. The free land attracted immigration, and such additions to the population increased the pressure upon our political boundaries, causing them to give way and then to be reconstructed far beyond the original line. The railroads opened up the land we had and made it accessible to the throng of settlers. But the most potent and persistent factor was the presence of farm, field, and forest to be had for the taking. This stimulated natural increase of population, lured foreign settlers, and encouraged the construction of far-reaching railroad lines, while it educated native and alien alike to the large ideas of landholding which kept the people spreading, until the expansion of the settled area from decade to decade almost kept pace with the growth of population.[1]

The barrier of the Atlantic and the early geographical isolation of the American continent made a basis of natural selection in the first colonists coming to this country. Immigration was voluntary except in the case of slaves and the indented servants who were imported for the distinct eco-

[1] Richmond Mayo-Smith, *Emigration and Immigration*, New York, 1890, p. 56.

nomic purpose of supplying the labor much needed in a new land. Even in the opening years of the nineteenth century, the long voyage across the ocean in a sailing vessel and the relatively high cost of the passage were still deterrents to the indigent and thriftless; but until the national policy of emigration restriction artificial influences of all kinds stimulated and assisted emigration from Europe, while fast steamers converted the ocean barrier into an open highway. The consequence was that in 1930 the whites of foreign birth and those of foreign parentage born in the United States comprised more than one fourth of our total population. In the North Atlantic division, which includes New England, New York, New Jersey, and Pennsylvania, these two elements represented 40 per cent (60 per cent in 1900) of the population, and in North Dakota, Wisconsin, and Minnesota the proportion ran from 51 to 62 per cent.[2]

INFLUENCE OF ABUNDANT LAND

Great as has been the immigration into the United States since 1820, it has been only commensurate with the early abundance of free land and the opportunities for work. By far the larger portion of these aliens have been unskilled laborers; but a new country with untouched resources, with forests to be cleared, land to be reclaimed, mines to be developed, and roads to be made, demands not so much skill as energy. Hence these crude foreign elements have served their purpose well, have contributed to the economic growth of the country, "quickened the pace of our development, and

[2] Recent population data in the chapter largely from "United States Summary: Composition and Characteristics of the Population," *Population Bulletin*, Second Series, *Fifteenth Census, 1930*, Washington, 1931.

made us do things rapidly and on a large scale." [3] Every advance of the frontier of settlement or expansion of the political boundary subjected them more and more to the most American of American conditions, abundant land, and accelerated their evolution from European peasants to self-reliant, enterprising American citizens.

The land has been the great solvent. This European invasion has had no terrors for the United States, because the vast territory has enabled it to take in and assimilate. The powerful trans-Atlantic influences to which the country has thereby been subjected [4] have been diluted in their mere distribution over a wide area, weakened by their remoteness from their source, neutralized in part by each other; and all the time the 3,025,600 square miles of land and the free institutions of this oversea republic have been asserting the potency of the American environment. Those immigrants who have settled upon the farms have rapidly assimilated American standards of life, political, social, and economic; even where, as in some Norwegian centers in Minnesota, they have retained their own language; but those who, like the Russians and Italians, have crowded into cities, have been less Americanized, have transferred a bit of Europe to United States soil, because in the congested districts of a New York or Chicago the immediate influence of the continental area is lost.

GEOGRAPHICAL DISTRIBUTION OF IMMIGRATION

The South. The most striking fact brought out by the geographical distribution of foreign population is the paucity

[3] Richmond Mayo-Smith, *op. cit.*, p. 62.
[4] Ratzel, F., *Politische Geographie der Vereinigten Staaten*, Leipzig, 1893, p. 355.

of alien elements in the southern states, owing to the presence of that most alien of all aliens, the negro. In this regard, the South presents a sharp contrast to the remainder of the country. The great bulk of the old slave territory is almost lacking in foreign elements. A narrow hem of immigrants along the Gulf coast, an occasional spot along the seaboard of Georgia and South Carolina, and a ragged band of varying width within the old slave periphery defined by the Ohio and the Mason and Dixon Line, bear witness to the accessibility of all coast regions to oversea neighbors and the character of every land frontier as a zone of assimilation. To counterbalance this foreign element in the frontier portions of the old "border states," the free states just north of the line show the effect of contact with the old slave territory in the considerable negro population of their southern counties. Maryland, with the largest percentage (7.0 per cent) of foreign born whites of all the old slave states in 1930, has a long frontier of contact with the old free states and an extensive coast on the Atlantic. Texas, with 2.3 per cent, and Florida, with 5.7 per cent, are young states with large unexploited resources inviting immigration, and are accessible from the Gulf. Louisiana, with 2.6 per cent, has a long coast-line and the port of a great inland waterway; it affords, moreover, a climate attractive to the Mediterranean peoples of Europe and a natural market for the fruit trade, a form of commerce for which these people show an appetency. In all the other southern states the percentage of foreign born is insignificant. North Carolina, with a total of 3,170,276 people, in 1930 was home to only 8,788 foreign-born whites. Only an occasional mining center in the southern Appalachians shows the presence of the immigrant laborer.

The Coasts. In the remaining portions of the United States where conditions of climate and soil permit settlement at all, the foreign-born element is universally found. But here again the highest percentages are shown by the coast regions and especially by the vicinity of important harbors like the Puget Sound district, the lower Columbia, and San Francisco Bay on the Pacific, and all the seaboard of the New England and middle states on the Atlantic. Here speaks the accessibility of the coasts. All immigrants, except those crossing the borders from Canada and Mexico, must enter this country by the seaports. Many find their enterprise and money exhausted by the time they reach the gateways of the land. Such are therefore stranded in or near the ports, whence they gradually spread to the nearest cities; for the land thereabouts has long since been taken up. The cities alone offer numerous openings for the predominant unskilled labor of the immigrant, and also employment in their particular trades for the skilled artisans.

Hence the region of the coast and the region of the large cities show a high percentage of foreign born. The states of the North Atlantic division, which have passed from the agricultural to the industrial stage of development and therefore show great concentration of population in urban centers, and which moreover are nearest to the teeming sources of the immigrant supply in Europe, show a higher percentage of foreign born than do the states of the Pacific coast. The 1930 census showed that in Rhode Island 25.2 per cent of the total white population was of alien birth, in Massachusetts 25.2 per cent, Connecticut 24.3 per cent, New York 26.3 per cent, and New Jersey 22.1 per cent. New Hampshire, with its short coast-line and industrial centers restricted to the southeast portion of the state, had nevertheless 17.8 per cent. Maine, which in relation to the rest of New England is a backwoods state with only limited industrial development and hence few cities, had only 12.6 per cent of its total population of foreign birth, in spite of an extensive coast-line. But as we have seen before in the history of this commonwealth, other geographical conditions of an unfavorable character have neutralized the advantage of an excellent seaboard. If to these percentages is added the quota of the native population of foreign parents (one or both) in each state, the figures are found in every case to be greatly increased. Since the 1890's the north Atlantic states have experienced a greater influx of foreigners than ever before, owing to a decided change in the character of immigration. In the years prior to restriction 58 per cent of all the immigrants reaching the United States shores came from eastern and southern Europe. These people, emanating from conditions of retarded economic development, recruit the lowest class of laborers. Hence the sweat-shops and cruder manufactures of the big cities, as also the mines and railroads of this section offer them the readiest opportunity to gain a livelihood.

The Interior. Next to this concentration of immigration along the accessible region of the northeastern coast lies an irregular inner zone of sparser foreign element, succeeded by an increasing proportion of foreign to native born from the interior towards the land frontiers. This is especially noticeable in the north central states, reaching from Ohio to Nebraska and from Missouri to the Canadian border, though the phenomenon can be detected also in New England and New York. Ohio shows a growing proportion of foreigner to native from its southern to its northern boundary. In the next three tiers of states toward the west, the same increase from south to north is observed.

In the successive stages of colonial and early national development, we have noticed the stratification of native and foreigner from the east towards the west, the later comer in general being located farthest towards the setting sun, on the abundant lands beyond the outskirts of continuous settlement. But in 1840, after the area of settlement defined on the north by the border of Lake Erie and the southern extremities of Lakes Huron and Michigan (42° N. L.) extended to the margin of the arid belt,[5] the frontier lay no longer towards the west but towards the north; and thither turned the immigrant. Hence the outlying states along the Canadian boundary show a large proportion of foreign born — North Dakota 15.7 (35.4 per cent in 1900), Minnesota 15.3 per cent (28.9 in 1900), Wisconsin 13.3 per cent (24.9 in 1900), and Michigan 18.1 per cent (22.4 in 1900).

In this region of the northwestern frontier we find particularly those nationalities who, like the Scandinavians, relatively recently began to come to this country, or who, like the Germans, have made especially large contributions for a longer period. The Scandinavians did not send any considerable numbers before the decade ending 1870, when they comprised 4.7 per cent of the total immigration.

The proportion reached a peak in 1890 of 10.8 per cent, composing only 5.7 per cent in the pre-War decade and 1.8 per cent in the first decade of restriction of immigration. These figures suggest the general decrease of arrivals from northern Europe and the increase from eastern and southern Europe. The Scandinavians, except such as tarried by the

---

[5] *Eleventh Census, Population*, Part I, Map of Distribution of Population in 1840

Atlantic seaboard, located well towards the northwest frontier, where in 1930 they constituted 40.7 per cent of the total foreign born in North Dakota, 38 per cent in South Dakota, 45.3 per cent in Minnesota, and 17.2 per cent in Wisconsin. The Germans, who between 1860 and 1890 comprised from one-fourth to one-third of the total immigration, constitute a large part of the aggregate foreign born in the north central states, with a noteworthy concentration about Chicago and Milwaukee. In Wisconsin, in 1930 they furnished 33.2 per cent of the foreign-born whites and 44 per cent of the native whites of foreign or mixed parentage. The Scandinavian center, representing a later immigration, lies farther west along the upper Mississippi.

Trans-Rocky Mountains. The average percentage of foreign born in the outlying states of the central west is approximately reproduced in most of the states between the Rocky Mountains and the Pacific. These figures reflect clearly enough the general remoteness of the Cordillera district from the areas of older and denser settlement Among the several states, three stand out in consequence of the low ratio of European immigrants to total population. New Mexico in 1930 showed that 91.3 per cent of its population of European stock had native parentage, Arizona 79.5 per cent; Oregon had the highest percentage on the coast. These states owe this situation in part to the presence of a considerable native population — Spanish and American respectively — in proportion to their then arable soil, when the gold fever stimulated trans-Rocky expansion in the fifties. Although in both states subsequent progress has led to the utilizing of more land and other resources, the presence of low-cost Mexican labor in New Mexico and

Arizona and Oregon's more limited geographical advantages compared with Nature's munificence to other Pacific states have discouraged immigration. In the two southwestern states, lack of significant natural barriers on the border suggests the influx of Mexicans which has attained considerable proportions; 14 per cent of New Mexico's population is Mexican and in Arizona the ratio is the country's greatest, 26 per cent.

Owing to the predominant aridity of this western country, the foreign elements have found their best opportunities in the extensive mining regions of the Rockies, the Great Basin, and the Sierra Nevada; but they are distributed also among the irrigated valleys of the interior, and form a large continuous area of alien settlement along the Pacific seaboard, on the fertile slopes of the Coast Range, and in the long fruitful valleys behind. Here field, orchard, vineyard, and garden offer congenial employment particularly to Italians, Swiss and the Oriental.

Pacific Coast. The foreign elements in trans-Rocky America, however, do not represent only the outermost strata of European immigrants who have moved westward from the Atlantic ports of the United States or the Mexicans who have worked northward from the southern land borders. They include a large number of aliens whom the Pacific highway has brought from its farther shores to the western coasts, and who are only scantily represented in the eastern sections of the country. Here, therefore, in the case of these trans-Pacific immigrants we find an inverted west-to-east stratification, densest in the accessible regions of the Pacific coast, growing sparser with some regularity in the successive tiers of states towards the interior, and disappearing almost wholly in the eastern Mississippi

Valley, but appearing again in scattered patches about the large cities of the Atlantic seaboard.

The Chinese. China, Japan, Australia, and the Pacific islands have all, according to their ability, sent contributions to this country's population. China out of its abundance gave most for many years after the beginning of immigration from Asia. Immigration of the Celestials began soon after the discovery of gold in California. The first came in from Hawaii, where they already formed a considerable part of the laboring class. Between 1848 and 1852 some ten thousand arrived, and in the latter year the number leaped to twenty thousand, but soon declined to a few thousand annually. They found their first employment in the placer mines, either as under-laborers or working abandoned claims for themselves. Later, as the country became more densely populated and the crude industries of the mining camp became diversified, the Chinese supplied the laboring class which the phenomenally rapid growth of California under peculiar geographical conditions had not permitted to develop among the American population.

Measured in terms of comfort, money, and time, California was nearer to China than to the Mississippi prior to 1869, when the first overland railroad was opened. The easy, cheap ocean voyage from Shanghai or Canton to San Francisco Bay made an open highway for the Mongolian coolie, while the long caravan journey from the Missouri, measured in months and leagues, the expense and hardship of such travel, and the barrier of mountain and desert, kept out the large influx of Americans from the eastern states which might have yielded a laboring class. Moreover, those who came found such wealth of opportunity in the mines, the agricultural resources of the free lands, and in commercial ventures, that every American became his own master, and employees did not exist as a class except among the Chinese. These sturdy workmen, therefore, formed the sub-stratum of rough labor in the new state; on them rested the burden of cutting down forests, opening roads, reclaiming rich swamp lands, harvesting crops, acting as domestic servants, and in general developing the abundant resources of the young Pacific commonwealths.[6]

The Pacific as a geographic factor in the history of Chinese immigration has not operated with its full power, owing both to restrictive legislation in this country, beginning in 1855 and continuing in the Chinese exclusion bills, and also to peculiarities of the Chinese themselves, the absence among them of Chinese women and the family life, and the annual return of large numbers to their original home. Their immigration was first curtailed, then arrested, while the Chinese population which had effected an entrance before the barriers were raised has lacked natural increase and has been regularly depleted by repatriation. Smuggling by way of the early negotiated Mexican and Canadian borders tends to maintain numbers, but in comparison with 107,488 Chinese in 1890 the country now holds 74,954. Thus the factor of the Pacific highway has been steadily weakened so far as Chinese immigrants are concerned and with a few more extensions of the exclusion bill it will be nullified.

The distribution of the Chinese in the United States illustrates their relation to the Pacific. More than 55 per cent of them are located in the trans-Rocky states and territories, and the heaviest proportions are found in the seaboard commonwealths. California heads the list with

6 Richmond Mayo-Smith, *op. cit.*, pp. 236–46.

37,361. As a consequence of particularly violent local agitation against the unwelcome visitors, Washington and Oregon muster only 4270. Outside the limits of the United States proper, Alaska formerly with over 3000 Chinese, and Hawaii, the great cross-roads stations of the Pacific, today with 27,179 demonstrate the uniting influence of an ocean upon its bordering lands. The second tier of states from the Pacific, including Arizona, Nevada, Idaho, and also Montana, which owing to its close approach to Oregon properly belongs to this group, have less than 1200 each; while in the next tier to the east the figure drops under 400 each, thus showing the attenuation of the geographic influence of the Pacific in proportion to the distance from its coast.

The Japanese. The distribution of the 138,834 Japanese in the United States in 1930 illustrates the same principle. Of this total 87 per cent are found in the western division, where the largest numbers are located near the seaboard in California (97,456), Washington (17,837), and Oregon (4958); Hawaii has 139,631. The development of Japanese exclusion has had results more serious than those of anti-Chinese measures. It has caused dangerous friction between the two leading powers having a Pacific frontage. Difficulties began soon after the commencement of Japanese immigration in the early 1880's. For a time the new supply of cheap labor replacing the excluded Chinese allayed the worries of the anti-Asiatics. Shortly the rapidity with which the new arrivals increased led to agitation recalling the earlier Chinese affairs. The efficiency and ambitions of the Japanese immigrants added coals to the fire of racial prejudice. In 1924 the selective immigration act quieted the local question (in the year ended June 30, 1930, only fifteen Japanese quota immigrants entered the United States), but initiated international complications of utmost delicacy. Interference with the principle of dissemination of peoples about the shores of a great sea not only has focussed world attention upon the community of interests of countries facing a common ocean but has accelerated the rise to world significance of the Pacific area.

Immigrants from the Hawaiian group and the other Pacific islands are distributed chiefly in the Pacific coast states. California alone in 1930 claims more than one-third of the 30,849 Australians settled in the United States and almost three-fourths of the country's 45,208 Filipines. Here not only relative proximity but doubtless also similarity of climate has influenced the choice of the home-seekers. Many of the Pacific Islanders, owing to their mid-ocean position, have found it almost as easy to reach New York and Massachusetts; but Hawaii, which is only five days distant by steamer from San Francisco, has felt all the attracting power of California and the western states.

FRONTIER ZONES OF ASSIMILATION

A frontier, as we have seen, is always a zone of assimilation, but the intensity of the assimilation varies under different geographic conditions. A sea frontier, in consequence of the accessibility of the average coast to all the ships of the world, shows a degree of ethnic mixture not attained on a land frontier. China, which in consequence of geographic conditions and of national characteristics engendered largely by these conditions has almost no aliens in its vast interior, shows a considerable representation of the leading commercial nations of Europe and America in its great seaports. The delta region of ancient Egypt was the first part of that peculiarly isolated country ever to see foreigners peacefully settling within its boundaries. That occurred when under Psammetichus I the Greeks settled in Naucratis and Sais. Later the Nile delta became the cosmopolitan area of the Mediterranean, while the ethnic simplicity of middle and upper Egypt was almost untouched. So today the streets of Alexandria and Cairo echo many languages. The southern seaboard of France has various Mediterranean elements in its population, with an alarming amount of the Italian constituent. Greater New York contains Russian, Polish, Italian, German, and Chinese towns within its city limits. Boston, New Orleans, and San Francisco can show almost as multifarious ethnic elements. A comparison of all the maps showing the distribution of foreign born in the United States according to their nationality, proves how varied is the mixture of population along the Pacific and northern Atlantic coasts.

Along a land frontier, on the contrary, the assimilation is as a rule limited to the two contiguous elements. The proximity of the two areas, however, the similarity of climatic and hence of economic conditions which usually prevail, and the intercourse across the boundary in spite of trade restrictions, all stimulate the shifting of population back and forth across the line. Any special advantage offered now by this, now by that side, will be the signal for migration. The large German population in the former Baltic provinces of Russia today records the Teutonic expansion under the Sword Brothers eastward across the Niemen and Duna as far as Lake Peipus in the thirteenth century, while Slav place names in eastern Germany attest not only the expansion of Prussia over Polish territory, but also an earlier

Slav encroachment towards the west, when these people extended to the river Elbe. Persecuted Russian Jews and German-Russians, restive under the harsh Russification process which for long prevailed in the Baltic provinces, sought refuge across the boundary in Germany. The different frontier zones in Switzerland are strongly assimilated in language and race to their French, German, and Italian neighbors.[7] So, too, the northern land frontier of the United States is in no small degree Canadian, as the southern is strongly Mexican.

The Mexicans. There were 1,422,533 Mexicans in the United States in 1930. Of these, 86 per cent were in the southern tier of states along the Mexican border, and, with few exceptions to be specially explained, the largest proportions were found in the southernmost counties in those states. Even these large figures take no account of the strong infusion of Mexican blood in this border population which originated in the days of Spanish and Mexican supremacy here, and has been augmented ever since by a steady tide of immigrants in sombrero and zarape from across the line. Of the 368,013 Mexicans in California in 1930, more than seventy-five per cent were located in the three southern tiers of counties, the proportions increasing towards the coast about Los Angeles and San Diego. The only other considerable areas of these people were found about San Francisco Bay, where a little over seventeen thousand were distributed in San Francisco, Santa Clara, and Alameda counties, and in Fresno County where intensive agriculture had attracted some ten thousand. Here speaks the accessibility of a seaboard country which draws not only from trans-oceanic sources of population, but also

[7] Ripley, W. Z., *The Races of Europe*, New York, 1899, chap. XI.

from the neighboring coasts of its own continent and its own hemisphere; for movements of population tend to follow the coastwise trade. Mexico therefore contributes inhabitants both to the sea and the land frontier of California.

The 114,173 Mexicans in Arizona in 1930 were found chiefly in the two southern tiers of counties, and New Mexico's 59,340 were located chiefly in Dona Anna and Grant counties in the southwest corner of the state, and in Eddy County in the southeast corner. A line of Mexican element extended northward from these into Bernalillo County, which forms one of the rural areas contiguous to Santa Fé, then east into San Miguel County about the old Spanish town of Las Vegas, and north across the Colorado boundary along the old line of communication, now the route of the Piedmont railroad, as far as Denver. The old Mexican centers and the old routes have still the power to attract.

Texas counted 683,681 Mexicans among its citizens in 1930. In all the counties along the Rio Grande, except those arid sections almost without inhabitants, they are found in numbers varying from one to seventy-seven thousand, and constitute in some cases considerably more than half of the total population. Two concentrations mark their settlement along the frontier, one in the far west, in El Paso County, the other in the southeastern corner whither they came by sea as well as land. The old Spanish administrative center of San Antonio in the interior of the state has also become a gathering-place for Mexicans, who are strongly represented in Bexar and the adjoining counties. In addition, the rapid growth of Texas cities has afforded many opportunities as a result of which the Mexican forms a conspicuous element of cities far inland. Dallas County contains 7699, Tarrant County (Fort Worth) 4553.

The zone of assimilation characteristic of every political boundary is further illustrated in the case of the Mexican frontier by the incursions into United States territory made for many years by Mexican outlaws and Indians to steal cattle and horses, by the hot pursuit of the tireless Texas Rangers down to the Rio Grande and across the line, and the unrecorded battles or rope-end administration of American justice on Mexican soil. In the stirring days of the seventies and early eighties the security of the border settlements depended upon the sleepless vigilance of the Rangers, their skill in trailing the marauders through the brush of southwestern Texas and over the plains of Mexico, the tenacity of purpose which kept them days and nights in the saddle on a dash of three or four hundred miles, and their grim disregard of international law which put a certain finality upon their accomplished tasks. More recent punitive expeditions bear further witness to the character of this typical zone of assimilation.

Other southern neighbors, though not in immediate contact with the frontier, have contributed elements to the American population; and their distribution is interesting as illustrating the geographic control of location and climate, the accessibility of coast regions, and the tendency of population to follow the coastwise trade. In 1930 the census returns gave 63,648 persons of foreign white stock from Cuba and the West Indies. Of these 21,891 fell to Florida alone, of whom almost two thirds live in Hillsborough County, which encloses Tampa and Tampa Bay, the great southern port for commercial intercourse with Cuba. This county contains also a goodly sprinkling of Spaniards, who have evidently drifted in here from the southern island. The attraction of a congenial climate, similar to that from which they came, and geographical proximity have drawn thither these Cubans and West Indians. The 21,289 of them in New York City show the effect of the great seaports and ship lines of this section. Owing to the great distance, this Caribbean district sends only a small contingent to the Pacific coast states.

In the distribution of immigrants from Central and South America, on the other hand, our two opposite coasts are more nearly on a par; and the Gulf seaboard, owing to the marked eastward projection of Brazil, loses its advantage of proximity for all immigrants coming from points south of the equator. For such the port of New York is quite as near as New Orleans. In 1930, New York City had almost one third of the 58,745 Central and South Americans in the country. The very small number of immigrants from Central and South America in the United States reflects the existence of broad undeveloped areas especially in Argentina and southern Brazil, and in other areas the indolence of peoples accustomed to tropical climates. The presence of immigrants from Cuba, the West Indies, Mexico, Central and South America in Missouri, Illinois, and Ohio, states bordering on the Mississippi and the Ohio, shows the geographic control exerted by the great central river system in the distribution of these southern elements, and the repelling influence of a harsh climate farther north.

The Canadians. The influence of immediate contact along a frontier upon immigration from the neighboring land is more strikingly illustrated in experience with Canada than with Mexico. In the north a longer frontier, bordering moreover upon the most densely populated belt of Canada, a greater similarity in race elements, and the proximity of superior economic conditions, all combined to produce a great exodus from Canada into the United States which has been going on for the past seventy-five years. We notice here two outgoing currents. One sets strongly from the coast regions of eastern Canada to the northern Atlantic states, where Canadian immigrants are densely distributed along the whole littoral from Passamaquoddy to Raritan Bay. Hither they have come in vast numbers from Newfoundland, Nova Scotia, New Brunswick, and French Canada to find work in the great manufacturing centers, especially in those of New England, where in 1930 they formed almost 30 per cent of the foreign-born population. There were 288,051 in Massachusetts, 73,743 in Maine, 50,959 in New Hampshire, 39,278 in Rhode Island, 27,182 in Vermont, and 37,808 in Connecticut. Near-by New York State had 147,874.

But not all the British Americans in these states were deposited by this coastwise current. The northern borders of New York, Vermont, New Hampshire, and Maine make a long line of contact with the Canadian boundary, and have been the scene of that frontier ethnic assimilation which we have come to know. Owing to the extreme narrowness of the United States territory in this northeastern corner, moreover, some of these border Canadians doubtless found their way by land routes southward to the Atlantic coast and contributed to the strong representation there.

The data showing the distribution of Canadians in this country according to the Census of 1890 show how the northern neighbors spread over into the United States territory all along the frontier from the St. Croix River to Puget

Sound, the distribution growing sparser from the border towards the interior, except where it increases again along our northern Atlantic coast. This incoming tide from Canada has met and mingled with that larger west and north bound current of European immigrants from the Atlantic ports. Hence the Canadian border, in point of ethnic elements, forms an exception to the rule of land frontiers inasmuch as it presents a varied mixture of nationalities, unlike the simple Mexican and American constituents along the southern boundary.

The distribution of British Americans in the United States is much denser along the eastern half of the frontier than along the western stretch beyond the head of Lake Superior. The eastern half is contiguous to the older, more densely populated provinces, and hence to more abundant sources of immigrants than is the western; and from New York to northern Minnesota, the Great Lakes have facilitated and guided this northern immigration. The deep indentation of Lake Michigan has placed a large colony of Canadians in Illinois, in the very heart of the Northwest, and brought them within easy reach of the middle Mississippi and Missouri. The southern rims of Lakes Ontario and Erie have a strong Canadian population. The two peninsulas of Michigan, being enclosed by Lakes Huron, Michigan, and Superior, are distinguished by the interior's heaviest Canadian concentration across their whole width; the state in 1930 had 202,316 Canadian born residents. The whole line of the St. Lawrence and the Great Lakes has helped this stratification towards the west, bringing the wheat-fields of Dakota and Minnesota and the forests of Michigan near the centers of population in eastern Canada.

The proportion of Canadians to the total population is

greatest in the frontier states, and in this group is greatest in those older states which, owing to geographic conditions, have still a large backwoods area, like Maine, New Hampshire, Vermont, and the Adirondack region of New York, or in the newer states to the west which have been more recently reclaimed from the wilderness. Such regions in their extensive forests offered congenial employment to Canadian lumbermen, practiced in the woods of Canada, or farther west in the prairie lands provided farms for those of agricultural tastes. The first motive located Canadians in the forests of Maine, the Adirondacks, Michigan, and Wisconsin; the second distributed them in central Minnesota, in North Dakota along the Red River of the North, and in the rich grain lands of Iowa. In North Dakota in 1890 they formed 12.61 per cent of the total population and 28.29 per cent of the foreign born; today they are exceeded only by the Scandinavian and Russian elements. After the Scandinavians, they are more strongly represented than any other alien people in Montana, and also in several counties of Idaho; and in Washington they form nearly one fifth of the total foreign born, being distributed most densely along the eastern and southern shores of Puget Sound. One center of greater density is found immediately on the land frontier, and another about the head of the inland sea, showing the tendency to coastwise expansion.

This tendency is demonstrated also by a continuous band of Canadian elements along the whole Pacific coast south to the Mexican boundary and by the location of all the denser centers immediately on the seaboard or at points like Portland and the Willamette Valley readily accessible therefrom. The old pioneer highway down the great Pacific Valley has also contributed to this distribution along the Pacific slope.

All these coast states offered in their farming, grazing, and timber lands congenial employment to Canadian settlers. Later the urban developments heightened the attractions, Los Angeles now having more than 30,000 Canadian born. An isolated area of great density in northern California on Humboldt Bay in the days prior to phenomena, such as Los Angeles, exemplified the affinity of the Canadian for much of the west coast and was explained by the important lumber industry of Humboldt County and by the port of Eureka, the best along this whole coast between the Golden Gate and the mouth of the Columbia.

A temporary peak of Canadian immigration into the United States came in the decade 1881–90. In that period almost 400,000 were domiciled in this country. For the next twenty year period the total is less than half this figure and emigration to Canada from the United States far exceeded the reverse flow. The problems of the War and post-War periods in the main returned to the United States its greater magnetic power, a development greatly favored after 1921 by the invitation to Canadians in their freedom from quota restrictions. Despite the resumption of large-scale Canadian arrivals, the movement in the opposite direction initiated at the turn of the century retains considerable importance. Once the trend set in late in the nineteenth century, it rapidly gathered momentum. In the quinquennium 1910–14 immigrant arrivals from the United States totaled 605,498. Ease of access, special inducements by the Canadian government, and the productive lands of the prairie provinces for a long period made the United States the premier source for Canadian immigration. With the diminution of European settlement occasioned by the World War, the tide from the United States attained even greater relative proportions, in 1918 reaching 90 per cent of the aggregate. As this country started in its unprecedented economic development following the war, the attractiveness of Canada paled, and by 1925 only 14 per cent of Canadian immigrants came from the United States. Subsequently the growing difficulties of the farmer in this country encouraged a new flight to Canada's comparatively uncrowded plains. Between 1927 and 1929 United States arrivals grew by almost one half while those from Europe had an increase of some eleven per cent.[8]

The sudden turning of the tide of migration in the 1890's marked the exhaustion of free arable land in the United States. This fact marked a significant readjustment in the relations of population to area. Abundance of free land gave the United States the distinguishing characteristic of a youthful country; but the fierce rush to the Cherokee strip in 1893 and the ten applicants for every one of the fourteen thousand homesteads opened for occupation in the Kiowa-Comanche district in 1901, the invasion of Indian reservations by American cattlemen, and this efflux of American farmers across the northern border, all indicated that the United States had reached an important milestone. Canada then represented the lusty junior of the North American continent. Its vast area gave it great capacity for assimilation. As the only country in the north temperate zone offering free land to home-seekers, for long it retained its own citizens, drawing a stream of emigrants from the United States, and was destined to attract the great tide of agricultural immigrants from Europe which had flowed into the United States.[9] Canadian immigration agents were at

[8] *Canada Yearbook, 1930*, Ottawa, 1930, p. 164.

[9] Whelpley, J. D., "The Isolation of Canada," *Atlantic Monthly*, 88 (1901), 196–204.

work in most of the states; wonderful exhibits of Canadian grasses and grains were made at state and county fairs, posters illustrating the northward bend of the isothermal lines west of Lake Superior and the ameliorating effects of the warm chinook winds were displayed in market-places and school-houses; and finally the transfer of the migrating American was made as simple, comfortable, and cheap as possible. The consequence was that thousands of settlers crossed the border to choose homesteads from the abundant grazing and farming lands of the Canadian Northwest.

The American emigrants were and are mostly from the border states of the Dakotas, Montana, Minnesota, Wisconsin, and Michigan; from interior regions of uncertain rainfall like Kansas and Nebraska; and from some of the older states like Ohio, Illinois, and Missouri, where land has risen in value and in many cases will sell for a good sum which can be reinvested in the cheaper land of Canada for the rising generation. Many of the emigrants are people who had moved to the United States from the older provinces of Canada. The number includes also a goodly sprinkling of Germans, Swedes, and Norwegians who have been in the United States long enough to learn the principle of prairie farming, and hence are a vast improvement over the raw immigrants from Europe. These people are drawn from that part of our country which has received the largest portion of the vigorous Teutonic stock of Europe. When we yield them up, therefore, we lose a valuable element of the population.

Such people we can ill afford to lose. And yet these are just the people who are alert to new advantages and who will seek them without hesitation. Migration is in their blood. Their local attachment is small. Bred in the large opportunities of a new country, they desire the same advantages for their offspring. Their table of square measure runs in terms of quarter sections and square miles. They want big farms and ranches for themselves and their children, and thus are unwilling to adopt the cramped standards of size and the intensive agriculture of a denser population and an older civilization. The demand that faced us at the beginning of the twentieth century, therefore, was more arable land on American soil. The amount and character of this American emigration proved that the demand was not a fanciful one. These facts made the development of government fostered irrigation seem urgent, although irrigation farming would not prove a powerful lure for the farmer accustomed to his broad acres.

CHAPTER XVI

GEOGRAPHICAL DISTRIBUTION OF CITIES AND INDUSTRIES

A COUNTRY in the germ, like the human embryo, passes rapidly through all the lower phases of development before it evolves to the type of the parent stock. Such was the history of colonial America. The settlers who came to people this country brought their best capital in the elements of European civilization. As exponents of this civilization they represented the forces of heredity. What transformed them was their environment, always the most potent factor for a young growth. The wide surrounding wilderness necessitated a return to a primitive type of living in order to cope with primitive conditions, but it generated a new order of adaptability, which is the strongest guarantee of a higher development. The men who learned the law of the wilderness gained the secret of its mastery. For the products of English garden and farm they accepted the savage commissariat of game, maize, and berries; for the busy London shops, Indian barter; for carriage and cart on well-built road, the highway of the streams with swift moving canoe or the blazed trail through forest and glade for the noiseless tread of moccasined feet.

Character of Early Settlements. Their settlements reflected in part the needs of defense which dictated the isolated, inaccessible sites of towns in the militant past. Fear of Indian attack located their first home on Roanoke, Jamestown, Manhattan, and New Orleans islands, like the ancient Mediterranean cities of Tyre, Alexandria, Syracuse, and the Ionian colonies off the Asia Minor coast; or it placed their stockaded forts on hills or eminences as best protected against unexpected assault, like the Tuscan towns crowning high spurs of the Apennines, or the walled "burg" or citadel which characterizes the mediæval cities of Germany. Danger of aggressions from rival colonies along the coast suggested a retired location at the inner end of long, narrow inlets or estuaries, according to the instructions given the Jamestown settlers, just as the same motive of security located Rome, Ephesus, Smyrna, Troy, and Athens well beyond reach of the Mediterranean pirates.

Such were the temporary concessions made to the militant conditions of their savage environment by the early settlers. In conflict with the moulding influence of this environment were the commercial needs and purposes which an industrial, commercial people had brought with them from their trans-Atlantic homes. Firearms and the strength of increasing numbers soon emancipated them from rigid geographic control in the selection of their village sites. Still encircled by their stockades, however, the settlements lined up along the rivers to the head of navigation in order to command the sole means of communication with the interior, while their accessibility to the coast guaranteed the trade with the mother country, the constant source of the commercial influence. At the meeting-points of sea and inland navigation grew up the large towns, those with the best harbors and the easiest, most extensive lines of communication with the back country gradually gaining pre-eminence. For a long time, however, there was slight distinction between the small harbor and the large entrepôt; differentiation had not yet gone so far. The evolution of seaports in this country has been marked by increase or size attended by decrease of number.[1]

NATURE OF AMERICAN CITIES

Colonial Commercial Cities. The colonial cities of America were essentially commercial centers, not industrial. They were markets where the country's new products were exchanged for the manufactured wares of England. The colonies as a whole were still in the agricultural stage of development. Only in New England had the geographical conditions of an excessively glaciated surface, abundant water-power, and accessibility by sea to outside sources of raw materials, curtailed the agricultural period and introduced the industrial. The New England towns became therefore manufacturing as well as commercial centers, but the products of their artisan labor were limited in variety, simple in character as a rule, and formed but a small part of the total exchanges. New York, Philadelphia, Baltimore, and later New Orleans became the typical commercial ports of a highly productive agricultural country.

Industrial Development. The industrial phase of city development began with the close of the Revolution and the effort to gain industrial as well as political autonomy. It advanced most rapidly in those parts of the country where, from conditions of soil and topography, arable land was limited in supply and soon felt the competition of other agricultural areas more favored by nature; where the labor thus released from the farm sought other outlets for its energy, and where the laboring class thus formed received largest accessions from European immigration; where an

[1] Compare list of ports in Brownell's *History of Immigration Between 1818 and 1840.*

invigorating climate stimulated the human energy necessary for the sustained labor of manufacture; and where superior routes of communication with other parts of the country, whether by sea, river, lake, or land, facilitated exchanges between such industrial centers and the agricultural areas. These conditions are found in the northeastern part of the United States, shading off in intensity towards the south and west, increasing towards the Atlantic coast. Hence the accompanying map shows that three fourths of the ninety-three cities of the United States, each having a population of one hundred thousand or more, fall within a zone lying between thirty-seven and forty-three and a half degrees north latitude, and stretching from the ocean on the east to the ninety-seventh meridian just beyond the Missouri River on the west.

It is impossible to separate the commercial and industrial aspects of a city because of the close interrelation between the two; now one aspect, now the other predominates, or again they may be equally strong, each contributing its part to the city's growth. The area of greatest urban development in the United States is the area of most abundant elements of production — labor, capital, water-power, fuel, and raw material of all kinds — as also of most numerous and varied routes of communications, not only with different parts of this country but also with Europe. Hence commercial and industrial activities are blended in all these urban centers in varying proportions which are determined largely by geographical conditions.

Characteristics of the Modern City. The modern city is essentially a point for collecting, producing, and distributing commodities of all kinds. Its location must be as accessible as possible. The site of the metropolis is at the cross-roads of the great world thoroughfares, where its markets can receive the products of all continents and all climes. All seaport towns are on the world's greatest and cheapest highway, the ocean. This is their first and greatest advantage. Their further development depends upon the area, fertility, and population of the back country which they command, and their means of communication with the same. The country for which Liverpool is the entrepôt is limited in extent, but vast in its content, in the amount and value of its products and in the size and demands of its population. Adelaide and Melbourne are good ports, but their growth will be limited by the desert character of the interior of Australia. New York and San Francisco are on opposite sides of the same country, command therefore the same area, and have equally good harbors; but while New York is connected by cheap waterways and almost level railroads with the interior, for San Francisco the high freight rates over the Rocky Mountains are prohibitive except for merchandise of small bulk and large value, and the arid plains and highlands of the west can never support the same density of population as the fertile region which lies within the range of attraction of the Hudson River port. Moreover, San Francisco's trans-oceanic connections are longer than those of New York, and the outbound cargo to the Orient finds a far more restricted market than the highly progressive countries of Europe offer to the commerce of our Atlantic cities.

Coast cities develop because they are middlemen in the commerce of all the bordering continents. Cities located on a land frontier share essentially in the trade only of two countries, their own and their neighbor's. Differences of geographical location, climate, soil, and degree of development tend to differentiate the products of the two communities and hence stimulate exchanges. Commerce between the two will depend upon the amount and kinds of their respective products. Interior cities are merely local distributing-points, in which commercial activity is determined by command of routes of communication, and the contrast in economic development of the areas which they serve.

GEOGRAPHICAL DISTRIBUTION OF URBAN CENTERS

In the light of these general principles, let us examine the geographical distribution of urban centers in the United States (Fig. 19). Of the twenty largest cities, each having more than 365,000 people, nine (Boston, New York, Newark, Philadelphia, Baltimore, New Orleans, Los Angeles, San Francisco, and Seattle) are located on the coast, five more along the northern lake frontier (Buffalo, Cleveland, Detroit, Chicago, and Milwaukee), and five in the Mississippi system (Pittsburgh, Cincinnati, St. Louis, Kansas City, and Minneapolis). The remaining city in this group is Washington, the national capital.[2] Though many of these owe their size in part to their industries, nevertheless commercial facilities have made an important contribution to their growth.

Seaports. The development of the large seaports in the

---

[2] *Fifteenth Census, United States Summary, Population Bulletin,* First Series, Washington, 1931, pp. 34–37.

Note to Fig. 19:

The great concentration of cities in the northeastern part of the country emphasizes for this area the potent arteries of trade, and the production of agricultural, forest, mineral, and manufactured products. How many cities of more than 100,000 lie outside this area? Of 50,000 to 100,000? How many cities of more than 100,000 lie west of 98° west longitude?

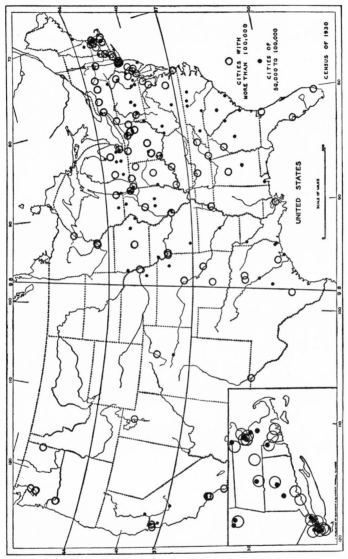

FIG. 19. THE LOCATION OF CITIES OF 100,000 AND
50,000 INHABITANTS IN 1930 (See note at foot of page 340)

United States reflects the advantages of a trans-oceanic market and of coastwise trade with other parts of the American continents. The active commerce which has long existed between New Orleans and the northern Atlantic states by sea would have been prohibited by the high freight charges of inland transportation, whether by rail or by river and canal. Three of the five cities with a population of over 1,000,000 are located on the Atlantic coast, and the other two, Detroit and Chicago, are accessible from the ocean to sea-going vessels through the St. Lawrence River, the Canadian canals, and the Great Lakes. The same rule holds on the Pacific slope. West of the Rockies there are ten cities with a population exceeding 100,000, and eight of these (San Diego, Long Beach, Los Angeles, San Fran- cisco, Oakland, Portland, Tacoma, and Seattle) are located on the seaboard; two (Salt Lake City and Spokane) in the interior. Though climatic conditions and the great fertility of the western coast region favor increase of population and hence of urban centers, nevertheless trade with the Yukon and Asia and the lumber industry of the northwest have been the making of Seattle, while Asiatic commerce has stimulated the growth of San Francisco and Portland. Los Angeles began to exploit this field of wealth on a larger scale following the government improvements on the deep-sea harbor at San Pedro.

Lake Ports. The cities along the Great Lakes, though located on the inland periphery of the United States, yet enjoy the advantages of water transportation for a brisk interior coastwise trade with eight states of the Union and foreign trade with Canada. The most populous and pro- ductive provinces of Canada are located along the borders of these lakes. Hence a considerable part of our large commerce ($1,452,000,000 in 1929 [3]) with our northern neighbor moves across this lake frontier and is forwarded by our lake cities. The long chain of inland seas gives a wide range in the distribution of these exchanges. Chicago's markets in Canada stretch from Quebec to Port Arthur, and Canada lumber seeks the furniture factories at Chicago or Grand Rapids as readily as it does the wood-pulp mills of northern New York and New England.

River Ports. The cities on the Ohio and Mississippi are located on the outer margin of the urban industrial area and on the inner margin of the southern and western agricultural section. It is not a chance fact that St. Louis early developed the largest mercantile hardware house in the world. The city stands near the southwestern apex of the industrial peninsula, and the farming, mining, and grazing interests of the wide surrounding territory demands hardware more than any other one class of commodities. The two chief items of capital on a Texas or Nebraska ranch are so many heads of cattle, so many miles of wire fence. This same distributing function characterizes also in a less degree the cities lining the Mississippi, Missouri, and Ohio rivers.

Growth of Major Urban Areas. An active commercial center necessarily possesses several of the qualifications of a successful manufacturing town. Situated on the focus of converging routes of communication, it commands abundant raw materials of various kinds and also an extensive market for the sale of its finished products. Its commercial interests insure the accumulation of capital necessary for industrial enterprises. Its labor supply, the last important factor in production, will depend upon the density and character of the surrounding population, and the conditions

[3] *Commerce Yearbook, 1931*, Washington, 1931, I, 117.

of climate under which its laborers must work. The urban development of a country is a fairly accurate index of its industrial progress. The accompanying map [4] shows the striking contrast in point of city life between the North and South on the one hand and the East and West on the other (Fig. 20). It is a climatic line (approximately 37° N.L.) which divides the urban North from the rural South, the area of abundant skilled white labor from the area of unreliable, unskilled negro labor. Even when skilled workmen are imported from the North to some particularly favored center of industry in the South, an enervating climate makes their labor far more difficult and less efficient. Even the entrepreneur does not escape the paralyzing touch of heat and moisture.

The contrast between the East and West in point of industrial and urban development is based upon a difference of geographical conditions and density of population. The territory lying east of the ninety-seventh meridian and north of the Potomac, Ohio, and Missouri Compromise Line contains about half of the total population of the United States, but comprises only about twenty-two per cent of its land area. Beyond the margin of aridity, stock-r ising, agriculture, and mining employ most of the inhabitants except in Colorado, California, and Washington, where again certain geographic influences raise the proportion of the urban population. But in general, conditions of prevailing aridity limit the number of people the country can support, while the exclusion of all but costly railroad transportation across long stretches of desert and over mountain barriers discourages industrial progress and its concomitant urban development.

[4] *Fifteenth Census, op. cit.*

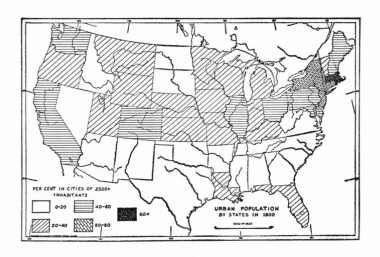

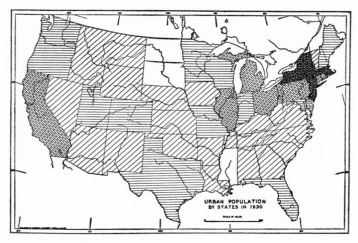

FIG. 20. URBAN POPULATION IN 1900 AND 1930

In 1930 only three states had less than 20 per cent of their population classed as urban; since 1900 a marked increase in urbanization has taken place in the south and in some of the western states. Compare with Fig. 19.

ROLE OF INDUSTRY IN URBAN CONCENTRATION

The area of intensest urban and industrial development is found in New England and the other states north of the Ohio–Potomac line (excluding Maryland and Delaware) and east of the Mississippi, an area in which urban life composes almost seventy-five per cent of the total. This development has been due to special local causes besides those general ones before enumerated as operating in the whole urban zone from the Atlantic to the Missouri River. The local advantage earliest felt was the water-power of New England and that developed in central New York with the construction of the Erie Canal. The whole Atlantic slope of the Appalachian Mountains naturally generates water-power. The rivers draining eastward cross an upland of resistant rock from which they descend to the coastal plain as cascades or rapids. This "fall line" stretches from the Delaware and Schuylkill southward as far as northern Georgia and Alabama, retreating farther and farther from the coast. In the lower courses of the New England streams, rapids and falls occur within a short distance of tidewater.

Besides this advantage of accessibility from the coast, as opposed to the long tortuous avenues of approach formed by the rivers of the most southern states, New England's water-power comes from concentrated falls due to the predominance of hard metamorphic rocks like granite, while in the interior and southern states softer rocks give rise to shoals and rapids, often too long and too wide to be utilized without heavy outlay. This is especially true of the larger streams. The Susquehanna has very little power economically available. In the southern states there are numerous abrupt falls on the small head streams, which, however, are subject to violent freshets due to the steep slope and heavy rainfall. In New England and part of the interior states, on the other hand, a more advantageously distributed rainfall, a larger precipitation in the summer and autumn than in the winter and spring, compensates for the evaporation during the heated term, and interior lakes of glacial origin regulate the flow of the drainage streams all the year round. Hence water-power was more readily available in the North Atlantic states.[5] There it was developed earliest and most extensively, though it was brought into requisition also for simple industries along the southern Piedmont. In 1870 it was used as much as steam in all the Atlantic coast states.[6] In New England it furnished 70.3 per cent of the total power used for manufacturing purposes, in the interior states 50 per cent, and in the southern 49.8 per cent of the total employed in these different sections, though the water-power utilized in the southern states amounted to less than half that employed in either of the other sections.[7] This was doubtless a result of retarded industrial development quite as much as less favorable geographic conditions in the mountain streams, as recent progress goes to prove.

The Cotton Industry. Local water-power determined the beginning of Lewiston, Manchester, Lowell, Lawrence, Pawtucket, Waterbury, and Fall River in New England,

[5] For exhaustive discussion, see article by Professor G. F. Swain in *Tenth Census, Water-Power of the United States*, I, Introduction. Also W. M. Davis, *Physical Geography of Southern New England*, National Geographical Monographs, I, No. 9; and Israel Russell, *Rivers of North America*.

[6] Other forms of power, particularly electricity and steam, have greatly lessened the significance of water-power. Nevertheless, the latter retains considerable importance. Although of the aggregate of power used in manufactures in the United States this type in 1927 produced only four per cent, for New England it furnished seventeen per cent. Furthermore, a large part of electrical power owes its origin to watercourses. *Statistical Abstract of the United States, 1931*, Washington, 1931, p. 815.

[7] *Twelfth Census*, Bulletin 247, pp. 23, 24.

and a line of towns along the Erie and Ohio canals. It has
been an especially important factor in the localization of the
textile industry, the manufacture of hosiery and knit goods,
and of wood pulp and paper. The cotton industry has
centralized chiefly in the water-power localities of New England and in the Piedmont region of South Carolina, North
Carolina, and Georgia. For the country as a whole, more
than ten per cent of the power used in manufacturing cotton
goods still comes directly from water wheels or water
turbines.[8]

Abundant water-power, accessibility to the raw material,
low cost of living, and peculiarly free conditions of labor
(for many years unrestricted employment of women and
children retarded development of labor unions) brought
about a rapid advance of cotton manufacture in the South,
and started a migration of the industry from New England
to the southern Piedmont. As an outcome of that migration, the South has achieved first rank in the nation's cotton
manufactures. In 1929, southern states embracing chiefly
North Carolina, South Carolina, Georgia, and Alabama had
more than half of the country's spindles and consumed
three fourths of the cotton used in the United States. In
keeping with this phenomenal expansion, water-power development has covered vast areas of the Piedmont south
with a network of electric transmission lines. At the beginning of 1931, the four leading states had a developed
water-power of 3,183,000 horse-power, North Carolina taking third place among the states as a producer of water-
power, Alabama fourth place, South Carolina sixth place.[9]
In contrast to the small scattered power developments of

[8] *Census of Manufactures, 1927*, Washington, 1930, p. 1275.
[9] *Statistical Abstract, 1931*, p. 392.

early days, many of the plants of today are gigantic, this by virtue of the impounding of vast artificial water bodies, a practice encouraged by the deep narrow valleys of the mountain streams, the relatively constant water-flow resulting from copious and fairly well-distributed rainfall in the forested watersheds, and the sparse population along such watercourses.

Power transmission and distribution by the use of an electric current has robbed water-power of that immobility which was its greatest disadvantage. It gives rise in the vicinity of large falls to urban centers of manufacture marked particularly by the lack of a congested factory district and by a predominance of the suburban character. The wide distribution of possible plant sites, as opposed to the crowding of the mills about the falls as we see them in Minneapolis today, is limited only by facilities of transportation. Decentralization of industry has progressed so rapidly in recent years that the philosophy of urban geography has undergone a profound realignment. And even the style of the buildings is modified, for massive walls to support heavy machinery are no longer necessary. Where smaller heads of water are used for the generation of electricity at commercially inaccessible points, as in the Sierras, the tendency is to concentrate this motive force at distant urban points in the lowlands, where raw materials and means of communication become determinants of the localization.

Paper. Water-power has been in many industries superseded or reinforced by steam, but in paper and wood-pulp manufacture it has remained supreme, constituting one third of all the power used for this purpose in 1927. The localization of this industry is instructive as showing the power of geographic control. The factors determining it are proximity to the supply of spruce and fir, the timber chiefly used in making wood pulp, and found in its greatest abundance near our northern frontier and in Canada;[10] water-power to operate cheaply the heavy grinding machinery; clear water for mixing pulp; and a near-by market in the newspaper presses and publishing houses of the large northern cities.[11]   Hence we find this industry localized along the Penobscot, Kennebec, Androscoggin, and Connecticut rivers; in Coos County in northern New Hampshire; in New York at the outskirts of the Adirondack Mountains. where water-power is abundant and the local supply of wood can be supplemented readily from the Canadian forests by the St. Lawrence River and the Champlain Canal; and in Wisconsin, where the abundant water-power north of Lake Winnebago and west of Green Bay, clear streams from the gravel-covered surface of an old glacial area, a large forest of northern woods, and proximity to the large Lake cities, which are made economically nearer by cheap water transportation, offer all the conditions necessary for the successful conduct of this industry.

Iron and Steel.   Where steam takes the place of water-power in the operation of manufactures, fuel becomes an important factor in the localization of industries, especially where it is found near iron, the other raw material fundamental to industrial progress, or where the two can be readily brought into conjunction by cheap transportation. The anthracite coal-fields and iron-mines of the eastern Appalachians in Pennsylvania explain the numerous in-

[10] The perfection of the "sulphate" process in paper manufacture has drawn also northern hemlock and southern pine into the rank of pulp-woods.

[11] *Twelfth Census*, Bulletin 244, p. 17.

dustrial towns of that section.   These owe their origin or
development to blast-furnaces, rolling-mills, and foundries.
Water transport on the lower Delaware and Hudson and
freight cars moving for the greater part of the way on a
downward grade from mines to seaboard have brought fuel
and iron at low cost to New England and the middle Atlantic states, and furnished the chief basis for the later industrial development of this section.   Accessibility to the
Pennsylvania mines explains the activity of iron and steel
shipbuilding from the coast of Virginia to that of Maine,
wherein the New York Harbor and lower Delaware River
districts contest the primacy.

The momentum of an early start and an extensive market
have combined to keep eastern Pennsylvania an important
area of iron and steel production; but rivals elsewhere have
taken the lead.   The barrier of the Appalachians, as we
have seen in a previous chapter, and the consequent higher
freight charges across them, soon after the Revolution
stimulated the exploitation of mining resources on the
western slope of the mountains, and gave rise to industrial
centers along the southern head streams of the Ohio.   With
the introduction of coke instead of anthracite as a fuel in
blast-furnaces, and the increased use of ores from the Lake
Superior mines, the center of the iron and steel industry
migrated across the mountains to the Connelsville district,
spreading from the sources of the Ohio northwestward to
Lake Erie, developing Johnstown, Pittsburgh, McKeesport,
Duquesne, and Newcastle in Pennsylvania, Wheeling in
West Virginia, Youngstown, Cleveland, and numerous other
towns in Ohio.   Connelsville grew up about its coke-ovens,
which at one time furnished forty-eight per cent of all the
coke manufactured in the United States.   Ohio owed its

phenomenal industrial progress to its position midway between the ore barges on Lake Erie coming from Superior mines, and the coal arriving by canal, river, and rail from the fields of western Pennsylvania and West Virginia.

But this westward migration of the iron and steel industry did not stop at Cleveland. Other lake ports were accessible to the northern ores and to Pennsylvania coal and coke. Hence we find this industry contributing to the growth of Buffalo, Lorain, Toledo, Detroit, Milwaukee, Chicago, Gary, and Duluth. The presence of iron, steel, and fuel early stimulated in this vicinity the establishment on a large scale of related manufactures, such as iron pipes, machinery, engines, and locomotives. Combined with a supply of hard woods from the adjacent northern forests, they gave rise to yet other industries. The whole line of the Great Lakes has a large production of steel ships and barges for the lake trade, while a broad zone of cities between the lakes and the Ohio make agricultural implements and automobiles and trucks (formerly farm-wagons) for the grain belt near by. The manufacture of agricultural implements, which must stand heavy freight charges on account of bulk and weight, became largely localized in the state of Illinois, which makes half of the total, and in Ohio, Wisconsin, and Indiana. The industry has migrated westward in the wake of expanding grain-lands. In the case of the automobile industry, advantages for wagon-making attributable to lake and rail transport facilities and the proximity of once abundant supplies of hard woods were major factors in the meteoric rise of Michigan's greatest industry. Well over half of the country's output of motor cars comes from this state.

The potency of iron ore and coal in giving rise to urban centers is demonstrated in the mineral belt at the foot of the Appalachian Mountains in northern Alabama, where the mere names of some of the towns and settlements — Birmingham, Sheffield, Bessemer, Irondale, Ironton, Dolomite, Newcastle, Connelsville, Carbonville, Coalberg, Coal City, and Coaldale — suggest the cause of their existence. Despite a late start, adverse labor conditions, an enervating climate, and, until the improvement of the Warrier and Tombigbee rivers, the lack of a cheap waterway to the sea, the Birmingham district holds third place among the leading iron and steel centers of the country. It is surpassed only by the Pittsburgh–Cleveland and the Chicago–Gary concentrations.

All the industrial centers which we have considered in relation to iron and coal production have had a close geographical connection with the Appalachian Mountains: they have been on the slopes of this upland area or have been readily accessible to it by rail, canal, and ocean on the east, or by the Great Lakes, rail, and Ohio River on the west. They may be called the cities of the iron belt, and hence show industries sprung purely from the products of farm and field, just as some of the outermost towns of this zone, in turn, coincide with the few marginal manufacturing points of the grazing belt beyond. There is just one spot where all these belts overlap, where the industries emanating from the products of mine, forest, grain-field, and cattle ranch all come together, and that is Chicago. Hence its growth from a village of two hundred and fifty inhabitants in 1832 to a metropolis with a population of almost three and a half million a brief hundred years later.

Flour. The flour-milling industry shows features of both strong localization and wide distribution. As flour and grist mills answer chiefly only local demand and do not belong by nature to city industries, we find them widely distributed; only those large establishments producing for a big domestic and foreign market contribute to urban development (Fig. 21). Hence Minnesota's eighteen per cent of the country's total production represents a strong localization. The principal factors, aside from the concentration of population in the middle west and northeast, are the proximity of Minneapolis to the spring wheat region, the power of the upper Mississippi, and the access to lake and railroad. Similarly, Buffalo counts for most of New York's ten per cent of national output, by combining the advantages of its position as eastern terminus of the Great Lakes (for the United States), its power resources in Niagara, and the access to the Erie Canal belt of transportation facilities.

Liquors. Proximity to the great central grain-fields favored the production of malt liquor in St. Paul, Milwaukee, Chicago, St. Louis, and Cincinnati, though a local demand from a large German population also contributed to the result; and the same factor of location was operative in the manufacture of distilled liquors in Illinois, Kentucky, Indiana, and Ohio, the chief states in this industry, before prohibition. The increased production toward the margin of the western and southern agricultural area was striking. Distilled liquors, owing to their relatively small bulk and large value, could bear the cost of transportation far better than the raw materials from which they were made; hence the industry showed a strong tendency to localize near the grain supply.[12] It was a marked factor in urban development only in the case of Peoria and Louisville. In Kentucky especially it was distributed in small establishments in the rural districts, generally wherever a large spring or

[12] *Twelfth Census*, Bulletin 180, pp. 7, 21, 22.

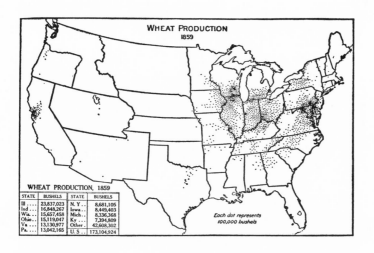

WHEAT PRODUCTION 1859

Each dot represents 100,000 bushels

WHEAT PRODUCTION, 1859

STATE	BUSHELS	STATE	BUSHELS
Ill	23,837,023	N. Y ..	8,681,105
Ind ...	16,848,267	Iowa..	8,449,403
Wis..	15,657,458	Mich..	8,336,368
Ohio..	15,119,047	Ky ...	7,394,809
Va ...	13,130,977	Other .	42,608,302
Pa. ...	13,042,165	U. S ..	173,104,924

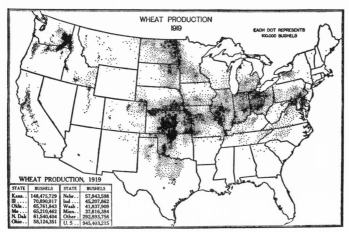

WHEAT PRODUCTION 1919

EACH DOT REPRESENTS 100,000 BUSHELS

WHEAT PRODUCTION, 1919

STATE	BUSHELS	STATE	BUSHELS
Kans..	148,475,729	Nebr..	57,843,598
Ill	70,890,917	Ind ...	45,207,862
Okla..	65,761,843	Wash..	41,837,909
Mo ...	65,210,462	Minn..	37,616,384
N. Dak	61,540,404	Other .	292,893,756
Ohio..	58,124,351	U. S ..	945,403,215

FIG. 21. WHEAT PRODUCTION IN 1859 AND 1919

The first important milling centers of the country developed east of the Appalachians; with the migration of population to the west, wheat production and milling centers grew up in new western areas. Except for a few great centers favored by power or special transportation facilities the flour milling centers are widely distributed over the areas of great production. (Courtesy of the United States Department of Agriculture.)

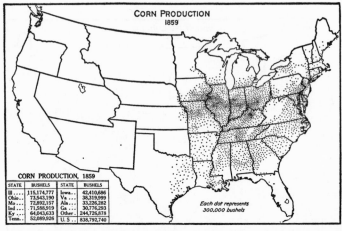

CORN PRODUCTION
1859

Each dot represents
300,000 bushels

CORN PRODUCTION, 1859

STATE	BUSHELS	STATE	BUSHELS
Ill	115,174,777	Iowa...	42,410,686
Ohio ..	73,543,190	Va ...	38,319,999
Mo ...	72,892,157	Ala ...	33,226,282
Ind ..	71,588,919	Ga ...	30,776,293
Ky ...	64,043,633	Other .	244,726,878
Tenn..	52,089,926	U. S ..	838,792,740

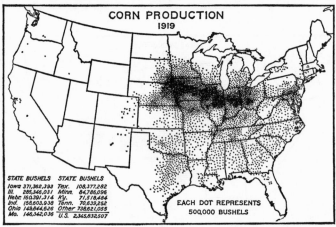

CORN PRODUCTION
1919

EACH DOT REPRESENTS
500,000 BUSHELS

STATE	BUSHELS	STATE	BUSHELS
Iowa	371,362,393	Tex.	108,377,282
Ill.	285,346,031	Minn.	84,786,096
Nebr.	160,391,314	Ky.	71,518,484
Ind.	158,603,938	Tenn.	70,639,252
Ohio	149,844,626	Other	738,621,055
Mo.	146,342,036	U.S.	2,345,832,507

FIG. 22. CORN PRODUCTION IN 1859 AND 1919

From the shores of Massachusetts and Chesapeake Bays to the Great Plains corn was the principal pioneer crop; it was planted among girdled trees, had a long harvest period and kept with little protection; it furnished food, shelter and bedding for the pioneer and his stock. Its importance is emphasized by the correspondence of early population and corn maps; the map of 1859 shows large corn production in areas of denser settlement, as on the Piedmont, in the Nashville and Lexington Basins, along the Old National Highway from Wheeling to St. Louis and in other areas. The Corn Belt of today has come to be the great swine and cattle fattening area of the country. (Courtesy of the United States Department of Agriculture.)

stream of limestone water furnished this desirable ingredient of the Bourbon product.

Meat. There has been a steady westward migration, following the advance of population, of all industries based upon cereal production; and these have been closely attended in their westward course by the allied industry of slaughtering and meat-packing. The herd and the cattle ranch naturally precede the corn and wheat field in the order of economic development (Fig. 22). Hence we find that whereas flour and grist milling is most highly specialized on the Mississippi, slaughtering and meat-packing has its most striking localization farther west on the Missouri. Here, however, an arid climate has reinforced the effects of later settlement.

The historical geography of this industry is instructive (Fig. 23). It began, as we have seen, in the early backwoods farms beyond the Alleghenies with the salting of hog products for export down the Mississippi to New Orleans and thence to the eastern seaboard cities. The Ohio, Illinois, and eastern Mississippi valleys were the chief stock-raising region of that day. Hogs especially ran wild in the "range" feeding on roots and nuts, or were fattened in the sty on corn. The salt came chiefly from the abundant mines on the Great Kanawha to the river towns. After the opening of the Ohio and Erie Canal, Cincinnati could command also the product of the Ontario mines in central New York; hence its supply of salt was assured. Its hams and bacon had a large market, particularly in the South.

The industry arose in Cincinnati in 1818 and had its chief center there until 1861–62, but numerous packing establishments sprang up in Columbus, Chillicothe, Circleville, and Hamilton, all of which were located on the Ohio canals; in

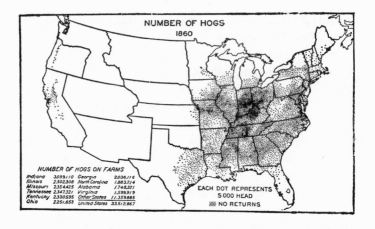

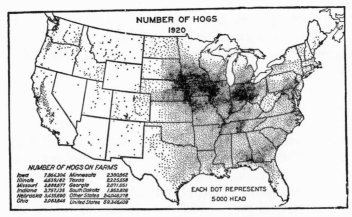

FIG. 23. NUMBERS OF SWINE IN 1860 AND 1920

The swine industry migrated with the settlers from the seaboard to the Great Plains; swine, fattened on the mast of the forest, supplied needed food and products for export of the early trans-Appalachian settlements, first down the Mississippi and later over the Appalachians. In the fertile upper Mississippi Valley so great was their production that in years of depression the steamboats at times found in bacon and salt pork a hot and cheap fuel. Today the distribution of swine emphasizes the productivity of the cereal lands of the upper Mississippi Valley. (Courtesy of the United States Department of Agriculture.)

several towns along the Ohio, notably Louisville, along the Wabash, Illinois, and Mississippi rivers; and in Chicago, where the industry began to develop in earnest only after 1850.[13] In 1862 the center migrated westward from Cincinnati to Chicago, where it has remained ever since, though the most striking industrial specialization is found beyond on the Missouri.

The slaughtering and meat-packing business had come in the meantime to include the preparation of cattle and sheep for the market, and the ranching frontier had been pushed farther west (Fig. 24). Extended railroad systems and the introduction of refrigerator cars for the transportation of meat rendered it more economical to kill on the border of the cattle belt and save freight costs on waste product. Thus have Kansas City (Kansas), Omaha, Fort Worth, St. Louis, and St. Paul become great packing centers. Almost three-fourths of the population in Kansas City earn their livelihood from the slaughtering industry, the city ranking next to Chicago in value of meat products. Chicago's location near the margin of the grazing lands to the west and the corn area just to the south, and its unsurpassed means of transportation, especially for the export trade, has assured it the primacy. An important part of the commercial activity of the city centers about its stockyards, packing establishments, and the dozen or more considerable industries which have developed to utilize the waste products of the slaughter-houses. Some of these are the manufacture of soap, candles, glue, fertilizer, gelatin, glycerine, ammonia, bonemeal, neat's-foot oil, felt, pepsin, margarine, brushes, and knife-handles.

The strong localization of the slaughtering and packing

[13] *Twelfth Census*, Bulletin 217, pp. 29, 30.

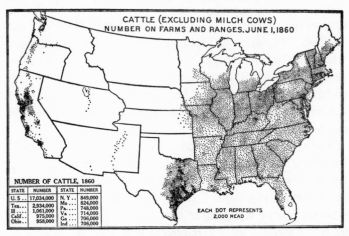

CATTLE (EXCLUDING MILCH COWS)
NUMBER ON FARMS AND RANGES, JUNE 1, 1860

EACH DOT REPRESENTS
2,000 HEAD

NUMBER OF CATTLE, 1860

STATE	NUMBER	STATE	NUMBER
U.S ..	17,034,000	N. Y ..	849,000
		Mo ...	824,000
Tex...	2,934,000	Pa. ...	748,000
Ill ...	1,061,000	Va ...	714,000
Calif..	975,000	Ga ...	706,000
Ohio..	958,000	Ind ...	706,000

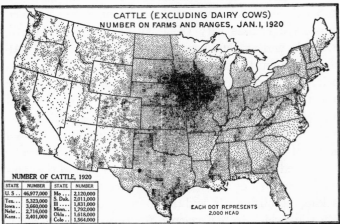

CATTLE (EXCLUDING DAIRY COWS)
NUMBER ON FARMS AND RANGES, JAN. 1, 1920

EACH DOT REPRESENTS
2,000 HEAD

NUMBER OF CATTLE, 1920

STATE	NUMBER	STATE	NUMBER
U.S ..	46,977,000	Mo ...	2,120,000
		S. Dak.	2,011,000
Tex...	5,323,000	Ill	1,831,000
Iowa..	3,660,000	Minn..	1,792,000
Nebr..	2,716,000	Okla..	1,618,000
Kans..	2,401,000	Colo ..	1,564,000

FIG. 24. NUMBERS OF CATTLE IN 1860 AND 1920

In the frontier march across the continent the "ranchers" frontier preceded close settlement and the production of cereals and swine. From the early settlements in the west cattle were driven over the Appalachians to the seaboard markets; these drives had almost ceased by 1860. The map of 1860 shows the areas of early settlement in the far west; Santa Fé region, California Valley and Willamette Valley; the cattle industry in 1860 had not reached the Great Plains area, later the great domain of range cattle; the chief beef cattle region today is the Great Plains and the western part of the Corn Belt.

industry in the central West is indicated by the fact that the solid block of six states in the corn belt — Illinois, Kansas, Nebraska, Indiana, Missouri, and Iowa — in 1900 yielded together 77 per cent of the total product of the United States reckoned in value and in 1931 51 per cent. Illinois led with 22 per cent of the total, Kansas produced 8 per cent, Iowa 7, Nebraska 6, Missouri 5, and Indiana 3.[14] A line of cities on the Missouri River, frontier posts of the urban area, manifests a very intense specialization in this industry, for it yields to Omaha 60 per cent of the value of all its manufactured products and to Kansas City, Kansas, 80 per cent.

"Black Gold." Intense specialization of another sort has converted many a cattleman into a type that his forbears of the open plains would have found incomprehensible. The origins of the change date to 1859, when one of the world's paramount industries reached commercial birth in the Titusville well in Pennsylvania. Thence production in the United States spread rapidly to Ohio, West Virginia, Kentucky, and Tennessee. These states, like Pennsylvania, have portions of their territory in the Appalachian plateaus, where porous sandstones in geologic age closely related to coal-bearing strata afford conditions conducive to the accumulation of petroleum in sizable underground pools. Success in the eastern mountains stimulated drilling in all parts of the country. By 1886, a Lima–Indiana field had become well defined. Oklahoma oil came to light in 1891. The Gulf Coast riches were adumbrated in 1901, those in Wyoming in 1912. On the west coast. California had found oil in good quantity by 1890; remoteness and coincident lack of capital retarded full exploitation for many years.[15] Today

[14] *Census of Manufactures, 1927,* Washington, 1930, pp. 172–86.

[15] Arnold, R. and Kemmitzer, W. J., *Petroleum in the United States and Possessions.* New York, 1931.

the petroleum fields *par excellence* are the Gulf Coast (Texas and Louisiana), the mid-continent (northern Texas, Oklahoma, and Kansas), and the California. Nature has labored mightily to concentrate the energy of numberless organisms in a form so readily utilized by human industry that almost all other activity gives ground where the irresistible force of petroleum development appears.

Petroleum and its derivatives have had a remarkable rise to indispensability in American economy. The precious fluid, of which the United States has such fortunate abundance, has proved so instrumental in nurturing many of the country's major lines of industrial activity that the western Crœsus' international standing is inconceivable without these riches. The latest prodigy — the recrudescent natural-gas industry — bids fair to outstrip all other in its speed of progress.

No less striking than the rise of petroleum as a barometer of national and world-wide industrial well-being has been the development of cities in areas of production and refining. The outstanding instances belong to Oklahoma. Oklahoma City, which in 1900 had a population of 10,000, now boasts 185,000, and Tulsa has sprouted from a hamlet of 1000 in 1900 to a now somewhat overgrown center of 141,000. The latter in particular illustrates the frenzied energy imparted to the rudiments of a city by the development of petroleum. Oklahoma City and Tulsa surpass other cities in their heavy specialization in petroleum. Yet the same astonishing power of city-nourishment appears to considerable degree in many other urban centers, among them most notably Los Angeles, and the first, second, and fourth cities in Texas — Houston, Dallas, and Fort Worth. Refining centers, in some cases more than a thousand miles from the well but closely tied to the producing district by pipe-line, show similar effects. These lie in areas of heavy consumption or in ports. New Jersey, for example, produces no oil, but only Texas and California eclipse it in the refining of petroleum.

Industrial Advance and the Frontier. Each frontier belt tends to pass more or less rapidly through all the stages of economic evolution, from ranch to field and from field to factory. The rate of progress is determined mainly by the extent of the zone in question, the quantity and quality of its arable soil, and the geographic conditions regulating competition. In the pastoral and agricultural stages competition hastens, in the industrial it hinders incipient development. Beyond the Great Plains, the corn and pasture lands of which support the packing industry of the central West, lies the vast territory between the Rocky Mountains and the Sierra Nevada, a region of scattered but productive agriculture where irrigation is possible, of wide cattle ranges, and abundant mines. It is a land of limited population, which the live-stock interest tends to distribute widely, but which the mines and intensive agriculture dependent upon irrigation canals tend to concentrate in certain small, favored areas, while wide stretches of desert and bare mountains are left wholly uninhabited. These facts seem to be the explanation of the rise in urban percentages in many of the far western states; but the striking urban development of Colorado, California, and Washington is determined in great part also by certain other geographic conditions.

Colorado Industries. Colorado's cities and towns have naturally sprung up in the vicinity of its mines and of its upland water supply for irrigation. This state, in addition to gold, silver, copper, and lead, has also an abundant supply of iron and coal, the essentials of manufacture, found notably along the one hundred and fifth meridian at the eastern base of the mountains. Remoteness from the centers of manufactures east of the Mississippi, the lack of cheap water communication, and the prohibitive freight charges on the bulky and heavy commodities required by a mining and agricultural population not only in this state but also in the vast intermontane territory behind it, have combined to exclude competition and force the industrial development of Colorado. Denver's geographical location at the foot of the Rocky Mountains, near three of the natural passways to the Far West followed by the Union Pacific, the Denver and Rio Grande, and the Santa Fé railroads, has made it a distributing-point for a large hinterland. It has a population of 288,000. Just to the south Pueblo, with a similar location and a population of 50,000, and Colorado Springs (population 33,000), have a predominant industrial development growing out of remoteness and mines. But the Colorado urban industries include also extensive smelting works, the manufacture of iron and steel, of foundry and machine products to answer the local demand; slaughtering and packing, owing to the adjacent live-stock area; flour and grist milling which avails itself of the abundant grain crops nearby; and a large tourist industry.

The Pacific Coast. On the Pacific seaboard, also, remoteness from the eastern manufacturing centers and the consequent lack of competition early gave an impulse to industrial development. The presence of trans-oceanic markets on the populous coasts of Asia and coastwise trade along the western shore of the American continents widened the market which inland was limited for most commodities by a mountain barrier. Abundant products of forest, ranch, field, orchard, and vineyard furnished many of the raw materials of manufacture. However, the lack of coal and iron and of the cheap and reliable labor developing with a dense population proved a great drawback, but did not suffice to counterbalance certain local advantages. In Washington and Oregon abundant water-power, especially on the Columbia and Willamette rivers, has in part compensated for the lack of coal for many years. California is finding a valuable substitute for coal in the products of its extensive oil-fields in the south, and in the generation and transmission of electrical energy from the plunging streams of the Sierra Nevada in the region of abundant rainfall in the north. In 1929 the state obtained 293,000,000 barrels of petroleum from its myriad oil-wells, of which quantity it used more than one third. How well the people have met the problem of poor coal resources is further evidenced by the fact that California leads the country in the production of hydro-electric power, generating one fifth of the aggregate for the United States. Moreover, the states' activity in the stupendous Boulder Dam project indicates the future of hydro-electric power on the Pacific coast.

The Pacific coast states, like Colorado, are industrial epitomes in consequence of their isolation; but the list of their leading manufactures marks them still a comparatively undeveloped country where land is abundant and the resources of forest, pasturage, and field are still ample. Even the motion picture phenomenon does not lessen the validity of such a statement. Lumber and timber industries, flour and grist milling, and slaughtering are prominent in all three states. In Washington and Oregon fish canning and preserving, which springs from the run of the salmon in the northern streams, is balanced by the canning of fruit and vegetables in California. Allied to these industries are planing-mills, paper and wood-pulp mills in the northern states, where, in consequence of a heavier rainfall and more recent exploitation, timber is most abundant. Car construction and repair-shops tell of the western termini of the great continental railroads. The rank of sugar and molasses refining among the industries of California points to the proximity of the Hawaiian Islands, whose raw sugar seeks San Francisco as the nearest port of entry into the United States.

All of these industries are due to abundant raw materials. The manufacture of foundry and machine products, on the other hand, in spite of the high prices of coal and iron, has developed to large proportions purely as a result of geographical isolation in response to a local demand for mining tools and machinery. This has been the case especially in California, though to no small degree also in Washington and Oregon. The year following the discovery of gold in California (1849) saw the first foundry established in that state; and in 1860 San Francisco alone had fourteen foundry and machine shops. The stimulant of a strong local demand has brought the industry now to such development that even in the face of existing disadvantages certain lines of its products not only control the local markets but also enter the markets of the world. The next step has been the rise of iron and steel shipbuilding.

The marked industrial character of the cities in the Pacific coast states is indicated by the fact that urban manufactures constitute the bulk of the total industries of this section. There is far less of the "neighborhood industry," production for local consumption, which characterizes all the states between the Sierras and the Missouri River except

Colorado, and most of the region south of the Ohio River. Despite the remarkable advance of recent years, it is safe to say that the industrial and hence urban development of the Pacific coast region will make great strides in the future. The questions of paucity of population and power have lost their weight and the quality of labor and market is well attested by the many recent establishments built to repre-sent eastern manufactures in this growing market. Already the local population in itself constitutes a significant pur-chasing power. With the trend towards trans-Pacific outlets for American products well defined, the western coast will continue to have great attraction for eastern population and capital.

CHAPTER XVII

THE GEOGRAPHICAL DISTRIBUTION OF RAILROADS

THE internal commerce of any country is based upon geographical conditions of size, location, zonal extent, and various topographical features tending to modify soil and climate. The larger a country, the greater in general are its chances of a diversified surface, contrast in climate, and hence the multiplicity of products which leads to exchanges. Large extent means wide climatic variation such as that between New England and Florida, Minnesota and Louisiana. China's location between the twentieth and fifty-fifth parallels gives it a basis for internal commerce similar to that of the United States between the twenty-fifth and forty-ninth. Mere zonal extent is not enough, however. Russia's long stretch from the fortieth to the seventieth parallel affords no advantages equal to those of China and the United States, because so much of the area falls within the polar and sub-polar region; yet in view of its monotonous lowland surface, only this great extent makes possible an internal Russian commerce between the forested north and the grain-fields and cattle pastures of the south. Everywhere along its southern border, from the Black to the Japan Sea, Russia has gradually enlarged its limits, with the result that it has diversified its products, as the cotton-fields of Russian Turkestan show, while it has striven to secure for the same an outlet to the sea. In the widely distributed British Empire, the distinction between internal and foreign commerce is lost; but the enormous size of that

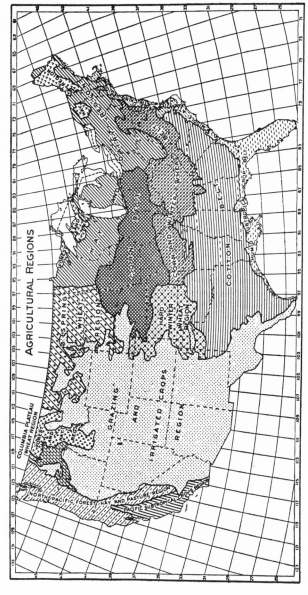

FIG. 25. AGRICULTURAL REGIONS OF THE UNITED STATES

This map shows the variety of agricultural and forest products of contrasted regions of the country. To it may be added the coal, iron, water power, and manufactures of the eastern United States and the mineral and oil sections of the west. The great railway net of the continent closely binds together the area of greatest production. Compare with Fig. 31. (Courtesy, U.S. Dept. of Agriculture.)

commerce, however it may be classified, has its basis in the area and the almost unlimited variety of geographical conditions embraced within the British possessions.

DIVERSITY OF PRODUCTS AND RAILROAD DEVELOPMENT

No other continuous political area in the world, with the possible exception of China, shows so many different geographical divisions distinguished by different staple products as the United States (Fig. 25).   Underlying such diversity of products is the great variety of physical conditions — physiographic, climatic, soil, vegetational, mineral (Figs. 26 and 27).   The interrelationships of these factors have produced a country more nearly self-sufficient than any other.   Within its boundaries, however, the specialization of activity fostered by variety in resources and facilities of transportation has caused no section to become self-sufficing and each depends upon all the rest.   The stock of the Rocky Mountains and the Great Plains moves now to the packing-houses on the Missouri and the Great Lakes which are feeding the concentrated industrial region of the Northeast; now to those on the Pacific coast which are furnishing meat for the growing Hawaiian, Alaska, and Asiatic trade.

Note to Fig. 26:

   This map represents some of the most significant facts in the history of the United States.   It pictures an enormous land which for thousands of miles on its coasts receives enough precipitation to give the landscape at least the appearance of habitability.   Such appearance and the rivers to enhance that impression, particularly in the lands east of the 20-inch line, lured the *conquistadores* and *voyageurs* far into the interior, with the result that development of the agricultural regions shown in Fig. 25 had the opportunity to begin early.   It is true that conditions of transportation long arrested that progress, but the knowledge of the country which such early explorations provided proved of incalculable value.   (Courtesy of the United States Department of Agriculture.)

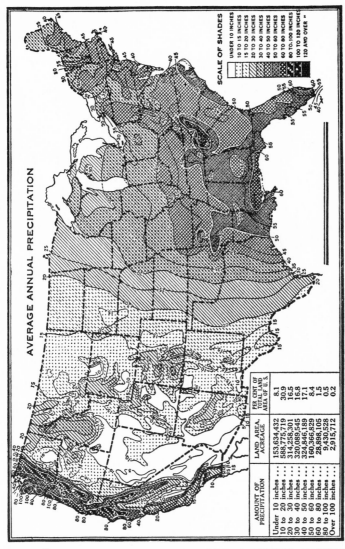

FIG. 26. ANNUAL RAINFALL MAP OF THE UNITED STATES

(See note at foot of page 370)

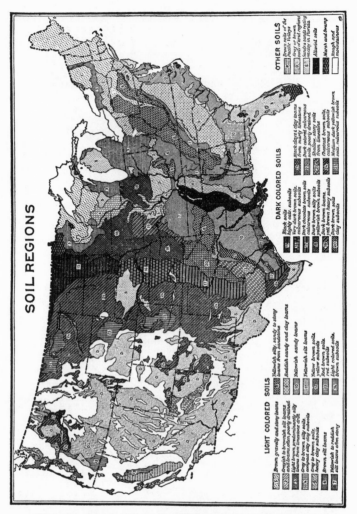

FIG. 27. SOIL REGIONS OF THE UNITED STATES

The early visitors drawn inland by the appearance of a well-watered land had little concern for soil science. Indeed, when they came upon that matchless expanse of prairie provided by nature in a generous mood, they deemed the soil of little value, for according to their experience forested areas inasmuch as the vegetation grew so much taller, had greater productivity. Their descendants now survey the richest agricultural region in the world, a region enjoying that preëminence because of the rich soils which rainfall and vegetation have evolved in the sedimentary and glacial deposits of the interior lowlands. (Courtesy of the United States Bureau of Soils.)

The Columbia and Puget Sound regions send their lumber, canned fish, and wool to supply the East and get in exchange the finished merchandise which goes to swell the current of commerce. Cotton moves from the Gulf states to supply the spindles of more northern states and coal from the Appalachian mines supplies the plantations of the South. "The statistics of internal trade movements show that both the outgoing foreign and the domestic commerce of the country depend principally upon the industries engaged in the production of these staple products. These industries are known as the fundamental or extractive industries, and include agriculture, mining, stock-raising, lumbering, and fisheries. Manufactures and merchandise contribute a comparatively minor portion of the total tonnage carried in a given year. The dividend-earning tonnage of the western roads, for example, is found chiefly in the volume of the grain and cattle shipments. Lake transportation is supported primarily by ore, grain, and coal freight. The southern railroads rely on cotton, lumber, coal, and fruits for their prosperity." [1] As much today as at the time they were penned in 1900, the preceding quoted statements testify to the nation-building qualities of a diversified continental area.

The vast scale of this geographical specialization of products involves enormous movements of freight. It has brought about the evolution of the American railroad system. As with the products, the railroads manifest the influences of variety in physical conditions, by falling into several well-defined divisions. Because chiefly of differences in population, however, these divisions do not

[1] From *Internal Commerce of the United States, Summary of Commerce and Finance*, January, 1901.

wholly correspond to those formed by forest, mine, crop, or factory. The section in which the greatest movements of internal commerce occur has become the channel of practically all the great trunk lines reaching from the interior to the Atlantic seaboard. This channel is constricted on the north by the downward bend of the Great Lakes and the geographical location of the Mohawk depression, and on the south by the rough upland of the Cumberland Plateau, the determining line of the Ohio Valley, and the central gaps of the Appalachian Mountains. Norfolk and Boston, together with all the intervening ports, are its eastern termini on the Atlantic coast. To the west, so many different railroad lines extend to the foot of the Rockies within the limits of the thirty-seventh and forty-third parallels that a railroad map of Kansas and Nebraska looks like a closely striped fabric. The meridional division of the sections of production in the Far West allows to the overland railroads a wider north-and-south distribution, so that their course is determined chiefly by the best passes through the Rocky Mountains and the location of the few good ports on the Pacific. One road ships eastward fresh fruits from southern California and Arizona, while a more northern line brings similar products from Oregon and Montana.

BASES FOR THE CHARACTER OF THE NATIONAL SYSTEM

The great breadth of the United States and its highly favored interoceanic position has given to its railroads a predominant east-and-west direction. The expansion of the American people from seacoast to the interior, and from the interior on to the sea again, has been repeated in the history of American railroads, but at a tremendously accelerated rate.[2]   Compare a transportation map of Oklahoma or Texas of 1900 with one of 1932 to gain an adequate idea of how accelerated that rate became.   The star marking the center of population was poised on the

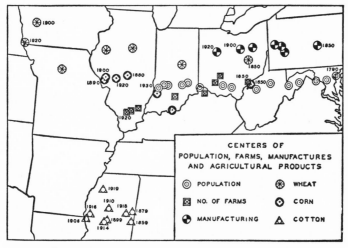

FIG. 28. CENTERS OF POPULATION AND PRODUCTION

The center of population from 1790 to 1930 has moved from the head of the Chesapeake to western Indiana along the 39° parallel; the centers of wheat production show the influence of the early development of the Red River Valley of the north and later the southern Great Plains, while the center of all farms has moved slightly to the southwest.   Data for the centers of manufacturing, wheat and corn for 1910 are not compiled.   (From the United States Census.)

summit of the Alleghenies in 1830, while infant railroads only here and there were crawling up the first easy grade of the Atlantic coastal plain (Fig. 28).   Twenty-one years

[2] Land speculation had an important part in this expansion of railroads in a picturesque though not altogether legitimate manner. The speculators contrived to gain bloated values for their holdings, then used such values and political pressure to justify demands for railway service. The United States owes much to such activity, despite a considerable amount of unnecessary construction which stimulated the consolidation of many early lines.

later a line of rails stretched through central New York to Lake Erie, and the Baltimore and Ohio road had reached an equally western point in Piedmont, West Virginia (79° W.L.), close on the trail of the star, which was moving down the sunset slope of the Allegheny Plateau towards Parkersburg and the Ohio. But eighteen years after that, an overland express drew in to the shores of San Francisco Bay, while the star still lingered in the valley of the upper Ohio.

Railroad development in the United States proceeded with amazing rapidity, so that it soon outstripped that in all other countries, with the result that this country now has one third of the world's railway mileage. Although consolidations and the many-sided competition of truck, bus, private automobile, and airplane have in recent years led to an actual decline in mileage, the country still enjoys the facilities of 250,000 miles of trackage. (See Fig. 31.) The great size of the territory, its long distances, made railroad communication more necessary than in Europe. Its simple continental build, yielding long stretches like the Atlantic plain, the Mississippi Valley, the prairies, and the Pacific Valley, was favorable to railroad construction because of the relatively few obstacles which it presented.[3] Moreover, the oneness of our country, as opposed to the political dismemberment of Europe, was conducive to the operation of great through lines and that consolidation of interests which early appeared.

In the first decade of their history, these roads, which in forty years were to rib the continent with steel, were merely accessories to established routes of water travel; or they united some adjacent interior town with the seaboard; or

[3] Ratzel, F., *Politische Geographie der Vereinigten Staaten,* Leipzig, 1897, p. 553.

they served as a short cut across the land between two ports which had previously established active intercourse by more devious coastwise communication.

Influence of Established Routes of Water Travel. Among those railroads having for objective an established waterway, we find the short line running sixteen miles from Carbondale to Honesdale (1828) and connecting the Lackawanna coalmines with the Delaware and Hudson Canal; the line of seventeen miles from Albany to Schenectady, opened in 1831 to accommodate passengers on the Erie Canal by saving them the long détour of the waterway between these two points; the road southward from Saratoga to Schenectady (21.5 miles) opened in 1832, and the branch off this line from Ballston to the Hudson at Troy (25 miles), completed in 1835; the road from the head of Lake Cayuga southward to navigation on the Susquehanna River (34 miles), opened in 1834; the railways over the high land between Philadelphia and Columbia on the lower Susque- hanna (81 miles), and the Portage Road over the summit (2491 feet elevation) of the Allegheny Mountains (36 miles) just east of Johnstown, both opened in 1834, to form links in the canal route joining Pittsburgh and Philadelphia; the Baltimore and Ohio, which in 1833, after a piecemeal construction, extended to Harpers Ferry (81 miles) on the Potomac, and there tapped the canalled river whereby passengers avoided the long détour of water travel around the end of the Potomac peninsula; the short independent road from Harpers Ferry up the Shenandoah Valley to Winchester (32 miles), opened in 1836; the little roads in Louisiana from Port Hudson on the Mississippi (21.5 miles) northeast to Clinton, opened in 1833, from Bayou Sara in the same vicinity to the town of Woodville (27.5 miles),

RAILROADS
IN
OPERATION IN 1840

SCALE OF MILES
0 _____ 500

FIG. 29. RAILROADS IN 1840

opened in 1842, and that from New Orleans running eight miles to Carrollton, opened in 1835 (Fig. 29).[4]

All these roads, with the exception of two, were distinguished by very short length, which emphasized their auxiliary character. But the last one to be mentioned in this class, the road between Boston and Albany (1842), owing to the lack of inland waterways in New England, had to strike two hundred miles across hill country and river valley to reach the growing western commerce which was coming out by the Erie Canal. This road, therefore, owing to the side-tracked position of Boston in relation to the great interior routes of the country, had to leave the convenient level of the tidewater and lowland, and take a more difficult upland course to the debouchment point of the Erie Canal. Hence in point of length, which is the measure of urgency, it resembles the Baltimore–Potomac and the Philadelphia–Columbia lines; all three tap established routes to the productive trans-Allegheny country.

Advance in All-Rail Routes. The second class of early railroads comprises those aiming to connect inland points with the seaboard, which commands the world's great waterway. They are characterized as a whole by greater length than the first class. Among them we find the germ of the Boston and Albany, the road running from Boston to Worcester (44 miles), opened in 1835 and extended to Springfield in 1838; the line from Boston to Lowell (26 miles) in 1835; from New Haven to Hartford in 1839 and extended along the easy route up the well-populated Connecticut Valley to Springfield in 1844, to Greenfield in 1846, to South Vernon on the Vermont border in 1849, whence it

---

[4] *Poor's Manual of America Railroads*, issues of 1880–1890, for these and subsequent dates and statistics.

branched off up the little Ashuelot River to Keene, New Hampshire, in 1851; the road up the Housatonic Valley from Bridgeport, Connecticut, forming a conjunction with the Boston and Albany route at West Stockbridge on the New York state line in 1842; the Philadelphia and Reading road (98 miles) and a branch from Lancaster on the already established Columbia and Philadelphia line running off 54 miles to Harrisburg, both opened as early as 1838, and that in spite of competing canals; a line from Portsmouth at the mouth of the James River in Virginia running 80 miles back from the coast to Weldon, North Carolina, opened early in 1835; one from Charleston, South Carolina, to Hamburg on the Savannah River opposite Augusta, opened in 1833, when its 135 miles made it the longest continuous line in the world, and extended by a branch to Columbia in 1840, whereby the cotton of the interior could be more readily concentrated in the chief port of the southern Atlantic seaboard; and finally another road subserving a like purpose, opened in 1841 throughout the 192 miles between Savannah and Macon, Georgia.

Coastal Railroads.   The third class of early railroads was designed to connect coast points, and therefore, from Pamlico to the eastern end of Long Island Sound, had to compete with the inside coast passage of canal and bay and the highway of the open ocean.   But the circuitous ocean route from point to point and the slow progress through the canals, winter storms on the outside passage and ice blockade on the inner channels, necessitated more direct and reliable communication.   Hence we find the early development of what we may call the coast or "fall line" railroad. The dates of construction of this geographical line of roads, made piecemeal by different companies, as were all early ventures of this sort, are instructive as indicating the intensity of water competition, which varied with the directness of the sea route. The railroad from Boston to Providence appeared as early as 1835, because it cut off the long détour of the sea-way around Cape Cod. It was supplemented in 1837 by a road from Providence to Stonington, Connecticut, which landed passengers and goods at the entrance of the protected course of Long Island Sound and thus avoided the dangerous navigation around Point Judith at the southern extremity of Rhode Island. Otherwise this road, which ran along within two miles of the coast in order to avoid the hundred feet elevation line of the interior, did not greatly shorten the distance between Providence and Stonington. The Sound route from Stonington to New York is safe and direct. Hence we find the railroad from New York to New Haven did not open until 1849, and that from New Haven to New London in 1852. Along the eastern shore of Massachusetts, also, where exceptional maritime conditions had produced a race of seamen, railroads developed somewhat slowly in competition with coastwise communication. The Eastern Railroad, consolidated from several minor lines running directly northward near the coast, was opened between Boston and Portsmouth, New Hampshire, in November, 1840, and extended two years later to Portland, Maine. This road served the manufacturing area of eastern Massachusetts and competed with the longer sea route around Cape Ann; but its branch running from Beverly out to Gloucester and Rockport on the extremity of this peninsula was not constructed until 1847. Plymouth waited for rail connection with Boston until 1846.

"Fall Line" Roads. South of New York Bay, more

devious sea routes between the leading tidewater cities, due to the long projections of the New Jersey, Maryland, Virginia, and Carolina peninsulas, and incidentally the location of the national capital on the medial one of the series, early determined the construction of a chain of railroads across their base. The deep-running estuaries of this stretch of coast necessitated the location of the railroad approximately along the "fall line" from New York south to Goldsboro, North Carolina; but there it left the one hundred foot elevation line and dropped down to Wilmington at the mouth of the Cape Fear River.

Following this road in detail, we find that the earliest link in the chain reflected the active intercourse between New York and Philadelphia. It ran from Camden, on the Delaware River just opposite Philadelphia, 64 miles to South Amboy on Raritan Bay; it was begun in 1830 and finished in 1834, four years before the completion of the Delaware and Raritan Canal. In 1839 a second railroad (31 miles) was opened between Bordentown and New Brunswick, the termini of the canal, parallel to the first road in its eastern half. A line opened between Jersey City and New Brunswick (34 miles) in 1838 completing the communication with the Hudson River and New York.

From Philadelphia southward the railroad, following closely the line of one hundred feet elevation, was opened in 1837 through Wilmington, Delaware, to Baltimore; there it connected with the Washington branch of the Baltimore and Ohio, which had already been in operation three years. From Washington the Potomac, owing to its southward course as far as Acquia Creek, long persisted as a link in the line of communication between the national capital and Richmond. A road was opened in 1837 between Richmond and Fredericksburg on the Rappahannock near the bend of the Potomac, but not until 1872 was the line extended to Washington and the steamer trip from Acquia Creek dispensed with. A writer in 1873 deplores this as the sacrifice of "one of the most pleasurable features of the trip between Washington and Richmond." (See map of Virginia rivers, Chapter XIV.)

From Richmond a short line (22 miles) was finished southward to Petersburg in 1838, to complete connection with an existing road (since 1833) which ran closely along the one hundred foot elevation line across the base of the deep peninsula of southern Virginia directly southward through Emporia to Weldon, North Carolina. Difficulty of communication down the rivers of North Carolina, the long détour around Albemarle Sound, Chesapeake Bay, and the James River had undoubtedly dictated this cut-off road. The continuation of the line southward through Goldsboro to Wilmington was not made until 1840, a fact which reflects the slow economic development of North Carolina at that time.

To the geographer the interesting fact in this long chain of railways from New York City to southern North Carolina is its close adherence to the line of one hundred foot elevation. This is the line marking cities, mills, and the head of navigation on the rivers or their estuaries, retreating farther and farther from the seaboard from the mouth of the Hudson southward. This western limit of the coastal plain presented few problems to railway building beyond the bridging of the wide drainage streams, which in early days were crossed by ferries from station to station.

Piedmont Railways. The smooth, even slope of the Piedmont upland and the broad trough of the Appalachian Valley also offered few obstacles. Hence as the development of the hill and interior valley country progressed, these natural longitudinal routes were traced by a line of rails from northern Georgia to the Potomac. The Piedmont road, now the Southern system, runs at an elevation between five hundred and one thousand feet from Manassas Junction, whence it connects with Washington, southwest through Culpeper, Orange, Charlottesville, Lynchburg, and Danville in Virginia; Greensboro, Salisbury, and Charlotte, in North Carolina; Spartanburg, Greenville, and Westminster, in South Carolina, to Atlanta, Georgia.

Piedmont railways are a feature of every map. They mark the limit set by nature to economic construction of great routes of transportation along the flanking plain. Their elevation varies with the magnitude of the mountain system which they trace, and the surface features of the plateau base which they traverse. We see the piedmont railroad of the Atlantic slope reproduced in the piedmont lines at the eastern foot of the Rockies, running from Calgary (3388 feet elevation), at the base of the mountain wall in western Alberta, southeast through western Montana, where along the sources of the Missouri River, the Yellowstone, and the Big Horn it rises at times to an elevation of five thousand feet; thence south along the Laramie Range to Cheyenne and still at the same altitude along the eastern base of the Colorado Rockies through Denver and Pueblo to Las Vegas, whence it turns westward across the mountains by the old Santa Fé Trail to the valley of the Rio Grande, to follow this stream southward to El Paso.

Only the long, gradual upward slope of the Great Plains, which places the foot of the Rockies at a considerable elevation, renders possible railroads of such length at such an altitude. The steep grade of the Alps and the Himalayas from the Po and Ganges respectively eliminates the piedmont plain as a physical feature; hence the piedmont railways run along at a very low altitude. In the case of northern Italy, the deep reëntrant valleys of the Italian lakes conspire with the slope to force the railroad almost down into the plain of the Po. In northern India the piedmont railway begins at Peshawar at an altitude of only 1165 feet in the northern corner of the Punjab, falls to an altitude of 820 feet of Ludhiana — though Simla at the terminus of a branch road only about sixty miles northeast of this point lies at an elevation of 7116 feet — to 700 feet at Rampur, and to 255 feet at Gorakpur, where the Ganges begins to encroach still more upon the base of the Himalayas.

But unless a mountain system presents an almost insuperable barrier, as in the case of the Caucasus and the Himalayas, a piedmont railway, owing to the less fertile and productive character of the country which it traverses, unless valuable mines supply the motive for its early development, will in general be antedated by transmontane roads, because the over-mountain country with its different climate and products offers a better field for commerce. This was true in the United States in the case both of the Appalachians and the Rockies. Especially is this the order of development when beyond the mountains lies the sea. The purpose to reach Pacific ports pushed both the American and Canadian overland roads.

Trans-Appalachian Lines. The period from 1830 to 1860 saw six railroads constructed across the Appalachians at various points between the Mohawk Valley and northern Georgia, where the upland system dwindles away into low hills offering little obstruction to railway building (Fig. 30). The roads followed with slight variations the lines of least

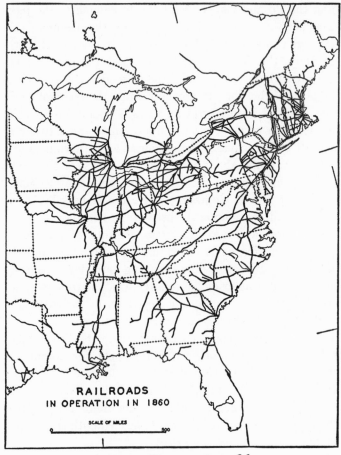

RAILROADS
IN OPERATION IN 1860

SCALE OF MILES

FIG. 30. RAILROADS IN 1860

resistance settled upon by the old trails of Indian, trapper, and western pioneer, and the later routes of proposed canals which were constructed in whole or in part, or were abandoned altogether as impracticable.   From New York to the

southern boundary of Virginia the lower altitude and dissected character of the Appalachian system afforded the first
routes for railways which were economically possible; but
from Virginia southward for a stretch of three hundred and
fifty miles, the massive wall of the Great Smoky Mountains
effectively discouraged the construction of a railway over
this barrier until 1882.

The route which saw the only through canal system across
the Appalachians saw naturally the first transmontane railroad.   From the little seventeen-mile road from Albany to
Schenectady as an embryo developed the different stages of
westward railroad advance along the line of the Erie Canal.
Year by year the links in the chain were added — Utica and
Schenectady in 1836, Syracuse and Utica in 1839, Auburn
and Syracuse in 1838, Rochester and Auburn in 1841,
Rochester, Lockport, and Niagara Falls in 1838.   In 1843 a
traveler could cross the state of New York by rail from Buffalo to Albany, but he was carried by sixteen different companies.   In 1851 the Hudson River railroad completed rail
connection between the Atlantic seaboard and Lake Erie.

To New York belongs the honor of having constructed
also the second railroad across the mountains.   The Erie
road, taking advantage of the dip in the mountains south of
the Catskills, started from Piermont on the lower Hudson,
taking seven years to crawl over the Highlands to Port
Jervis on the Delaware, whence it pushed rapidly westward
along the valley of the Susquehanna and its western tributaries, and over the second watershed to Dunkirk on Lake
Erie, in 1851, nowhere reaching an elevation of eighteen
hundred feet.   Thus in this year New York had two lines
from the harbor of the Hudson to the western lake.

The Erie was followed closely by the Pennsylvania, and

Baltimore and Ohio railroads, opened respectively in 1854 and 1853. The impracticability of a canal between the Potomac and the Ohio forced the development of the more southern road. It reached the old pioneer station of Cumberland, at the northern bend of the Potomac, as early as 1842; but from that point the discouragement to construction over the rough surface of the Allegheny Plateau and the high altitude to which it had to ascend (2620 feet) retarded its completion to Wheeling and the Ohio until January of 1853. The Pennsylvania line extended westward from Harrisburg, which since 1838 had had rail connection with Philadelphia, followed the canal route up the Juniata River to Huntingdon and Holidaysburg, passed thence over the summit of the mountains to Johnstown and down the valley of the Conemaugh River to the Allegheny, and down this stream to Pittsburgh. Difficulty of construction over the main crest of the mountains delayed the road for two years, so that through connection was not made until 1854.

With the completion of these four roads across the mountains, the competition of rail and waterways began, but at first very slowly. In 1852 the through freight east on the Erie Canal was twenty-six times that carried by the Central and Erie lines, but in 1853 it was only fifteen times greater. In one year more the absolute decline of tonnage on the canal began to be alarming, so much was being diverted to its rivals. In Pennsylvania the inadequacy of the canal system as a transit route over a mountainous country had long been apparent, and its early (1857) purchase by the railroad company eliminated the last vestige of competition it might have offered.

In the meantime, the opportunity for a railroad around the southern extremity of the Appalachians along the route known to the early Cherokee traders was being exploited, and a chain of many links from Savannah and Charleston through Atlanta and Chattanooga, the two "gate" cities, to river navigation at Nashville was completed in 1854, while another line from Chattanooga through Stevenson, Alabama, to Memphis opened connection with the Mississippi in 1858. The lack of river communication along this east and west route, the impracticability of Gallatin's proposed canal, the adaptation of the face of the country to railway building, and the need of access from the southern states of the Mississippi Basin to the Atlantic seaboard, all combined to push the construction of this southern line.

Chattanooga had now a central position on a great route east and west, and in its rear lay the Appalachian Valley, affording a natural route of communication with the northeast. Hence we find that the next transmontane line, though starting in Virginia, had Chattanooga for its objective. From its seaboard terminus, Norfolk, at the entrance of Chesapeake Bay, it ran westward along the low watershed between the James and Roanoke rivers to Lynchburg, which it reached in 1854. Thence it passed through the Blue Ridge by the water-gap of the James, turned southward up the Valley of Virginia by the path of the old Wilderness Road to Bristol on the upper Holston, in 1857, and down the valley of East Tennessee to Knoxville and Chattanooga by 1858. Though so late in being constructed, its value as a link in the great through road between New Orleans and the eastern cities was soon appreciated. Subsequently it became a main trunk line from which one branch turned off eastward at Morristown up the French Broad River to Paint Rock, on the western slope of the Great Smoky Mountains, in 1861, and there in 1882 formed a junction with a line which came up from Salisbury on the eastern piedmont railroad and crossed this forbidding range by way of Swannanoa Gap and the upper valley of the French Broad. Another branch from the Tennessee Valley railroad turned westward to Cumberland Gap, and there united in 1890 with another line passing down to central Kentucky; and a third one turned westward a little farther north at the elbow of the New River in western Virginia, passed down that stream for about thirty miles, and over the watershed to the Tug Fork of the Big Sandy by the old war-trail of the marauding Shawnees, and continued down that river to the Ohio and the railroads traversing its banks.

In the meantime, however, before these branch roads from the Great Valley thoroughfare had multiplied the rail routes over the Appalachians, another road was planning to utilize the pioneer trail from the western sources of the James over the mountains to the Greenbrier branch of the Kanawha. As early as 1857 a road passing along the head streams of the Shenandoah and the James had reached the base of the main Allegheny range at Covington. The extension to navigation at Huntington on the Ohio was undertaken entirely by the state of Virginia, which still cherished its old dream of being a great transit region, a dream which the river paths of the Virginia Mountains had awakened in the minds of Washington and Jefferson. The difficulty of construction down the New River cañon and the interruption of the Civil War retarded the construction of the work until 1873.

Three out of the four earliest trans-Appalachian railroads, as we have seen, followed the routes of finished or unfinished canals; and even after reaching the interior basin of the country, the railroads continued to search out the domain of the waterway as if to challenge its competition. The geographical facts are these. The waterways, whether lake or canal, traced the line of least elevation and hence least resistance. The westward trend of the Great Lakes brought the terminus of the water route near to the natural concentrating channel of the Mississippi River, and the western canals united the Lakes with the Ohio. Both lakes and canals, Ohio and Mississippi, were dotted with the largest cities of the western country. Commerce had been started in its course along these waterways. The limitation of canal navigation, due to shallow draft vessels and the short open season in these northern latitudes, soon proved a serious stumbling-block as western resources were developed and commerce grew. The lines of traffic which the canals had created the railroads fell heir to; the transmontane roads did not begin to come into their full heritage, however, until railways began to spread over the interior basin between the Ohio and the Lakes, and the produce of western farms could be loaded first into freight cars instead of canal-boats. Thus the strategy of transportation patronage lay in the question of reloading. When railroads by their wide expansion had gained this point, by their rapidity and reliability they surpassed their rival. Hence we find the western trunk lines seeking the path of the waterways.

Development of Interior Systems. Just as Ohio was the first western state to follow the example of New York in canal building, so now she was the first to imitate her in the construction of railroads. Here again geographical location on the constricted area between free navigation on the Ohio and the Great Lakes was a potent factor in transportation development. It made a short passway for the steel arteries of commerce as before for water channels. The Mad

River railroad, begun in 1832, was opened in 1848 between Sandusky on Lake Erie and Dayton, a city which already had canal communication with the Lake through Toledo. This road in connection with a previously (1846) completed line, the Little Miami between Springfield and Cincinnati, which was also in canal communication with Toledo, formed the first through line from the Ohio to Lake Erie. A second line in operation in 1851 connected Columbus with Cleveland, and a third opened communication between Cleveland and Pittsburgh in 1852.

Thus Ohio had three railroads across the state from north to south when the New York trans-Appalachian lines began to push westward along the southern rim of Lake Erie, from Buffalo to Erie, Pennsylvania, in February, 1852, from Erie to Cleveland later in the same year, and from Cleveland to Toledo in January, 1853. This was the last link in the line between New York and Chicago, because the approximation of the heads of Lakes Erie and Michigan had some years before suggested the plan of a railway short cut across the base of the Michigan peninsula. This line, first projected to run from Monroe just north of Toledo over to New Buffalo (a suggestive name) on Lake Michigan opposite Chicago, was pushed half of the distance to Hillsdale in 1843; but when reorganized under a new company was diverted to Chicago and the road from lake to lake opened in 1852 with the eastern terminus at Toledo.

No sooner had the New York roads connection with the lines of the Lakes and the Ohio Basin than an enormous increase of their commerce ensued. To this the state of Ohio contributed a large measure. In spite of slack water navigation on its canals, traffic had previously followed its drainage streams, owing chiefly to the different areas of production in the state. About two thirds of the wheat had sought an outlet by the Lakes and the Erie Canal; corn, which was grown largely in the southern part of the state, and all other provisions went out by the Ohio River to New Orleans, whence they were transported to the Atlantic seaboard. Of the exports of beef from Cincinnati in 1851, the year prior to the through railway communication with the East, 97 per cent went down the river and only 2 per cent northward to the Lake. Of the Indian corn, the river traffic got 96 per cent and the Lake 3 per cent; of the flour, the former got 97 per cent and the latter 1 per cent. Lard, pork, and bacon sought these outlets in about the same proportion.[5] A small quantity of all these articles supplied the demand in the growing city of Pittsburgh. The heavy movement of provisions to the South was due in part to the fact that animals could not be slaughtered until cold weather had set in, closing navigation on the canals. Hence the provision trade was readily diverted to the railroads, and with the growing demand in the eastern markets attending increase of population and of industrial development, it soon came to constitute an important part of the through traffic.

When the Pennsylvania road completed its connection with Pittsburgh, its rail communication with Cleveland was already established. The next year after the Baltimore and Ohio came into Wheeling a line was opened from Bellaire in Ohio, nearly opposite Wheeling, westward to Columbus; and another road, branching off northwestward from this at Newark, established communication with Sandusky and the Shore line in 1856. Thus the region of the Ohio and the Lakes was rapidly drawn into the sphere of influence of the four eastern roads.

[5] *Poor's Manual of Railroads, 1881,* p. xvii.

But beyond lay the Mississippi, and already the traffic of this great waterway was being tapped by the Chicago and Rock Island railroad, which was completed in 1854. Prior to this time the canals from Lake Michigan had exerted little influence in directing the Mississippi trade eastward to the Lake route. All the produce along its western tributaries and most of that from its eastern bank went down the river to New Orleans. The current of the Illinois River carried southward most of the products of central Illinois, and only those from the northern part of the state sought the Lake outlet. But from this time the stream of traffic was deflected at right angles toward the eastern markets. Between 1855 and 1856 Chicago became the center of roads radiating to the Mississippi — to Galena, Alton, Burlington, Quincy, and the mouth of the Ohio. In 1858 the Milwaukee and La Crosse road struck the Mississippi higher up. The next step was to the Missouri, from Hannibal to St. Joseph through northern Missouri, in 1859, and an extension of the Galena line through Iowa to Council Bluffs in 1866.

The intense localization of our industrial and urban development in the northeastern part of the United States, the concentration here of our great commercial ports, and the distribution of our chief foreign markets across the Atlantic yet farther east in Europe, were the main factors in determining the early east-and-west direction of our principal railroads (Fig. 31). When the Mississippi Valley was finally opened to the eastern lines, railroad building progressed rapidly, finding in its gentle slopes and low watersheds slight obstacles to construction. The bridging of its wide streams was one of the most serious problems. We notice today certain large features of railroad distribution in the

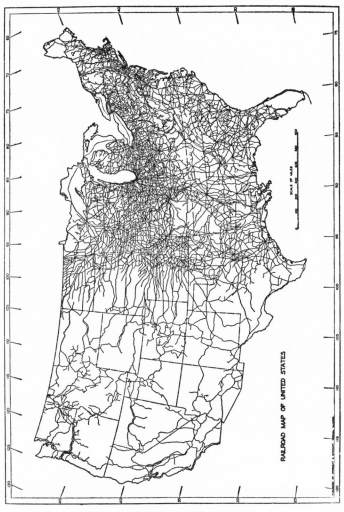

FIG. 31. RAILROADS IN 1930
(Courtesy of McKnight and McKnight.)

United States.   The most striking of these is the coincidence
of the area of intensest urban development with that of the
greatest railroad development.   Here the network of steel
rails is thickest.   It tells the story of incoming raw materials
and of outgoing finished commodities, of many mouths to
feed, bodies to clothe, houses to build, and of many factories
to be supplied with fuel.   We notice particularly how all the
great lines from the Northwest have to turn the corner
sharply at Chicago, owing to the deep indenting inlet of Lake
Michigan, and thus produce a congestion of railroads which
has been the making of that city.   We next observe a thin-
ning of this steel network in the agricultural South and the
arid West; the occurrence of certain "vacant spots" where
the mesh becomes still wider, spots already familiar as areas
of sparse population, in the swamp region of southern
Florida, in the lumber region of northern Maine and Minnesota, in the barren Ozark Mountains of Missouri and
Arkansas, and in the rough upland of the Cumberland
Plateau in West Virginia, Kentucky, and Tennessee.   The
few railroads which enter the latter region, with only one
exception, strike across the axis of the Appalachians, indicating their primary character as transit lines.   The
western base of this mountain system, owing to the irregular
limit of the Allegheny and Cumberland plateaus, has developed no well-defined piedmont railroad such as outlines
the eastern foot of the Appalachians.

We notice lastly beyond the eastern margin of the arid
belt a marked predominance of east-and-west roads and a
sudden decrease, almost a cessation of railroads running
north and south.   West of this limit we find few such roads.
The outstanding are three: the Cordilleran piedmont already mentioned; a second line running south from Helena

and Butte, Montana, diagonally across the axis of the Rocky Mountains and down the head stream of Snake River to Pocatello, whence along the western base of the Wasatch range to southwestern Utah it forms the piedmont road of this rim of the Great Basin; the Pacific Valley line running from Puget Sound along the old trails from the Nisqually to the Columbia and from the Willamette to San Francisco Bay, and on up the San Joaquin Valley to southern California.

The Transcontinental Roads. Across the belt of the Great Plains many lines strike out boldly for the Rocky Mountains, following sometimes the banks of the parallel drainage streams, more often seeking the solid ground of the watersheds between. Only seven pass the mountain barrier and reach the Pacific; but in view of the youth of the country, its arid and mountainous character, and the sparsity of its population, this number speaks eloquently for the power of attraction of two opposite coasts. Its situation between two oceans makes of the United States a great transit land; hence the amazing development of the transcontinental lines. The alternative of this overland transportation from New York to San Francisco, a distance of three thousand miles, until the Panama Canal was completed, meant a voyage over four times as long around the Horn. The wide separation of the Baltic and Pacific coasts of Russia, with the choice of a long voyage through arctic or through tropical seas, has forced upon the Muscovite the construction of the great Siberian Railroad. A similar situation in Canada called forth its first overland road. All these great lines had a political as well as a commercial motive; the political was immediate, however, and the commercial was largely a matter of faith in the future. The Russian line was purely a

government undertaking; the first in Canada began as a
government project, but later was released to a subsidized
syndicate; but in the United States political urgency dictated a gigantic system of land grants and subsidies to the
transcontinental roads, which, owing to the character of the
country which they traversed, were most expensive in construction and along certain stretches could probably never
count upon the support of local traffic.[6]

These overland railroads, for a great part of their way,
keep to the old California, Oregon, Santa Fé, and Gila River
trails.   The more northern ones follow for shorter distances
the footsteps of Lewis and Clark and other early explorers.
But the engineer straightens the routes which Nature made
and avoids détours which were the traders' only paths.
The zonal distribution of these transcontinental roads is
interesting.   We find three northern lines starting from the
western Great Lakes.   In the stretch from the Red River
of the North to Puget Sound a number of cross-lines connect them with the Canadian railways of the prairie provinces and British Columbia, arteries through which so much
rich American blood has been poured into the infant giant of
the Far North.   The main lines are dotted every few hundred miles with railroad plexus, all lying in so narrow a belt
as to stress the directness of the connection between eastern
and western termini which is permitted by the far-flung
plains spanning the distance between the Great Lakes and
the Rockies.

The same phenomenon is observed in the other overland

[6] In this way the government has granted more than eight per cent of its continental area — 245,000 square miles — to aid railway construction.   Typical of the
early generosity was the Northern Pacific grant, consisting of a band forty miles
wide across Minnesota and eighty miles wide across North Dakota, Montana,
Idaho, and Washington.   United States Department of Agriculture, *Yearbook, 1898*,
Washington, 1916, pp. 327–29.

routes. The next one to the south takes its course almost along the forty-second parallel from Chicago through Council Bluffs, Omaha, Cheyenne, and Ogden to the northern end of Great Salt Lake; thence it deviates from its adopted path, sending one branch off along the old Oregon Trail to the Columbia and Portland, another southwest by the California Trail to San Francisco Bay. A third artery between the Pacific and the Salt Lake oasis follows approximately the old Spanish Trail southwest across the Mohave Desert and through Cajon Pass to Los Angeles. Thus Salt Lake City has become preëminently the railroad center of the Great Basin. In addition it is entered from the east by the fifth trans-Rocky railroad, which, adhering closely to the thirty-ninth parallel, moves straight across the country from St. Louis through Kansas City, Pueblo, Salida, Glenwood Springs, and Grand Junction to the Green River at the town of Greenriver, and thence turns sharply northward to join the Wasatch piedmont road at Utah Lake.

The destiny of the Salt Lake oasis as a concentrating point is assured, because for a stretch of almost two hundred miles across northwestern Arizona the cañon of the Colorado River acts as a barrier to deflect overland railroads either northward towards Salt Lake or southward below the outlet of this mighty trench. Hence we find the next overland route leading directly west along the thirty-fifth parallel from Albuquerque, New Mexico, to Mojave, California, where it unites with the Pacific Valley line. For a time this Santa Fé system was the only road across the great western highlands to make a distinct bend, either north to Pueblo or south to El Paso, to establish its eastern connections. The desolate expanse of the Llano Estacado of northwestern Texas, flanked on the west by the barren mesa-dotted high-

lands of eastern New Mexico and on the east by the undeveloped area of the Indian Territory, proved an uninviting
field for railroad enterprise.

Farther south, the Gila River depression, the gap in the
mountain wall at El Paso, the grass highlands of central
Texas, and direct connection with the earlier roads eastward
from the Mississippi Valley around the southern end of the
Appalachians, have determined the line of the remaining
transcontinental route.   This also adheres closely to one
parallel, the thirty-third, near which it leaves the Mississippi River and passes through Dallas and Fort Worth in
Texas; but then it drops southward one degree for the
mountain gap at El Paso and the easy route over the Sierra
Madre Plateau, followed by Cooke's wagon-trains in 1846.
It strikes the thirty-third parallel again on the Gila River,
and this line it keeps to southern California, where mountains deflect it north to Los Angeles and bar it from San
Diego, its natural Pacific terminus.

The striking facts in these overland railroads are their
distribution in northern, central, and southern groups; the
directness of the lines of connection from east to west; the
development of an interior concentrating point in the Salt
Lake oasis and of two marginal ones on the Pacific.   One of
these is located near the Canada boundary about Puget
Sound, which receives three of the American transcontinental roads and is in close communication with the Canadian
roads where they issue from the mountains at the mouth of
Fraser River; and the other is near the Mexican frontier at
Los Angeles, which to its two overland railroads has added
two lines from the interior deserts of the Great Basin and
another pair giving it coastal and valley communication
with San Francisco and the north.   To San Francisco re-

mains always the advantage of its central location and its direct line of communication with the northern Atlantic seaboard.

The Pacific coast is remarkable for the fairly even distribution of its active ports along all its great length — Seattle and Tacoma at about 47° 30' N.L., Portland at 45° 30', San Francisco at 37° 45', and San Pedro, the harbor of Los Angeles, at 33° 45'. In this it presents a striking contrast to the Atlantic coast, which has all of its important seaboard points crowded together between Boston (42° 20' N.L.) and Norfolk (36° 50' N.L.), a stretch of five and a half degrees of latitude as opposed to nearly fourteen degrees between extreme ports on the Pacific. The explanation of this phenomenon is to be sought in the various geographic influences already discussed, which have determined economic development and railroad distribution in the whole northeastern section of the United States.

CHAPTER XVIII

THE UNITED STATES IN RELATION TO THE AMERICAN MEDITERRANEAN

MEASURED in terms of length and configuration of coastline, which are the determinants of a seaboard base, and gauged by the productiveness and extent of the contiguous hinterland, the United States has a greater claim to strength as a Gulf power than as a Pacific. Its foothold upon the western ocean measures only 1810 miles, and except for a narrow coast strip, excessive aridity limits the productiveness of much of the country naturally tributary thereto. The deep inlet of the Gulf of Mexico creates for the United States a southern seaboard measuring 1852 miles, back of which lies the rich Mississippi Basin, its slope emphasizing the leaning of the country towards the Gulf.[1] The Pacific coast, in view of natural disadvantages, has achieved an amazing development; and yet this is only a promise of what is to come. For many years the possibilities of our Gulf development were neither recognized nor utilized. The narrow circle of the Caribbean lands formed the natural field of its foreign commerce. Their products too, like those of the Mississippi Valley, are agricultural though tropical. Countries where pack-trains of burros are the prevailing means of transportation do not offer conditions for extensive exchanges. Where the Gulf ports have sought outside markets in Europe, they have suffered from the competition of the commercially developed centers lying between Massachusetts and Chesapeake bays. The southwestward trend

[1] Ratzel, F., *Politische Geographie der Vereinigten Staaten*, Leipzig, 1897, p. 17.

of the Atlantic coast from Cape Cod to the extremity of Florida brings Tampa Bay, our most eastern port on the Gulf, in the longitude of Sandusky, and Corpus Christi in that of Fargo, North Dakota; so that wheat from the famous Red River Valley takes a shorter trip to England than do the products of the Texas fields.

The advantages of the Gulf coast over the Atlantic seaboard earlier lay only in its greater proximity to Mexico, Central America, and the Caribbean coast of South America; but with the opening of the interoceanic canal this advantage was extended to the whole Pacific coast of the two continents. The consequences of the Spanish-American War reflect full cognizance of these facts. They gave additional impetus to the shifting of the country's commercial center of gravity towards the south, a movement amply illustrated in the trend of population in the western Gulf states.[2]

OLD-WORLD AND NEW-WORLD MEDITERRANEANS

The Gulf–Caribbean Basin was the first part of the western hemisphere to be actively developed. The wealth of the Spanish possessions in Mexico and Peru made it a thoroughfare for galleons from Vera Cruz or Porto Bello on the Isthmus, where they had received the burdens of heavily laden mules bringing gold over the highway from Panama. This old preëminence passed from it, to be revived for a season when the tide which set toward California

[2] With the exception of the Pacific and Mountain states, the 1930 census category of the West South-Central States — Arkansas, Louisiana, Oklahoma, and Texas — shows the greatest proportionate increase in the country since the Spanish-American War. *Fifteenth Census, United States Summary, Population Bulletin*, First Series, Washington, 1931, p. 4.

in 1849 took largely this channel until the opening of the overland railroad. On a relative basis the area probably will never regain its rank. Nevertheless, the Spanish-American War, the Panama Canal, and the progress of South America have given it powerful stimuli. This historical rise, decline, and rise again of great sea basins is not new. The ascendency that once belonged to the Baltic has been lost and so far never regained; had it become the terminus of German and Russian railroads the Persian Gulf would have had its eminence restored. The sleep which descended upon the Mediterranean at the middle of the fifteenth century was broken by the shouts of de Lesseps' workmen on the Suez Canal, but the completion of the canal has not fully restored to its bordering land the old maritime energy. The Mediterranean and the Persian Gulf regained their importance when they became avenues to the Pacific, and it is this world ocean which is to determine the final significance of the Caribbean Sea and Gulf of Mexico.

The two Mediterraneans are alike in many respects. Both wash the shores of three great land masses with their tideless waters. Both have two basins each, a northwestern and a southeastern; but the Gulf of Mexico manifests a resemblance also to the Black Sea. Like the latter it lies apart from the marine path of interoceanic travel and is such a landlocked sea that Spain, prior to the loss of Mexico, was geographically in a position to block American commerce passing out into the Caribbean Sea, just as Turkey, when it enjoyed a bi-continental location, could bar Russia from the Ægean. Both Mediterraneans have seen their several basins, like so many segregated land areas, follow different lines of historical development, resulting largely from differences of geographical location. Each sea has an outer or Latin basin. In the Old World Mediterranean the inner basin has been marked above everything else by the constant recurrence of Asiatic influences emanating from the Phœnicians, Syrians, Persians, Saracens, and Turks; in the New World sea, the inner basin gets its stamp from the youngest, freshest, most progressive civilization of the Anglo-Saxon race. Thus these two present the most marked contrast, and are in a large sense representative of their respective hemispheres.

The two Mediterraneans, though interesting as areas of differentiated local development, focus upon themselves the attention of the world at large because by their east-and-west extension and location in or near the belt of the northeast trade-winds, which was so long the pathway of circum-mundane travel, they form links in the chain of oceanic communication around the world. Both being inlets of the same ocean, they extend the reach of the Atlantic from Suez to Panama. But at these extremities a slender belt of sand and a low line of hills have blocked the path of navigation. These narrow necks of land have debarred the Atlantic side of their respective hemispheres from intercourse with the same countries — the rich, historic lands of eastern Asia; and both have pointed to the expensive and dangerous alternative of doubling a great continent by a long voyage. The American isthmus was discovered because the Asiatic one existed; in trying to avoid Suez, the early mariners found the Isthmus of Panama.

The American Mediterranean, in spite of its more southern location between the tenth and thirtieth parallels, is quite as near to the center of maritime activity in North America between Baltimore and Boston (39° 20′ to 42° 20′ N.L.) as the Straits of Gibraltar (36° N.L.) to the leading ports of Europe between the forty-ninth and fifty-fourth parallels, at Havre, Antwerp, Rotterdam, Hamburg, Bremen, Southampton, London, and Liverpool. And though the Atlantic entrance to the Suez route is located so far north, its exit into the farther ocean at Aden (12° 45′ N.L.) falls almost as far south as the Pacific end of the Panama Canal (9° N.L.).

Function of the Mediterraneans. Both Mediterraneans therefore seem destined by nature as great transit basins; but whereas in the European body of water one narrow, easily guarded channel secures connection with the main Atlantic, in the American a dozen or more straits of varying breadth and depth afford free access to the commerce of the world. The Gulf of Mexico, almost encircled by the sweep of broad land masses from the extremity of Florida to the tip of the Yucatan peninsula, backed everywhere by a hinterland of abundant resources, has nevertheless only one direct avenue of approach from the Atlantic, Florida Strait; and the control of this is shared by the United States, Cuba, and the British Bahamas just outside the passage. The Yucatan Channel, the natural line of communication between the mouth of the Mississippi and the Isthmus of Panama, connects the Gulf with the Caribbean.

This sea presents a marked contrast to the northern basin. A narrow rim of isthmus lands on the west and of islands on the north and east make it appear like a mirror in a delicate frame. The thickly strewn islands of the Lesser Antilles border it on the east for four hundred miles, affording harbors and passages in plenty for vessels bound for Caribbean ports or for the Panama Canal; for this is the focus of navigation lines in the American Mediterranean. On the north the land frame is more continuous. For twelve hundred miles the rather compact line of the Greater Antilles forms the containing wall from the western point of Cuba to the eastern end of Porto Rico, except where broken by the Windward and Mona passages. Hence this northern rim of the Caribbean presents the more highly strategic positions from the military standpoint,[3] and to the United States the more important locations from a commercial. because its channels form the natural avenues of approach for all vessels from New York seeking the Panama Canal.

Europe first gained a foothold in the western hemisphere along the Atlantic or island rim of the Caribbean Sea, and there she longest maintained her claim. Until the end of the Spanish-American War the eastern marge still belonged to Europe, while the western held typically New-World republics. Wedged in between Spanish Cuba and Porto Rico, republican San Domingo presented as much of an anomaly in its colonial surroundings as formerly democratic Switzerland in the heart of feudal Europe. The only exception to be found on the mainland shore was in British Honduras. Of the original Spanish empire in America, Cuba and Porto Rico alone remained to the descendants of the first discoverers; but they too have slipped from the nerveless grasp of a decadent despotism. North of these lie the Bahamas, which England appropriated when her colonists settled the Carolina coast near by, and which now are island remnants of vast continental possessions reaching to Florida and the Mississippi. To the south is Jamaica, which Cromwell took to adorn the cap of the Commonwealth. In the Lesser Antilles, British, French, and Dutch, have established themselves at the cost of Spain; for many years the Danes too had a foothold, but strategic

[3] Mahan, A. T., *The Interest of America in Sea Power*, Boston, 1897, p. 303.

value impelled the United States to purchase in 1917 their right to the Virgin Islands. Formerly even Sweden was represented by the island of St. Bartholomew. The British possessions in this group are most numerous and extensive, though the French hold the two largest islands, Guadeloupe and Martinique.

Islands in a Mediterranean. Islands are detached areas physically and are detachable areas politically. They tend to fall to the nearest political domain; this is what we may call the politico-geographical law of gravity. But the attraction of a larger and stronger country may prove more potent than that of a nearer but smaller land. According to this law Corsica belongs to France, Sardinia and Sicily to Italy, though Sicily in its checkered political career has experienced the sway of Carthaginians, Romans, Saracens, Spaniards, and Italians. The Cretan War, late in the last century, was in certain aspects an expression of this politico-geographical law of gravity. The American annexation of Hawaii illustrates the same principle. Cyprus acknowledged once the supremacy of Phœnicia, later that of Turkey, which holds the near-by coast of Asia Minor and Syria; but still later it was alienated to Great Britain, which was operating on another geographical principle, the control of strategic points on a transcontinental waterway. Hence the world at large, and especially the most interested parties, have looked to see the Greater Antilles obey the law of their geographical location and fall to the United States; and there are some who anticipate that the same great magnet will eventually draw to itself the other fragments of European empires in the Caribbean Sea.

THE UNITED STATES IN THE CARIBBEAN

The irresistible strength of the magnet has had repeated demonstration. Some of the political entities concerned prefer to regard the attracting power not as a magnet but as an extremely horrendous octopus. Whatever such opinions be, the needs of the greater land require satisfaction; no amount of animus would have prevented the United States from attempting the acquisition of an Isthmian Canal. In its early phases, the magnetic principle in the Caribbean took the form of guardianships with a view in some cases to eventual annexation. The latter step has materialized only in a few instances, notably Porto Rico and the Virgin Islands. The later phases, dictated by growing requirement for greater Caribbean security and for tropical foodstuffs, were facilitated by the unparalleled expansion in national wealth. The epithet "dollar diplomacy" was a foreign reaction to this expansion. In this case the power of attraction depended merely upon placing the southern neighbor in debt to American interests, as a consequence of which the United States has direct means of exercising a potent influence in the affairs of all republics facing the Caribbean.[4] In addition to the discussions of a Nicaraguan Canal, two recently advanced ideas, seriously considered by some who have an eye to the remote future, show how much strength the magnetic principle has today. One would have England cede Jamaica to the United States as a solution to our war-debt problem. The other gives Cuba to the United States to

[4] Witness American investments in these lands. In 1913, this country had placed $1,247,000,000 in Mexico, the West Indies, and the two South American republics of the Caribbean, Venezuela and Colombia. In 1928, the total had reached the staggering amount of $3,716,000,000. (Winkler, M., *Investments of United States Capital in Latin America*, Boston, 1928, pp. 274-78.)

help the island out of its financial troubles, these due in large part to duty-free Hawaiian, Porto Rican, and Philippine cane-sugar and to domestic beet-sugar.

The isolation which makes an island readily detachable, and its prevailing small size, which renders it easily controlled from within and, with the exception of those occupying important strategic positions, less an object of conquest from without because of its limited resources, have combined to maintain European powers in the West Indies. "Such a parti-colored sample card of political areas as is afforded by the Antilles is the expression of the geographical independence of islands; it makes a contrast to the magnitude of the political territories which we elsewhere find in America." [5] This bizarre arrangement would be impossible on any continent today. But these island fragments of broken empires are found everywhere. Tiny St. Pierre and Miquelon off the southern coast of Newfoundland are all that remain to France of its vast Canadian domain. The Channel Isles are the last geographical evidence of England's former dominion in France, as Cuba and Porto Rico were of Spain's supremacy in continental America. First detached from the common history of Mexico, Central America, and Peru, they are now detached in turn from the destiny of their mother country and follow the law of their geographical being. Although only Porto Rico and the Virgin Islands have become a part of the United States, the limited suzerainty established over Cuba, Haiti, and the Dominican Republic by the terms of treaties brings these islands in effect under the operation of this principle.

The expulsion of Spain from the Antilles was only the

[5] Ratzel, F., *Anthropogeographie*, Stuttgart, 1882, p. 575.

finishing touch in an historical process which had been going on for a century, and which the United States constantly aided and abetted. The only astonishing thing is that an operation which was so early accomplished on the mainland should have been arrested when extended to the islands. Geographical location and isolation have been two factors in bringing about this result.

The United States and Cuba. West Florida was acquired from Spain by the natural expansion of the American people, just as Texas was from Mexico. But there is a vast difference between proximity and contact. Cuba, although so near the mainland, has felt the isolation of island environment. The hundred-mile stretch of Florida Strait constituted an absolute boundary. This was sufficient to bar an influx of American immigration like the steady lapping of the human tide across the Mexican border. Isolation robbed Cuba of adequate support from American volunteers in its uprisings. Filibuster expeditions by sea could be more readily checked at the port of departure or arrival than the silent slipping of resolute men across a land frontier several hundred miles long. Moreover, the peninsula of Florida, which seems almost to bridge the sea to Cuba, was in fact almost wholly inoperative as a connecting link because of its extensive swamp lands, which render the lower third of the peninsula almost uninhabitable. There was here, therefore, no chance of an increasing population which should outgrow the narrow limits of a peninsula and overflow into adjacent islands, as exemplified everywhere else by peninsula history. By the Everglades of Florida and the barrier of the Strait, Cuba was removed nearly three hundred miles from the American frontier of settlement.

Nevertheless the interest of the United States in Cuba was close. By its size and location it presented a parallel to Ireland's politico-geographical relation to England. Its acquisition by a strong foreign power was always to be dreaded. When in 1823, it seemed that Cuba and Porto Rico were to be the price of England's support of Spain in a war with France, John Quincy Adams thus wrote to the American minister at Madrid: "These islands are natural appendages to the North American continent. One of them, Cuba, lying almost within sight of our shores, is an object of transcendent importance to the commercial and political interests of our Union. It commands the entrance to the Gulf of Mexico and the West Indian seas. The character of its population, its situation midway between our southern coast and Santo Domingo, its safe and capacious harbor of Havana fronting hundreds of miles of our coast destitute of such ports, the nature of its productions and its wants furnishing the supplies and needing the returns of a commerce immensely profitable, give to Cuba an importance in our national affairs with which no other foreign country can be compared. Such are the interests of that island and this country — geographical, moral, and political — that, in looking forward to the probable course of events for half a century, it is impossible to resist the conviction that the annexation of Cuba to the United States will be indispensable to the Union itself.... The transfer of Cuba to Great Britain would be an event unpropitious to the interests of the United States."

The annexation of Cuba was a constantly recurring proposition from 1807, when the seizure of the Spanish colonies in the Gulf region by either England or France seemed probable, up to 1898. But the United States had committed itself to a continental policy which it was loath to abandon, though statesmen again and again declared for island expansion. Jefferson advocated the acquisition of Cuba, because it could be defended without a navy, but opposed any farther seaward advance beyond the mainland.

The influence of the slave power came in to complicate the question, forbidding the liberation of Cuba by Mexico and Colombia in 1825 because the proximity of the island to the southern states made it an undesirable neighbor if a free-soil republic; Haiti was near enough. Later this very proximity, the adaptation of Cuba's products to the plantation system, and hence its ready incorporation into the body politic of the South, became reasons for its acquisition as a slave state in the view of the Southern party. This of course was opposed by the North; but from 1848 until the Civil War, repeated offers to purchase the island and numerous filibuster expeditions for its conquest attested the eagerness of the party in power to annex the island.

After the war, between 1867 and 1869, the advent of a spirit of expansion led to plans for the acquisition of San Domingo and the Danish Isles; but the American people as a whole were apathetic about the advantages to be gained and the old continental policy was not abandoned. Nevertheless, from the time (1868) Cuba began to make a sustained effort to secure its freedom, the United States became deeply concerned for the fate of the island.[6] The Cuban question, which had been almost perennial since 1807, now became a daily one in the discussions of the President and his cabinet. Cuba lay just at this country's doors, and everything which influenced it fundamentally

[6] For relations of the United States to Cuba in this period, see Albert Bushnell Hart, *Foundations of American Foreign Policy*, 1901, pp. 108–33.

touched American commercial interests, which had been growing steadily since 1850. The peace and prosperity of this market of purchase and sale were of moment to the United States. Moreover, the proximity of its shores made the United States a natural base for filibustering expeditions, which, in spite of deeply aroused sympathies, the government was bound to prevent. Nearby ports became the refuge for Cuban exiles, the home of the Cuban Junta. Persecution started an exodus of Cuban subjects to the United States, where they became naturalized. Consider the large proportion of these people in the southern counties of Florida. From their adopted home they returned to transact business in Cuba, but their naturalization papers did not always outweigh their Spanish names and swarthy complexions to save them from mistreatment at the hands of Spanish officials. Thus the close relations, ethnic, commercial, and political, which grew out of geographic conditions, had their logical consequence in the expulsion of Spain from a last foothold in the western hemisphere.

From the war with Spain the United States issued as a Caribbean power. Hitherto limited to the segregated basin of the Gulf of Mexico by her virtual protectorate over Cuba, the pledge of naval stations on its coast, the possession of Porto Rico and two small islands in the Virgin Passage, and the purchase of the Virgin Islands, the United States has a base of thirteen hundred miles along the northern rim of the Caribbean. The possession of St. Thomas gives us control of the Anegada Passage, the doorway for many of the steamship lines from Europe and the easternmost important channel into this sea from the north.

THE PANAMA CANAL

The American advance into the West Indian sea derived its great significance from the paramount interest of the United States in an interoceanic canal to connect the Atlantic and Pacific shores of the country and secure closer communication with the new island possessions in the Orient. The war which yielded Porto Rico, and thereby raised the geographical status of the United States in the American Mediterranean, created also a more urgent necessity for a perfected transit route to the Pacific, magnified the country's interest in the canal, and at the same time increased its power to control it.

The configuration of that part of the North American continent which forms the western rim of the Caribbean Sea complicated the question of the location and construction of a transit channel. Nature unequivocally limited the Suez Canal to its present site; but geographical conditions in this western Mediterranean are quite different. The American isthmus is about fourteen hundred miles long, extending from the Isthmus of Tehuantepec in Mexico to the Atrato River in western Colombia. For the south-eastern stretch of six hundred miles the width of this isthmus is comparatively narrow, varying from a minimum of barely thirty miles to a maximum of one hundred and twenty miles, contracting to this last width again farther north at the Bay of Honduras and at Tehuantepec.

Isthmian Routes. The outlines of the map therefore would indicate numerous possible canal routes. A broad ridge of seven hundred feet elevation, too high and wide to be cut, eliminates Tehuantepec, though its nearness to the United States speaks eloquently in its favor. This was the line of Eads's proposed ship railway. A mountain range disposes of the Bay of Honduras. In southern Nicaragua, the San Juan River and Lake Nicaragua, forming links in an interoceanic route, and a passway over the mountain divide at only 153 feet elevation promise better conditions; they involve, however, earthquake dangers, a rather long (184 miles) transit route and the construction of artificial harbors at the termini.[7] Three possible lines, known as the Panama, San Blas, and Caledonian, terminate in the Gulf of Panama on the Pacific side. The first, with a summit elevation of less than three hundred feet and a width of thirty-six miles, though necessitating a canal of forty-nine miles, seemed to have most in its favor. The last two had the advantage in shorter length and superior ports on the Atlantic; but the height of the dividing ridge (681 ft.) would involve a tunnel canal which would outweigh the other advantages. Still farther south, the Atrato River, which is only seventy miles from tidewater on the Pacific at the nearest point, offered a possibility.[8]

In the early days of Spanish supremacy the long Atrato Valley was a natural transit route especially between the Gulf of Darien and Peru, but Philip II issued one of his genial decrees forbidding the navigation of the river on pain of death. The San Juan River was a regular line of communication for Spanish vessels plying between Cuba and Granada on Lake Nicaragua up to 1639; and again in 1850, when the rush of the gold-seekers to California put a strain on Isthmian transportation, this route was brought into

[7] Despite such problems this route seems destined for the second Isthmian Canal. In addition to proximity to the United States, arguments in favor of the Nicaraguan project include the difficulties of increasing capacity at Panama and the strategic value of an alternative passage between the oceans.

[8] *Report of the Isthmian Canal Commission, 1899 to 1901*, Washington, 1901, pp. 69–72.

requisition. Likewise the Chagres River, which is navigable for skiffs and light-draft vessels halfway across the Panama Isthmus to Cruces, was opened in 1534 for the Spanish trade, served later for California emigrants, guided the surveyors of the Panama Railroad, and later the engineers of the Panama Canal. Thus history repeats itself along even an insignificant watercourse which serves an important connection.

Owing to the threefold predominance of water on the earth's surface and the consequent development of marine transportation as commerce tends more and more to encircle the world, an isthmus soon loses its importance as a link between land masses, and becomes instead a barrier between water areas, which political and commercial exigencies require to be converted into an artificial strait. The Isthmus of Panama served as a passway for the aimless wanderings of the primitive tribes of Central and South America and was a factor in early ethnic distribution. But for centuries it acted only as a barrier to interoceanic navigation.

The supreme interest of the United States in an Isthmian Canal, the strength of its geographic location in relation to the same, its natural office as guarantor of the neutrality of the channel and the political stability of the country through which it passes, finally the abundant wealth, the resources of the Anglo-Saxon republic, and the steadily developed aptitude of its citizens for vast enterprises, all combined to lay the task of its construction upon the United States. The geographic influences which brought forth the fishermen of Gloucester, the spinners of Rhode Island, the fur-trading expansionists of the Far West, and the courageous manufacturers of the Pacific states have been only so many remote antecedent causes, stable, persistent, of the American control of the Panama Canal today.

Construction of the Canal. A "battle of routes" ensued when the United States finally determined to build a canal. By the middle of 1902, however, the Panama route prevailed. The means of obtaining rights to the passageway greatly lowered American prestige in Latin America. On the other hand, the country would have suffered more if it had allowed the Pacific and Atlantic seaboards to remain so far distant by water and if it had neglected to draw the west coast of South America closer to industrial centers of the northern hemisphere. Steps previous to actual construction comprised the acquisition of the French Canal Company, the severance of Panama from Colombia, the establishment of the new Republic of Panama, acquisition of rights to the needed "Canal Zone" late in 1903, clearing the path of all obstacles except the stupendous difficulty of sanitation in the Canal Zone and of cutting the canal.

In the years following 1903 the epic struggle with the physical geography of the Isthmus succeeded. By August, 1914, man had eradicated yellow fever and plague and had lessened greatly the ravages of malaria and other diseases of a humid tropical climate; he had lessened the likelihood of land slides fostered by steep slopes and heavy rains; he had negotiated a water channel with a rise to an elevation of eighty-five feet by a Gargantuan series of locks and a vast artificial lake. Most important, man had caused another rearrangement of the trade routes of the world. In 1930, the passage of 6185 vessels carrying 30,000,000 tons of freight emphasizes the meaning of this achievement.[9] The Suez

[9] *Annual Report of the Governor of the Panama Canal 1931*, Washington, 1931, p. 157.

of the West in a few years had outstripped the premier canal of the eastern hemisphere.

Control of the Canal involves naval supremacy in the American Mediterranean. No other country has here a base so broad and full of natural resources. The long sweep of mainland and islands from the Rio Grande to St. Thomas leaves little to be desired. The extension of the American coast-line following the acquisition of Porto Rico and the Philippines, the rapid expansion of American foreign commerce, and the creation of a trans-Pacific colonial trade, finally the construction of the Isthmian Canal, which constitutes in effect a bit of American seaboard, must call forth a navy whose strength shall be commensurate with the importance of extra-continental interests. Such a navy insures command of the Caribbean Sea.

Great Britain's holdings in these waters are numerous and well distributed for naval control. Especially Jamaica, by its almost central location in the Caribbean, occupies a strategic position similar to that of Malta in guarding the approaches to the Suez Canal. The limited resources of England's West Indian possessions are compensated for by the political and maritime position of the British Empire. France's positions are all on the outskirts. So were those of Denmark; the pivotal location of St. Thomas at the angle of the Greater and Lesser Antilles lends it considerable significance.[10]

The position of the Dutch near this northeast angle in St. Martin (half French), St. Eustatius, and Saba Isle, and in Buen Aire, Curaçao, and Aruba off the northwest coast of Venezuela, gives them a near and remoter base in the

---

[10] For strategic aspects, see Mahan, *Interest of America in Sea Power*, Boston, 1897, chap. VIII.

approaches to the Isthmus of Panama. This excellent distribution reflects the interest of Holland in an alternative line of communication with her vast colonial possessions (730,000 square miles) in the East Indies, should the Suez route be at any time impassable for her. The holdings of the French and British in the Caribbean Sea also gain an added significance when viewed in relation to the territories of these nations in the Orient.

CARIBBEAN COMMERCE

While the United States had abundantly proved its political ascendency in the American Mediterranean, and while its naval strength there had been sufficient for long, it did not show the commercial development in this region which its proximity and facility of communication, the adaptation of exports to the needs of its population, and the extensive importation of tropical products, would lead one to expect.[11] The balance of trade with the countries and islands bordering on the Caribbean has been almost always against the United States. The proximity, however, has been in the past perhaps more apparent than real, in consequence of the concentration of the industrial and commercial activities of this country in the northeastern states. The distance by sea from New York to Vera Cruz, Mexico, or to Bluefields, Nicaragua, is over two thousand miles. New Orleans is little over half as far from Bluefields and only 788 miles from Vera Cruz; a fact well mirrored in the rank of New Orleans as a port for Caribbean products.[12]

[11] Compare the situation today. In 1929, more than sixty per cent of all Caribbean purchases abroad came from the United States; in return, this country took a like part of Caribbean exports. In all, the United States accounted for $796,000,000 of a total commerce of $1,273,000,000. ("Latin American Foreign Trade in 1929," *Foreign Trade Series*, No. 81, Pan-American Union, Washington, 1931.)

[12] The city has embarked upon a plan of port improvement ultimately to require $100,000,000.

An additional factor in the deceptive nature of proximity to the Caribbean arose from the fact that prior to the Spanish-American War the United States was distinctly a one-language country. Geographical isolation has operated against Americans becoming linguists. Marked ethnic differences have prevented any but limited affiliation with the nations to the south, and they are the only neighbors speaking a different language except the negligible numbers of the French *habitant*. Now the United States has a large number of Spanish-speaking citizens, pleasure cruises have taken hundreds of thousands of Americans to Caribbean countries, and the importance of Spanish is growing in the national consciousness.

Commercial Relations with South America. In South America, the United States had even more discouraging commercial situations than characterized its nineteenth-century relations with the Caribbean. The bold eastern projection of the continent which brings Cape St. Roque some forty degrees of longitude, or twenty-six hundred miles east of New York, has the effect of placing New York, Hamburg, and Liverpool at about equal distances from South America and therefore so far on an equal footing of competition in the markets south of Pernambuco on the Atlantic side and all along the Pacific coast. But almost all the steamship lines to South American ports were controlled by European capital. They carried European merchandise to the southern markets, exchanged their cargoes for rubber, coffee, wool, and hides, which they brought up to our Atlantic seaboard cities, reloaded there again with grain and provisions, since the United States' exports to Europe so much exceeded the imports from that continent, and having reached the home ports, after making the vast

circuit (Plymouth, Montevideo, New York, Plymouth —
fifteen thousand miles), took on a fresh cargo for South
America again. By this system, New York's goods shipped
to Montevideo by way of Europe were at a disadvantage,
in competition with English or German merchandise having
direct steamship connection with the port of destination.
The obvious remedy for this condition was to build up a
native merchant marine.

The opening of the Panama Canal and the outbreak of the
World War shortly after gave the United States two powerful stimuli for its program devoted to a realization of geographic advantages in Latin America. The Canal gave an
almost due south route from New York and New Orleans
to the west coast of South America, shorter by more than
two thousand miles than the routes to Europe. On the
Atlantic, South American ports had the advantage of
distance, but lack of facilities lessened the commercial
significance of Nature's generosity; Buenos Aires lies 5870
miles from New York and 6240 miles from Liverpool.
Disruption of shipping services resulting from the War
augmented the impetus arising from these facts of physical
distance. The strength of these facts is evidenced by the
preëminence of United States trade at the present, more than
a decade having elapsed to test Europe's hold upon South
America.

Amplification of American shipping lines constituted a
basic step in the development of the southern markets.
Prior to the World War no American line regularly served
either the west or east coast. Now United States vessels
afford the fastest service available, though as yet not the
most widespread. Closely allied to the growth of shipping,
cable services have shown an even more remarkable ex-

pansion, American cables now surpassing in mileage all those controlled by Europe. A third vital form of communication, as yet in its infancy but certain to develop huge proportions, has arisen with the introduction of regular airplane schedules to all the republics. In this field, the United States has far outstripped its competitors. For a cogent example of the force of the airplane in South America, consider that in four days planes carry mail from Buenos Aires to the United States by way of Valparaiso, a route which requires more than two weeks by rail and steamer. In addition to such more tangible modes of *rapprochement*, there have developed two factors of incalculable value in the past development and future maintenance of South American contacts. One of these, the Bureau of Foreign and Domestic Commerce, largely by the dissemination of geographic information relative to the southern continent, has achieved wonders in facilitating commercial intercourse between South America and this country. The flood of inquiries it handles daily suggests how indispensable the Bureau has become to American commerce. In another direction, the Pan-American Union has fashioned an imperishable bond between north and south. The multiplicity of its activities, recently directed particularly towards exchange of educational facilities, makes the Union an outstanding factor in the relations of the United States with every republic of the southern continent. All of these powerful influences bespeak the close interdependence which proximity and differences in physical geography, as well as in stages of economic development, have made inevitable.[13]

Progress so prodigious necessarily has had its basis first

[13] Jones, C. F., *Commerce of South America*, Ginn and Co., Boston, 1928. By the same author, *South America*, Henry Holt & Co., New York, 1930.

in the exchange of produce. To the United States, South America has furnished raw materials in great abundance and variety. Coffee, ores and metals, hides and skins, nitrates, flaxseed, wool, cacao, sugar, quebracho, and rubber; these, with later important developments such as petroleum in Venezuela, have filled the holds of a constantly growing number of vessels. In return the northern country, as a demonstration of its advancing industrialism, has sent an endless variety of manufactures. Most of these products are of the sort required by areas beginning to develop along twentieth-century lines, notably heavy goods of iron and steel, durable and inexpensive textiles, fuels, and a few foodstuffs.

The enormous trade fostered by such exchanges has led to the second stage in the advance of the United States in South America. By the actual exploitation of resources with American capital, the country has virtually increased its stores of raw materials. Furthermore, it has given assurance to the future of trade in both directions through affording the northern manufacturer vast opportunities in supplying the needs of the industries created by his fellow-citizens.[14]

As interest in the Caribbean region and in South America grew, the significance of the Gulf seaboard increased. The trend received additional impetus from the rapid use of population and industry in the rich lands of Texas and

[14] Since 1913, American investments in South America have grown thirteen-fold; they now exceed $2,300,000,000. British capital still is twice as large, but in the years since 1913 it has increased less than twelve per cent. Adequate explanations for such features lie in trade statistics, which show the United States to be much the largest factor in both export and import movements. Of the total of South American exports, this country takes more than one-quarter; it supplies almost one-third of the imports. Immediately previous to the World War, the respective shares amounted to eighteen per cent and sixteen per cent. (Winkler, M., *op. cit.*, pp. 274–85.)

Oklahoma. Railroads rediscovered the Mississippi and a
new era of transportation added to the South's advantages
in trade with Latin America. By no means were these
developments the result only of Latin American potenti-
alities; domestic possibilities far surpassed all others. The
fruitful expanses of the Southwest in reality constituted
another land of raw materials which required the manufactures of the North. Ports and railroad centers under-
went miraculous transformation. New Orleans is the classic
example. In the days before its majority, the city utilized
few of its geographic attractions. Unsightly and unhealth-
ful, the port merited the ill-repute attached to its name.
Pressure from the interior and the powerful pull from the
Caribbean finally roused the city to a comprehension of its
bright future, with the result that the publicly owned port
facilities are a show-place of the South. In value of total
trade, New Orleans now stands sixth among the country's
ports. In value of foreign trade it acknowledges superiority
only to New York.[15]

Advance in commerce and industry and improvements in
sanitation, education, and transportation will strengthen
the geographical ties between the United States of America
and the lands of the Caribbean, tropical South America, and
the mineralized areas of the Andes. As the United States
cannot produce the many tropical products, its supplies
must continue to originate to a large degree in these areas;
as most of the minerals of the entire area are alloy minerals,
they will continue to move to the great coal and iron regions
— the great industrial areas — for fabrication. In turn,
without the facilities for the development of huge manufac-

[15] *Commercial Statistics, Water-Borne Commerce of the United States*, War Department, Washington, 1930, pp. 5–13.

turing enterprises, the Caribbean and South American lands will draw in greater quantities from the United States their needs in a variety of manufactured commodities. This potent movement, already of large proportions, emphasizes the attraction of near-by complementary areas, and focuses critical attention on the activities and policies of the leading nation of the area. The leading rôle assumed by the United States, because of geographical conditions, cannot readily be shifted.

CHAPTER XIX

THE UNITED STATES AS
A PACIFIC OCEAN POWER

HISTORIC areas of civilization are most naturally indicated by the seas which they encompass. The Ægean, Mediterranean, the Atlantic, Pacific mark eras of progress, of which the seafaring nations of the world have been the first apostles. Every maritime expansion of civilization draws with it in its train the smaller water area which constituted its previous field, operates for a long time under the influence of the latter, and while robbing it of its former preëminence, contributes finally to its absolute activity. This has been the history of the Ægean in relation to the Mediterranean, of the Mediterranean and Baltic-North in relation to the Atlantic. We speak of the Pacific as the "ocean of the future," but this means in reality the final expansion of the maritime field by which it embraces this last great basin and advances to active exploitation of the world ocean. For the sea is always one. The little harbor of Batum at the innermost corner of the Euxine is just as much a port of the world ocean as New York, Honolulu, or Hongkong.

When the commercial and maritime drama of Europa was shifted from the stage of the Mediterranean to the Atlantic, those nations which had the front seats got most out of it, as we have seen. They furnished the best trained actors in the stirring scenes of exploration, colonization, and trade, and drew in the largest rewards. Their advantages were fundamentally the product of geographical location. The same principle must hold on the "ocean of the future"; but the development of the world ocean will mean the exploitation of the Pacific from the basis of the Atlantic. The preëminence which the Atlantic has gained will long dominate the Pacific, and geographic conditions make it doubtful whether this supremacy will ever pass to the larger basin. Therefore, those countries which have a foothold on both these oceans possess the vantage-ground; and their potential strength will be in proportion to the length and proximity of their two ocean frontages and the resourcefulness of their respective hinterlands.

THE PACIFIC BASIN

Rivers. A narrow ocean, near-lying continents, remote watersheds, long navigable river systems, accessible inland regions, a large back country to draw upon — that is the Atlantic field. A vast ocean, remote continents, a few, fall-broken rivers, mountain walls hugging the coast, and inaccessible interior, limited back country — that is the Pacific field. The Pacific, though twice the size of the Atlantic has a drainage basin less than half as large. The reason for this disparity lies in the fact that the primary highlands of Asia, Australia, North and South America are situated on the Pacific coasts of those continents. In Australia and South America the mountains rise directly from the sea, and only short, plunging torrents erode their slopes, while all the extensive drainage is in another direction. In the northern continents the watershed is a thousand miles or more inland, and thereby furnishes almost the whole drainage area of the Pacific; but this location of the divides does not mean navigable streams to the coast. The unfavorable character of Pacific rivers of the United States has been explained. Those of Canada are no better. Only the faraway Yukon, by sweeping around to the north of the coast range, affords a navigable course for vessels of light draft for 1370 miles to Dawson; but the nature of the country through which the Yukon flows and its ice-bound condition most of the year render it of little commercial importance.

The Asiatic rivers of the Pacific are much more important. The Amur with its tributaries affords hundreds of miles of navigable waterways, but the sharp northward bend of its course just before reaching the ocean discharges the stream into the Okhotsk Sea, where its port is frozen six months of the year. The next great river, the Hwang-ho, though flowing with a sluggish current through the great plain of eastern China, is too shifting in its course to be relied upon for navigation. The Yangtse-kiang alone is comparable to the great streams of the Atlantic. It is navigable for one thousand miles from its mouth and for most of the year admits even ocean-going vessels six hundred and thirty miles up to Han-Kow, where they take on cargoes of cotton, wood and nut oils, dried eggs, beans, tea, and silk. In the Si-kiang and Mekong navigation is much impeded by rapids. Therefore of all the rivers flowing east and west into the Pacific, only the Yangtse-kiang affords a good route of communication between seaboard and interior. Hence we find it lined with free ports all the way from Shanghai, on the coast, and Chin-kiang, at the juncture with the Grand Canal, to Ichang, a thousand miles up its course.[1] The Yangtse-kiang is the one valuable river adjunct of sea

[1] Arnold, J., *China, Commercial and Industrial Handbook*, Trade Promotion Series, No. 38, Bureau of Foreign and Domestic Commerce, Washington, 1926, pp. 433, 706–07.

power in the Orient; hence the discerning eye of the English early appropriated it as the British "sphere of influence"; [2] and hence in the attempt to coerce China, Japan in 1932 struck at Shanghai, the great entrepôt for the valley.

Lands. China, by reason of its long irregular coast-line stretching through twenty-one degrees of latitude, the possession of the most navigable river of the whole Pacific, its central geographical location in the temperate zone, and its large territory of abundant resources, has a strong position on the Pacific; but dominated by a nomad people from the inland steppes of Asia, bred to isolation by the great sweep of mountains behind them, and unreceptive to the vitalizing influences of the Atlantic civilization, the Chinese have not profited by the advantages of their location. Russia's frontage on the Pacific finds its value much reduced by its sub-Arctic situation. Japan has central location, a long island base, and the spirit of progress which has developed at a wonderful rate the maritime activity of the kingdom; but inadequacy of area hampers expansion, a difficulty which has led to the acquisition of Formosa in 1895, Korea in 1910, and which ultimately may bring Manchuria into the island's empire. England's possessions in India, Australia, New Zealand, North Borneo, New Guinea, Hongkong, and the Malay Peninsula give it a broad enough base in the Pacific; but their scattered location, remoteness from the national center of strength in the Atlantic, and also from the storm-center of the "problem of Asia," between the thirtieth and fortieth parallels, all combine to reduce the value of its Pacific position, though the maritime strength of Great Britain makes it a powerful factor in the Eastern Question.

[2] Mahan, A. T., *The Problem of Asia*, New York, 1900, pp. 41, 65, 120.

China is the only power on the western shores of the Pacific to whom geographic conditions might have given political and commercial preëminence, except for the one thing needful, contact with the Atlantic. This the United States has, besides the requisites of a long Pacific coast-line, central location in the temperate zone, and a large territory of abundant resources. To balance the teeming plains of eastern China, it has the long Pacific Valley with its enterprising if not dense population. A coast-line of 1810 miles, which rises to 8900 miles if all the inlets, bays, estuaries, and islands are included, a few evenly distributed ports for larger vessels and numerous safe roadsteads for smaller craft, yield a fair degree of contact with the sea from San Juan Strait to the excellent harbor of San Diego, in spite of the mountain range which faces the coast.

ADVANTAGES OF THE UNITED STATES AS A PACIFIC POWER

The great advantage of the United States is its inter-oceanic location. This it shares with Mexico, the Central American republics, Colombia, and nominally with Chile, which has stretched a narrow tape of territory around the southern extremity of the continent to the Atlantic entrance of the Straits of Magellan; but obvious geographic limitations of climatic situation, natural features, and size restrict the political and commercial ambitions of all these countries, even if we ignore the inferiority of their Latin-American populations. To the north, Canada has also a broad frontage on both oceans, and as part of the British Empire has also like the United States mid-sea islands in the Pacific to serve as way-stations to the opposite coasts. British

Columbia, with its one thousand miles of seaboard and its excellent harbors, occupies a fine position in relation to trade with China and Japan, Russia and Manchuria.   It has also considerable natural resources, especially abundant water power and coal of good quality.   British Columbia has moreover the resources of all Canada at its back; but when full weight is given to all these favorable conditions,[3] the disadvantage of a location too far north, and hence the restriction of area adapted for the support of a dense population and the production of superfluous wealth which may enter the markets of the world as capital, place British Columbia and Canada far behind the United States in the rivalry for the commerce of the Pacific.

The Pacific Northwest.   The first weak foothold of the young Republic in the far-away station of Astoria at the mouth of the Columbia River, and that early trade in furs with China, seemed prophetic of the destiny of the nation. The never abandoned purpose to widen the frontage on the western ocean, the obstinate debate of the "Oregon Question," and the conquest of California, committed the United States to the career of a Pacific power.   Wide though the ocean is — ten thousand miles at the Equator, eighty-five hundred at the Tropic of Cancer between Hongkong and Mazatlan on the Mexican coast, and forty-seven hundred and fifty between Yokohama and San Francisco approximately along the thirty-seventh parallel — and sparse though the islands are for a belt of two thousand miles off its American shores, the mere presence of the United States on the Pacific has been a sufficient reason for concern in all matters pertaining to this ocean.

Alaska.   Such was the ground on which Russia in 1867

[3] Colquhoun, A. R., *The Mastery of the Pacific*, New York, 1902, pp. 217, 225.

pressed Alaska upon the United States, strengthening this country's base on the Pacific and weakening that of Russia's hereditary enemy in British Columbia by placing this English colony between the fires of American enterprise on both its northern and southern borders. The "ten marine leagues," moreover, which fix the width of the long "panhandle" of southern Alaska, cut off a thousand miles of the natural Pacific frontage of British Columbia; while the possession of the peninsula and the Aleutian Islands gives the United States' Pacific base a reach of over four thousand miles from San Diego to Attu, three hundred miles from the nearest Japanese islands. The acquisition of Alaska brought Russia for a near neighbor in Bering Strait. The ownership of the Pribilof Islands in Bering Sea, which the seals have adopted as their breeding-grounds, made the United States the most interested party in the controversy of the seal fisheries, and involved the country in negotiations with Russia, Japan, and England, which resulted in the Paris Commission of 1895.

Possession of Alaska has proved a powerful factor in turning the eyes of the country towards the Pacific. It greatly favored development in the Pacific Northwest states. Moreover, this influence has scarcely begun to exert its strength and in all probability will continue semi-dormant for many decades. Eloquent commentaries are the facts that a land of 586,400 square miles contains 59,000 people (1930 — 64,000 in 1910) and that more than 99 per cent of the territory remains in the hands of the federal government. The largest cities — Juneau and Ketchikan — in 1930 had populations respectively of 4043 and 3796. Riches Alaska undeniably has: its handful of people in 1929 engaged in $98,000,000 of trade, each person having a representation

of $1660; for a resident of the United States, the corre-
sponding figure is only seventy-eight dollars.[4]

Mining activities in Alaska have been concerned largely
with the precious minerals; Alaska has some of the largest
coal reserves of the world, but remoteness of the country,
the distribution and condition of the coals and the large
supply of coals in the United States will cause the coal resources to remain largely undeveloped for some time.

Also, human endeavor has so much land on which to expend its energy in areas nearer present centers of population
that the population and transportation needed to develop
Alaska will be slow in arriving.   A pioneer land Alaska will
long remain, gaining a livelihood chiefly from the extractive
industries on which it now depends — fish, minerals, furs
and forests.

The Philippines and Oceania.   The possession of the
Philippines, which lent a new importance to the neglected
province of the north, was the signal for the United States
to profit by certain other advantages which lay at its door
or within its hands and had been ignored.   Dewey's victory
in Manila Bay made imperative the annexation of Hawaii,
Wake Island, and the retention of Guam, the southernmost
isle of the Ladrones group, so that a direct mid-ocean line of
communication between the home shore and the oriental
colony might be assured.   Just as England on the route
between London and India acquired first the remote extremity in the Orient, and then filled in the intermediate
points — Gibraltar, Malta, Cyprus, Suez, and Aden —
which were to secure its long line of communication, so the
United States had to turn its attention to getting way-

[4] *Commerce Yearbook, 1931*, Bureau of Foreign and Domestic Commerce, Washington, 1931, I, pp. 662–67.

stations across the Pacific. Far back between 1841 and 1867, it had claimed Wake and Midway Islands by right of discovery, but failed to enter into their active possession for many years. In 1898, when a location between Guam and Hawaii indicated its natural province as a Pacific cable-station, Wake Island became definitely an American possession. Cable requirements likewise brought under United States control the Midway Islands, which lie twelve hundred miles northwest of Hawaii.

After 1889 the position of the United States as a Pacific power was attested by its share in the tripartite government of the Samoan Islands. This share was converted into the absolute ownership of Tutuila and Manua in 1899 by the acquiescence of England and Germany. The fact that the superior harbor of Pago-pago on Tutuila was ceded to the United States as a coaling-station as early as 1872, but was not actively occupied till 1898, bears witness to the American change of policy. The whole Samoan group is of great strategic value. It is situated at about 14° south latitude and 170° west longitude, on the direct path from Puget Sound to Sydney, Australia, and on a line from the Isthmus of Panama to east Australian ports. Herein lies its significance for the United States.

The island world which, like a vast continental nebula, occupies the expanse of the Pacific, becomes more and more rarified in the direction of the American mainland, until it finally leaves a wide gap of ocean space between the outlying groups of Hawaii and the Low Archipelago on the two Tropics and the mountain-bound coasts of the Western Hemisphere. Neither North nor South America finds at its western door natural stepping-stones for advance into the Pacific. Hence the Hawaiian group, the only place in the whole Pacific north of the Equator and east of the continental islands festooning the coast of Asia where the nebula has condensed into a constellation, by their location, their magnitude, and their isolation become the paramount strategic position west of the American shores.   They afford the first ocean-station on a trans-Pacific line of communication.

The Hawaiian Islands.   Political gravitation has drawn the Hawaiian Islands to the dominion of the United States. Their location in relation to the American shores at an early date made them a wintering place and a port of call for New England trading-vessels on their way to the north-west coast or to China.[5]   Their situation at the great cross-roads of the Pacific tended to make their population a precipitate of all the races traversing this ocean, but the American element predominated.   An island environment suffers always from the limitation of its size, especially in commerce.   England had to go out in search of the markets of the world.   Where the English found none, they created them by forming colonies.   Japan is on the same keen hunt today.   Cuba cannot survive without the markets of the United States.   The nearest market is the logical one because of economy in transportation.   Hawaii from the beginning of its sugar culture needed American buyers.   In 1851 a strong effort, emanating from the Islands themselves, was made for annexation; but the United States Senate refused to ratify the treaty offered by the Hawaiian Parliament, and instead promised protection.   Meanwhile trade between the two countries was growing and with it the sentiment of annexation in Hawaii, while the big Republic held to its continental policy.   Sugar became the chief interest of the Islands; it was almost wholly in the hands of Americans,

[5] Dulles, F. H., *The Old China Trade*, Boston, 1930, pp. 55–63, 66–71.

who formed the monied and the ruling class, but who found a naturally remunerative industry almost hopelessly crippled by the heavy duties on their products at the port of San Francisco. Annexation would make them rich, so the agitation was kept up. Here again that extra-territorial expansion which had fixed the destiny of West Florida and Texas was doing its work. In 1876 a compromise was effected. The chief Hawaiian products were admitted to the United States free of duty, and the United States was given a naval station in the vicinity of Honolulu. The barrier was beginning to fall. The Islands were commercially within the sphere of the United States, and the United States had advanced to the strategic outpost on the Hawaiian shores. This status of overlapping boundary was maintained until 1898.

In the meantime, however, this country was not so indifferent to the fate of Hawaii as it seemed. Twice it interfered in Hawaii's behalf with England, and in 1850 it warned off the French. In 1843, when there was danger of acquisition by England, Daniel Webster declared that no other power ought to get possession of these islands either by conquest or for the sake of colonization. There was much of the dog in the manger in this attitude. Prior to the acquisition of the Philippines, Hawaii possessed far greater political utility for British Columbia than for the United States, because it was the one East Pacific station on the long intercontinental sea route between Vancouver and Sydney. From a military standpoint, however, it was quite as important to this country, because Hawaii as a coaling and naval station, two thousand and eighty miles from San Francisco and not more than twenty-five hundred from any point on our western

coast, in the hands of any foreign power would have
been a standing threat.[6] So held, it would have paralleled the Bermudas, which were the source of discom-
fort enough to the mainland in the Revolution and the
War of 1812.

The Hawaiian Islands, Wake Island, and Guam form to
Manila a line of communication lying between the narrow
limits of the thirteenth and twenty-first parallels. The
American termini of this line are located at San Francisco
(38° N.L.), Los Angeles (34° N.L.), and Panama (9° N.L.),
to all three of which Honolulu holds a central position. The
preëminence which it now enjoys as the focus of the great
commercial routes of the Pacific was enhanced with the
opening of the Isthmian Canal, because it lay in the path
of an increasing file of vessels moving along from Panama
to China, Japan, or Asiatic Russia. At the western end of
this island chain of communications are the Philippines,
by reason of which the United States has become an Asiatic
power. This large group, scattered over an area measuring
one thousand miles, is located wholly within the tropics,
and distributed around it in a wide-sweeping semicircle are
the oriental countries where vast populations make the
markets of the East.

Commercial Relations with the Islands. These islands with
a combined population approaching 12,500,000 in themselves
form a valuable market. The foundations of trade between
the United States and its satellites are solid ones; they arise
from the almost undiluted tropical conditions of the fertile
Pacific lands and the need for products of such areas by the
mother country. To promote such production and con-
currently to enlarge the outlets for its manufactures, the

[6] Mahan, A. T., *Interest of America in Sea Power*, Boston, 1897, p. 48.

United States has furnished many encouragements. The results comprise an exchange between Hawaii and the United States in 1929 amounting to $189,000,000, Hawaii shipping principally sugar and pineapples, and receiving factory products and a few foodstuffs. In the Philippines a similar exchange obtains. The archipelago, so far as indispensable tropical materials are concerned, has a stronger place in American commerce than Hawaii, primarily in consequence of differences in size and climate. Sugar, hemp, coconut oil, copra and tobacco account for the bulk of exports to the United States; in 1929 these shipments had a value of $124,000,000 and total trade amounted to $217,000,000.[7]

The strides of American foreign trade in the Pacific suggest the country's rise to a Pacific power of first magnitude. Asia and Oceania in 1929 purchased goods from the United States having a value of $835,000,000, while the return movement attained $1,335,000,000. That year showed Japan as going to the United States for 30 per cent of its imports; China for 18 per cent; Australia for 25 per cent: conversely, the United States took 43 per cent of Japanese exports; 17 per cent of Chinese; but only 4 per cent of Australian, similarity of leading agricultural products with those in America giving Australia little opportunity in markets here. The trend towards the Pacific appears further to advantage in a comparison of percentages of all United States exports going to the various major political divisions of the world. In 1880, this country sent to Asia and Oceania 2.8 per cent of its exports; in 1929 the ratio was 16 per cent. This sixfold growth in percentage dwarfs that in any other major area (North America, South America, Europe, Africa). In the fifty-year period, Atlantic

[7] *Commerce Yearbook*, Washington, 1931, I, 667-81.

exports — that is, to Europe — diminished from 83 per
cent of the total to 45 per cent.[8]

These commercial achievements have carried the United
States inevitably forward into the maelstrom of Asiatic
affairs, because there lay the center of the new interests.
The proximity of Cuba to American shores was the far-
away factor which placed the Stars and Stripes in the
Philippines and accelerated the progress of history; but this
or some other base, perhaps on the Chinese mainland, would
have been inevitable.   The commercial strength of the
American Republic was bound sooner or later to find a
political expression in that international struggle for existence, which is a struggle for space, going on in Asiatic
territory.   A chain of historical events, largely geographical
in their causes, determined that the Philippines should be
the channel of American influence in the East.   The detachable character, inner weakness, and protected isolation of
every island group maintained Spain in its insular possessions here, as in the Antilles; so that the blow which despoiled
the Spanish of one took all.   Now this same protection
against international entanglements which is yielded by an
insular position accrues to the United States, makes the
situation in the Orient analogous to the continental location
at home, and gives it the best possible base from which to
protect its interests.

These interests, chiefly of a commercial nature, are well
worth guarding.   The needs of much of the Orient are those
of an old, crowded country which, however, has not advanced
into the modern industrial stage of development, except
for Japan.   The demand comes therefore for grain and
flour, refined oil, wood and leather manufactures, tobacco,

[8] *Commerce Yearbook*, Washington, 1931, I, 77–121.

cotton goods of all kinds, agricultural implements, and all forms of iron and steel manufactures. These the United States can provide; and the advantages arising from abundant natural resources, the extensive organization of industry which reduces the cost of production, and the superior character of our industrial methods, enable the American merchant to compete in these distant markets with other nations which operate from a base thousands of miles nearer. On the other hand, the products originating in the trans-Pacific lands have secured near-indispensability in American industry. Their importance to the United States derives either from the lack of domestic areas physically capable of such production or from the low labor costs of the densely peopled eastern lands. The vast size of the home country, affording a wide field for raw materials, for concentration, and hence organization of industries, for the development of transportation facilities, and the maintenance of an extensive and varied domestic market, has been in the past the dominant factor in the evolution of the American entrepreneur. The other factor has been vigor of character and tenacity of purpose. Here heredity and environment have combined to do their utmost, and the result has not been small. The United States is today the world's greatest producer of manufactures, and as an exporter of domestic products it ranks side by side with Great Britain.

The Atlantic has given us near access to Europe, and the "American invasion" has followed. The Pacific has opened to us, though at longer range, the markets of the Orient, and the flag has been set up on an outlying fragment of the Asiatic continent. "Enthroned between her subject seas," the United States has by reason of large area and geographical location the most perfect conditions for attaining preëminence in the commerce of the world ocean.

If the tree planted by the fathers of the Republic has lifted its head high and spread its branches afar, due must be given to the great, generous land which has nourished and the seas which have watered its wide-running roots.

SUPPLEMENTARY READINGS

THESE readings by no means represent a definitive reference list for the subject of American history and its geographic conditions. While the references embrace the salient features of the several chapters, they are arranged according to the major subjects of each chapter. Such a grouping will prove helpful in making special studies of different topics and in suggesting leads for further research, involving reading far beyond the scope of the lists to follow. To this end, full use of bibliographies given in many of the more comprehensive works is recommended. For greatest benefit in amplifying the subject-matter of the book, a constant regard for geographic relationships should accompany the quest for additional materials. This viewpoint has influenced the selection of such works as are here cited.

CHAPTER I

Relation of Medieval Europe to the Far East

1. Cheyney, E. P., *European Background of American History 1300–1600*, New York, 1904, chapters 1–4.
2. Fiske, J., *The Discovery of America*, Boston, 1892, I, 261–294.
3. Yeats, J., *The Growth and Vicissitudes of Commerce*, London, 1872, pp. 13–21, 37–47, 73–111.
4. Semple, E. C., *Geography of the Mediterranean Region*, New York, 1931, pp. 156–171.
5. Beazley, C. R., "Marco Polo and the European Expansion of the Middle Ages," *Atlantic Monthly*, CIV (1909), 493–501; Hildebrand, J. R., "The World's

Greatest Overland Explorer," *National Geographic Magazine*, LIV (1928), 505–568.

6. Hunter, W. W., *History of British India*, New York, 1899, pp. 17–53.

Europe Turns Toward the Atlantic

7. Beazley, C. R., *Prince Henry the Navigator*, New York, 1923, chapters 2, 7–10, 12, 20.

8. Thördarson, M., "The Vineland Voyages," *Research Series, No. 18*, American Geographical Society, New York, 1930, pp. 1–68.

9. Gray, E. F., *Leif Eriksson, Voyager to Vinland*, New York, 1930.

10. Thacher, J. B., *Christopher Columbus*, New York, 1903, I, portions of chapters 27, 47, and 60; or Fiske, J., *The Discovery of America*, I, portions of chapters 5 and 6.

11. Nunn, C. E., "Geographical Conceptions of Columbus," *Research Series, No. 14*, American Geographical Society, New York, 1925, pp. 1–90.

12. Tyler, L. G., *England in America*, New York, 1904, chapters 1 and 2.

13. Munro, W. B., *Crusaders of New France*, New Haven, 1921, portions of chapters 2 and 3.

14. Parkman, F., *The Old Régime in Canada*, Boston, 1901, chapter 17.

15. Fiske, J., *The Dutch and Quaker Colonies in America*, Boston, 1899, I, chapters 1 and 3.

CHAPTER II

Search for the Northwest Passage

16. Parkman, F., *La Salle and the Discovery of the Great West*, Boston, 1903, chapters 1–6.

17. Asher, G. M., *Henry Hudson the Navigator*, the Original Documents, Hakluyt Society, London, 1860, selected portions of pp. 100–194.

18. Greely, A. W., *A Handbook of Polar Discoveries*, Boston, 1910, chapters 2, 7, 8.
19. Burpee, L. J., *The Search for the Western Sea*, London, 1908, pp. 13–60.

The Early Fur Trade

20. Buffinton, A. H., "The Policy of Albany and Westward Expansion," *Mississippi Valley Historical Review*, VIII (1922), 327–366.
21. "New England and the Western Fur Trade, 1629–1675," *Publications of the Colonial Society of Massachusetts*, XVIII (1916), 160–192.
22. Broshar, H., "The First Push Westward of the Albany Traders," *Mississippi Valley Historical Review*, VII (1920), 228–241.
23. Morrison, A. J., "The Virginia Indian Trade to 1763," *William and Mary Quarterly Historical Magazine*, I (1921), 217–236.
24. McIlwain, C. H., *Wraxall's Abridgement to the New York Indian Records* (1915), Cambridge, Mass., chapters 1 and 2.
25. Turner, F. J., "The Character and Influence of the Indian Trade in Wisconsin," *Johns Hopkins University Studies*, IX (1891), 547–615.
26. Pinkerton, R. E., *Hudson's Bay Company*, New York, 1931, portions of pp. 7–110.

Rivers and French Exploration and Settlement

13. Munro, *op. cit.*, chapters 6, 9–11.
14. Parkman, F., *op. cit.*, chapters 20 and 21.
16. Parkman, *op. cit.*, chapters 6, 8, 10–12, 19–21, 24.
27. Peattie, R., "The Isolation of the Lower St. Lawrence Valley," *Geographical Review*, V (1918), 102–118.
28. Semple, E. C., "The Influence of Geographic Environment on the Lower St. Lawrence," *Bulletin of the American Geographical Society*, XXXVI (1904), 449–466.

29. Hulbert, A. B., "Portage Paths," *Historic Highways of America*, VII (1903), 9–84, 151–194.
30. Surrey, N. M. M., "The Commerce of Louisiana During the French Régime, 1699–1763," *Studies in History, Economics, and Public Law, Columbia University*, LXXI (1916), 21–95, 256–303.
31. Campbell, E. F., "New Orleans in Early Days," *Geographical Review*, X (1920), 31–36.

Rivers and the English Colonies

12. Tyler, *op. cit.*, "Virginia," pp. 34–54; "Maryland," pp. 118–132; "Plymouth," pp. 149–162; "Massachusetts," pp. 196–209; "Connecticut, Maine and New Hampshire," pp. 229–281.
32. Fiske, J., *Old Virginia and Her Neighbours*, Boston 1897, pp. 91–98, and portions of chapter 4.

CHAPTER III

The Appalachian Barrier

33. Brigham, A. P., *Geographic Influences in American History*, Boston, 1903, pp. 3–36, 70–86, 86–88.
34. Bailey, W., "The Northern Appalachians," in *The Physiography of the United States*, New York, 1896, pp. 169–198.
35. Hayes, C. W., "The Southern Appalachians," in *The Physiography of the United States*, New York, 1896, pp. 305–332.

Lines of Development in New England

36. Davis, W. M., "The Physical Geography of Southern New England," in *The Physiography of the United States*, New York, 1896, pp. 269–305.
12. Tyler, *op. cit.*, chapter 19.
37. Bullock, C. J., *Selected Readings in Economics*, Boston, 1907, pp. 13–14.

38. Thwaites, R. G., *The Colonies, 1492–1570*, New York, 1902, pp. 178–190.
39. Weeden, W. B., *Economic and Social History of New England*, Boston, 1891, I, 15–22, 88–116, 244–247; II, 594–598.
40. Brigham, A. P., *Cape Cod and the Old Colony*, New York, 1921, chapters 2, 6, "The Harvest of the Waters."
41. Duncan, N., "Newfoundland Fisheries," *World's Work*, III (1904), 554–567.
42. La Gorce, J. O., "Fishes and Fisheries of Our North Atlantic Seaboard," *National Geographic Magazine*, XLIV (1923), 567–634.
43. Wallace, W., "Life on the Grand Banks," *National Geographic Magazine*, XL (1921), 1–31.

Lines of Development in the Middle Colonies
32. Fiske, *op. cit.*, pp. 174, 176–177, 185–188, 223–237, 273–275.
12. Tyler, *op. cit.*, pp. 100–104, 113–118, and 126–130.
44. Surface, G. T., *Studies on the Geography of Virginia*, Philadelphia, 1907, pp. 1–10, 11–14.
37. Bullock, *op. cit.*, pp. 14–18.
38. Thwaites, *op. cit.*, pp. 96–104, 106–109, 218–231.
15. Fiske, *op. cit.*, II, 324–326.
45. Bruce, P. A., *Economic History of Virginia in the Seventeenth Century*, New York, 1907, I, 75–81, 102–113, 130–135, 198–201, 210–220, 254–255, 260–265, 302, 321–323, 424–425, 428, 459–461, 492, 584–587; II, 495–497.
46. Becker, C. L., *Beginnings of the American People*, Boston, 1915, pp. 133–134.

Relation of Geographical Conditions to Campaigns of the Revolution
47. Nickerson, H., *The Turning Point of the Revolution*, Boston, 1928, pp. 38–40, 47–57, 129–158.
48. Channing, E., *History of the United States*, New York, 1912, III, chapters 6, 8, 9, 11, pp. 279–283.

49. Van Tyne, C. H., *The American Revolution*, New York, 1905, chapters 7–8, 10, 16–17.
46. Becker, *op. cit.*, pp. 253–272.
50. Caldwell, R. G., *A Short History of the American People, 1492–1860*, New York, 1925, selected portions, and especially the maps, of chapters 7 and 8.

CHAPTER IV

Early Settlements in the Piedmont and the Great Valley

33. Brigham, *op. cit.*, pp. 97–98.
46. Becker, *op. cit.*, pp. 175–182.
51. Paxson, F. L., *History of the American Frontier, 1763–1893*, Boston, 1924, pp. 3–5, 7, 22–27.
52. Henderson, A., "Forces in Westward Expansion," *American Historical Review*, XX (1914–15), 90–97.
53. Henderson, A., *The Conquest of the Old Southwest*, New York, 1920, chapters 1–3.

Exploration of Trans-Allegheny Country

54. Roosevelt, T., *The Winning of the West*, New York, 1903, II, chapter 6.
55. Hulbert, A. B., *Boone's Wilderness Road*, Cleveland, 1903, chapter 2.
56. Henderson, A., "Forces in Westward Expansion," *American Historical Review*, XX (1914–15), pp. 86–90, and 97–108.
53. Henderson, *op. cit.*, chapters 7–1
57. Chalkey, L., "Before the Gates of the Wilderness Road," *Virginia Magazine of History and Biography*, XXX (1922), 183–202

Westward Movement Through the Appalachians

58. Campbell, J. C., *The Southern Highlander and His Homeland*, New York, 1921, chapter 3.
33. Brigham, *op. cit.*, pp. 99–104.
59. Speed, T., *The Wilderness Road*, Louisville, 1886.

55. Hulbert, *op. cit.*, chapters 1, 2, 5.
51. Paxson, *op. cit.*, pp. 27–33.

George Rogers Clark and the West in the Revolutionary War
54. Roosevelt, *op. cit.*, II, chapters 2, 3, 7, 13.
51. Paxson, *op. cit.*, pp. 35–39, 40–43.
55. Hulbert, *op. cit.*, chapter 4.
60. Bodley, T., *George Rogers Clark, His Life and Public Service*, New York, 1926. Selected portions on the war in the west.

CHAPTER V

Character of Frontier Settlements and Industries
61. Branch, E. D., *Westward: The Romance of American Expansion*, New York, 1930, pp. 75–92, 236–243.
62. Turner, **F. J.**, *Rise of the New West*, New York, 1906, pp. 67–83, 84–95, 96–110.
63. Turner, F. J., "Western State-Making in the Revolutionary Era," *The American Historical Review*, I (1895–96), 70–88.
64. Chambers, H. E., *Mississippi Valley Beginnings*, New York, 1922, chapters 27, 28.
54. Roosevelt, *op. cit.*, III, chapters 1, 2, 5, 6.
65. Bogart, E. L., and Thompson, C. M., *Readings in the Economic History of the United States*, New York, 1916, pp. 234–237, 241–244, 268.
66. Harrison, L. C., *The Salt Industry as a Factor in the History of the Middle West*, Chicago, 1919, chapters 2, 3.

Early Trade
67. Carson, W. W., "Transportation and Traffic on the Ohio and Mississippi before the Steamboat," *Mississippi Valley Historical Review*, VII (1920–21), 26–39.
68. McMaster, J. B., *History of the People of the United States*, New York, 1902, III, 459–487.

65. Bogart and Thompson, *op. cit.*, pp. 244–249, 379–385.
61. Branch, *op. cit.*, pp. 243–250.
69. Gronert, T. G., "Trade in the Blue-Grass Region, 1810–1820," *Mississippi Valley Historical Review*, V (1918–19), 313–323.

Importance of Mississippi (Separatist Movement)

70. Ogg, F. A., *The Opening of the Mississippi*, New York, 1904, pp. 415–460.
54. Roosevelt, *op. cit.*, III, chapter 3.
64. Chambers, H. E., *Mississippi Valley Beginnings*, New York, 1922, chapters 17, 18.
53. Henderson, *op. cit.*, chapter 20.
71. "Resolutions and Remonstrances of Westerners Affected by the Spanish Control of New Orleans," *William and Mary College Quarterly*, II (1922), 239–256.

CHAPTER VI

Early Settlements on the Mississippi

64. Chambers, *op. cit.*, chapters 12, 13, 19.
72. Coman, K., *Economic Beginnings of the Far West*, New York, 1912, II, chapter 1.

Interest of Different Nations in Louisiana

64. Chambers, *op. cit.*, chapters 20, 21.
51. Paxson, *op. cit.*, pp. 130–133.
54. Roosevelt, *op. cit.*, IV, 251–282.
73. Bruce, H. A., *The Romance of American Expansion*, New York, 1909, pp. 33–50.
48. Channing, *op. cit.*, IV (1917), chapter 11.

Results of the Purchase of Louisiana

70. Ogg, *op. cit.*, pp. 536–538.
74. Sparks, E. E., *The Expansion of the American People*, Chicago, 1900, chapter 18.
61. Branch, *op. cit.*, pp. 259–271.

75. Pelzer, L., "Economic Factors in the Acquisition of Louisiana," *Mississippi Valley Historical Proceedings*, VI (1912-13), 109-128.

CHAPTER VII

Shipbuilding

39. Weeden, *op. cit.*, I, 123-124, 128-129, 140, 143, 154, 162, 252-260, 363-369; II, 573-582, 613, 651-653.
76. Wright, C. D., *The Industrial Evolution of the United States*, New York, 1902, pp. 28-43.
77. Johnson, E. R., *Ocean and Inland Water Transportation*, New York, 1920, pp. 15-21.
78. Abbot, W. J., *The Story of Our Merchant Marine*, New York, 1919, pp. 10-17.

Whaling

39. Weeden, *op. cit.*, I, 430-447; II, 654-655, 828-830.
78. Abbot, *op. cit.*, chapter 4.
79. Tower, W. S., *A History of the American Whale Fishery*, Philadelphia, 1907, pp. 1-80.
80. Marvin, W. L., *The American Merchant Marine*, New York, 1919, chapter 8.

Intercoastal Trade

39. Weeden, *op. cit.*, I, 260-262, 375-378; II, 588-592, 760-761.
65. Bogart and Thompson, *op. cit.*, pp. 55-57, 203-204.
81. Van Metre, T. W., "American Coastwise Trade Before 1789," from Johnson, E. R., *History of Domestic and Foreign Commerce of the United States*, Washington, 1915, I, chapter 10.

West Indian Trade

39. Weeden, *op. cit.*, I, 137-139, 359; II, 584-585, 640-641, 753-758, 781, 827.

82. Pitman, F. W., *The Development of the British West Indies, 1700–1763*, New Haven, 1917, chapters 9, 12, 13.
65. Bogart and Thompson, *op. cit.*, pp. 71–82 (trade to West Indies and Europe), 134–139, 192–197.
83. Beer, G. L., *The Commercial Policy of England Toward the American Colonies*, New York, 1893, pp. 45–66, 66–90, 91–153.
84. Johnson, E. R., *History of Domestic and Foreign Commerce of the United States*, Washington, 1915, I, 93–100.
85. DuBois, W. E. B., "The Suppression of the African Slave Trade to the United States 1638–1870," *Harvard Historical Studies*, I, New York, 1904, pp. 1–6, 7, 9, 16–18, 25–26, 27–38, 39–52, 85–93, 109–118, 131–150, 162–167, 176–180.
86. Bell, H. B., "The West Indian Trade Before the American Revolution," *American Historical Review*, XXII (1916–17), 272–288.

European Trade

39. Weeden, *op. cit.*, I, 156, 232–244, 356–357, 362–363; II, 586–588, 617–620, 783–784.
65. Bogart and Thompson, *op. cit.*, pp. 69–71, 128–133, 185–192.
84. Johnson, *op. cit.*, I, 73–83, 106–107, 120–131.

Privateering

39. Weeden, *op. cit.*, I, 337–353; II, 598–607, 655–665, 769–778.
78. Abbot, *op. cit.*, chapter 5.
80. Marvin, *op. cit.*, pp. 12–18, 125–131.

Pacific Ocean Trade

39. Weeden, *op. cit.*, II, 820–827.
65. Bogart and Thompson, *op. cit.*, pp. 202–207.
87. Dulles, F. R., *The Old China Trade*, Boston, 1930, chapters 1, 3, 4, 6, 7.
88. Greenbie, L., and Greenbie, M., *Gold of Ophir*, New York, 1925, chapters 2–4.

CHAPTER VIII

The War of 1812

89. Coleman, C. B., "The Ohio Valley in the Preliminaries of the War of 1812," *Mississippi Valley Historical Review*, VII (1920), 39–50.
48. Channing, *op. cit.*, IV (1917), 456–478.
90. Babcock, K. C., *The Rise of American Nationality*, New York, 1906, chapter 6, pp. 106–121, 121–127, 132–149.
91. Elson, H. W., *History of the United States*, New York, 1920, pp. 415–443.
92. Morison, S. E., *The Oxford History of the United States, 1783–1917*, London, 1927, I, 286–302.
93. McClay, E. S., *History of the Navy*, New York, 1910, pp. 469–491, 603–621, 492–520.
68. McMaster, *op. cit.*, IV, 1–190.   (Refer to index for topics.)
94. Adams, H., *History of the United States*, New York, 1901, II (1809–1813), chapter 17.
95. Roosevelt, T., *The Naval War of 1812*, New York, 1903, chapter 10.
96. Krafft, H. F., and Norris, W. B., *Sea Power in American History*, New York, 1920, pp. 93–149.

CHAPTER IX

Movement into the Northwest Territory

51. Paxson, *op. cit.*, chapters 14 and 22.
97. Mathews, L. K., *The Expansion of New England*, Boston, 1909, chapters 2–4, 7–9.
62. Turner, *op. cit.*, chapter 5.
68. McMaster, *op. cit.*, IV, 381–395.
61. Branch, *op. cit.*, pp. 272–275, 281–291.
98. Hulbert, A. B., *The Cumberland Road*, Cleveland, 1904, pp. 15–189.
74. Sparks, *op. cit.*, pp. 259–289.
99. Paxson, F. L., "The Gateways of the Old Northwest,"

Michigan Pioneer and Historical Collections, XXXVIII (1912), 139–148.
100. Pease, T. C., *The Frontier State*, II, *Centennial History of Illinois*, Springfield, 1918, selected portions.

Expansion into the Trans-Mississippi Country
72. Coman, *op. cit.*, chapter 2.
51. Paxson, *op. cit.*, chapter 24.
61. Branch, *op. cit.*, chapter 17.
101. Bryan, W. S., "Daniel Boone in Missouri," *Missouri Historical Review*, III (1909), 89–98, 198–205.
102. Viles, J., "Missouri in 1820," *Missouri Historical Review*, XV (1920), 36–52; and Goodwin, C. "The American Occupation of Iowa," *Iowa Journal of History and Politics*, XVII (1919), 83–102.

The Texas Question
72. Coman, *op. cit.*, chapter 4.
51. Paxson, *op. cit.*, chapter 34.
50. Caldwell, *op. cit.*, chapter 15.
103. Garrison, G. P., *Westward Extension, 1841–1850*, New York, 1906, pp. 23–34, chapters 7, 8, 10.
73. Bruce, *op. cit.*, chapter 4.
61. Branch, *op. cit.*, chapter 20.
104. Riegel, R. E., *America Moves West*, New York, 1930, chapters 22, 25.

CHAPTER X

Hunters and Trappers on the Plains and in the Rocky Mountains

105. Chittenden, H. M., *The American Fur Trade of the Far West*, New York, 1902, selected portions of the following: I, Part I, chapters 1, 2, 4–6; Part II, chapters, 2–6, 15, 17, 18; II, Part III, chapters 6, 7; Part V, chapters 1–7.
54. Roosevelt, *op. cit.*, IV, 331–339.

106. Duffus, R. L., *The Santa Fé Trail*, New York, 1930, chapter 4.
 72. Coman, *op. cit.*, I, 300–301.
107. Gilbert, E. W., "South Pass: A Study in the Historical Geography of the United States," *The Scottish Geographical Magazine*, XLV (1929), 144–154.

Santa Fé Trade

 61. Branch, *op. cit.*, chapter 19.
 51. Paxson, *op. cit.*, chapter 36.
105. Chittenden, *op. cit.*, II, Part II, chapters 28–30.
108. Goodwin, C., *The Trans-Mississippi West, 1803–1853*, New York, 1922, pp. 137–146.
109. Harvey, C. M., "The Story of the Santa Fé Trail," *Atlantic Monthly*, CIV (1909), 774–786.
110. "Captain Thomas Becknell, 'Journal from Boone's Lick to Santa Fé,'" *Missouri Historical Review*, IV (1910), 65–81; Major Alphonso Wetmore, "Journal," *ibid.*, VIII (1914), 177–197.
111. Stephens, F. F., "Missouri and the Santa Fé Trade," *Missouri Historical Review*, X (1916), 234–262; XI (1917), 289–312.
106. Duffus, *op. cit.*, portions of chapters 6, 7, 8, 10, 11.
 72. Coman, *op. cit.*, II, chapter 3.

Advance to the Pacific and the California Trade

 51. Paxson, *op. cit.*, pp. 361–364.
108. Goodwin, *op. cit.*, pp. 146–147.
112. Cleland, R. G., *A History of California: The American Period*, New York, 1922, pp. 61–66, 81–86, 88–89.
 72. Coman, *op. cit.*, II, 213–214.

CHAPTER X.

British and American Claims to the Oregon Country

 72. Coman, *op. cit.*, I, 301–375; II, 113–148.
113. Harvey, C. M., "Fur-Traders as Empire Builders," *Atlantic Monthly*, CIII (1909), 304–305, and 523–535.

54. Roosevelt, *op. cit.*, IV, 308–331.
114. Skinner, C. L., *Adventurers of Oregon*, New York, 1921, chapters 2–6.
108. Goodwin, *op. cit.*, pp. 114–137, and 200–225.
104. Riegel, *op. cit.*, pp. 177–189.
115. Merk, F., "Oregon Pioneers and the Boundary," *American Historical Review*, XXIX (1923–24), 681–700.

The Oregon Trail and the Movement to Oregon

116. Young, F. G., "The Oregon Trail," *Quarterly of the Oregon Historical Society*, I (1900), 339–370.
117. Ghent, W. J., *The Road to Oregon*, New York, 1929, chapters 4, 7.
118. Dale, H. C., "The Organization of the Oregon Emigrating Companies," *Quarterly of the Oregon Historical Society*, XVI (1915), 205–227.
119. Paxson, F. L., *The Last American Frontier*, New York, 1922, chapter 5.
92. Morison, *op. cit.*, II, 46–54.
104. Riegel, *op. cit.*, chapter 23.

Settlements in Oregon and Washington

72. Coman, *op. cit.*, II, 148–161.
120. Skinner, C. L., *Adventurers of Oregon*, New York, 1921, pp. 217–273.
61. Branch, *op. cit.*, chapter 21.
108. Goodwin, *op. cit.*, chapter 9.
121. Wilson, W. J., "The Oregon Question," *Quarterly of the Oregon Historical Society*, I (1900), 3–59.

The California Trail and the Early Migration to California

72. Coman, *op. cit.*, II, 207–241.
122. Thwaites, R. G., *Rocky Mountain Exploration*, New York, 1914, chapter 13.
117. Ghent, *op. cit.*, pp. 50–58.
112. Cleland, *op. cit.*, chapters 5, 9.

108. Goodwin, *op. cit.*, pp. 426–456.
123. Bidwell, J., "The First Emigrant Train to California," *Century Magazine*, XIX (1890–91), 106–130.

Chief Events Leading to Treaty of 1848

112. Cleland, *op. cit.*, chapters 10–14.
73. Bruce, *op. cit.*, chapter 6.
108. Goodwin, *op. cit.*, chapter 14.
72. Coman, *op. cit.*, II, 241–248.

Influence of Discovery of Gold upon California

117. Ghent, *op. cit.*, chapter 8.
124. McMaster, J. B., *A History of the People of the United States*, New York, 1910, VII, 585–614.
72. Coman, *op. cit.*, II, 255–314.
125. Bidwell, J., "The Discovery of Gold in California," *Century Magazine*, XIX (1890–91), 525–537.
61. Branch, *op. cit.*, pp. 428–445.
104. Riegel, *op. cit.*, chapter 27.

CHAPTER XII

The Monroe Doctrine

126. Latané, J. H., *America as a World Power*, New York, 1907, pp. 255–268.
48. Channing, *op. cit.*, V (1921), 342–347.
92. Morison, *op. cit.*, I, chapter 26.
50. Caldwell, *op. cit.*, pp. 325–330.

Expansion to Continental Power

103. Garrison, *op. cit.*, "The Expansion Movement (1790–1841)," pp. 3–21; "The Field for Expansion (1800–1841)," pp. 22–42.
62. Turner, *op. cit.*, "The Far West," pp. 111-133.
127. Wertenbaker, T. J., *The American People*, New York, 1928, pp. 229–240, 396–414.
128. Hulbert, A. B., *Frontiers*, Boston, 1929, "The Soil Factor

in American Unification," pp. 34–57; "Frontiers Breed Frontiers," pp. 127–149; "Strands of Dusty Trails," pp. 161–180; "Bands of Tempered Steel," pp. 181–200.

61. Branch, *op. cit.*, "Concord Coaches on Western Trails," pp. 485–502; "The Miners' Frontier of the Northwest," pp. 503–520.

129. Turner, F. J., *The Frontier in American History*, New York, 1921, especially chapter 1.

130. Fish, C. R., *American Diplomacy*, New York, 1915, chapters 16–20.

Expansion and Scientific Boundaries

103. Garrison, *op. cit.*, pp. 67–84, 98–108, 157–173.

131. Garber, P. N., *The Gadsden Treaty*, Philadelphia, 1923, selected portions.

108. Goodwin, *op. cit.*, pp. 499–507.

132. Klotz, O., "The History of the Forty-ninth Parallel Survey West of the Rocky Mountains," *Geographical Review*, III (1917), 382–387.

130. Fish, *op. cit.*, pp. 148–151, 186, 194, 201–202, 218, 228–232, 271.

115. Merk, *op. cit.*, pp. 681–700.

CHAPTER XIII

Water Transportation in the Mississippi Valley

133. Meyer, B. H., *History of Transportation in the United States Before 1860*, Washington, 1917, pp. 94–116, 280–298.

134. Carson, W. W., "Transportation on the Ohio and Mississippi Before the Steamboat," *Mississippi Valley Historical Review*, VII (1920–21), 26–38.

78. Abbot, *op. cit.*, pp. 261–302.

135. Benton, E. J., "The Wabash Trade Route in the Development of the Old Northwest," *Johns Hopkins University Studies in Historical and Political Science*, XXI (1903), 1–112.

136. "Inland Water Transportation in the United States," Bureau of Foreign and Domestic Commerce, *Miscellaneous Series, 119*, Washington, 1923, pp. 5–18, 38–48, maps.

137. "Transportation in the Mississippi and Ohio Valleys," *Transportation Series No. 2*, War Department, Washington, 1929, series of tables and maps showing facilities and traffic.

138. Clowes, E. S., *Shipways to the Sea*, Baltimore, 1929, pp. 18–23, 32–46.

139. Daggett, S., *Principles of Inland Transportation*, New York, 1928, pp. 11-20.

Trans-Appalachian Canals

133. Meyer, *op. cit.*, pp. 161–206, 207–248, 249–279.

140. Hulbert, A. B., *Historic Highways of America*, Cleveland, 1904, IV, "The Erie Canal."

141. Hulbert, A. B., *Historic Highways of America*, Cleveland, 1904, XIII, "Chesapeake and Ohio Canal and the Pennsylvania Canal."

139. Daggett, *op. cit.*, pp. 18–29.

136. *Miscellaneous Series 119*, pp. 33–38.

142. Whitbeck, F., "New York State Barge Canal in Expectations and Realizations," *Economic Geography*, IV (1928), 196–206.

143. McFarlane, C. T., "The Erie Canal," *Journal of Geography*, X (1912), 219–228.

The Great Lakes and Canals

78. Abbot, *op. cit.*, chapter 7.

139. Daggett, *op. cit.*, pp. 29–39, 185–201.

138. Clowes, *op. cit.*, pp. 29–30, 58–72, 117–132, 170–180, 181–184.

136. *Miscellaneous Series 119*, pp. 48–67.

144. "Transportation on the Great Lakes," *Transportation Series No. 1*, War Department, Washington, 1930, tables and maps of traffic on the Great Lakes.

78. Abbot, *op. cit.*, pp. 227–260.

145. Van Cleef, E., "The Great Lakes Waterway as a Civic and National Asset," *Journal of Geography*, XVIII (1919), 18–24.

CHAPTER XIV

Causes of the War

146. Elson, H. W., *Sidelights of American History*, New York, 1900, chapter 4.
147. Chadwick, F. E., *Causes of the Civil War*, New York, 1906, chapters 1, 2, 4.
148. Phillips, U. B., "The Central Theme of Southern History," *The American Historical Review*, XXXIV (1928–1929), 30–44.
149. Emerson, F. V., "Geographic Influences in American Slavery," *Bulletin of the American Geographical Society*, XIII (1881), pp. 13–26, 106–118, 170–181.
150. Caldwell, R. G., *A Short History of the American People, 1860–1921*, New York, 1927, II, chapter 2.
151. Smith, E. F., *The Borderland in the Civil War*, New York, 1927, chapter 1.
152. Rhodes, J. F., *History of the Civil War, 1861–1865*, New York, 1917, numerous maps.

Campaigns in the East

33. Brigham, *op. cit.*, pp. 224–229.
153. Hosmer, J. K., *The Appeal to Arms, 1861–1863*, New York, 1907, chapters 4, 9–13, 16–19.
91. Elson, *op. cit.*, pp. 655–658, 669–676, 691–701, 706–712, 721–725, 739–746, 751–758, 765–767, 768–773.
48. Channing, *op. cit.*, VI, 1925, 447–453, 464–485, 560–562, 565–579, 630–636.
92. Morison, *op. cit.*, II, 219–231, 238–245, 259, 284–286, 288–298, 304–309, 314–321.
154. Muzzey, D. S., *The United States of America*, Boston, 1922, I, pp. 552–556, 562–573, 574–579, 586–592.
155. Fiske, J., *The Mississippi Valley in the Civil War*, Boston, 1900, numerous maps.

Campaigns in the West
  33. Brigham, *op. cit.*, pp. 202-223.
 153. Hosmer, *op. cit.*, chapters 6-8, 15.
  91. Elson, *op. cit.*, pp. 658-659, 676-691, 716-721, 732-739,
      748-751, 758-761, 765-768.
  48. Channing, *op. cit.*, VI, 453-464, 546-560, 562-565.
  92. Morison, *op. cit.*, II, 208-219, 279-284, 298-304.
 154. Muzzey, *op. cit.*, I, pp. 556-562, 573-574, 579-586.

CHAPTER XV

Growth and Distribution of Immigration
 129. Turner, *op. cit.*, chapter 8.
 150. Caldwell, *op. cit.*, I, 91-97, 434-437; II, 262-268.
 156. Burr, C. S., *America's Race Heritage*, New York, 1922,
      chapters 2, 3.
 157. Siegfried, André, *America Comes of Age*, New York,
      1927, chapter 1.
 158. Stephenson, G. M., *A History of American Immigration*,
      Boston, 1926, chapters 1, 10-17.
 159. Fairchild, H. P., *Immigration*, New York, 1913, chapters
      2-8.
 160. Willcox, W. F., "The Distribution of Immigrants in the
      United States," *The Quarterly Journal of Economics*,
      XX (1906), 523-546.

Nationality and Assimilation
 158. Stephenson, *op. cit.*, chapters 2-9.
 161. Johnson, S. C., *A History of Emigration from the United
      Kingdom to North America*, New York, 1914, chapters
      1, 2, 8, 9.
 162. Faust, A. B., *The German Element in the United States*,
      New York, 1927.
 163. Van Cleef, E., "The Finns in America," *Geographical
      Review*, VI (1918), 185-214.
 164. Renner, G. T., "Chinese Influences in the Development

of the United States," *Annals of the American Academy of Political and Social Science*, CLII (1930), 356–370.

165. Millis, H. A., *The Japanese Problem in the United States*, New York, 1915, chapter 1.

166. Gamio, M., *Mexican Immigration to the United States*, Chicago, 1930, chapters 2, 13.

167. Jackson, G. E., "Emigration of Canadians to the United States," *Annals of the American Academy of Political and Social Science*, CVII (1923), 25–35.

168. Foerster, R. F., *The Italian Emigration of Our Times*, Cambridge, 1919, chapters 17–20.

Public Domain and Free Land

169. Smith, J. R., *North America*, New York, 1925, chapter 2.

170. Hill, R. T., *The Public Domain and Democracy*, New York, 1910, chapters 1, 2, 7, 8.

171. Treat, P. J., *The National Land System*, New York, 1910, chapter 14.

172. Trimble, W. J., "The Influence of the Passing of the Public Lands," *Atlantic Monthly*, CXIII (1914), 755–767.

173. Connor, L. G., "A Brief History of the Sheep Industry in the United States," *American Historical Association Report*, I (1918), 89–197.

174. Fletcher, R. S., "The End of the Open Range in Montana," *Mississippi Valley Historical Review*, XVI (1929), 188–211.

174. Teele, R. P., *The Economics of Land Reclamation in the United States*, Chicago, 1927, chapters 2, 3, 10.

CHAPTER XVI

Geographical Factors in the Development of American Cities.

175. Ridgley, D. C., "Geographic Principles in the Study of Cities," *Journal of Geography*, XXIV (1925), 66–79.

176. Jefferson, M., "How American Cities Grow," *Bulletin of the American Geographical Society*, XLVII (1915), 19–37.

177. Roth, L. V., "The Growth of American Cities," *Geo graphical Review*, V (1918), 384–398.
178. Brigham, A. P., *The United States of America*, London, 1927, chapter 4.
179. Southworth, G. V. D., and Kramer, S. E., *Great Cities of the United States*, Syracuse, 1916.
169. Smith, *op. cit.*, pp. 78–91, 121–144, 176–182, 189–195, 201–203, 268–273, 314–319, 327–329, 361–365, 376–388, 541–549, 561–564, 590–597, 604–614.
180. Miller, G. J., and Parkins, A. E., *Geography of North America*, New York, 1928, pp. 119–155, 204–221, 304–335, 396–414.
181. Goodrich, E. P., "Growth of New York City," *Geographical Review*, II (1916), 184–205.
182. Goode, J. P., *The Geographic Background of Chicago*, Chicago, 1926.
183. Parkins, A. E., *Historical Geography of Detroit*, Lansing, 1918.

Urban Concentration and Industry

184. Whitbeck, R. H., "Manufacturing in the United States," *Journal of Geography*, XXVII (1928), 207–219.
185. Huntington, E., and Williams, F. E., *Business Geography*, New York, 1926, chapters 21, 22, 25.
178. Brigham, *op. cit.*, pp. 160–180.
186. Clark, V. S., *History of Manufactures in the United States*, Washington, 1916, 1928, I, chapters 1, 4, 5, 13, 14, 19–21; II, chapters 1, 16–19, 31, 34, 37, 39–43, 46, 65.
187. Keir, M., *Manufacturing*, New York, 1928.
188. Whitbeck, R. H., and Finch, V. C., *Economic Geography*, New York, 1924, pp. 99–103, 114–119, 125–142, 151–155, 156–160, 161–202.
189. Burgy, J. H., *The New England Cotton Textile Industry*, Baltimore, 1932.
190. Hartshorne, R., "Location Factors in the Iron and Steel Industry," *Economic Geography*, IV (1928), 241–252.

191. White, L., "The Iron and Steel Industry of the Pittsburgh District," *Economic Geography*, IV (1928), 115–139.

192. Kuhlmann, C. B., *The Development of the Flour-Milling Industry in the United States*, Boston, 1929, pp. xiii-xvii, chapters 1–8.

193. Clemen, R. A., *The American Livestock and Meat Industry*, New York, 1923, chapters 1–4, 8–13, 19.

194. Newell, F. H., "Water," in Van Hise, C. R., and Havemeyer, L., *Conservation of Our Natural Resources*, New York, 1930, pp. 115–226.

CHAPTER XVII

Geographic Bases for Rapid Growth of Railroads in the United States

178. Brigham, *op. cit.*, chapter 10.

128. Hulbert, *op. cit.*, chapter 12.

188. Whitbeck and Finch, *op. cit.*, pp. 215–223.

185. Huntington and Williams, *op. cit.*, pp. 149–167.

133. Meyer, *op. cit.*, chapters 11–17, maps following p. 654.

186. Clark, *op. cit.*, I, chapters 5, 14.

139. Daggett, *op. cit.*, chapters 4, 11–14.

195. Johnson, E. R., and Van Metre, T. W., *Principles of Railroad Transportation*, New York, 1913, chapters 2, 3, 6.

196. Newcombe, H. T., "Railway Progress and Agricultural Development," *Yale Review*, IX (1900), 33 ff.

197. Bogart, E. L., "Early Canal Traffic and Railroad Competition in Ohio," *Journal of Political Economy*, XXI (1913), 56–70.

Railroad Development East of the Appalachians

104. Riegel, *op. cit.*, pp. 369–378.

198. Parkins, A. E., "A Comparison of Trans-Appalachian Railroads," *Journal of Geography*, IX (1909), 113–118.

133. Meyer, *op. cit.*, chapters 12–14.

199. Murphy, H. K., "The Northern Railroads and the Civil

War," *Mississippi Valley Historical Review*, XIV (1918), 324–339.
200. Hungerford, E., *The Story of the Baltimore and Ohio Railroad*, New York, 1928, I, chapters 1, 5, 9, 12, 14.

Expansion of the Interior System
104. Riegel, *op. cit.*, pp. 378–382.
133. Meyer, *op. cit.*, chapters 15, 16.
201. Parkins, A. E., "Development of Transportation in Pennsylvania," *Bulletin of the Geographical Society of Philadelphia*, XV (1917), 1–18.
202. Shippee, L. B., "The First Railroad Between the Mississippi and Lake Superior," *Mississippi Valley Historical Review*, V (1918), 121–142.
203. Markham, C. H., "The Development, Strategy, and Traffic of the Illinois Central System," *Economic Geography*, II (1926), 1–19.

Transcontinental Lines
204. Parkins, A. E., "The Transcontinental Lines of the West," *Journal of Geography*, VIII (1909), 97–109.
104. Riegel, *op. cit.*, chapters 32, 33, 38.
205. Sabin, E. L., *Building the Pacific Railway*, Philadelphia, 1919, chapters 2–9.
206. Cotterill, R. S., "The Beginnings of Railways in the Southwest," *Mississippi Valley Historical Review*, V (1921), 318–326.
207. Daggett, S., *History of the Southern Pacific*, New York, 1922, chapters 1–4.
208. Hedges, J. B., "The Colonization Work of the North Pacific Railroad," *Mississippi Valley Historical Review*, XIII (1926), 311–342.

CHAPTER XVIII

Broader Aspects of the Caribbean Relations of the United States
169. Smith, *op. cit.*, chapters 38, 39.
130. Fish, *op. cit.*, chapter 31.

209. Jones, C. L., *Caribbean Backgrounds and Prospects*, New York, 1931, chapters 1, 15.
210. Crowther, S., *The Romance and Rise of the American Tropics*, New York, 1929, chapters 1–4, 19.
127. Wertenbaker, *op. cit.*, chapter 24.
211. Whittlesey, D. S., "Geographic Factors in the Relations of the United States and Cuba," *Geographical Review*, XII (1922), 241–256.

The West Indies and the Caribbean Mainland

169. Smith, *op. cit.*, chapters 40–46.
180. Miller and Parkins, *op. cit.*, pp. 525–565, 568–580.
188. Whitbeck and Finch, *op. cit.*, chapter 19.
212. Bennett, H., "Agriculture in Central America," *Annals of the Association of American Geographers*, XVI (1926), 63–84.
213. Whitbeck, R. H., "Geographical Relations in the Development of Cuban Agriculture," *Geographical Review*, XII (1922), 223–240.
214. Fairchild, F. R., "The Problem of Santo Domingo," *Geographical Review*, IX (1920), 121–138.
215. Clark, V. S., and Associates, *Porto Rico and Its Problems*, Washington, 1930, chapters 1, 19.
216. Diffie, B. W., and Diffie, J., *Porto Rico: A Broken Pledge*. New York, 1921. Selected portions on trends of production of sugar, tobacco, coffee, fruits and the problems introduced by changes in agriculture.
217. De Booy, T., "The Virgin Islands of the United States," *Geographical Review*, IV (1917), 359–373.
218. "Nicaragua, a Commercial and Economic Survey," *Trade Promotion Series, Number 54* (1927), Bureau of Foreign and Domestic Commerce, Washington.
219. Sanders, E. M., "The Natural Regions of Mexico," *Geographical Review*, XI (1921), 212–226.

The Panama Canal

220. Herbert, J. W., "The Panama Canal: Its Construction

and Its Effect on Commerce," *Bulletin of the American Geographical Society*, XLV (1913), 241–254.

126. Latané, *op. cit.*, chapter 12.

92. Morison, *op. cit.*, II, 439–443.

221. Miller, H. G., *The Isthmian Highway*, New York, 1929, chapters 2, 3.

222. Bishop, J. B., *The Panama Gateway*, New York, 1913, Part I, chapters 3–7; Part III, chapter 1.

180. Miller and Parkins, *op. cit.*, pp. 565–568.

Commercial Relations of the United States and Latin America

209. Jones, *op. cit.*, chapters 11–14.

223. Lahee, A. W., *Our Competitors and Markets*, New York, 1924, chapters 8–10.

210. Crowther, *op. cit.*, chapter 18.

224. Jones, C. F., *Commerce of South America*, Boston, 1928, chapter 13.

225. Reynolds, P. K., *The Story of the Banana*, Boston, 1929, pp. 1–40.

226. Denny, L., *The Fight for Oil*, New York, 1928, chapters 4–7.

CHAPTER XIX

Lands and Activities of the Pacific Basin

227. Wood, G. L., *The Pacific Basin*, Oxford, 1930, chapters 1–6, 26.

223. Lahee, *op. cit.*, chapters 11–15.

228. Brooks, A. H., "The Value of Alaska," *Geographical Review*, XV (1925), 25–50.

229. Freeman, O. W., "The Economic Geography of the Hawaiian Islands," *Economic Geography*, V (1929), 260–277.

230. Eldridge, F. R., *Trading with Asia*, New York, 1921, chapters 1, 5, 6, 9, 11, 12, 20, 22, 24.

231. Orchard, J., *Japan's Economic Position*, New York, 1930.

232. "China," *Annals of the American Academy of Political*

and Social Science, CLII (1930), 1–9, 109–195, 278–292, 356–369.

233. Arnold, J., and Associates, "China," *Trade Promotion Series, No. 38*, Washington, 1926, pp. 26–54, 206–207, and 272–279.

234. Roxby, P., "Distribution of Population in China," *Geographical Review*, XV (1925), 1–24.

235. Foscue, E. J., and La Fleur, A., "Agricultural Production in China," *Economic Geography*, III (1927), 297–309.

236. Roosevelt, N., *The Philippines*, New York, 1926, chapters 1, 7, 15.

237. Butler, O. M., "The Philippine Islands," *Trade Promotion Series, No. 52*, Washington, 1927, pp. 1–130.

238. Waters, H. J., "Development of the Philippine Islands," *Geographical Review*, V (1918), 282–292.

239. "An Economic Survey of Australia," *Annals of the American Academy of Political and Social Science*, CLVIII (1931), 1–94.

Rise of the United States to a Pacific Power

87. Dulles, *op. cit.*, chapters 1, 4–9.

240. Dennett, T., *Americans in Eastern Asia*, New York, 1922, chapters 1–3, 13, 30, 31.

241. Roosevelt, N., *The Restless Pacific*, New York, 1928.

126. Latané, *op. cit.*, chapters 6, 9.

130. Fish, *op. cit.*, chapters 28, 32.

242. Ogg, F. A., *National Progress*, New York, 1918, chapter 17.

169. Smith, *op. cit.*, chapters 34–36.

180. Miller and Parkins, *op. cit.*, chapter 21.

FOR GENERAL REFERENCE

Paullin, C. O., *Atlas of Historical Geography of the United States*. New York, 1932.

166 plates comprising more than 620 separate maps. xiv + 145 pages. Of great value to any student of geographic relationships to American history.

LITERARY READING LISTS

THE following list of books is merely typical and suggestive. It is designed to broaden the geographical knowledge of the student; to reveal the rich material often contained in general literature coming from writers familiar with certain regions where they have lived and worked; to encourage an appreciation of a choice literary style, even in dealing with scientific facts; and finally to feed the imagination of youth, rather than restrict it to the starvation diet which constitutes the major part of American education.

ELLEN CHURCHILL SEMPLE

I. ALASKA, NORTH ARCTIC AMERICA, AND CANADA

The literature of this region shows the adjustment of life to local geographic conditions; transportation in a sub-arctic climate; exploitation of food supply; trapping and fur-trading; survival of native Indians as laborers under harsh climatic conditions; mixture of native and white races by marriage of white men with Indian women.

Food was supplied by fish caught in the streams and in the waters along the coast and by the meat of northern mammals, such as beaver, bison, musk-ox, bear, and seals. The wild animals of the region — buffalo, beaver, bear, and fox; otter and seal, found along the coast, and muskrat on the northern marshes, especially around Hudson Bay at a later period, provided furs for native clothes. Skins supplied leather for various articles of dress, as well as covering for tipi or wigwam and for Eskimo kayak. Sinews of animals furnished thread, and their bones provided material for articles like bodkins or needles. Transportation was provided by means of kayaks and dugout boats

along the coast, and in summer on interior streams, by birch
bark canoes, propelled by paddles, and carried over the portages
between rivers and lakes or around rapids. The winter demanded dog-sleds for the frozen areas. Birches furnished bark
for the canoes, various woods provided paddles, and the Pacific
coast forests supplied the large dugouts. Driftwood was found
on the northwest coast beyond the range of tree growth. Fuel
was provided by wood, the blubber of sea animals, and by buffalo dung in the semi-arid plains of the interior.

Cather, Willa, *Shadows on the Rock.* Knopf, New York, 1931.
A beautiful story of pioneer life in French Quebec.

Davis, Mary Lee, *Uncle Sam's Attic.* Wilde, Boston, 1930.
The intimate story of Alaska.

We are Alaskans. Wilde, Boston, 1931.
The author has lived in Alaska many years.

Gaither, Frances, *The Fatal River.* Holt, New York, 1931.
A dramatic narrative of the life and death of La Salle.

Grenfell, Wilfred, *Labrador, the Country and the People.* Mac
millan, New York, 1922.

Hémon, Louis, *Maria Chapdelaine.* Macmillan, New York, 1921.
A poignant account of the impoverishment and isolation of the
lives of the women on a north Canadian small farm, the effect of
barren soil, a harsh climate, short growing season and constant danger to husband or lover of the blizzards when away from home on
long trapping or hunting expeditions.

Laut, Agnes C., *Conquest of the Great Northwest.* Doubleday
Doran, New York, 1919.
Radisson. Macmillan, New York, 1904.
Account of his life and explorations, vivid and
authoritative.

McLennan, John, *Louisbourg.* Macmillan, London, 1918.
Authoritative account of the famous French fortress on Cape
Breton Island, designed as an outpost for the St. Lawrence highway
and also as a base of trade with France in the early season, when the
St. Lawrence was endangered by icebergs and fogs. It figured in the
conflict of the French and English for the control of North America,
and was an active base for smugglers operating from New England

ports. This volume is an *édition de luxe*, amply supplied with maps and pictures, and provided with source material on Louisbourg.

Merk, Frederick, George Simpson's Journal, *Fur Trade and Empire*. Harvard University Press, Cambridge, 1932.
A journey made by a governor of the Hudson's Bay Company in 1824-1825 to the Oregon country and return.

Owl, Grey, *Men of the Last Frontier*. Scribner, New York, 1932.
A book about one of the last isolated spots in America, "The Haute Terre of Canada."

Parker, Gilbert, *The Right of Way*. Harper, New York, 1901.
Pierre and His People. Macmillan, New York, 1898.
Stories of Canadian lumbering and trapping.

Parkman, Francis, *The Jesuits in North America in the Seventeenth Century*.
La Salle and the Discovery of the Great West.
A Half Century of Conflict.
Count Frontenac and the New France under Louis XIV.
The Old Régime in Canada.
Montcalm and Wolfe.
Pioneers of France in the New World. Little, Boston, 1901–1903.
These are all delightful and reliable accounts of early French Canada, and show the relation between natural environment and development.

Pinkerton, Robert E., *The Hudson's Bay Company*. Holt, New York, 1931.
A popular and authoritative account of the development of the Canadian fur trade from 1667 to the present time. The Hudson's Bay Company played a big part in the opening up and early economic development of Canada; it exercised a great influence upon the American continent from the Missouri River to the Pacific and upon the political history of the young United States.

Radisson, Pierre E., *Relations*. Prince Society, Boston, 1885.
An account of his explorations of Canada from the St. Lawrence River and Hudson Bay westward nearly to the sources of the

Saskatchewan River, and south to the Iroquois territory and Dutch settlements on the Hudson River.

Robins, Elizabeth, *The Magnetic North*.   Stokes, New York, 1904.

> *Come and Find Me*.   Century, New York, 1908.
>
> Miss Robins has written interesting and vivid novels, based on a long residence, of life in Alaska and the Yukon country after the discovery of gold.

Thomas, Lowell J., *Kabluk of the Eskimo*.   Little, Boston, 1932.
The story of a rare and moving friendship between an Eskimo chief and a cultured French trader, who operated for the furrier firm of Revelton Freres in the pelts of Labrador.

White, Stewart E., *Conjuror's House*.   McClure, New York, 1904.

> *The Silent Places*.   Doubleday, New York, 1909.
>
> *The Land of Footprints*.   Doubleday, New York, 1904.
>
> *The Blazed Trail*.   Doubleday, New York, 1912.
>
> Stories of the Canadian Northwest depicting the geographic background for the fur trade.

II. THE NEW ENGLAND REGION

The geographic conditions of the New England region comprise a long, indented coast, abundant harbors, short rivers with falls providing water power and milling facilities near the shore line, an extensive interior granitic upland, excessively glaciated, characterized by poor soil, suited only for grazing on the hilltops, isolated hill and mountain valleys, remote from each other and from the coast; and extensive forests of conifers and some hardwood trees in southern portions, which together furnish wood for shipbuilding and naval supplies.   Hence, the principal industries engaged in were shipbuilding; fishing off the nearby

Grand Banks and Nantucket Bank; whaling by people from Massachusetts, eastern Connecticut, and eastern Long Island ports, such as New Bedford, New London, and Sag Harbor; exporting of fish and whale products, of wood and naval supplies to European and West Indian ports; importing of foodstuffs such as wheat and other grains; and finally an active trade with China and the Dutch East Indies, from which countries were imported valuable goods for the colonists, such as tea, coffee, silk, paper, ivory, and porcelains.

Bassett, Sara W., *The Taming of Zenas Henry*. Little, Boston, 1915.
> *The Harbor Road.* Burt, New York, 1919.
>> Stories describing the life and characters of Cape Cod.

Brown, Alice, *Meadow Grass*. Houghton, Boston, 1902.
> A study of New England environment both in a village and rural community.

Dulles, Foster R., *The Old China Trade*. Houghton, Boston, 1930.
> A valuable account of trade from Atlantic and Pacific ports with the Dutch Indies and China. The trade emanated chiefly from Salem, Boston, Cape Cod ports, and New York.

Esty, Annette, *The Proud House*. Harper, New York, 1932.
> A study of Polish settlers on New England farmland in Vermont.

Ferber, Edna, *American Beauty*. Doubleday Doran, New York, 1931.
> Another study of Polish settlers, the scene laid in the Connecticut Valley.
> Both this novel and *The Proud House* are full of beauty and deal with the fundamental realities of life and physical conditions.

Green, Anne B., *The Lone Winter*. Century, New York, 1923.
> A remarkable early story — partly autobiographical — of struggle and courage on a Vermont farm, depicted against a fine background of animal lore.

Hawthorne, N., *The House of Seven Gables*. Houghton, Boston, 1893.
> Depicting the effects of poverty, family pride, and traditional customs, which were encouraged by isolation and limited contacts.

Hergesheimer, Joseph, *Java Head*. Knopf, New York, 1919.
An interesting and reliable account of Salem vessels, trading in Dutch East Indies and China ports.

Jewett, S. O., *The Country of the Pointed Firs*. Houghton, Boston, 1929.
An excellent story of New England life.

Judd, Silvester, *Margaret*. Little, Boston, 1902.
A story of "blight and bloom" of the discouraging effects of a harsh climate and a narrow environment.

Kipling, Rudyard, *Captains Courageous*. Doubleday, New York, 1923.
A study of the Gloucester fishermen. Compare Pierre Loti's *Iceland Fishermen*, and Harriet Martineau's *Seals on the Fjord*, more artificial but sound facts.

Lambert, M. R., *Old Boston*. Houghton, Boston, 1930.

Lee, Jennette, *Uncle William*. Century, New York, 1906.
A story of the island of Monhegan, with vivid setting and characters.

Melville, Herman, *Moby Dick*. Boni, New York, 1925.
A story of whaling in the South Seas by New England vessels.

Sigourney, Lydia H., *The Farmer and Soldier: A Tale*. Carter, New York, 1836.
First published in 1833, and reprinted in *Olive Buds* in 1836.

Stowe, Harriet B., *The Pearl of Orr's Island*. Houghton, Boston, 1862.
Shows the dangers and romance of an island community in Maine.

Thompson, Daniel P., *The Green Mountain Boys*. Lee, Boston, 1901.
Deals with pioneer life in Vermont and the struggle for statehood against the efforts of New York to absorb the territory.

Wharton, Edith, *Ethan Fromme*. Scribner, New York, 1919.
Depicts life on an isolated New England farm.

Wilkins, Mary E., *Jane Field*. Harper, Boston, 1893.
A good picture of the bleak and narrow environment in a New England village, and its reaction upon a revolter.

III. THE HUDSON RIVER AND ATLANTIC COASTAL PLAIN

The geographic conditions of this section are fertile river valleys and a productive coastal lowland, bordered on the sea by deposit islands, defined inland by a "fall line" marking the head of sea navigation, and backed by a highland, for example, the Catskills, or a piedmont plateau characterized by low relief and good soil suited for fields and orchards.   Inlets, lagoons, and estuaries make an indented coastline, such as is found in Maryland, Virginia, and North Carolina.   A climate, increasing in mildness from the Hudson south to Florida, offered conditions for a wide range of agricultural crops raised by slave labor, especially tobacco, cotton, sugar, and rice on the swampy coasts.

Asher, G. M., *Henry Hudson, the Navigator*.   Original Documents, Hakluyt Society, London, 1860.
   The Journal of "The Third Voyage" gives a brief but interesting narrative of Hudson's exploration of the Hudson River, navigable for his ocean vessel with its deep keel to the head of the tides near the present town of Hudson.   This was the old Clavarack Landing where a group of Nantucket whaling folk established a settlement about 1783 for the distribution of whale oil to the interior.

Bancroft, Frederic, *Slave-Trading in the Old South*.   Furst, Baltimore, 1931.
   An interesting history of the American slave trade down to the Civil War.

Churchill, Winston, *Richard Carvel*.   Grosset, New York, 1917.
   A story of early Virginia.

Cooper, J. Fenimore, *The Pioneers*.   Houghton, Boston, 1898.
                        A story of life on the old New York Frontier.

                     The Last of the Mohicans.   Houghton, Boston, 1896.
                        Studies of native Indian life on upper Hudson.

Edmonds, Walter D., *Rome Haul*. Grosset, New York, 1931.
> Depicts life on the Erie Canal in the early days, a novel of considerable interest.

Fiske, John, *Old Virginia and Her Neighbours*. Houghton, Boston, 1897.
>> An excellent analysis of geographic causes, and economic and social effects.

>> *The Dutch and Quaker Colonies in America*. Houghton, Boston, 1899.
>>> A study of the English settlements on the Delaware River; and the development of the fur trade on the upper Delaware and Susquehanna rivers, and their western tributaries.

Glasgow, Ellen, *The Battle-ground*. Doubleday, New York, 1920.
>> *Barren Ground*. Doubleday, New York, 1925.
>>> The struggle of a Virginia family to make a living on the infertile ground of the piedmont country.

Heyward, Du Bose, *Porgy*. Doran, New York, 1925.
> A story of negro life and labor in Charleston, South Carolina.

Hughson, S. C., *Carolina Pirates and Colonial Commerce, 1670–1740*. Johns Hopkins University Studies in History and Political Science, Series 12, Nos. 5–7, Baltimore, 1894.
> An account of the sounds, lagoons and deposit islands of the North Carolina coast, used as lairs by American pirates and privateers, as they lay in wait for ships bound between New England and the West Indies, in an effort to nullify the obnoxious Navigation Acts. Here location and the nature of the coast afforded choice conditions for piratical activities.

Irving, Washington, *Knickerbocker's History of New York*. Doubleday, New York, 1928.
> Fiske's and Irving's books emphasize the distribution of land grants to the Dutch patroons along the Hudson River route. They also reveal the value of this stream for the interior fur trade in the early days, the concentration of the commerce in pelts at or near Albany; and the function of the Hudson as a link through Lake

Champlain with the St. Lawrence River, and through the Mohawk Gap and later the Erie Canal, with the Great Lakes.

Johnston, Mary, *To Have and to Hold.* Houghton, Boston, 1900.
  Audrey. Houghton, Boston, 1902.
  The Long Roll. Houghton, Boston, 1911.
  The Great Valley. Little, Boston, 1926.

Lovell, Caroline C., *The Golden Isles of Georgia.* Little, Boston, 1932.
 A story of the fertile "sea islands," a picture of life in the Old South along the coast.

Mitchell, Dr. Silas W., *Hugh Wynne.* Century, New York, 1922.
 A story of Philadelphia during the Revolution, the result of its geographic location and importance as the colonial capital.

Olmsted, Frederick, *A Journey in the Seaboard Slave States.* Putnam, New York, 1861, 2 vols.
 An absorbing account of geographic and especially economic conditions in the states dependent upon wasteful slave labor. Every page is as interesting as a novel.

Page, Thomas N., *Marse Chan and Other Stories.* Scribner, New York, 1902.
  Red Rock. Scribner, New York, 1926.
  Charming tales of plantation life in the slave state of Virginia.

Parkman, Francis, *Champlain.* Little, Boston, 1898.

Peterkin, Julia, *Black April.* Bobbs-Merrill, New York, 1927.
  Green Thursday. Knopf, New York, 1924.
  Accounts of negro life and labor on South Carolina plantations, where climate and soil offered an ample yield for certain crops, discouraged diversification and white labor.

Quick, Herbert, *Vandemark's Folly.* Bobbs-Merrill, New York, 1922.
 A story of the Erie Canal and its part in the great western trek to Minnesota.

Radisson, Pierre, *Relation.* Scull, Boston, 1885.

Smith, John, *True Travels, Adventures, and Observations in Europe, Asia, Africa and America*. Franklin Press, Richmond, 1819, 2 vols.

John Smith's pioneer experiences in the settlement of Jamestown in old Virginia. Interesting but not reliable, because the old man had embroidered his stories for years in Devonshire taverns before the Journal was written.

Ward, Christopher, *The Dutch and the Swedes on the Delaware, 1609–1664*. University of Pennsylvania Press, Philadelphia, 1930.

An interesting account of the trials of the trading settlements of the Swedes and the Dutch. The book gives a good picture of conditions of life in the colonies.

Weygandt, Cornelius, *The Red Hills*. University of Pennsylvania Press, Philadelphia, 1929.

A story of the Pennsylvania Dutch.

Wilstach, Paul, *Tidewater Maryland*. Bobbs-Merrill, New York, 1931.

An account of the influence of geographic conditions; the dependence of the state upon waterways for communication, the broad Potomac barrier separating Maryland from Virginia; hence the long preservation of the colonial atmosphere of the south with its manors and manorial institutions. The book is rich in geographic, economic, and social facts, establishing the distinctive character of the region and its inhabitants, maintained for 200 years. The Marylander of 1750 was an individual type, free from bigotry, regardless of his Puritan, Catholic, or Church of England ancestry. The capital, Annapolis, was "The Bath of America," center of culture, wealth, and social graces. Maryland's port, Baltimore, founded in 1729, fattened on the wheat and iron trade of its progressive hinterland. Its location left it unimpaired by the Revolution, and it seized the marine trade by its admirable clippers.

Tidewater Virginia. Bobbs-Merrill, Indianapolis, 1929.

The story of Tidewater Virginia from the coming

of the settlers; special phases and stages of development; the rivers of the regions and the families, plantations, and the picturesque and distinctive features of the life that grew up along their banks.

IV. THE APPALACHIAN MOUNTAIN REGION WITH A PURE BRITISH STOCK

The Appalachian Mountain region is made up of dissected plateaus and deep, V-shaped valleys, the soil being limited in area and generally poor in quality and exposed to excessive denudation.   Communication is difficult, both within and without the region, hence isolation prevails. The results of these conditions have been poverty, ignorance, feuds, illicit distilling, lack of roads, emigration of the better elements and stagnation of the inferior residue, excessive intermarriage within the valleys, and malnutrition, all working for the deterioration of the population.   They were furthered by the exploitation of the natives through the coal and iron mines of the region, and through mills where water power was developed.   The latter is a recent development.   These conditions and effects are reflected in the following books.

Bruce, H. A., *Daniel Boone and the Wilderness Road.*   Macmillan, New York, 1910.
    An excellent semipopular account of Boone and his associates.

Burke, Fielding, *Call Home the Heart.*   Longmans, New York, 1932.
    The story of a girl of the North Carolina mountains, who left the highlands to seek a different experience in a mill town.

Party Fixings and Other Plays of the North Carolina Country.   Playmaker's Series, First, Second, and Third.
    Illustrative of the life of mountain whites and tenant farming.

Chapman, Mariston, *The Happy Mountain*.   Allen, London,
      1931.
      The Weather Tree.   Viking, New York,
      1932.
      Both these stories reveal the conflict be-
      tween the stagnant human life of the moun-
      tains and its conflict with an intruding civili-
      zation, the intense conservatism of the iso-
      lated highlander contented with little as op-
      posed to the grasping and progressive "for-
      eigner."

Craddock, Charles E., *In the Tennessee Mountains*.   Houghton,
  Boston, 1884.
  Depicting adjustment of human life in the lonely "coves" of the
  Cumberland Plateau.
  See also other stories of this region by the same author.

Dargan, Olive T., *Highland Annals*.   Scribner, New York, 1925.
  A story of the rugged Unakas of North Carolina which imposed a
  life of poverty, ignorance, and isolation on the mountaineers.

Doyle, A. Conan, *The Valley of Fear*.   Burt, New York, 1920.
  A story of coal mining in the Pennsylvania anthracite region.

Fox, John, Jr., *The Cumberland Vendetta*.   Harper, New York,
      1896.
      A story of the feuds of the Kentucky Mountains
      in the isolated valleys of the Cumberland Plateau.
      The Little Shepherd of Kingdom Come.   Scribner,
      New York, 1931.
      The Trail of the Lonesome Pine.   Grosset, New
      York, 1923.
      Both stories depict various phases of life in this
      same geographic environment.
      Crittenden.   Scribner, New York, 1920.
      In this novel John Fox reveals the power of the
      mountain environment to produce vigorous, ener-
      getic characters, unspoiled by luxury, with unjaded
      nerves and high ideals — men like Abraham Lin-
      coln, Andrew Jackson, and more recently, Melvin
      Traylor of Chicago — men marked for success.

Furman, Lucy, *The Quare Women*. Little, Boston, 1923.

       The Glass Window. Little, Boston, 1925.

       Both novels give vivid and often humorous pictures of mountain life on Hell fur Sartain and Troublesome Creek.

Semple, Ellen C., "The Anglo-Saxons of the Kentucky Mountains," *Geographical Journal*, XVII, June, 1901, 588–623 (London), reprinted in the *Bulletin of the American Geographical Society*, XLII (1910) 561–594 (New York).

    A geographic, economic, and social study of this whole region.

Tome, Philip, *Pioneer Life; Thirty Years a Hunter*. Buffalo, 1854.

    Excellent pictures of backwoods life.

Verhoeff, Mary, *Kentucky River Navigation*. Morton, Louisville, 1917.

    Yields much valuable geographic and economic material about the large mountain area of the Kentucky River system.

V. THE MISSISSIPPI VALLEY AND THE MISSISSIPPI RIVER

The geographic conditions of this region comprise extensive lowlands or plains, with ample soil of great fertility, navigable rivers, and easy intercourse both by land and stream; widespread forests of hardwoods with some treeless prairies, varied with large stands of coniferous forests in the colder north; and a wide range of climate from the sub-tropical coast of the Gulf of Mexico, with a long frostless period suited to rice, cotton, and sugar cane culture, to the severe winters of the northern portions of the lowland, suited to the production of spring wheat and dairy farming, combined with extensive lumbering enterprises. From pioneer and even Indian days, farming was varied and productive, while the whole region was rich in game.

The human geography is complicated by a variety of race stocks — the large colonial French or Creole element in Louisiana, the negroes distributed over the southern half of the region from the Gulf of Mexico to the Mason and Dixon Line, intrusive

Americans from the eastern states occupying the old Northwest Territory where slavery was prohibited, and finally large numbers of immigrant Norwegians, Swedes, Germans, and Finns who settled in Michigan, Wisconsin, Minnesota, and Iowa, the colder section of the region..

Allen, James Lane, *The Choir Invisible.* Macmillan, New York, 1898.
> *The Reign of Law.* Macmillan, New York, 1900.
> *The Mettle of the Pasture.* Macmillan, New York, 1903.
> *A Summer in Arcady.* Macmillan, New York, 1896.
>> These novels picture the easy conditions of life in the Kentucky Bluegrass region, describe some of the economic processes, like hemp production, and show with great delicacy and charm the influence of the physical environment upon the character of the people. They cover a period from pioneer days to the late nineteenth century.

Bodley, Temple, *The Life of George Rogers Clark.* Houghton, Boston, 1926.
> A delightful biography which comprises material on the pioneers of Kentucky, and emphasizes the conquest of the old Northwest Territory during the Revolution by the self-equipped frontiersmen without financial or other aid from the government in Philadelphia or the continental army.

Cable, George, *Old Creole Days.* Scribner, New York, 1907.
> *The Grandissimes.* Scribner, New York, 1908.
> *Dr. Sevier.* Scribner, New York, 1908.
> *The Lovers of Louisiana.* Scribner, New York, 1918.
>> These four novels emphasize the charm and individuality of the old French population of New Orleans, while describing economic and social problems growing out of geographic conditions and slave labor.

Cannon, Cornelia J., *Red Rust*. Grosset, New York, 1930.
 Depicts life in the Minnesota wheatlands, the region of hard
 spring wheat, as the background for an industrious Swedish community. All is poetically portrayed, reflecting conditions of climate
 and soil to which an immigrant folk adjust themselves.

Chopin, Kate, *Bayou Folk*. Houghton, Boston, 1894.
 Characteristic short stories, popular between 1890–1899.

Churchill, Winston, *The Crisis*. Macmillan, New York, 1930.
 Presents an authoritative account of life in the rich prairie land of
 Illinois during the political contest between Abraham Lincoln and
 Stephen A. Douglas before the Civil War.

Davis, Reuben K., *Recollection of Mississippi and Mississip-
 pians in Ante-bellum Days*. Houghton, Boston, 1889.
 This is one of the most delightful books of the kind ever written.
 It is based on first-hand knowledge, gathered in a long life and varied contacts in the state.   The style is easy, flowing, stimulating,
 and the record is often relieved by gleams of humor.

Eggleston, Edward, *The Circuit Rider*.   Scribner, New York,
  1878.
   The Hoosier Schoolmaster.   Hurst, New
   York, 1891.
    Both novels depict life in rural Indiana in
    the sixties and seventies.

Ferber, Edna, *The Showboat*. Doubleday, New York, 1926.
 Describing a special phase of communication on the Mississippi
 which carried dramatic entertainment from one river town to another; a floating theater with its stock company.

Hatcher, M. A., *The Opening of Texas to Foreign Settlement*,
 1801–1821.   Austin, Rochester, 1912.

Hay, John, *Life of Abraham Lincoln*. Century, New York, 1894.
 Affords material on the Sangamon country and Springfield in
 Illinois.

Henshaw, Neville, *The Inheritance of Jean Trouvé*.   Bobbs-
   Merrill, New York, 1922.
   The Painted Woods.   Bobbs-Merrill, New
   York, 1924.
    These are two novels of life on the channels,
    bayous, oxbow lakes, and cypress swamps of

the lower Mississippi. They describe a poor population of coast fishermen, muskrat trappers, and outlaws, maintaining a precarious existence, both physical and economic, on the old levees and delta islands of the coast. The books are charmingly written in a vivid style, with unconscious emphasis on the geographic conditions.

King, Grace, *New Orleans*. Macmillan, New York, 1895.

Ogilvie, Frances, *Green Bondage*. Farrar, New York, 1931.
Life on small farms in the Kentucky tobacco land.

Oudard, Georges, *Four Cents an Acre*. Brewer and Warren, New York, 1930.
A detailed account of the story of Louisiana under the French.

Parkman, Francis, *The Jesuits in North America*. Little, Boston, 1901.
La Salle and the Discovery of the Great West. Little, Boston, 1903.
These books reveal the importance of the Mississippi as a highway of exploration and territorial expansion.

Roberts, Elizabeth M., *The Great Meadow*. Viking Press, New York, 1930.
A picture of pioneer life and Indian forest warfare in early Kentucky, a beautifully written novel of absorbing interest.
The Time of Man. Viking Press, New York, 1926.
A story of tenant farming and tobacco culture by "poor white" labor in the rich lands of Kentucky.

Saxon, Lyle, *Lafitte the Pirate*. Century, New York, 1930.
A fascinating story of the life and activities of Jean Lafitte and his brother Pierre in the bayous of the lower Mississippi near New Orleans and in the Gulf of Mexico.

Snider, D. J., *Lincoln and Anne Rutledge*. Sigma Publishing Company, St. Louis, Mo., 1912.
Pictures the semi-pioneer life in early Illinois.

Tarbell, Ida, *Life of Abraham Lincoln*. Macmillan, New York, 1917.
Affords material on the Sangamon country and Springfield in Illinois.

Tarkington, Booth, *The Gentleman from Indiana*. Doubleday, New York, 1920.
The Turmoil. Harper, New York, 1915.
The Magnificent Ambersons. Doubleday, New York, 1918.
All depict life in Indiana towns or cities.

Thompson, Maurice, *Alice of Old Vincennes*. Bobbs-Merrill, New York, 1908.
An interesting story of the George Rogers Clark campaign for the capture of the British post at Vincennes. This campaign clinched the conquest of the Northwest Territory, increasing the area of the young United States of 1783 by fully one third, advancing the frontier from the Ohio River to the Great Lakes and sources of the Mississippi River.

Tinker, Francis and Edward L., *Old New Orleans*. Appleton, New York, 1931.
Comprising four romances of social history and national elements in the great delta seaport of the Mississippi.

Twain, Mark, *Life on the Mississippi*. Harper, New York, 1927.
Indicates the economic importance of the great stream, its large cargo steamboats collecting freight along its banks, the bizarre assemblage of passengers, together with the humorous or sinister events which varied life on the river.
Adventures of Tom Sawyer. Harper, New York, 1917.
Huckleberry Finn. Harper, New York, 1903.
Depicting river life from the standpoint of two enterprising boys.

White, Stewart E., *The Riverman*. McClure, New York, 1908.
A story of lumbering on midwestern rivers and the exploitation of the northern forests of the old northwestern states.

Wilson, Margaret, *The Able McLaughlins*. Harper, New York, 1923.
A story of Wisconsin in the days of early settlement.

Wright, Harold B., *The Shepherd of the Hills*.   Appleton, New
     York, 1907.
     A story of the rugged Ozark Highlands of southern Missouri and
     northern Arkansas, an upland region abutting upon the Mississippi
     lowland, providing sawmills and certain minerals for the valley
     population.

VI. TRANS–MISSISSIPPI PRAIRIE PLAINS AND
THE HIGH PLAINS

This region embraces the second tier of states west of the Mississippi River and the territory thence to the Rocky Mountains,
extending from mid-Texas north to the Dakotas and the Canadian border.   The geographic conditions are conspicuous west of
the 98th meridian.   They comprise a gentle relief; a sub-humid
climate averaging less than 20 inches of annual rainfall, periods
of extreme drought with scant water supply, braided streams
bordered by slender coniferous forests whose delicate tracery
hardly breaks the continuity of the grassland; extreme continental climate except on the Texan coast, with blizzards in winter and scorching winds, destructive to crops, in summer, fan-
ning the grass fires aided by hot and arid conditions.   The
pioneers had to rely on sod houses, *bois de vache* or "buffalo
chips" instead of wood for fuel, grazing and ranching supplemented by a limited amount of dry-farming which gave an uncertain yield, owing to locust pests and blasting hot winds.
The 98th meridian was and is a climatic, economic, and social
"fault-line" in the Great Plains region.   The literature based on
this region reflects these conditions, and the race elements comprising Indians from the western reservations, Mexicans dating
from the old union of Texas with Mexico, hardy Norwegian and
Swedish immigrants in the north, and Canadians seeking to
escape the rigors of Manitoba — all animated by land hunger.

Adams, Andy, *The Log of a Cowboy*.   Houghton, Boston, 1927.
     Pictures vividly ranching on the "open range," and the transfer

in 1870 of a herd of ranch cattle from Texas to an Indian reservation in Montana.

Aldrich, Bess S., *A Lantern in her Hand*. Appleton, New York, 1928.

A beautiful story of pioneer life in the plains of Nebraska; a record of blizzards and cyclones, of droughts and locusts, of scorching winds and failing water, but also of heroic courage and determination to win.

Banning, William and George H., *Six Horses*. Century, New York, 1930.

A detailed portrayal of life along the western frontier of the fifties and sixties in one of the most romantic phases of the struggle to secure means of transportation over hundreds of miles of mountain and plain, an authoritative and engaging study of stagecoach days.

"Captain Thomas Bicknell, Journal from Boone's Lick to Santa Fé," *Missouri Historical Review*, IV (1910), 65–81.

Bojer, Johann, *The Emigrants*. Century, New York, 1925.

Has the same theme as Rölvaag's *Giants in the Earth*, and is a similar dramatic and heroic recital, authentic in the last detail to conditions of climate, soil, and remote frontier location.

Boynton, Percy H., *The Rediscovery of the Frontier*. University of Chicago Press, Chicago, 1931.

This book serves as a guide to the extraordinary group of novels about the American frontier that have appeared in recent years; but for the geographer it cannot take the place of the novels themselves.

Branch, E. D., *The Cowboy and His Interpreters*. Appleton, New York, 1926.

The Hunting of the Buffalo. Appleton, New York, 1929.

Buffalo Child Long Lance. *Long Lance*. Cosmopolitan Book Company, New York, 1928.

By the Siouan chief himself, depicting the Sioux of the western plains, sweeping broadly from the Missouri Valley, where they hunted the buffalo, northward into the Dakota country and west into the Columbia Valley and Cœur d'Alène region in search of wild horses and the disappearing game.

Canton, F. M., *Frontier Trails*. Houghton, Boston, 1930.

The biography of the author who in 1869 grazed his cattle on the open range of the Great Plains and guided a herd 1000 miles across the virgin country.   The book describes also the transition from "open range" to fenced farming under the Homestead Act, followed by the rapid appropriation of free land till the supply was exhausted by the settlement of the "Cherokee Strip."   Brilliant and vivid pictures of the old frontier life.

Cather, Willa, *O Pioneers!* Houghton, Boston, 1913.
> *My Ántonia.* Houghton, Boston, 1926.
>> Choice novels of pioneer life in Nebraska written out of the author's long residence in this region.

> *One of Ours.* Knopf, New York, 1922.

Coues, Elliott, *The Journal of Jacob Fowler.* New York, 1898.

Custer, Elizabeth, *Boots and Saddles.* Harper, New York, 1885.
> A vivid and delightful account of travel and life on the Great Plains in pioneer days, experienced by the young wife of General Custer as she accompanied the military expedition of the United States forces to the "Bad Lands" of Dakota soon after the Civil War.   The book gives entrancing pictures of the vast buffalo herds, Indian encampments and hunting parties, travel in "the covered wagon" or on horseback, and the swift emancipation from the impediments of a settled and civilized life for the freedom and simplicity of the frontier.   The book is a record of a charming and courageous personality, ready to meet the luck of the road.

Doneghy, Dagmar, *The Border, a Missouri Saga.* Morrow, New York, 1931.
> This is a dramatic story of the Civil War on the Kansas-Missouri border along the frontier of settlement, remote from centers of governmental control and betraying the typical disorders of such outlying districts.   It is a powerful, moving recital, authentic as an historical document because based on the actual experiences of the author's ancestors.

Ferber, Edna, *Cimarron.* Doubleday, New York, 1930.
> A brilliant narrative, depicting a late phase of the westward movement with the transformation of the old Indian Territory into the state of Oklahoma.   The appropriation or purchase of Indian lands, the opening of "the Cherokee Strip," the development of agriculture, oil resources, and pioneer urban centers are described in relation to local climate, soil, geology, and the on-sweeping tide of frontier settlers.

Garland, Hamlin, *A Son of the Middle Border*. Macmillan, New York, 1927.

A biographical study of pioneer life in Iowa and Nebraska in the early sixties, based on an unusual synthesis of personal, economic, and social conditions on the westward moving frontier. It pictures life in a new country of sparse population and meager contacts both human and economic, though endowed with ample resources in the favored prairie plains of eastern Nebraska.

Gates, Eleanor, *The Biography of a Prairie Girl*. Century, New York, 1902.

An early story of life on a western ranch, where neighbors were few, labor scarce, and the problem of providing water for the cattle a recurrent one. The book is entirely authentic and delightfully written.

Griffith, G. W., *My Ninety-Six Years in the Great West*. Published privately, Los Angeles, 1929.

A detailed account of pioneer life in Indiana from 1833 to 1855, the perils of covered wagon travel to Kansas and pioneer life in that area for a half century.

James, Marquis, *The Raven*. Bobbs-Merrill, New York, 1929.

A choice biography of Sam Houston, who epitomized in his daring and enterprise pioneer life in the Texas of American immigrants, a buffer state between old Mexico and the United States bristling with political problems and with opportunities. This is one of the best biographies of recent times, its theme an interesting character in critical time and place.

Linderman, F. B., *American*. Day, New York, 1930.

An account of Plenty Coups of the Crow tribe and the life of the mounted Indians north of the Platte River between 1850 and 1870, when buffalo were abundant and horses made hunting easy.

Neihardt, J. G., *Black Elk Speaks*. Morrow, New York, 1932.

A vivid record of life among the Ogalala Sioux. Like *Long Lance*, it describes the training of youth, the hunting of buffalo, and the conversion of the meat into pemmican by the women, the social and economic customs dating back to the time of the Coronado Expedition, when a stampede among the Spanish horses freed many of these animals (1542). Hence herds of wild horses flourished on the grasslands and provided the Indians with mounts.

Ostenso, Martha, *Wild Geese.* Dodd, New York, 1925.
>   *The Waters under the Earth.* Dodd, New York, 1930.
>   These are stories of the north middlewest in an isolated community, in which foreign immigrants of the peasant class predominate, people animated by land-hunger and competent for the struggle for existence.

Rölvaag, O. E., *Giants in the Earth.* Harper, New York, 1927.
>   *Peder Victorius.* Burt, New York, 1931.
>   *Their Fathers' God.* Harper, New York, 1931.
>   This is Rölvaag's impressive pioneer trilogy of Norwegian immigrants who braved the hardships of life, conquering the frontier land of Dakota for settlement and economic independence.

Scarborough, Dorothy, *The Stretch-Berry Smile.* Bobbs, New York, 1932.
A realistic romance of life on the sun-baked and wind-scorched plains of Texas, which have been subdued to human purposes by infinite labor. Like the author's earlier novels, the book deals especially with the cotton fields of her native state and the tenant farmers in their fight against poverty and drought.

Webb, Walter Prescott, *The Great Plains.* Ginn, Boston, 1931.

Wister, Owen, *The Virginian.* Macmillan, New York, 1902.
A charming story of ranch life and herding on the western plains.

VII. THE ARID AND SEMI-ARID BASINS OF THE WESTERN HIGHLANDS

This is a region of successive basins, linked by high and difficult passes, where the climate is arid or semi-arid, due to exclusion of the rain-bearing winds of the Rocky Mountains on the east and the Cascade-Sierra Nevada ranges on the west; of canyon streams whose deep trenches form barriers across the land and whose swift, variable current is little aid to navigation. Human adjustment to this environment resulted in isolation by mountains and deserts; limited irrigation tillage where the high ranges provided water to the piedmont or valleys below; extensive cattle grazing with transhumance in the hot season to the grass and shrub growth of the mountain forests; mining on a large scale where the outcrops disclosed rich minerals like gold, silver, and copper; development of water power in connection with streams for irrigated fields and placer mines — all summed up in a sparse population and almost complete dependence upon climatic conditions, while the prevailing low rainfall resulted in soil low in humus content. These physical conditions are reflected in the following literature, in which also the Indian population of the numerous western reservations, the intrusive Mexican elements, trappers and mining prospectors from various states add complex human ingredients to the dramatic episodes.

Austin, Mary, *The Land of Little Rain*. Houghton, Boston, 1927.
A story of sheep ranching and the effects of extreme isolation in this sparsely populated region of low rainfall.

Barker, Ruth L., *Caballeros*. Appleton, New York, 1931.
An historical and descriptive account of native Spanish-American life in Santa Fé and near-by districts of New Mexico, showing the survival of Spanish arts and architecture, besides the manners and customs adapted to natural conditions in the isolated valleys of the Rocky Mountains. Remoteness and enforced segregation, seconded by the desert environment, have protected the region from inundations of Americans.

Buck, Franklin A., *A Yankee Trader in the Gold Rush*. Houghton, Boston, 1930.
In its second half this journal gives a vivid picture of the climatic, geographic, economic and social conditions which combined in the early mining centers and ranches of Nevada. It is both authoritative and interesting, an absorbing journal.

Burnham, Frederick R., *Scouting on Two Continents*. Doubleday, New York, 1926.
The biography of a great scout, operating in the United States and South Africa. The first third of the book depicts life among the Indians and cattlemen of the arid southwest in the early nineties, as reflecting the climatic, economic, and social conditions, the raids

of Apaches from Mexico to despoil the ranches and drive away their herds, the effects of drought and the perils of a savage frontier.

Cather, Willa, *Death Comes for the Archbishop*.   Knopf, New York, 1927.
>A beautiful and moving story of pioneer days in the settlement of New Mexico, soon after the American conquest.   It shows the conflict between the Spanish and American cultures exemplified by the older Spanish occupants and the American intruders in the upper Rio Grande Valley, and depicts the social disorders on the remote frontier of ill-governed Mexico.

>*The Professor's House*.   Knopf, New York, 1925.
>A book in which is interpolated a vivid story of the exploration of prehistoric cliff dwellings on an almost inaccessible mesa of the arid southwest.

Coolidge, Mary R., *The Rain-Makers*.   Houghton, Boston, 1929.
>*Navajo Indians*.   Houghton, Boston, 1930.
>Written in coöperation with Dane Coolidge, these books depict the relations of these Indians to their geographic environment.   Included are small-scale irrigation gardening on the border of streams for the production of maize, beans, squash, and melons; raising of horses, sheep, and goats with careful discrimination in the use of the pasturage, especially the herding of sheep as the more economic product for food and clothing better adapted to the scant grassland; blanket-weaving as a tribal industry; and amazing tolerance of thirst by men and animals.

Dellenbaugh, Frederick S., *A Canyon Voyage*.   Yale University Press, New Haven, 1926.
The exploration of the Colorado River Canyon, by Major J. W. Powell, a vivid and authoritative account, since young Dellenbaugh accompanied Major Powell.   The book reveals the barrier character of these canyons which prevailed in this semi-arid west.

Glasscock, C. B., *The Big Bonanza*. Bobbs-Merrill, New York, 1931.
 A story of the Comstock Lode in Nevada, and the romantic careers of James Fair, John W. Mackay, Adolph Sutro, "Lucky" Baldwin, and other conspicuous figures in the spectacular mining town.

Grey, Zane, *Riders of the Purple Sage*. Harper, New York, 1921.
 The Light of Western Stars. Harper, New York, 1914.
 Arizona Ames. Harper, New York, 1932.

Irving, Washington, *The Adventures of Captain Bonneville*. Putnam, New York, 1868.
 An account of conditions in the Great Salt Lake Basin.

Werner, M. R., *Brigham Young*. Harcourt Brace, New York, 1925.
 Interesting geographic, economic, and social data.

Wilson, Harry L., *The Lions of the Lord*. Lothrop, New York, 1903.
 A narrative of the pioneer settlement of the Mormons in the Utah oasis.

VIII. THE TRANS–CONTINENTAL TRAILS: LINES OF WESTERN EXPANSION

The geographic conditions of these trails comprise those of the Great Plains west of the Missouri River, the Cordilleran Highlands and their vast intermontane basins, and the Pacific coast ranges down to the sunset shore of the young United States territory. Factors determining the lines of these trails were the river approaches to the Rocky Mountains and the western Sierras, streams and water holes in the arid stretches, water supply and fodder, the choice of mountain passes over the major divides, barriers of mountains and deserts, and finally the terminus of the trail in a fertile valley, protected seaport, or an old Spanish town or mission.

Bancroft, H. H., *History of Oregon*. Bancroft Co., San Francisco, 1886–1888, vols. 29–30.
 Contains a wealth of material on the penetration of trappers and

pioneer settlers into the Columbia River Plateau and Valley, both
by way of the Oregon Trail and from the Saskatchewan Valley,
where the headstreams of the Canadian River interlace with those
of the Columbia.

Brewerton, G. D., *Overland with Kit Carson.* Coward-McCann,
New York, 1930.

An account of the famous "Kit Carson's Ride" and the route he
followed when in 1846 he carried military dispatches for General
Kearney overland from Santa Fé to California. Any authoritative
life of Kit Carson contains an entrancing record of experiences on
the southern trails of California, and the personality of this frontier
hero.

Chapman, Arthur, *The Pony Express.* Putnam, New York,
1932.

Describing a romantic phase in the conquest of the Far West.

Coues, Elliott, *The Pike Expedition.* Harper, New York, 1895.

In two volumes. Contains authoritative material on the Santa
Fé Trail and the search for passes to the upper Rio Grande Valley.

Driggs, H. R., *Covered-Wagon Centennial and Ox-Team Days.*
World Book Co., Yonkers-on-Hudson, 1932.

The volume tells the story of the labors and achievements of the
Oregon Trail Memorial Association, which marked 3000 miles of
that historic way. The second part is devoted to Ezra Meeker's
story of boyhood days, the ox-team journey overland to Oregon and
adventurous years in the Northwest — Mr. Meeker's reminiscences
make a lively and graphic portrayal of one of the most dramatic
movements in our history.

Duffus, R. L., *The Santa Fé Trail.* Longmans, New York, 1930.

A short account of the trail from its outfitting point at Independence to its terminus in the old Spanish City in the upper Rio Grande
Valley, with its route, its facilities and obstacles, its perils and its
commerce in the decades of its preëminence.

Hulbert, Archer B., *The Forty-Niners.* Little, Boston, 1931.

An authoritative and brilliant chronicle of western expansion on
the overland trails to Oregon and California during the gold rush to
California. The emigrants endured thirst, poisonous alkaline water,
lack of food and fodder, and constant Indian attacks. They guided
their oxcarts and covered wagons over marshes, across rivers beset
with quicksand, over snow-blocked mountain passes, and up ap-

proaching valleys filled with torrents during storms or sudden thaws. The book depicts the sections of the trails and the methods of transportation as adjustments to geographic conditions; explains the outfitting points, the cut-offs and the western terminals in their relation to location and physiography. It describes in detail the route over the Sierra Nevadas from Ragtown on the Carson River, south of Lake Tahoe, by Carson Pass, and its course thence down to Hangtown near the present Placertown in California, but indicates the other pass routes available, as the Truckee Pass above Sutter's Fort and the Sacramento River. Based upon a mass of journals.

McGlashan, C. F., *History of the Donner Party*, 14 ed. Carlisle & Co., San Francisco, 1929.

The tragic story of the crossing of the snow-bound Sierras by the Donner Party in 1846-47.

Miller, Joaquin, *Overland in a Covered Wagon*. Appleton, New York, 1930.

The western poet's story of his own life gives interesting pictures of the trials of western migration.

Neihardt, John G., *The Splendid Wayfaring*. Macmillan, New York, 1920.

The record of trapping and trading on the upper Missouri and its headwaters by Jedediah Smith and Ashley in 1826, their discovery of South Pass, and experiences in a wild, unknown country on a remote and shifting frontier. The region from the Rockies westward was occupied only by Indians and game, but the lonely trappers were peering through the passes to the great beyond, and searching for the beaver dams in highland valleys for the sake of the pelts. The book records the beginning of a vast, unorganized but effective system of western exploration.

Parkman, Francis, *The Oregon Trail*. Houghton, Boston, 1925.

White, Stewart E., *The Long Rifle*. Doubleday, New York, 1932.

A vivid narrative of western exploration and expansion between 1810 and 1840. The actors are descendants of the lusty pioneers who penetrated Cumberland Gap into Kentucky and followed the rich beaver streams into the Rocky Mountains. They were the restless, tireless human stock of the "Long Hunters," described by Roosevelt, and carried their traps across the Great Divide into Spanish California. The writer gives authoritative descriptions of the

geographic conditions underlying his story, which deserves high
rank among modern regional novels.

Willsie, H. M., *We Must March.*   Stokes, New York, 1925.
An interesting story of the Oregon Trail.

Literature on the Mormons, the semi-arid and arid basins
of the West, and some on California will add further material
to this subject of the overland trails.

IX. THE PACIFIC COAST REGION

The geographic conditions of this region comprise a mild
marine climate, with a Mediterranean climate of winter rains
and summer droughts from the Mexican border to northern California; a scarcely indented coastline with rare embayments in
depressed areas, as in Humboldt Bay and San Francisco Bay
along the Californian coast, the estuary of the Columbia River
and Puget Sound in Oregon and Washington; ranges of mountains defining the Pacific seaboard, backed by long intermontane
valleys linked by moderately low passes, which afforded from
early times easy interior communication from north to south
through the length of the region; the Cascade Mountains and
the Sierra Nevadas, ending southward in the Sierra Madre of
Southern California, which together formed a high mountain
wall flanking the region on its landward side and attaining a
sufficient altitude to accumulate rain and snow from the moisture-laden winds from the Pacific.   These mountains have provided reservoirs of water to irrigate the semi-arid interior Valley
of California, extensive forests and pastures, while the rock-
outcrops were rich in minerals and especially gold, accumulated
in the placer deposits of the drainage streams.   Access to the
Pacific encouraged maritime trade along the coast from Chile to
Alaska and also an extensive trans-oceanic commerce with the
Orient from the late eighteenth century.

Atherton, Gertrude, *Before the Gringo Came.*   Stokes, New
York, 1915.
Comprising "Rezanov," dealing with Rus-

sian designs on northern California, and the "Doomswoman," dealing with the Spanish and American ideals in their struggle for supremacy.

California. . Boni & Liveright, New York, 1927.
Depicts the life of Spanish dons in early San Francisco.

Austin, Mary, *The Ford.* Houghton, Boston, 1917.
A story of the San Joaquin Valley.

Buck, Franklin A., *A Yankee Trader in the Gold Rush.* Houghton, Boston, 1930.
Comprising a series of letters that form a journal. It depicts every phase of California geography, climate, and economic activity; mining, irrigation, tillage, and ranching; the active and far-reaching trade, covering the Pacific islands and the mainland coast from Chile to Alaska, with the swift development of Oriental commerce.

Buffum, E. G., *Six Months in the Gold Mines.* Philadelphia, 1850.

Canse, John M., *Pilgrim and Pioneer.* Abingdon Press, New York, 1930.
An account of the work of Jason Lee, and other pioneer evange-lists, 100 years ago in what is now Oregon.

Christman, F. M., *One Man's Gold — The Letters and Journals of a Forty-Niner.* McGraw-Hill, NewYork, 1930.
A detailed account of the trying journey around the Horn which took from July 3, 1849, to February 9, 1850, and of the life in the Mariposa Diggings and the stirring events which took place as the forces of order gradually exerted themselves against the riff-raff of a dozen nations.

Coy, Owen C., *The Great Trek.* Powell Publishing Company, Los Angeles, 1931.

Dana, R. H., *Two Years before the Mast.* Houghton, Boston, 1911.
An outstanding work on California in 1834-1835 which everyone should read. It describes American smuggling in the ports of Mexi-

can California, the overbearing methods of the traders, and life in the Spanish settlements when few American colonists had arrived.

De Bra, Lemuel., *Ways that are Wary.* Burt, New York, 1927.
Stories of Chinatown and Chinese life in California.

Farquhar, Francis P., *Up and Down California in 1860–1864; The Journal of William H. Brewer.* Yale University Press, New Haven, 1930.
The account of an expedition which made the first scientific exploration of California.

Gabriel, Gilbert, *James Lewis.* Doubleday, New York, 1932.
Records the story of the first ship, Tonquin, sent around the Horn in 1811 to establish fur posts in the Pacific Northwest. Lewis was chief clerk of the expedition.

Gifford, E. W., *Californian Indian Nights Entertainments.* Clark, California, 1930.
An authoritative and valuable book.

Gross, William B., *The Conquest of California.* Stratford, Boston, 1930.
Depicting the experiences of Junipero Serra and his thirteen Franciscan friars in the exploration and settlement of California. A faithful study showing careful use of detail.

Harte, Bret, *Works.* Houghton, Boston, 1929.
Bret Harte has written many stories the scenes of which are laid in various counties of California in the gold rush days.

Irving, Washington, *Astoria.* Putnam, New York, 1900.
Describes the founding of John Jacob Astor's ill-fated fur station at the mouth of the Columbia River in 1811.

Irwin, Wallace A., *Seed of the Sun.* Grosset, New York, 1923.
Dealing with the Japanese problem as presented in Santa Clara County.

Jackson, Helen H., *Ramona.* Little, Boston, 1916.
A vivid story of Indian life and Spanish-California ranches in early California.

Kennan, George, *The Salton Sea.* Macmillan, New York, 1917.
Describes the break of the Colorado River into the Imperial Valley.

King, Clarence, *Mountaineering in the Sierra Nevadas.* Scribner, New York, 1902.
A book everyone should know.

Kroeber, A. L., *Handbook of the Indians of California.* Government Printing Office, Washington, 1925.
History, customs, culture, and arts of fifty former Indian tribes of California, showing response to environment of fragmentary native stocks. Smithsonian Institution, Bureau of American Ethnology Bulletin 78.

Kyne, Peter B., *Pride of Palomar.* Cosmopolitan Book Co., New York, 1921.
Deals with the Japanese peril.

Valley of the Giants. Grosset, New York, 1920.
Laid in the redwood country of Humboldt County.

Mitchell, Ruth C., *Water.* Appleton, New York, 1931.
A story of irrigation and dairy ranching in the San Joaquin Valley.

Norris, Frank, *The Octopus.* Doubleday, New York, 1930.
Deals with the conflict between the wheat grower and railroad trust in a new country of sparse population.

Ross, Blake, *The Golden Crucible.* Elder, San Francisco, 1930.
An introduction to the history of California.

Saunders, Charles F., and O'Sullivan, St. John, *Capistrano Nights.* MacBride, New York, 1930.

Stevenson, Robert Louis, *The Silverado Squatters.* Scribner, New York, 1904.

Twain, Mark, *Roughing It.* Harper, New York, 1904.

White, Stewart E., *The Story of California.* Doubleday, New York, 1927.
A trilogy containing "Gold," "Gray Dawn," and "Rose Dawn." This triology describes the gold rush, San Francisco under Vigilante rule, and the land boom of later days.

Wright, Harold B., *The Winning of Barbara Worth.* Book Supply Co., Chicago, 1911.
A story which describes the reclamation of the Imperial Valley.

X. URBAN GEOGRAPHY AND THE NATURAL ENVIRONMENT

Geographic conditions comprise location on coast or river, local resources, means of communication, town sites, and elements of populations. Many literary authorities cited above are applicable, such as Grace King's *New Orleans*, Willa Cather's *Shadows on the Rock*, and others. Excellent books may be obtained on most of the large cities of the United States.

Bolton, Herbert E., *Outpost of Empire*. Knopf, New York, 1931.
   The story of the founding of San Francisco.

Blumenthal, Albert, *Small-Town Stuff*. University of Chicago, 1932.
   A study of a mining town near Butte, Montana, based geographically on its remote location on the western slope of the Rocky Mountains at an altitude of 5000 ft.; its abundant resources of lead, silver, zinc, and manganese; and finally its limited export of livestock and farm produce.

Buck, F. A., *A Yankee Trader in the Gold Rush*. Houghton, Boston, 1930.
   Discusses geographic factors of development in San Francisco, Maryville, Sacramento, and other Californian cities.

Campbell, J. B. T., *Rose of Los Angeles*. Published by the author, Los Angeles, 1929.
   A romance of Los Angeles with an historical background.

Cooney, P. J., *Dons of the Old Pueblo*. Rand, McNally, Chicago, 1914.
   A story of Los Angeles in the last days of Mexican rule.

Ferber, Edna, *So Big*. Neinemann, New York, 1931.
   A study of Chicago in relation to its suburban market-gardens and its stockyards.

Luther, Mark L., *Boosters*. Bobbs-Merrill, New York, 1924.
   A satire on Los Angeles.

Lynd, Robert S., and Lynd, Helen M., *Middletown*. Harcourt, New York, 1929.
   A study of an Indiana town of 50,000 population, chiefly in its economic and social aspects.

Parkins, Albion, *Detroit*. Lansing, Michigan, Historical Commission, 1918. Mich. Historical Publications, University series III.

A geographic and economic study of the city from its origin as a fur station up to the time of its great industrial development.

XI. THE CARIBBEAN ISLANDS

The geographic factors of these islands comprise location in relation to Panama, Mexico, and the United States; their size, climate, and soil; their value in early colonial trade in tropical and sub-tropical products; their significance as lurking places for illicit slave-ships, pirates, and smugglers; and the variety of the racial elements in their populations — Spanish, French, Danish, Dutch, and negro.

Bedford-Jones, H., *Drums of Dambala*. Covici, New York, 1932.

A thrilling novel of San Domingo when Toussaint L'Ouverture was struggling to maintain his power against revolt and treachery.

Bigelow, John, *Jamaica in 1850*. New York, 1851.

Cundall, Frank, *Jamaica in 1928*. Institute of Jamaica, Kingston, 1928.

Describes the physical, social and economic conditions of Jamaica.

Cundall, Frank, Editor, *Lady Nugent's Journal*. Kingston, Jamaica, 1906.

Covering the period from 1801 to 1815, when the Napoleonic wars increased the demand for sugar and rum, when both the slave trade and commerce in these colonial commodities yielded big profits, and plantations were principally estates.

Davis, H. P., *Black Democracy*. Dial Press, New York, 1928.

Franck, Harry A., *Roaming through the West Indies*. Century, New York, 1920.

Freeman, Lewis R., *Afloat and Aflight in the Caribbean*. Dodd, New York, 1932.

A voyage of adventure and close observation from Antigua to Dominica, and from the Virgin Islands to Panama. This book has both geographic and economic value.

Gardner, W. J., *History of Jamaica*. Appleton, New York, 1909.
Depicts life in the island when it was England's chief source of sugar, when hundreds of plantations were worked by thousands of slaves on this most prosperous island colony of the British Empire.

Hearn, Lafcadio, *Two Years in the French West Indies*. Harper, New York, 1923.
Authoritative, varied, and brilliant book written by one who traveled among the islands extensively.

Niles, Blair, *Black Haiti*. Putnam, New York, 1926.

Phillpotts, Eden, *Black, White and Brindled*. Macmillan, New York, 1923.
Vivid stories of the West Indian islands, illustrative of their mixed race elements, superstitions, smugglers, and slaves.

Pitman, F. W., *The Development of the British West Indies 1700–1763*. Yale Historical Publications Series 4, Yale University Press, New Haven, 1917.

Ragatz, L. J., *The Fall of the Planter Class in the British Caribbean*. Century, New York, 1928.

Rubens, Horatio S., *Liberty*. Brewer, New York, 1932.
The story of Cuba's fight for freedom.

Vandercook, John W., *Black Majesty*. Blue Ribbon Books, New York, 1930.
A gripping account of the life of Christophe and his mountain fortress and his effort to throw off French control in Haiti. It reveals the savage and fanatical life of the native negro population, and the truculent methods of the French in strengthening the long arm of authority.

Van Dyke, John C., *In the West Indies*. Scribner, New York, 1932.
A series of delightful descriptions.

Waxman, Percy, *The Black Napoleon*. Harcourt Brace, New York, 1931.
The story of Toussaint L'Ouverture, who transformed San Domingo from a French colony to a republic.

XII. POEMS WITH A GEOGRAPHICAL BACKGROUND

CANADA

Drummond, William H., *The Habitant and Other French Canadian Poems*. Putnam, New York, 1905.
The Voyageur and Other Poems. Putnam, New York, 1910.
Johnnie Courteau and Other Poems. Putnam, New York, 1911.
Phil-o-Rum's Canoe and Madeleine Verchers. Putnam, New York, 1911.
Service, Robert W., *Ballads of a Cheechako* (complete). Barse and Hopkins, New York, 1917.
Rhymes of a Rolling Stone, containing Athabasca Dick, The Nostomaniac, The Trapper's Christmas Eve, Death in the Arctic, Little Moccasins, The Squaw Man, Song of the Camp Fire. Dodd, New York, 1912.

NEW ENGLAND

Bryant, William C., To a Waterfowl, Green River, Monument Mountain, Autumn Woods, A Forest Hymn, The Prairies, Thanatopsis, The Death of the Flowers, Summer Winds. Contained in *William Cullen Bryant's Complete Poems*. Appleton, New York, 1903.
Emerson, Ralph W., The Rhodora, Woodnotes, The Snow Storm, Two Rivers, Musketaquid, My Garden. In *Emerson's Complete Poems*. Houghton, Boston, 1876.
The River. In Page, Curtis H., *Chief American Poets*. Houghton, Boston, 1905.

Frost, Robert, New Hampshire, Evening in the Sugar Orchard, Our Singing Strength. In *New Hampshire,* Holt, New York, 1923.
   Birches, Christmas Trees, Snow. In *Mountain Interval*. Holt, New York, 1916.
   The Mountain. In *North of Boston*, Holt, New York, 1914.

Longfellow, Henry W., Evangeline, The Building of the Ship, The Song of Hiawatha, The Courtship of Miles Standish, The Birds of Killingworth, My Lost Youth. Contained in *Complete Works of Longfellow*. Houghton, Boston, 1902.

Lowell, Amy, Lilacs, Meeting House Hill, Charleston, South Carolina. In *What's O'Clock?* Houghton, Boston, 1925.
   Monadnock in Early Spring. In *A Dome of Many Coloured Glass*. Houghton, Boston, 1921.

Lowell, James R., An Indian Summer Reverie, Sunthin' in the Pastoral Line. Contained in *Complete Poems of James R. Lowell*. Cambridge Edition. Houghton, Boston, 1897.

Whittier, John G., The Ranger, The Merrimac, Summer by the Lakeside, The Barefoot Boy, Snow Bound, The Wreck of the Rivermouth, The Dead Ship of Harpswell. In *Complete Poetical Works*, Houghton, Boston, 1894.
   Songs of Labor, The Trailing Arbutus, Storm on Lake Asquam, Sweet Fern. In Page, Curtis H., *Chief American Poets*. Houghton, Boston, 1905.

GENERAL DISTRIBUTION

Lanier, Sidney, *Poems*. Scribner, New York, 1906. The Song of the Chattahoochee, The Marshes of Glynn, From the Flats.
Whitman, Walt, *Leaves of Grass*. Small, Boston, 1899. Song of Myself, Crossing Brooklyn Ferry, I saw in Louisiana a Live Oak Growing, Night on the Prairies, A Magnet-South, Man-

nahatta, A Broadway Pageant, Pioneers! O Pioneers, Spirit
that Formed this Scene, A Prairie Sunset.

INTERIOR PLAINS AND HILLS

Lindsay, Vachel, *Collected Poems*.   Macmillan, New York, 1927.
A Gospel of Branty — Kansas, My Father Came from Kentucky, The City that Will Not Repent, The Golden Whales
of California.

URBAN LIFE

Sandburg, Carl, *Chicago, Skyscraper*.   Holt, New York, 1916.
   Smoke and Steel.   Omaha, Tangibles, The Sins
    of Kalamazoo.   Harcourt, New York, 1921.
   The Windy City.   Harcourt, New York, 1922.
   Santa Fê Sketches.   The Corn Belt (28 poems),
    Flat Waters of the West in Kansas.   Har-
    court, New York, 1928.
   Joliet.   Prairie, Prairie Waters by Night,
    Laughing Corn.   Holt, New York, 1918.

CALIFORNIA

Poems of Joaquin Miller.   Putnam, New York, 1923.
Poems of Edward R. Sill.   Houghton, Boston, 1906.
Poems of Ina Coolbrith.   Houghton, Boston, 1929.

INDEX